CHILTON'S REPAIR & TUNE-UP GUIDE
MUSTANG II 1974-78

Mustang II • Hardtop • 2 + 2 • Mach 1

President LAWRENCE A. FORNASIERI
Vice President and General Manager JOHN P. KUSHNERICK
Executive Editor KERRY A. FREEMAN, S.A.E.
Senior Editor RICHARD J. RIVELE, S.A.E.
Editor JOHN M. BAXTER

CHILTON BOOK COMPANY
Radnor, Pennsylvania
19089

SAFETY NOTICE

Proper service and repair procedures are vital to the safe, reliable operation of all motor vehicles, as well as the personal safety of those performing repairs. This book outlines procedures for servicing and repairing vehicles using safe, effective methods. The procedures contain many NOTES, CAUTIONS and WARNINGS which should be followed along with standard safety procedures to eliminate the possibility of personal injury or improper service which could damage the vehicle or compromise its safety.

It is important to note that repair procedures and techniques, tools and parts for servicing motor vehicles, as well as the skill and experience of the individual performing the work vary widely. It is not possible to anticipate all of the conceivable ways or conditions under which vehicles may be serviced, or to provide cautions as to all of the possible hazards that may result. Standard and accepted safety precautions and equipment should be used when handling toxic or flammable fluids, and safety goggles or other protection should be used during cutting, grinding, chiseling, prying, or any other process that can cause material removal or projectiles.

Some procedures require the use of tools specially designed for a specific purpose. Before substituting another tool or procedure, you must be completely satisfied that neither your personal safety, nor the performance of the vehicle will be endangered.

Although the information in this guide is based on industry sources and is as complete as possible at the time of publication, the possibility exists that the manufacturer made later changes which could not be included here. While striving for total accuracy, Chilton Book Company cannot assume responsibility for any errors, changes, or omissions that may occur in the compilation of this data.

PART NUMBERS

Part numbers listed in this reference are not recommendations by Chilton for any product by brand name. They are references that can be used with interchange manuals and aftermarket supplier catalogs to locate each brand supplier's discrete part number.

ACKNOWLEDGMENTS

Chilton Book Company expresses its appreciation to the Ford Motor Company, Dearborn, Michigan, and to George Ruggiere Ford, Devon, Pennsylvania for the technical information and illustrations contained in this book.

Manufactured in the United States of America
    0   8765

Chilton's Repair & Tune-Up Guide: Mustang II 1974–78
ISBN 0-8019-6812-7 pbk.
Library of Congress Catalog Card No. 78-22143

CONTENTS

Quick Reference
Specifications For Your Vehicle

Fill in this chart with the most commonly used specifications for your vehicle. Specifications can be found in Chapters 1 through 3 or on the tune-up decal under the hood of the vehicle.

 Tune-Up

Firing Order_____

Spark Plugs:

    Type_____

    Gap (in.)_____

Point Gap (in.)_____

Dwell Angle (°)_____

Ignition Timing (°)_____

    Vacuum (Connected/Disconnected)_____

Valve Clearance (in.)

    Intake_____   **Exhaust**_____

Capacities

Engine Oil (qts)

    With Filter Change_____

    Without Filter Change_____

Cooling System (qts)_____

Manual Transmission (pts)_____

    Type_____

Automatic Transmission (pts)_____

    Type_____

Front Differential (pts)_____

    Type_____

Rear Differential (pts)_____

    Type_____

Transfer Case (pts)_____

    Type_____

FREQUENTLY REPLACED PARTS
Use these spaces to record the part numbers of frequently replaced parts.

PCV VALVE   **OIL FILTER**   **AIR FILTER**

Manufacturer_____   **Manufacturer**_____   **Manufacturer**_____

Part No._____   **Part No.**_____   **Part No.**_____

General Information and Maintenance

HOW TO USE THIS BOOK

This book has been written to aid the Mustang II owner perform maintenance, tune-ups and repairs on his automobile. It is intended for both the novice and for those more familiar with auto repairs. Since this book contains information on very simple operations (Chapters 1 and 2) and the more involved ones (Chapters 3–11), the user will not outgrow the book as he masters simple repairs and is ready to progress to more difficult operations.

Several things were assumed of you while the repair procedures were being written. They are mentioned here so that you will be aware of them. It was assumed that you own, or are willing to purchase, a basic set of hand tools and equipment. A skeletal listing of tools and equipment has been drawn up for you.

For many repair operations, the factory has suggested a special tool to perform the repairs. If it was at all possible, a conventional tool was substituted for the special tool in these cases. However, there are some operations which cannot be done without the use of these tools. To perform these jobs correctly, it will be necessary to order the tool through your local Ford dealer's parts department.

Two basic rules of automobile mechanics deserve mentioning here. Whenever the left-side of the car is referred to, it is meant to specify the driver's side. Likewise, the right-side of the car means the passenger's side. Also, most screws, nuts, and bolts are removed by turning counterclockwise and tightened by turning clockwise.

Before performing any repairs, read the entire section of the book that deals with that job. In many places a description of the system is provided. By reading this first, and then reading the entire repair procedure, you will understand the function of the system you will be working on and what will be involved in the repair operation, prior to starting the job. This will enable you to avoid problems and also to help you learn about your car while you are working on it.

While every effort was made to make the book as simple, yet as detailed as possible, there is no substitute for personal experience. You can gain the confidence and feel for mechanical things needed to make auto repairs only by doing them yourself. If you take your time and concentrate on what you are doing, you will be amazed at how fast you can learn.

TOOLS AND EQUIPMENT

Now that you have purchased this book and committed yourself to maintaining your car, a small set of basic tools and equipment will prove handy. The first group of items should be adequate for most maintenance and light repair procedures:

- Sliding T-bar handle or ratchet wrench;
- ⅜ in. drive socket wrench set (with breaker bar) (metric);
- Universal adapter for socket wrench set;
- Flat blade and phillips head screwdrivers;
- Pliers;
- Adjustable wrench;
- Locking pliers;
- Open-end wrench set (metric);
- Feeler gauge set;
- Oil filter strap wrench;
- Brake adjusting spoon;
- Drift pin;
- Torque wrench;
- Hammer.

Along with the above mentioned tools, the following equipment should be on hand;

- Scissors jack or hydraulic jack of sufficient capacity;
- Jackstands of sufficient capacity;
- Wheel blocks;
- Grease gun (hand-operated type);
- Drip pan (low and wide);
- Drop light;
- Tire pressure gauge;
- Penetrating oil (spray lubricant);
- Waterless hand cleaner.

In this age of emission controls and high priced gasoline, it is important to keep your car in proper tune. The following items, though they will represent an investment equal or greater to that of the first group, will tell you everything you might need to know about a car's state of tune:

- 12-volt test light;
- Compression gauge;
- Manifold vacuum gauge;
- Power timing light;
- Dwell-tachometer.

MODEL IDENTIFICATION

Mustang II hardtop

Mustang II 3-door 2 + 2

Mustang II Mach 1

Mustang II Ghia

$$\mathscr{F}\ 4S56H100001\mathscr{F}$$

(VEHICLE IDENTIFICATION NUMBER)

Vehicle identification label

SERIAL NUMBER IDENTIFICATION

Vehicle Identification Number

The official vehicle identification number for title and registration purposes is stamped on a metal tag, which is fastened to the top of the instrument panel. The tag is located on the driver's side, visible through the windshield. The first digit in the vehicle identification number is the model year of the car (4—1974, 5—1975 etc.). The second digit is the assembly plant code for the plant in which the vehicle was built. The third and fourth digits are the body serial code designations (2-dr sdn, 3-dr sdn, etc.). The fifth digit is the engine code which identifies the type of engine originally installed in the vehicle (see "Engine Codes" chart). The last six digits are the consecutive unit numbers which start at 100,001 for the first car of a model year built at each assembly plant.

Vehicle Certification Label

The vehicle certification label is attached to the rear face of the driver's door. The top half of the label contains the name of the vehicle

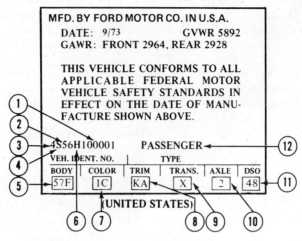

1. Consecutive unit no.
2. Body serial code
3. Model year code
4. Assembly plant code
5. Body type code
6. Engine code
7. Color code
8. Trim code
9. Transmission code
10. Rear axle code
11. District—special equipment
12. Vehicle type

Vehicle certification label

manufacturer, date of manufacture and the manufacturer's certification statement. The top half of the label also contains the gross vehicle weight rating and the front and rear gross vehicle axle ratings. The gross vehicle weight rating is useful in determining the load carrying capacity of your car. Merely subtract the curb weight from the posted gross weight and what is left over is how much you can haul around. The bottom half of the vehicle certification label contains the vehicle identification number (as previously described), the body type code, the exterior paint color code, the interior trim color and material code, the rear axle code (see "Rear Axle Codes" chart), the transmission code (see "Transmission Codes" chart) and the district and special order codes.

The vehicle certification label is constructed of special material to guard against its alteration. If it is tampered with or removed, it will be destroyed or the word "VOID" will appear.

Engine Codes

Engine No. Cyl Displacement cu in. (cc)	Bbl	'74	'75–'78
4—140 (2300)	2	Y	Y
6—170 (2800)	2	Z	Z
8—302 (4900)	2		F

Rear Axle Codes

Ratio	'74	'75–'76 °	'77–'78
2.79 : 1	—	3	3
3.00 : 1	—	6 (O)	6
3.18 : 1	—	—	4
3.40 : 1	—	7	7
3.55 : 1	G (X)	G (X)	—

* Figures in parentheses designate locking differential

Transmission Codes

Type	'74	'75–'76	'77–'78
4-speed manual	5	5	6
4-speed manual	6	6	7
C3 automatic	V	V	V
C4 automatic	W	W	W

ROUTINE MAINTENANCE

Maintenance Interval Chart

The numerals in the maintenance chart represent the suggested intervals between service in thousands of miles or number of months, whichever occurs first. For example:

Where the number 4 appears, the intervals are 4,000 miles or 4 months, whichever interval elapses first.

In the case of oil changes, however, where the mileage interval is 7,500 or 10,000, the time interval is 6 months rather than 7½ months or 10 months. Thus, in that case only, the number 7.5 means 7,500 miles or 6 months, whichever interval has elapsed first, etc.

Double the oil change frequency when trips are generally less than 10 miles and the weather is consistently 10 degrees F. or less, or when driving in very dusty conditions.

If the designation "@" appears, specific mileages/months figures are given rather than intervals.

1974–76
ENGINE

Oil change 6
Oil filter replacement 12
Oil filler breather cap cleaning 12
Fuel filter replacement 6
Air filter cleaning 12
Air filter replacement 24
Carburetor idle fuel mixture, fast idle speed, curb idle speed, and throttle solenoid positioner off-speed adjustment (4 cyl) . . 12
Carburetor idle fuel mixture, fast idle speed, curb idle speed, and throttle solenoid positioner off-speed adjustment (V6 and V8 engines) 24
Throttle and choke linkage check, delay and deceleration valve (fuel or spark) check (4 cyl) 12
Throttle and choke linkage check, delay and deceleration valve (fuel or spark) check (V6 and V8 engines) 24
Valve clearance adjustment (V6) 12
Crankcase breather filter (in air cleaner) replacement 24
Intake manifold bolt/nut torque check . . . 12
Evaporative emission system vapor lines emission canister and fuel filler cap check 24
Positive crankcase ventilation (PCV) valve replacement 24
PCV system hoses and tubes check/cleaning 12
Ignition timing adjustment 12
Distributor breaker point inspection (1974 only) 6
Distributor breaker point replacement (1974 only) 12
Distributor cap and rotor inspection (4 cyl) 12

Distributor cap and rotor inspection (V6 and V8 models) 24
Spark plug replacement; plug wire inspection 12
Spark control system (spark delay valve, etc.) operational check 12
Air cleaner temperature control system operational check 12
Thermactor air injection operational check 24
Belt-driven accessories mounting bolt torque check (4 cyl) 24
EGR system check and cleaning (using leaded gas) 12
(Using unleaded gas, EGR system requires no scheduled maintenance)
Drive belt tension check 12
Coolant antifreeze protection check; system leakage check 12
Coolant draining and flushing 36

CHASSIS

Automatic transmission fluid level check . . 12
Brake master cylinder reservoir fluid level check 12
Steering linkage free-play check; rubber seal damage check 12
Front suspension ball joint lubrication 36
Rear axle fluid level check 12
Automatic transmission band adjustment . 12 *
Brake lining check 24
Front wheel bearings cleaning, repacking and adjusting 24
Manual transmission fluid level check 12
Clutch pedal free-play adjustment 6

---

* Normal service—adjust at 12,000 miles only unless abnormal transmission operation is noticed
Severe service—adjust at 12,000 mile intervals starting at 6,000 miles

1977
2.3 LITER, 2.8 LITER ENGINES

Maintenance Operation	Sticker Designation	
	"A"	"B"
Change Engine Oil	10	10
Replace Oil Filter	20	30
Replace Spark Plugs	20②	30②
Check V6 Valve Clearance	@ 5, 20, etc.	@ 10, 30, etc.
Check Coolant Condition & Protection	Annually	Annually
Replace Coolant	40①	40①
Check Cooling System Hoses & Clamps	40①	40①

Maintenance Operation	"A"	"B"
Check Drive Belt Tension	20	@ 10, 30
Replace 2.3 Liter Engine PCV Valve	20	30
Check 2.3 Liter Engine Idle Mixture	20	30
Check/Adjust Fast Idle	@ 5	@ 10
Check/Adjust Idle Speed	@ 5, 20	@ 10, 30
Check/Adjust TSP Off Speed	5	10
Check Choke	10	@ 30
Replace PCV Air Filter	30	30
Replace Air Cleaner Element	30	30
Check Air Cleaner Temperature Control	@ 40	@ 30
Check Thermactor Delay Valve (if equipped)	20	30
Inspect Evaporative Emissions System	40	30
Adjust Ignition Timing	5	10

Maintenance Operation	"A"	"B"
Check Choke	22.5	30
Replace Air Cleaner Element	30	30
Replace PCV Filter	30	30
Check Air Cleaner Temperature Control	30	45
Check Thermactor Delay Valve	22.5	30
Inspect Evaporative Emissions System		
Check/Adjust Ignition Timing	7.5	7.5

1. At specified mileage or at 36 months
2. Clean and regap plugs every 6,000 miles under severe service—i.e. prolonged idling, trailer towing, or short trips in cold weather.

1. At specified mileage or at 36 months
2. Clean and regap plugs every 6,000 miles under severe service—i.e., prolonged idling, trailer towing, or short trips in cold weather.

302 V8 ENGINE

Maintenance Operation	Sticker Designation "A"	Sticker Designation "B"
Change Engine Oil Change Oil Filter	7.5 @ 7.5, 22.5, etc.	7.5 @ 7.5, 22.5, etc.
Check Coolant Condition & Protection	Annually 45①	Annually 45①
Replace Coolant	45①	45①
Check Cooling System Hoses and Clamps	45①	45①
Check Belt Tension & Condition	22.5	@ 7.5, 30
Replace Spark Plugs	22.5②	30②
Replace PCV Valve (if specified on sticker)	22.5	30
Check Idle Fuel Mixture (if specified on sticker)	22.5	30
Check/Adjust Fast Idle Speed	7.5	7.5
Check/Adjust Idle Speed	@ 7.5, 22.5	@ 7.5, 30
Check/Adjust "TSP" Off Speed	7.5	7.5

1978

2.3 LITER, 2.8 LITER ENGINES

Maintenance Operation	Sticker Designation "A"	Sticker Designation "B"
Change Engine Oil	10	10
Change Oil Filter	10	10
Check Cooling System Hoses & Clamps	50①	50①
Check Coolant Condition & Protection	Annually	Annually
Replace Coolant	50①	50①
Check Belt Tension & Condition	20	@ 10, 30, etc.
Replace Air Cleaner Element	30	30
Replace Crankcase Emission Filter	30	30
Replace Spark Plugs	20	30
Replace PCV Valve	20	30
Check Idle Mixture (If there are enrichment specifications on sticker)	20	30
Check Thermactor Delay Valve	20	30
Check Choke System	20	30
Check V6 Valve Clearance	@ 5, 20, etc.	@ 10, 30, etc.
Check Idle Speeds (except below)	@ 5, 10	@ 5, 10
Check Idle Speed (2.3 engine w/Feedback carburetor)	—	@ 5

1. At specified mileage or 36 months.

302 V8 ENGINE

Maintenance Operation	Sticker Designation	
	"A"	"B"
Change Engine Oil	7.5	7.5
Change Oil Filter	@ 7.5, 22.5, etc.	@ 7.5, 22.5, etc.
Check Cooling System Hoses & Clamps	52.5①	52.5①
Check Coolant Condition & Protection	Annually	Annually
Replace Coolant	52.5①	52.5①
Check Belt Tension & Condition	22.5	@ 7.5, 30, etc.
Replace Air Cleaner Element	30	30
Replace Crankcase Emission Filter	52.5	52.5
Replace Spark Plugs	22.5	22.5
Replace PCV Valve	36	48
Check Idle Mixture (If there are enrichment specifications on sticker)	@ 22.5	@ 30
Check Thermactor Delay Valve	22.5	30
Check Choke System	22.5	30
Check Curb and Fast Idle Speeds	7.5	7.5

1. Every 3 years or at mileage indicated.

1977–78

CHASSIS

Maintenance Operation	Sticker Designation	
	"A"	"B"
Inspect Exhaust System Heat Shields	@ 22.5, 37.5, etc.	@ 22.5, 37.5, etc.
Inspect Brake Lining, Lines, Hoses, and Repack Front Wheel Bearings	30	30
Lubricate Front Suspension and Steering Linkage	30	30
Check Brake Fluid Level	30	30
Check/Adjust Clutch Pedal Free Play	@ 15, 22.5, etc.	@ 15, 22.5, etc.
Change Automatic Transmission Fluid	22.5①	22.5①
Adjust Automatic Transmission Bands	7.5①	7.5①

1. In severe service, such as prolonged idling, continuous operation at low speeds, or trailer towing. Figure refers to mileage only.

Air Filter Replacement

At the recommended intervals in the maintenance schedule, the air filter element must be replaced. If the vehicle is operated under dusty conditions, the element should be changed sooner. On all V8 models, the air filter cover is retained with a single wing nut atop the cover. On 4 cylinder and V6 models, the cover is retained by either two wing nuts or by four metal clips.

To replace the element, unscrew the wing nut(s) or unsnap the metal clips, lift off the cover and discard the old element. While the cover is removed, check the choke plate and external linkage for freedom of movement. Brush away all dirt and spray the plate corners and linkage with a small amount of penetrating cleaner/lubricant. Wipe the air filter housing clean with a solvent-moistened rag and install the new element with the word "FRONT" facing front. Then install the cover and fasten the clips or wing nut(s).

NOTE: *Make sure that all of the emission control hoses and ducts fit tightly to their connections at the air cleaner.*

Crankcase Ventilation Filter Replacement

At the recommended intervals in the maintenance chart, or sooner if the car is operated in dusty areas, at low rpm, for trailer towing,

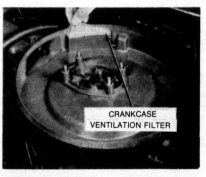

Crankcase ventilation filter

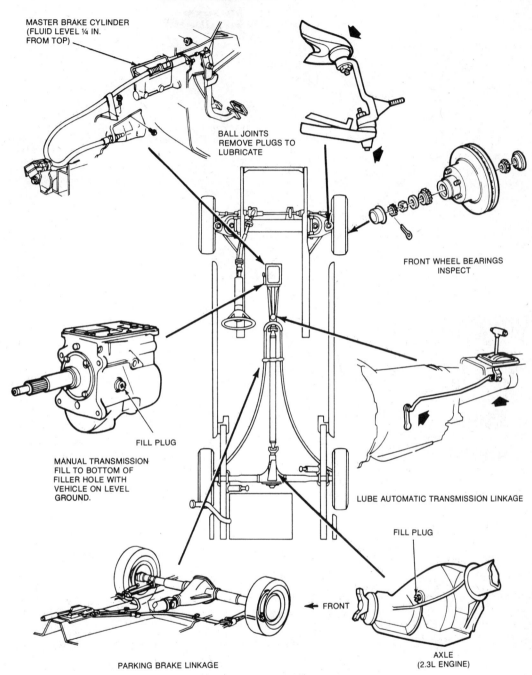

LUBRICATE CLUTCH LINKAGE

MASTER BRAKE CYLINDER
(FLUID LEVEL ¼ IN.
FROM TOP)

BALL JOINTS
REMOVE PLUGS TO
LUBRICATE

FRONT WHEEL BEARINGS
INSPECT

FILL PLUG

MANUAL TRANSMISSION
FILL TO BOTTOM OF
FILLER HOLE WITH
VEHICLE ON LEVEL
GROUND.

LUBE AUTOMATIC TRANSMISSION LINKAGE

FILL PLUG

◀ FRONT

PARKING BRAKE LINKAGE

AXLE
(2.3L ENGINE)

Chassis lubrication diagram

or if the car is used for short runs preventing the engine from reaching operating temperature, the crankcase ventilation filter in the air cleaner must be replaced. Do not attempt to clean this filter.

To replace the filter, simply remove the air filter cover and pull the old crankcase filter out of its housing. Push a new crankcase filter into the housing and install the air filter cover.

Positive Crankcase Ventilation (PCV) Valve

See "Emission Controls Component Service" in Chapter 4.

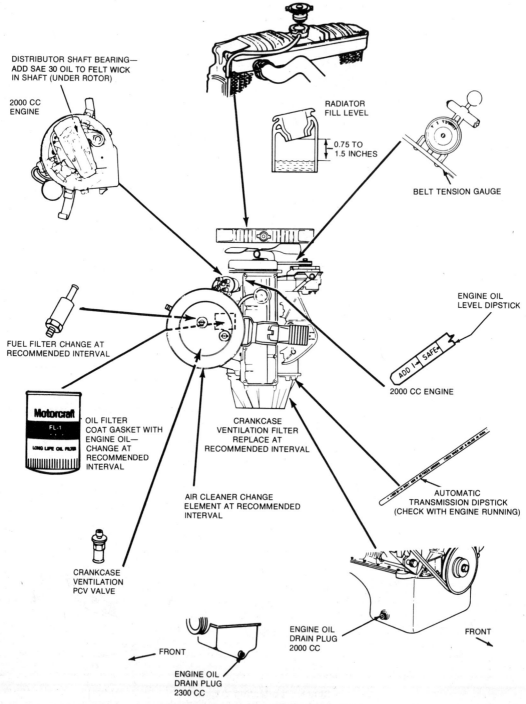

DISTRIBUTOR SHAFT BEARING—
ADD SAE 30 OIL TO FELT WICK
IN SHAFT (UNDER ROTOR)

2000 CC
ENGINE

RADIATOR
FILL LEVEL

0.75 TO
1.5 INCHES

BELT TENSION GAUGE

ENGINE OIL
LEVEL DIPSTICK

ADD   SAFE

2000 CC ENGINE

FUEL FILTER CHANGE AT
RECOMMENDED INTERVAL

Motorcraft
FL-1
LONG LIFE OIL FILTER

OIL FILTER
COAT GASKET WITH
ENGINE OIL—
CHANGE AT
RECOMMENDED
INTERVAL

CRANKCASE
VENTILATION FILTER
REPLACE AT
RECOMMENDED INTERVAL

AUTOMATIC
TRANSMISSION DIPSTICK
(CHECK WITH ENGINE RUNNING)

AIR CLEANER CHANGE
ELEMENT AT RECOMMENDED
INTERVAL

CRANKCASE
VENTILATION
PCV VALVE

FRONT

ENGINE OIL
DRAIN PLUG
2000 CC

FRONT

FRONT

ENGINE OIL
DRAIN PLUG
2300 CC

Four-cylinder engine lubrication points

Evaporative Control System Canister

See "Emission Control Component Service" in Chapter 4.

Exhaust Gas Recirculation System Component Cleaning

See "Emission Controls Component Service" in Chapter 4.

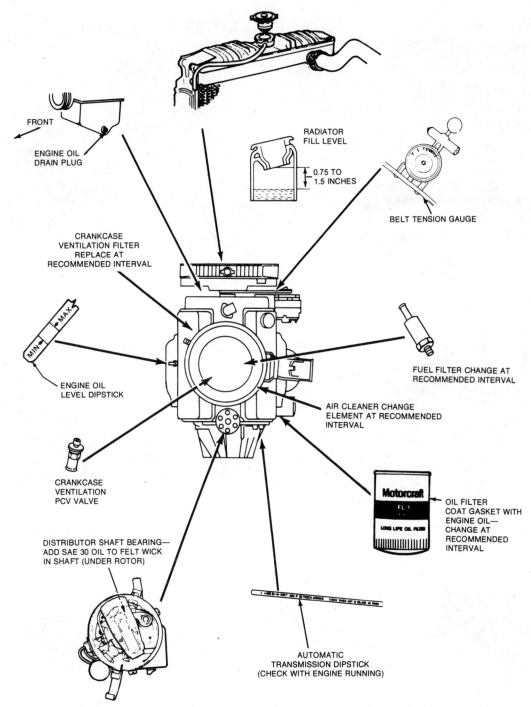

V6 engine lubrication points

Belts

DRIVE BELT ADJUSTMENT

Once a year or at 12,000 mile intervals, the tension (and condition) of the alternator, power steering (if so equipped), air conditioning (if so equipped), and Thermactor air pump drive belts should be checked, and, if necessary, adjusted. Loose accessory drive belts can lead to poor engine cooling and diminish alternator, power steering pump, air conditioning compressor or Thermactor air pump output. A belt that is too tight places a severe strain on the water pump, al-

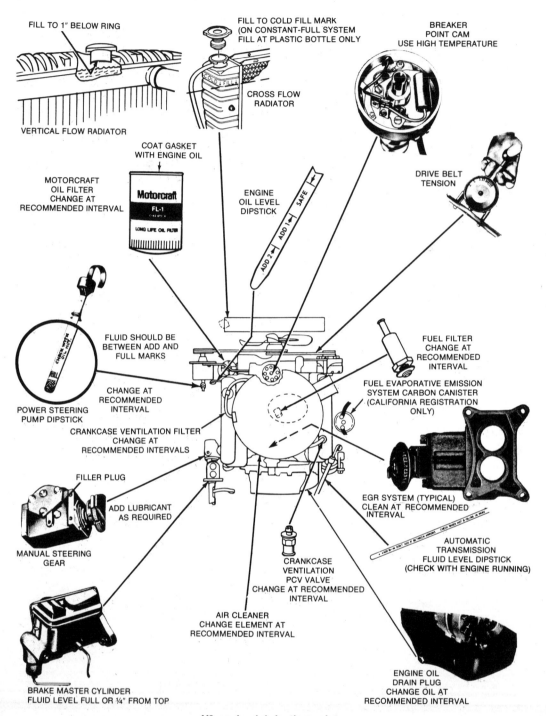

FILL TO 1" BELOW RING

VERTICAL FLOW RADIATOR

FILL TO COLD FILL MARK
(ON CONSTANT-FULL SYSTEM
FILL AT PLASTIC BOTTLE ONLY

CROSS FLOW
RADIATOR

BREAKER
POINT CAM
USE HIGH TEMPERATURE

COAT GASKET
WITH ENGINE OIL

MOTORCRAFT
OIL FILTER
CHANGE AT
RECOMMENDED INTERVAL

Motorcraft
FL-1
LONG LIFE OIL FILTER

ENGINE
OIL LEVEL
DIPSTICK

DRIVE BELT
TENSION

FLUID SHOULD BE
BETWEEN ADD AND
FULL MARKS

CHANGE AT
RECOMMENDED
INTERVAL

POWER STEERING
PUMP DIPSTICK

FUEL FILTER
CHANGE AT
RECOMMENDED
INTERVAL

FUEL EVAPORATIVE EMISSION
SYSTEM CARBON CANISTER
(CALIFORNIA REGISTRATION
ONLY)

CRANKCASE VENTILATION FILTER
CHANGE AT RECOMMENDED INTERVALS

FILLER PLUG

ADD LUBRICANT
AS REQUIRED

MANUAL STEERING
GEAR

EGR SYSTEM (TYPICAL)
CLEAN AT RECOMMENDED
INTERVAL

AUTOMATIC
TRANSMISSION
FLUID LEVEL DIPSTICK
(CHECK WITH ENGINE RUNNING)

CRANKCASE
VENTILATION
PCV VALVE
CHANGE AT RECOMMENDED
INTERVAL

AIR CLEANER
CHANGE ELEMENT AT
RECOMMENDED INTERVAL

BRAKE MASTER CYLINDER
FLUID LEVEL FULL OR ¼" FROM TOP

ENGINE OIL
DRAIN PLUG
CHANGE OIL AT
RECOMMENDED INTERVAL

V8 engine lubrication points

ternator, power steering pump, compressor or air pump bearings.

Replace any belt that is so glazed, worn or stretched that it cannot be tightened enough for it to run without slippage. On vehicles with matched belts, replace both belts. New belts are to be adjusted to a tension of 140 lbs

(½ in., ⅜ in., and ¹⁵/₃₂ in. wide belts) or 80 lbs (¼ in. wide belts) measured on a belt tension gauge. Any belt that has been operating for a minimum of 10 minutes is considered a used belt. In the first 10 minutes, the belt should stretch to its maximum extent. After 10 minutes, stop the engine and recheck the

Checking alternator belt tension

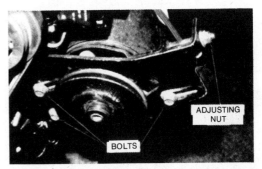

Adjusting power steering reservoir drive belt tension—V6 and V8

belt tension. Belt tension for a used belt should be maintained at 110 lbs (all except ¼ in. wide belts) or 60 lbs (¼ in. wide belts). If a belt tension gauge is not available, the following procedures may be used.

Alternator (Fan Drive) Belt

1. Position a ruler perpendicular to the drive belt at its longest run. Test the tightness of the belt by pressing it firmly with your thumb. The deflection should not exceed ¼ in.

2. If the deflection exceeds ¼ in., loosen the alternator mounting and adjusting arm bolts.

3a. On 4 and 6 cylinder models, use a pry bar, such as a pipe or broom handle, to move the alternator toward or away from the engine until the proper tension is reached. CAUTION: *Apply tension to the front of the alternator only. Positioning the pry bar against the rear end housing will damage the alternator.*

3b. On V8 models, place a 1 in. open-end or adjustable wrench on the adjusting arm bolt and pull on the wrench until the proper tension is achieved.

4. Holding the alternator in place to maintain tension, tighten the adjusting arm bolt. Recheck the belt tension. When the belt is properly tensioned, tighten the alternator mounting bolt.

Power Steering Drive Belt

ALL MODELS

1. Position a ruler perpendicular to the drive belt at its longest run. Test the tightness of the belt by pressing it firmly with your thumb. The deflection should be about ¼ in.

2. To adjust the belt tension, loosen the three bolts in the three elongated adjusting slots at the power steering pump attaching bracket.

3. Turn the steering pump drive belt adjusting nut as required until the proper deflection is obtained. Turning the adjusting nut clockwise will increase tension and decrease deflection; counterclockwise will decrease tension and increase deflection.

4. Without disturbing the pump, tighten the three attaching bolts.

Air Conditioning Compressor Drive Belt

1. Position a ruler perpendicular to the drive belt at its longest run. Test the tightness of the belt by pressing it firmly with your thumb. The deflection should not exceed ¼ in.

2. If the engine is equipped with an idler pulley, loosen the idler pulley adjusting bolt, insert a pry bar between the pulley and the engine (or in the idler pulley adjusting slot), and adjust the tension accordingly. If the engine is not equipped with an idler pulley, the alternator must be moved to accomplish this adjustment, as outlined under "Alternator (Fan Drive) Belt."

3. When the proper tension is reached, tighten the idler pulley adjusting bolt (if so equipped) or the alternator adjusting and mounting bolts.

Thermactor Air Pump Drive Belt

4 CYLINDER AND V8 MODELS

1. Position a ruler perpendicular to the drive belt at its longest run. Test the tightness of the belt by pressing it firmly with your thumb. The deflection should not exceed ¼ in.

2. To adjust the belt tension, loosen the single bolt in the elongated hole of the adjusting bracket.

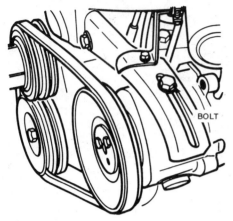

Adjusting Thermactor air pump drive belt tension—4 cylinder

NOTE: *On V8 Models, the adjusting bolt is UNDERNEATH the pump.*

3. Using a broom handle or other suitable lever, move the air pump away from (to tighten) or toward (to loosen) the engine until the proper tension is reached.

4. Without disturbing the setting, tighten the adjusting bolt.

V6 MODELS

The drive belt for the Thermactor air pump on V6 models is the same belt which drives the alternator. Follow the procedure outlined under "Alternator (Fan Drive) Belt" on these models.

Air Conditioning

AIR CONDITIONING REFRIGERANT CHECK

Once a year, before hot weather sets in, it is advisable to check the refrigerant charge in the air conditioner system. This may be accomplished by looking at the sight glass located in the engine compartment, next to the radiator. First, wipe the sight glass clean

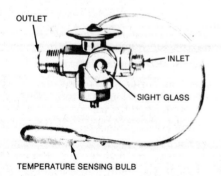

Air conditioning sight glass—typical

with a cloth wrapped around the eraser end of a pencil. Connect a tachometer to the engine with the positive line connected to the distributor side of the ignition coil and the negative line connected to a good ground, such as the steering box. Have a friend operate the air conditioner controls while you look at the sight glass. Have your friend set the dash panel control to maximum cooling. Start the engine and idle at 1,500 rpm. While looking at the sight glass, signal your friend to turn the blower switch to the High position. If a few bubbles appear immediately after the blower is turned on and then disappear, the system is sufficiently charged with refrigerant. If, on the other hand, a large amount of bubbles, foam or froth continue after the blower has operated for a few seconds, then the system is in need of additional refrigerant. If no bubbles appear at all, then there is either sufficient refrigerant in the system, or it is bone dry. The way to clear this question up is to have your friend turn the blower switch off and on (engine running at 1,500 rpm) about every 10 seconds or so while you look at the sight glass. This will cycle the magnetic clutch. If the system is properly charged, bubbles will appear in the sight glass a few seconds after the blower is turned off and disappear when the blower is turned on although they may linger awhile in extremely hot weather. If no bubbles appear when the blower is in the "OFF" position, then the system should be serviced by an authorized dealer and checked for leaks.

Fluid Level Checks
ENGINE OIL

The oil level in the engine should be checked at fuel stops. The check should be made with the engine warm and switched off for a period of about one minute so that the oil has time to drain down into the crankcase. Pull out the dipstick, wipe it clean and reinsert it. The level of the oil must be kept within the "SAFE" area, above the "ADD 1" mark on the dipstick. If the oil level is kept above the "SAFE" area, heavy oil consumption will result. If the level remains below the "ADD 1" mark, severe engine damage may result. The "ADD 1" and "ADD 2" refer to US measure quarts. Remember that in Canada, the Imperial measure quart is used and it is equal to $5/4$ of a US quart. When topping up, make sure that the oil is the same type and viscosity rating as the oil already in the crank-case.

MANUAL TRANSMISSION FLUID

At the recommended intervals in the maintenance schedule, the fluid level in the manual transmission should be checked. With the car standing perfectly level, apply the parking brake, set the transmission in Neutral, stop the engine and block all four wheels. Wipe all dirt and grease from the filler plug on the side of the transmission. Using a sliding T-bar handle or an adjustable wrench, remove the filler plug. The lubricant should be level with the bottom of the filler hole. If required, add SAE 80 manual transmission fluid to the proper level using a syringe. Install the filler plug.

AUTOMATIC TRANSMISSION FLUID

At the recommended intervals in the maintenance schedule, the automatic transmission fluid level should be checked. The level should also be checked if abnormal shifting behavior is noticed. With the car standing on a level surface, firmly apply the parking brake. Run the engine at idle until normal operating temperature is reached. Then, with the right foot firmly planted on the brake pedal, shift the transmission selector through all of the positions, allowing sufficient time in each range to engage the transmission. Shift the selector into Park (P). With the engine still running, pull out the transmission dipstick, located at the right rear of the engine compartment. Wipe it clean and reinsert it, pushing it down until it seats in the tube. Pull it out and check the level. The level should be between the "ADD" and "FULL" marks. Add ATF Type F as required through the dipstick tube.

CAUTION: *Do not overfill the transmission, as foaming and loss of fluid through the vent may cause the transmission to malfunction.*

BRAKE MASTER CYLINDER FLUID

At the recommended intervals in the maintenance schedule, the fluid in the master cylinder should be checked. Before checking the level, carefully wipe off the master cylinder cover to remove any dirt or water that would fall into the fluid reservoir. Then push the retaining clip to one side and remove the cover and seal. The fluid level should be maintained at ¼ in. from the top of the reservoir.

Top up as necessary with heavy-duty brake fluid meeting SAE 70 R3 specifications.

COOLANT

The coolant level in the radiator should be checked on a monthly basis, preferably when the engine is cold. On a cold engine, the coolant level should be maintained at one inch below the filler neck on vertical flow radiators, and 2½ in. below the filler neck at the "COLD FILL" mark on crossflow radiators. Top up as necessary with a mixture of 50% water and 50% ethylene glycol antifreeze, to ensure proper rust, freezing, and boiling protection. If you have to add coolant more often than once a month or if you have to add more than one quart at a time, check the cooling system for leaks. Also check for water in the crankcase oil, indicating a blown cylinder head gasket.

CAUTION: *Exercise extreme care when removing the cap from a hot radiator. Wait a few minutes until the engine has time to cool somewhat, then wrap a thick towel around the radiator cap and slowly turn it counterclockwise to the first stop. Step back and allow the pressure to release from the cooling system. Then, when the steam has stopped venting, press down on the cap, turn it one more stop counterclockwise and remove the cap.*

REAR AXLE FLUID

At the recommended intervals in the maintenance schedule, the rear axle fluid level should be checked. With the car standing perfectly level, apply the parking brake, set the transmission in Park or 1st gear, stop the engine and block all 4 wheels.

Wipe all dirt and grease from the filler plug area. Using a sliding T-bar handle (⅜ in.) or an adjustable wrench, remove the filler plug. The fluid level must be maintained at ¼ in. from the bottom of the filler plug hole. To check the fluid level in the axle, bend a clean, straight piece of wire to a 90° angle and insert the bent end of the wire into the axle while resting it on the lower edge of the filler plug hole. Top up as necessary with SAE 80 or SAE 90 hypoid gear lube, using a syringe. Install the filler plug.

POWER STEERING RESERVOIR FLUID

At the recommended intervals in the maintenance schedule, the fluid level in the power steering reservoir (if so equipped) should be checked. Run the engine until the fluid

Capacities

Year	Model	Engine Displacement Cu In. (cc)	Engine Crankcase (qts)		Transmission (pts)		Drive Axle (pts)	Gasoline Tank (gals)	Cooling System (qts)	
			With Filter	Without Filter	Manual 4-spd	Automatic			W/ AC	W/O AC
'74	All	4—140 (2300)	5.0	4.0	4.0	16.0	4.0	13.0	9.2	8.8
	All	6—170 (2800)	5.0	4.5	4.0	15.0	4.0	13.0	12.8	12.5
'75–	All	4—140 (2300)	4.5	4.0	3.5	16.0	4.0②	13.0①	9.1	8.5
'76	All	6—170 (2800)	5.0	4.5	3.5	15.0	4.0②	13.0①	13.2	12.3
	All	8—302 (4900)	5.0	4.0	—	15.0	4.0②	13.0①	16.3	16.3
'77	All	4—140 (2300)	4.5	4.0	3.5	16.0	3.0④	13.0	8.5	9.1
	All	6—170 (2800)	5.0	4.5	3.5	16.0	4.5	13.0	8.8③	9.0
	All	8—302 (4900)	5.0	4.0	3.5	18.0	4.5	16.5	16.3	16.3
'78	All	4—140 (2300)	4.5	4.0	3.5	16.0	3.0	13.0	8.8	9.1
	All	6—170 (2800)	5.0	4.5	3.5	16.0	4.5	13.0	8.8③	9.0
	All	8—302 (4900)	5.0	4.0	3.5	13.4	4.5	16.5	16.3	16.3

① 16.5 with auxiliary tank
② 6.75 in. axle—3.0; 8 in. axle—4.5
③ Applies to automatic only; manual—8.3
④ 4.5 w/Traction–Lok differential

reaches operating temperature. Turn the steering wheel from lock-to-lock several times to relieve the system of any trapped air. Turn off the engine. Check the level on the reservoir dipstick. The level must be maintained on the crosshatch pattern between the Full mark and the end of the dipstick. Top up as necessary with ATF Type F.

MANUAL STEERING GEAR LUBRICANT

If there is binding in the steering gear, or if the wheels do not return to a straight-ahead position after a turn, the lubricant level of the steering gear should be checked.

Remove the filler plug and upper cover bolt from the cover using a 9/16 in. wrench. With the holes exposed, have a friend slowly turn the steering wheel to the right until it stops. At this point, lubricant should be rising within the upper cover bolt hole. Then, have your friend slowly turn the steering wheel to the left until it stops. At this point, lubricant should be rising in the filler plug hole. If lubricant does not rise in the respective holes during either of these operations, top up as necessary with SAE 90 steering gear lube for rack and pinion type steering. Steering gear capacity is 0.44 pints. Replace the cover bolt and filler plug when finished.

Battery Care

Every six months or 6,000 miles, the battery's state of charge should be checked with a hydrometer. A fully-charged battery should have a hydrometer reading of 1.260–1.310 specific gravity at 80°F electrolyte temperature. To correct readings for temperature variations, add 0.004 to the hydrometer reading for every 10°F that the electrolyte is above 80°F; subtract 0.004 for every 10°F below 80°F electrolyte temperature. The readings obtained in all six cells should be nearly equal. If any cell is markedly lower, it is defective. If this low reading is not improved by charging, the battery should be replaced, particularly before cold weather sets in. When charging a weak or sulphated (brownish color of electrolyte) battery, the slow charging method must be used. Never allow electrolyte temperature to exceed 120°F during charging.

Inspect the battery terminals for a tight fit on the poles and check for corrosion. Remove any deposits with a wire brush and coat the terminals, after placing them on the poles, with petroleum jelly to prevent further corrosion. Check the battery case for cracks or leakage.

Tires

The tread wear of the tires should be checked about twice a year. Tread wear should be even across the tire. Excessive wear in the center of the tread indicates overinflation. Excessive wear on the outer corners of the tread indicates underinflation. An irregular wear pattern is usually an indication of improper front wheel alignment or incorrect wheel balance. On a vehicle with improper front wheel alignment, the car will tend to pull to one side of a flat road if the steering wheel is released while driving the car. Incorrect wheel balance will usually produce vibrations at high speeds. When the front wheels are out of balance, they will produce vibration in the steering wheel, while rear wheels out of balance will produce vibration in the floor pan of the car.

TIRE PRESSURE

One way to prolong tire life is to maintain proper pressure in the tires. This should be checked at least once a month and should be done with the tires cold (not driven for one hour). If you check the tire pressure when the tires are warm, you will obtain a falsely high reading. Refer to the accompanying tire inflation chart, or to the sticker attached to the right-hand door lock pillar. Sustained high speed driving requires adjustment of tire pressure levels to 4 psi over the normal rating, front and rear, as long as this does not cause the pressure to exceed the maximum rating stamped on the tire. Snow tires require a 4 psi cold increase in the rear tire pressure above that listed in the chart. For example, a B78 x 13 snow tire will require 30 psi to be properly inflated. Under no circum-

stances must the maximum inflation pressure, which is stamped on the sidewall of the tire, be exceeded. If you plan to do any trailer towing, it is recommended that tire pressure (cold), be increased by 6 psi on the rear wheels, again being careful not to exceed the maximum inflation pressure.

Tire Inflation Chart—1974–76 (cold psi)

Tire Size	Front	Rear
B78 x 13	26	26
BR78 x 13	26	26
BR70 x 13	26	26
CR70 x 13	26	26
195/70 x R13 (302 only)	26	26

TIRE ROTATION

Another way to prolong tire life is to rotate the tires at regular intervals. These intervals depend on the type of tire and on the type of driving you do, but generally they should be about 6,000 miles or twice a year, or sooner if abnormal wear due to front end misalignment is apparent. Follow the accompanying tire rotation diagram for the type of tires your car is equipped with; conventional (bias-ply or bias-belted) or radial-ply. Because of the design of radial-ply tires, it is imperative that they remain on the same side of the car and travel in the same direction. Therefore, in a 4-tire rotational sequence, the front and rear radial tires of the same side are merely swapped. Studded snow tires, radial or conventional, are just as choosy about the direction they travel in. If you equip your car with

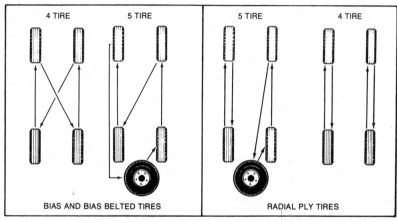

BIAS AND BIAS BELTED TIRES   RADIAL PLY TIRES

Tire rotation diagrams

studded snow tires, mark them "Left" or "Right" prior to removal so that next year they may be installed on the same side of the car. If a studded snow tire that was used on the left rear wheel one year is installed on the right rear wheel the next year, the result will be a dangerous condition where the studs pull out of the tire and are flung to the rear. Remember, never mix radial, belted, and/or conventional type tires on your car. Always make sure that all tires and wheels are of the same size, type and load-carrying capacity.

Fuel Filter Replacement

Every 12,000 miles or 12 months, the fuel filter must be replaced. The filter is located inline at the carburetor inlet on most models. Some 1974–76 V6 equipped Mustang IIs use an inline fuel filter located near the fuel pump. The procedure for replacing the fuel filter (except inline filter) is as follows:

1. Remove the air filter.
2. Loosen the retaining clamp(s) securing the fuel inlet hose to the fuel filter. If the filter is located in-line, also loosen and remove the outlet hose clamp. If the hose has crimped retaining clamps, these must be cut off and replaced.
3. Pull the hose off the fuel filter.
4. Unscrew the fuel filter from the carburetor and discard the gasket, if so equipped.
5. Install a new gasket, if so equipped, and screw the filter into the carburetor.

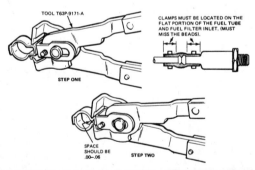

Installing crimp-type fuel line clamps using Ford special tool

6. Install a new retaining clamp onto the fuel hose. Push the hose onto the fuel filter and tighten the clamp.
7. Start the engine and check for leaks.
8. Install the air filter.

On V6 equipped Mustang IIs with the inline filter, replacement is a simple procedure of loosening the hose clamps, removing

the old filter and installing a new one. Always make sure that the clamps have enough tension to prevent fuel leakage at the filter connections.

2700 VV CARBURETOR ONLY

1. Remove the air cleaner.
2. Loosen the screw type or remove the spring type fuel line clamp from the inlet line, and disconnect the line.
3. Unscrew the fuel inlet fitting and remove the filter, gasket, and spring.
4. To install the new filter, put the filter spring, filter, inlet fitting gasket, and inlet fitting into position on the carburetor (in that order). Then, screw in the inlet fitting.
5. Put the fuel line and clamp into position and tighten the clamp.
6. Start the engine and check for leaks.
7. Replace the air cleaner.

LUBRICATION

Oil and Fuel Recommendations
FUEL

It is important that you use fuel of the proper octane rating in your car. Octane rating is based on the quantity of anti-knock compounds added to the fuel and it determines the speed at which the gas will burn. The lower the octane rating, the faster it burns. The higher the octane, the slower the fuel will burn and a greater percentage of compounds in the fuel prevent spark ping (knock), detonation and preignition (dieseling).

As the temperature of the engine increases, the air-fuel mixture exhibits a tendency to ignite before the spark plug is fired. If fuel of an octane rating too low for the engine is used, this will allow combustion to occur before the piston has completed its compression stroke, thereby creating a very high pressure very rapidly.

Fuel of the proper octane rating, for the compression ratio and ignition timing of your car, will slow the combustion process sufficiently to allow the spark plug enough time to ignite the mixture completely and smoothly. Mustang II non-catalyst models are designed to run on regular fuel. The use of some "super-premium" fuel is no substitution for a properly tuned and maintained engine. Chances are that if your engine exhibits any signs of spark ping, detonation or preignition when using regular fuel, the ignition timing should be checked against specifications or the cylinder head should be removed for decarbonizing. This, of course, does not apply if a former owner or yourself has had the cylinder head shaved (raising the compression ratio) or has bumped ahead (advanced) the ignition timing for increased performance. If the engine has been modified, then you will have to try different fuels until you find one that works best.

If you find yourself out of fuel in some remote place and the only fuel available is of a lower octane than that required by your engine, you may use a small quantity of it after retarding the ignition timing a maximum of 2 degrees from its stock setting. This will reduce performance a bit, but it will get you to the next gas station.

Some 1975 and all 1976 and later Mustang IIs are equipped with catalytic converters which require the exclusive use of unleaded fuel.

OIL

When adding oil to the crankcase or changing the oil or filter, it is important that oil of an equal quality to original equipment be used in your car. The use of inferior oils may void your warranty. Generally speaking, oil that has been rated "SE, heavy-duty detergent" by the American Petroleum Institute will prove satisfactory.

Oil of the SE variety performs a multitude of functions in addition to its basic job of reducing friction of the engine's moving parts. Through a balanced formula of polymeric dispersants and metallic detergents, the oil prevents high temperature and low temperature deposits and also keeps sludge and dirt particles in suspension. Acids, particularly sulphuric acid, as well as other by-products of combustion of sulphur fuels, are neutralized by the oil. These acids, if permitted to concentrate, may cause corrosion and rapid wear of the internal parts of the engine.

While your owner's manual may specify oils rated either "SE" or "SE/CC", the specifications for the 2300 engine have been upgraded to permit use of "SE" oil *only*. If you are using any other type of oil in a four cylinder engine, it would be best to change oil and filter as soon as possible, using "SE" oil only.

It is important to choose an oil of the proper viscosity for climatic and operational conditions. Viscosity is an index of the oil's thickness at different temperatures. A thicker oil (higher numerical rating) is needed for high temperature operation, whereas thinner oil (lower numerical rating) is required for cold weather operation. Due to the need for an oil that embodies both these characteristics in parts of the country where there is wide temperature variation within a small period of time, multigrade oils have been developed. Basically, a multigrade oil exhibits less sensitivity to temperature change than a single weight oil. For example, a 20W-40 oil exhibits the characteristics of a 20 weight oil when the car is first started and the oil is cold. Its lighter weight allows it to travel to the lubricating surfaces quicker and offer less resistance to starter motor cranking than, let's say, a straight 30 weight oil. But after the engine reaches operating temperature, the 20W-40 oil begins acting like a straight 40 weight oil, its heavier weight providing greater lubricating protection and less suceptibility to foaming than a straight 30 weight oil would at that temperature. Whatever your driving needs, the "Oil Viscosity–Temperature" chart should prove useful in selecting the proper grade. The SAE viscosity rating is printed or stamped on the top of every oil container.

Oil Viscosity— Temperature Chart

When outside temperature is consistently . . .	Use SAE viscosity number . . .
SINGLE GRADE OILS	
—10° F to 32° F	10W
10° F to 60° F	20W-20
32° F to 90° F	30
Above 60° F	40
MULTIGRADE OILS	
Below 32° F	* 5W-30
—10° F to 90° F	10W-30
—10° F to 90° F	10W-40
Above 10° F	20W-40

* When sustained high-speed operation is anticipated, use the next higher grade.

Changing Engine Oil and Filter

At the recommended intervals in the maintenance schedule, the oil and filter are changed. After the engine has reached operating temperature, shut it off, firmly apply the parking brake, block the wheels, place a drip pan beneath the oil pan and remove the drain plug. Allow the engine to drain thoroughly before replacing the drain plug. Place the drip pan beneath the oil filter. To remove the filter, turn it counterclockwise using a strap wrench. Wipe the contact surface of the new filter clean of all dirt and coat the rubber gasket with clean engine oil. Clean the mating surface of the adapter on the block. To install, hand-turn the new filter clockwise until the gasket just contacts the cylinder block. Do not use a strap wrench to install. Then hand-turn the filter $1/2$ additional turn. Unscrew the filler cap on the valve cover and fill the crankcase to the proper level on the dipstick with the recommended grade of oil. Install the cap, start the engine and operate at fast idle. Check the oil filter contact area and the drain plug for leaks.

Certain operating conditions may warrant more frequent oil changes. If the vehicle is used for short trips, where the engine does not have a chance to fully warm-up before it is shut off, water condensation and low temperature deposits may make it necessary to change the oil sooner. If the vehicle is used mostly in stop-and-go traffic, corrosive acids and high temperature deposits may necessitate shorter oil changing intervals. The shorter intervals also apply to industrial or rural areas where high concentrations of dust and other airborne particulate matter contaminate the oil. Finally, if the car is run at high speeds for an extended period of time, a severe load is placed on the engine causing the oil to "thin-out" sooner, making necessary the shorter oil changing intervals.

Transmission and Rear Axle Fluid Changing

The lubricant originally installed in the transmission and rear axle is designed to last the life of the vehicle. No regular changing of fluids is scheduled. However, if the transmission or rear is torn down for repairs, new fluids must be used. Consult the transmission and rear axle "Fluid Level Checks" section in this chapter for the type of lubricants used.

Chassis Greasing

FRONT SUSPENSION BALL JOINTS

Every three years or 36,000 miles on 1974–76 cars, and every 30,000 miles or 30 months on 1977 and 1978 cars, the upper and lower ball joints must be lubricated. The Mustang II is not equipped with grease fittings at the ball joints. Instead, it uses plugs, one at the top of the upper ball joint and another at the underside of the lower ball joint, which must be removed prior to greasing.

If you are using a jack to raise the front of the car, be sure to install jackstands, block the rear wheels and fully apply the parking brake. If the car has been parked in a temperature below 20°F for any length of time, park it in a heated garage for a half an hour or so until the ball joints loosen up enough to accept the grease. Wipe all accumulated dirt from around the ball joint lubrication plugs. Remove the plugs with a $3/16$ in. socket wrench. Using a hand-operated, low pressure grease gun fitted with a rubber tip and loaded with a suitable chassis grease, force lubricant into the joint only until the joint rubber boot begins to swell.

NOTE: *Do not force lubricant out of the rubber boot as this destroys the weathertight seal.*

Install the grease plugs.

CLUTCH LINKAGE

On models so equipped, apply a small amount of chassis grease to the pivot points of the clutch linkage as per the chassis lubrication diagram.

AUTOMATIC TRANSMISSION LINKAGE

On models so equipped, apply a small amount of 10W engine oil to the kickdown and shift linkage pivot points of the transmission linkage.

PARKING BRAKE LINKAGE

Whenever binding of the parking brake is noticed, apply a small amount of chassis grease to the friction and pivot points of the parking brake cable linkage, as per the chassis lubrication diagram.

BODY LUBRICATION

At the recommended intervals in the maintenance schedule, door, hood and trunk hinges, checks, and latches should be greased with a white grease such as Lubriplate®. Also the lock cylinders should be lubricated with a few drops of graphite lubricant.

DRAIN HOLE CLEANING

The doors and rocker panels of your car are equipped with drain holes to allow water to

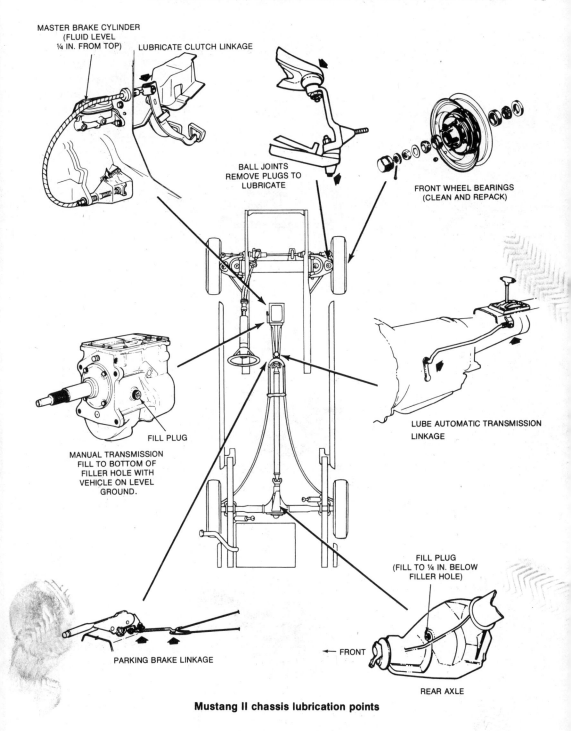

MASTER BRAKE CYLINDER
(FLUID LEVEL
¼ IN. FROM TOP)

LUBRICATE CLUTCH LINKAGE

BALL JOINTS
REMOVE PLUGS TO
LUBRICATE

FRONT WHEEL BEARINGS
(CLEAN AND REPACK)

FILL PLUG

MANUAL TRANSMISSION
FILL TO BOTTOM OF
FILLER HOLE WITH
VEHICLE ON LEVEL
GROUND.

LUBE AUTOMATIC TRANSMISSION
LINKAGE

FILL PLUG
(FILL TO ¼ IN. BELOW
FILLER HOLE)

PARKING BRAKE LINKAGE

← FRONT

REAR AXLE

Mustang II chassis lubrication points

drain out of the inside of the body panels. If the drain holes become clogged with dirt, leaves, pine needles, etc., the water will remain inside the panels, causing rust. To prevent this, open the drain holes with a screwdriver. If your car is equipped with rubber dust valves instead, simply open the dust valve with your finger.

WIPER BLADE REPLACEMENT

Depending on the type of weather, amount of use or the amount of snow removing chemicals used in your area, the recommended interval for replacement of wiper blades will vary. After making sure that the windshield glass surface is free of all oil, tree sap or other

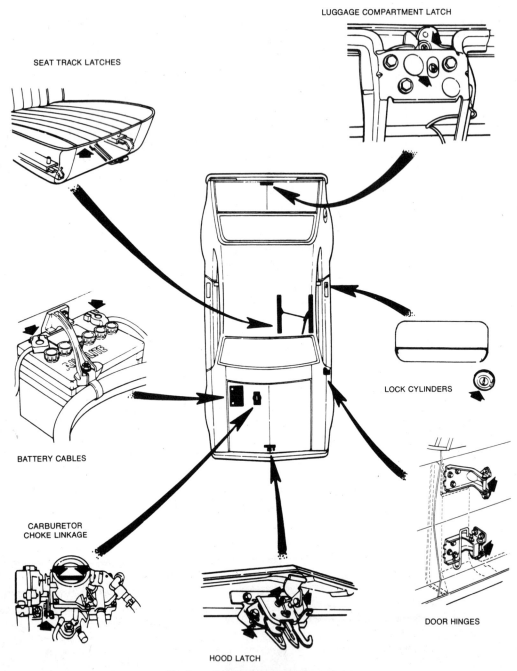

SEAT TRACK LATCHES

LUGGAGE COMPARTMENT LATCH

BATTERY CABLES

LOCK CYLINDERS

CARBURETOR
CHOKE LINKAGE

DOOR HINGES

HOOD LATCH

Mustang II general lubrication points

foreign substance that cannot be easily wiped off, check the wiper pattern for streaking. If the blades are cracked or the pattern is streaked or uneven, replace the blades. Replace any blade in question. It will be far cheaper than replacing a scratched windshield later.

PUSHING, TOWING, AND JUMP STARTING

Some day, when you least expect it, you will stroll out to your car, hop in, turn on the key and nothing will happen. At this point, your main interest will be in getting the engine

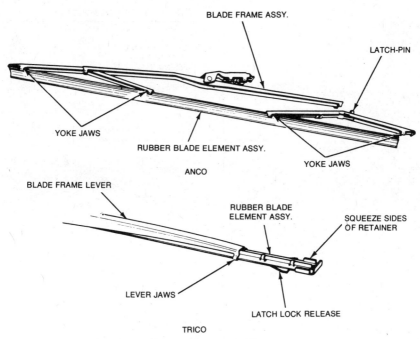

BLADE FRAME ASSY.

LATCH-PIN

YOKE JAWS

RUBBER BLADE ELEMENT ASSY.

YOKE JAWS

ANCO

BLADE FRAME LEVER

RUBBER BLADE
ELEMENT ASSY.

SQUEEZE SIDES
OF RETAINER

LEVER JAWS

LATCH LOCK RELEASE

TRICO

Wiper blade element refill

started or repaired so that it will start in the future. If the car is in a reasonably good state of tune and you haven't flooded the engine but the battery is dead or dying, the car may be jump started by means of jumper cables. All you need is a willing assistant with either a good 12 volt battery or a running engine with a 12 volt electrical system or both.

When using jumper cables to jump start a car, a few precautions must be taken to avoid both charging system damage and damage to yourself should the battery explode. The old "positive to positive and negative to negative" jumper cable rule of thumb has been scrapped for a new revised procedure. Here it is. First, remove all of the battery cell covers and cover the cell openings with a clean, dry cloth. Then, connect the positive cable of the assist battery to the positive pole of your battery and the negative cable of the assist battery to the engine block of your car. This will prevent the possibility of a spark from the negative assist cable igniting the highly explosive hydrogen and oxygen battery fumes. Once your car is started, allow the engine to return to idle speed before disconnecting the jumper cables, and don't cross the cables. Replace the cell covers and discard the cloth.

If your car fails to start by jump starting and it is equipped with manual transmission, it may be push started. Cars equipped with automatic transmission cannot be push started. If the bumper of the car pushing you

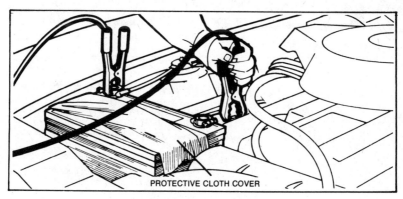

PROTECTIVE CLOTH COVER

Jumper cable installation

MUSTANG-FRONT

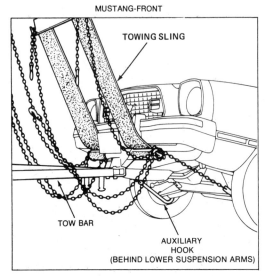

TOWING SLING

TOW BAR

AUXILIARY
HOOK
(BEHIND LOWER SUSPENSION ARMS)

MUSTANG-REAR

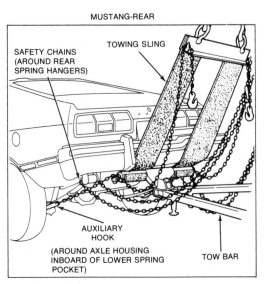

TOWING SLING

SAFETY CHAINS
(AROUND REAR
SPRING HANGERS)

AUXILIARY
HOOK
(AROUND AXLE HOUSING
INBOARD OF LOWER SPRING
POCKET)

TOW BAR

Towing sling and tow bar installation

and your car's bumper do not match perfectly, it is wise to tie an old tire either on the back of your car or on the front of the pushing car. This will avoid unnecessary trips to the body shop. To push start the car, switch the ignition to the "ON" position (not the "START" position) and depress the clutch pedal. Place the transmission in Second gear and hold the accelerator pedal about halfway down. When the car speed reaches about 10 mph, gradually release the clutch pedal and the engine should start.

If all else fails and the car must be towed to a garage, there are a few precautions that must be observed. If the transmission and rear axle are in proper working order, the car can be towed with the rear wheels on the ground for distances under 15 miles at speeds no greater than 30 mph. If the transmission or rear is known to be damaged or if the car

has to be towed over 15 miles or over 30 mph, the car must be towed with the rear wheels raised and the steering wheel locked so that the front wheels remain in the straight-ahead position.

NOTE: *If the ignition key is not available to unlock the steering and transmission lock system, it will be necessary to dolly the car under the rear wheels with the front wheels raised.*

JACKING AND HOISTING

When it becomes necessary to raise the car for service, proper safety precautions must be taken. The Mustang II is equipped with a scissors jack. These jacks are fine for changing a tire, but never crawl under the car when it is only supported by the scissors jack.

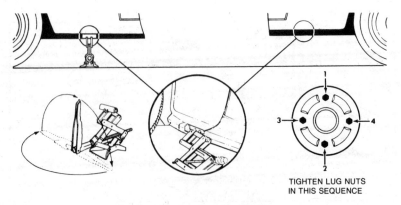

TIGHTEN LUG NUTS
IN THIS SEQUENCE

Scissors jack usage instructions

FRONT RAIL TYPE FORK LIFT
OR FLOOR JACK CONTACT AREA

FRONT FRAME CONTACT AREA

Hoist contact areas—typical front

REAR FRAME CONTACT AREA

REAR RAIL TYPE, FORK LIFT OR
FLOOR JACK CONTACT AREA

Hoist contact areas—typical rear

If the jack should slip or tip over, as jacks sometimes do, you would be pinned under 3,000 lbs of automobile.

When raising a car with the scissors jack to change a tire, follow these precautions. Jack only at one of the four reinforced jacking locations shown in the accompanying illustration. Firmly apply the parking brake, block the wheel diagonally opposite the wheel to be raised, and place the gear lever in Park (automatic) or 1st or Reverse gear (manual), making sure that the jack is firmly planted on a level, solid surface.

If you are going to work beneath the car, always install jackstands under an adjacent reinforced frame member or crossmember, beneath a front suspension lower control arm or the rear axle housing.

When using a hydraulic floor jack, the car may be raised at either the #2 front crossmember, the rear axle housing, or at any one of the four scissors jacking points. Never attempt to raise the car by its bumpers, as this will result in damage to the car.

The best way to raise a car for service is to use a garage hoist. There are several different types of garage hoists, each having their own

special precautions. Types you most often will encounter are the drive-on (ramp type), frame contact and the twin post or rail type. When using a drive-on type, make sure that there is enough clearance between the upright flanges of the hoist rails and the underbody. When using a frame contact hoist, make sure that all four of the adapter pads are positioned in the center of the adapter contact areas (shaded area of hoist contact area illustrations). On unibody cars such as the Mustang II, the shaded areas are reinforced steel box members (subframes). When using a twin-post or rail type, make sure that the front adapters are positioned squarely beneath the lower control arms and the rear adapters positioned carefully beneath the rear axle housing at points not farther outboard than one inch from the circumference welds near the differential housing (to prevent shock absorber damage). Always raise the car slowly, observing the security of the hoist adapters as it is raised.

NOTE: *If it is desired to unload the front suspension ball joints for purposes of inspection, position the jack beneath the lower control arm of the subject ball joints.*

Tune-Up

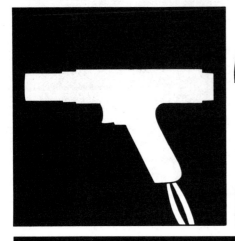

TUNE-UP PROCEDURES

The tune-up is a routine maintenance operation which is essential for the efficient and economical operation, as well as the long life of your car's engine. The interval between tune-ups is a variable factor which depends upon the way you drive your car, the conditions under which you drive it (weather, road type, etc.), and the type of engine installed in your car. It is generally correct to say that no car using leaded fuel should be driven more than 12,000 miles between tune-ups, especially in this age of emission controls and fuel shortages. If you plan to drive your car extremely hard or under severe weather conditions, tune-ups should be performed at closer intervals. High performance engines require more frequent tuning than other engines regardless of weather or driving conditions.

The replaceable parts involved in a conventional tune-up include the spark plugs, breaker points and condenser (unless equipped with breakerless ignition), distributor cap, rotor, spark plug wires and the ignition coil high-tension (secondary) wire. In addition to these parts and the adjustments involved in properly adapting them to your engine, there are several adjustments of other parts involved in completing the job. These include carburetor idle speed and air/fuel mixture, ignition timing, dwell angle (unless equipped with breakerless ignition) and valve clearance adjustments.

This section gives specific procedures on how to tune-up your Mustang II and is intended to be as complete and basic as possible. In chapter 11 there is another, more generalized section for tune-ups which includes trouble-shooting diagnosis for the more experienced weekend mechanic.

CAUTION: *When working with a running engine, make sure that there is proper ventilation. Also make sure that the transmission is in Neutral (unless otherwise specified) and that the parking brake is fully applied. Always keep hands, long hair, clothing, neckties and tools well clear of the hot exhaust manifold(s) and radiator and fan. When the ignition is turned on and the engine is running, do not grasp the ignition wires, distributor cap, or coil wire, as a shock in excess of 20,000 volts may result. Whenever working around the distributor, even if the engine is not running, make sure that the ignition is switched off.*

Spark Plugs

The job of the spark plug is to ignite the air/fuel mixture in the cylinder as the piston approaches the top of the compression stroke. The ignited mixture then expands and forces the piston down on the power stroke. This turns the crankshaft which then turns the remainder of the drive train. If the transmission is in gear and the brakes are not applied, the vehicle will move.

The average life of a spark plug is approximately 12,000 miles. This is, however, dependent on the mechanical condition of the engine, the type of fuel that is used, and the type of driving conditions under which the car is used. For some people, spark plugs will last 5,000 miles and for others, 15,000 or 20,000 miles.

Your car came from the factory with resistor spark plugs. Resistor spark plugs help to limit the amount of radio frequency energy that is given off by the automotive ignition system. Radio frequency energy results in the annoying buzzing or clicking you sometimes hear on your radio or the jumping picture you see on your TV when a car pulls into the driveway.

The electrode end of the spark plug (the end which goes into the cylinder) is also a very good indicator of the mechanical condition of your engine. If a spark plug should foul and begin to misfire, you will have to find the condition which caused the plug to foul and correct it. It is also a good idea to occasionally give all the plugs an inspection and cleaning to get an idea how the inside of your engine is doing. A small amount of deposit on a spark plug, after it has been in use for any period of time, should be considered normal.

REMOVAL AND INSTALLATION

Every six months or 6,000 miles, the spark plugs should be removed for inspection. At this time they should be cleaned and regapped. At 12-month or 12,000-mile intervals, the plugs should be replaced.

Prior to removal, number each spark plug wire with a piece of masking tape bearing the cylinder number. Remove each spark plug wire by grasping its rubber boot on the end and twisting slightly to free the wire from the plug. Using a $^{13}/_{16}$ or $^5/_8$ in. spark plug socket, turn the plugs counterclockwise to remove them. Do not allow any foreign matter to enter the cylinders through the spark plug holes.

On Mustang IIs with the V6 engine, to gain access to the first spark plug on the right-side, you must reposition the alternator. This can be done by loosening the mounting and adjustment bolts and sliding the alternator upward. On the V8, to gain access to the last two plugs on the right side, you must remove the battery and battery holder. Also, the Thermactor by-pass valve should be repositioned for easy access to the first two plugs on the right-side.

Consult the spark plug inspection chart in the "Color" insert of chapter four when in doubt about plug condition. If the spark plugs are to be reused, check the porcelain insulator for cracks and the electrodes for excessive wear. Replace the entire set if one plug is damaged. Clean the reusable plugs with a stiff wire brush, or have them cleaned in a plug sandblasting machine (found in many service stations). Uneven wear of the center or ground electrode may be corrected by leveling off the unevenly worn section with a file.

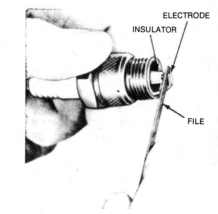

Cleaning plug with file

The gap must be checked with a feeler gauge before installing the plug in the engine. With the ground electrode positioned parallel to the center electrode, a wire gauge of the proper diameter must pass through the opening with a slight drag. If the air gap between the two electrodes is not correct, the ground electrode must be bent to bring it to specifications.

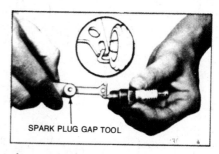

Gapping spark plug

Tune-Up Specifications

When analyzing compression test results, look for uniformity among cylinders, rather than specific pressures.

Year	Engine Displacement (Cu In.)	Spark Plugs Type	Gap (in.)	Distributor Point Dwell (deg)	Point Gap (in.)	Ignition Timing (deg) MT	Ignition Timing (deg) AT	Intake Valve Opens (deg)	Fuel Pump Pressure (psi)	Idle Speed (rpm)° MT	Idle Speed (rpm)° AT	Valve Clearance (in.) In	Valve Clearance (in.) Ex
1974	140	ARGF-52	.044	35–41	.027	6BTDC[1]	6BTDC[1]	22BTDC	3.5–4.5	750 (N)	750 (D)	Hydraulic	Hydraulic
	170	AGR-42	.034	35–41	.024	12BTDC[1]	12BTDC[2]	20BTDC	3.5–4.5	750 (N)	650 (D)	.014	.016
1975 (49 states)	140	AGRF-52	.034	Solid State		6BTDC[4]	6BTDC[4]	22BTDC	3.5–4.5	750 (N)	650 (D)	Hydraulic	Hydraulic
	170	AGR-42	.034	Solid State		6BTDC[5]	10BTDC[6]	20BTDC	3.5–4.5	850 (N)	700 (D)	.014	.016
	302	ARF-42	.044	Solid State		—	6BTDC[2]	20BTDC	5.5–6.5	—	700 (D)	Hydraulic	Hydraulic
1975 (Calif.)	140	AGRF-52	.034	Solid State		6BTDC[4]	10BTDC[4]	22BTDC	3.5–4.5	750 (N)	650 (D)	Hydraulic	Hydraulic
	170	AGR-42	.034	Solid State		6BTDC[5]	8BTDC[6]	20BTDC	3.5–4.5	850 (N)	700 (D)	.014	.016
	302	ARF-42	.044	Solid State		—	6BTDC[2]	20BTDC	5.5–6.5	—	700 (D)	Hydraulic	Hydraulic
1976 (49 states)	140	AGRF-52	.034	Solid State		6BTDC[4]	20BTDC[4]	22BTDC	3.5–4.5	850 (N)	750 (N)	Hydraulic	Hydraulic
	170	AGR-42	.034	Solid State		10BTDC[5]	12BTDC (D)[6]	20BTDC	3.5–4.5	850 (N)	700 (D)	.014	.016
302 (49 states)	302	ARF-42	.044	Solid State		—	6BTDC[2]	20BTDC	5.5–6.5	—	700 (D)	Hydraulic	Hydraulic
1976 (Calif.)	140	AGRF-52	.034	Solid State		6BTDC[4]	20BTDC[4]	22BTDC	3.5–4.5	850 (N)	750 (D)	Hydraulic	Hydraulic
	170	AGR-42	.034	Solid State		8BTDC[5]	6BTDC[2]	20BTDC	3.5–4.5	850 (N)	800 (D)	.014	.016
	302	ARF-42	.044	Solid State		—	8BTDC[7]	16BTDC	5.5–6.5	—	700 (D)	Hydraulic	Hydraulic
1977 (49 states)	140	AWRF-42	.034	Solid State		6BTDC	20BTDC	22BTDC	5.5–6.5	850 (N)	800 (D)	Hydraulic	Hydraulic
	170	AWSF-42	.034	Solid State		8BTDC	12BTDC	20BTDC	3.5–5.8	850 (N)	700 (D)	.014	.016
	302	ARF-52	.050	Solid State		12BTDC	4BTDC	16BTDC	5.5–6.5	850 (N)	700 (D)	Hydraulic	Hydraulic
1977 (Calif.)	140	AWRF-42	.034	Solid State		6BTDC	20BTDC	22BTDC	5.5–6.5	850 (N)	750 (D)	Hydraulic	Hydraulic
	170	AWSF-42	.034	Solid State		[8]	[8]	20BTDC	3.5–5.8	850 (N)	750 (D)	.014	.016
	302	ARF-52-6	.060	Solid State		[8]	12BTDC	16BTDC	5.5–6.5	850 (N)	700 (D)	Hydraulic	Hydraulic

Year	Engine	Spark Plug	Gap	Ignition						Idle Speed	Idle Speed	Valve Clearance
1978 (49 states)	140	AWRF-42	.034	Solid State	6BTDC	20BTDC	22BTDC	5.5–6.5	850 (N)	800 (D)	Hydraulic
	170	AWSF-42	.034	Solid State	10BTDC	12BTDC	20BTDC	3.5–5.8	700 (N)	650 (D)	.014 .016
	302	ARF-52	.050	Solid State	6BTDC	4BTDC	16BTDC	5.5–6.5	900 (N)	700 (D)	Hydraulic
1978 (Calif.)	140	AWRF-42	.034	Solid State	6BTDC	20BTDC	22BTDC	5.5–6.5	850 (N)	750 (D)	Hydraulic
	170	AWSF-42	.034	Solid State	⑧	6BTDC	20BTDC	3.5–5.8	700 (N)	600 (D)	.014 .016
	302	ARF-52-6	.060	Solid State	⑧	12BTDC⑨	16BTDC	5.5–6.5	900 (N)	700 (D)	Hydraulic

① At 750 rpm
② At 650 rpm
③ Lowest reading within 75% of highest
* (N)—adjust idle speed with trans. in Neutral; (D)—adjust idle speed with trans. in Drive (parking brake applied)
④ At 550 rpm
⑤ At 850 rpm
⑥ At 700 rpm
— Not applicable
⑦ At 500 rpm
⑧ See engine compartment sticker
⑨ 9 degrees BTDC—altitude emissions package

NOTE: The underhood specifications sticker often reflects tune-up specification changes made in production. Sticker figures must be used if they disagree with those in this chart.

After the plugs are gapped correctly, they may be inserted into their holes and hand-tightened. Be careful not to cross-thread the plugs. Torque the plugs to the proper specification with a $^{13}/_{16}$ or $^5/_8$ in. (302 V8) socket and a torque wrench. Install each spark plug wire on its respective plug, making sure that each spark plug end is making good metal-to-metal contact in its wire socket.

BREAKER POINTS AND CONDENSER

The points and condenser function as a circuit breaker for the primary circuit of the ignition system. The ignition coil must boost the 12 volts (V) of electrical pressure supplied to it by the battery to about 20,000 V in order to fire the spark plugs. To do this, the coil depends on the points and condenser for assistance.

NOTE: *All 1975 and later models are equipped with breakerless (solid state) ignition systems. These systems eliminate the breaker points and condenser completely. For a description of this system, see "Ignition System" in Chapter 3.*

The coil has a primary and a secondary circuit. When the ignition key is turned to the "on" position, the battery supplies voltage to the primary side of the coil which passes the voltage on to the points. The points are connected to ground to complete the primary circuit. As the cam in the distributor turns, the points open and the primary circuit collapses. The magnetic force in the primary circuit of the coil cuts through the secondary circuit and increases the voltage in the secondary circuit to a level which is sufficient to fire the spark plugs. When the points open, the electrical charge contained in the primary circuit jumps the gap which is created between the two open contacts of the points. If this electrical charge was not transferred elsewhere, the material on the contacts of the points would melt and that all-important gap between the contacts would start to change. If this gap is not maintained, the points will not break the primary circuit. If the primary circuit is not broken, the secondary circuit will not have enough voltage to fire the spark plugs. Enter the condenser.

The function of the condenser is to absorb the excessive voltage from the points when they open and thus prevent the points from becoming pitted or burned.

If you have ever wondered why it is necessary to tune-up your engine occasionally, consider the fact that the ignition system must complete the above cycle each time a spark plug fires. On a four-cylinder, four-cycle engine, two of the four plugs must fire once for every engine revolution. If the idle speed of your engine is 800 revolutions per minute (800 rpm), the breaker points open and close two times for each revolution. For every minute your engine idles, your points open and close 1,600 times ($2 \times 800 = 1,600$). And that is just at idle. What about at 65 mph?

There are two ways to check breaker point gap: with a feeler guage or with a dwell meter. Either way you set the points, you are adjusting the amount of time (in degrees of distributor rotation) that the points will remain open. If you adjust the points with a feeler gauge, you are setting the maximum amount the points will open when the rubbing block on the points is on a high point of the distributor cam. When you adjust the points with a dwell meter, you are measuring the number of degrees (of distributor cam rotation) in which the points will remain closed before they start to open as a high point of the distributor cam approaches the rubbing block of the points.

There are two rules which should always be followed when adjusting or replacing points. *The points and condenser are a matched set; never replace one without replacing the other. If you change the point gap or dwell of the engine, you also change the ignition timing. Therefore, if you adjust the points, you must also adjust the timing.*

INSPECTION

To ease access to the distributor, remove the air cleaner and position it to one side.

Disconnect the secondary cable from the coil at the center of the distributor cap. On distributors using clasps to secure the cap, pry the retaining clasps from either side of the cap using a flat blade screwdriver. On distributors using cross-head screws with "L-shaped" levers to secure the cap, press down on the screw head with a flat blade screwdriver and while maintaining pressure, rotate the screw head and retaining lever in either direction to free it from the distributor body. Then, lift of the cap (wires installed) and position it to one side.

Mark the position of the rotor by scribing a mark on the distributor body. Pull the rotor

Examining breaker point contacts

Rotating engine manually

straight up and off. Discard it if it is cracked, burned or excessively worn at the tip. Insert a screwdriver between the stationary and breaker arms of the points and examine the condition of the contacts. Replace the points if the contacts are blackened, pitted, or if the metal transfer exceeds that of the specified point gap (see "Tune-Up Specifications"). Also replace the points if the breaker arm has lost its tension (nonadjustable types) or if the rubbing block has become worn or loose. Contact points which have become slightly burned (light gray) may be cleaned with a point file.

In order for the points to function properly, the contact faces must be aligned. The alignment must be checked with the points closed. To close the points, install an open-end wrench on the crankshaft pulley/damper bolt and turn the engine over in its normal direction of rotation until the points can be seen to close.

NOTE: *This may be more easily accomplished with the spark plugs removed.*

If the contact faces are not centered, bend the stationary arm to suit. Never bend the breaker arm. Discard the points if they cannot be centered correctly.

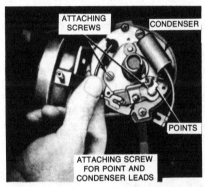

Removing points and condenser

REPLACEMENT

To replace the points and condenser, loosen the nut at the center of the point assembly

CONDITION	POSSIBLE CAUSE
BURNED	INCORRECT VOLTAGE REGULATOR SETTING. RADIO CONDENSER INSTALLED TO THE DISTRIBUTOR SIDE OF THE COIL.
EXCESSIVE METAL TRANSFER OR PITTING	INCORRECT ALIGNMENT. INCORRECT VOLTAGE REGULATOR SETTING. RADIO CONDENSER INSTALLED TO THE DISTRIBUTOR SIDE OF THE COIL. IGNITION CONDENSER OF IMPROPER CAPACITY. EXTENDED OPERATION OF THE ENGINE AT SPEEDS OTHER THAN NORMAL.

Breaker point troubleshooting

and slide the distributor primary lead and the condenser lead away from the terminal. Then remove the condenser retaining screw and the point assembly retaining screw(s) and remove the points and condenser. While the points are out, clean the distributor base plate with an alcohol soaked rag to remove any oil film which might impede completion of the ground circuit. Also, lubricate the breaker cam lobes with a very light coating of silicone base grease.

Install the new points and condenser and tighten their retaining screws. Connect the electrical leads for both at the primary terminal. Make sure that the contacts are aligned horizontally and vertically as previously described.

The breaker points must be correctly gapped beore proceeding any further. Install an open-end wrench on the crankshaft pulley-damper bolt and turn the engine over by hand in the normal direction of rotation until the rubbing block on the point assembly is resting on the high point of a breaker cam lobe. Loosen the point attaching screws slightly. Insert a feeler gauge of the proper thickness between the point contacts (see "Tune-Up Specifications").

NOTE: *Wipe the feeler gauge clean of any grease or oil which will contaminate the point contacts.*

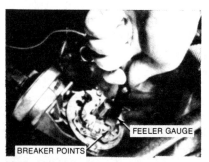

Checking point gap

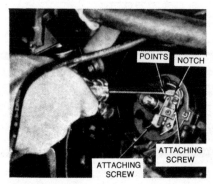

Adjusting point gap

The gap is correct when the loosely held feeler gauge passes through the contacts with a slight drag. If the gap needs adjusting, insert the tip of a screwdriver in the notch beside the points and twist to open or close the gap as necessary. Then, without disturbing the setting, tighten the breaker point attaching screw(s). Recheck the gap after tightening.

If a dwell meter is available, proceed to "Dwell Angle Setting." If the meter is not available, replace the rotor on top of the distributor shaft, making sure that the tab inside the rotor aligns with the slot on the distributor shaft. Position the distributor cap on top of the distributor. On distributors using clasps to secure the cap, snap the clasps into the slots in the cap. On distributors using cross-head screws with "L-shaped" levers to secure the cap, press down on the screw head and rotate the retaining lever until it is beneath the retaining boss on the distributor body, and then release the screw. Check that the cap is fully seated, and that the spark plug wires fit snugly into the cap. Connect the secondary cable from the coil at the distributor cap. Proceed to "Ignition Timing Adjustment."

Dwell Angle Setting

The dwell angle is the number of degrees of distributor cam rotation through which the breaker points remain fully closed (conducting electricity). Increasing the point gap decreases dwell, while decreasing the point gap increases dwell.

NOTE: *On cars equipped with breakerless (solid state) ignition, dwell is electronically controlled and cannot be adjusted.*

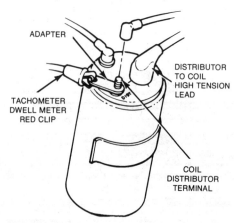

Installing dwell/tachometer adapter on coil (1974 models)

Using a dwell meter of known accuracy, connect the red lead (positive) wire of the meter to the distributor primary wire connection on the positive (+) side of the coil, and the black ground (negative) wire of the meter to a good ground on the engine (e.g. thermostat housing nut).

The dwell angle may be checked either with the distributor cap and rotor installed and the engine running, or with the cap and rotor removed and the engine cranking at starter speed. The meter gives a constant reading with the engine running. With the engine cranking, the reading will fluctuate between zero degrees dwell and the maximum figure for that angle. While cranking, the maximum figure is the correct one for that setting. Never attempt to change dwell angle while the ignition is on. Touching the point contacts or primary wire connection with a metal screwdriver may result in a shock.

To change the dwell angle, loosen the point retaining screw slightly and make the approximate correction. Tighten the retaining screw and test the dwell with the engine cranking. If the dwell appears to be correct, install the breaker point protective cover, if so equipped, the rotor and distributor cap, and test the dwell with the engine running. Take the engine through its entire rpm range and observe the dwell meter. The dwell should remain within specifications at all times. Great fluctuation of dwell at different engine speeds indicates worn distributor parts.

Following the dwell angle adjustment, the ignition timing must be checked. A 1° increase in dwell results in the ignition timing being retarded 2° and vice versa.

Ignition Timing

Ignition timing is the measurement in degrees of crankshaft rotation of the instant the spark plugs in the cylinders fire, in relation to the location of the piston, while the piston is on its compression stroke.

Ignition timing is adjusted by loosening the distributor locking device and turning the distributor in the engine.

Ideally, the air/fuel mixture in the cylinder will be ignited (by the spark plug) and just beginning its rapid expansion as the piston passes top dead center (TDC) of the compression stroke. If this happens, the piston will be beginning the power stroke just as the compressed (by the movement of the piston) and ignited (by the spark plug) air/fuel mixture starts to expand. The expansion of the air/fuel mixture will then force the piston down on the power stroke and turn the crankshaft.

It takes a fraction of a second for the spark from the plug to completely ignite the mixture in the cylinder. Becase of this, the spark plug must fire before the piston reaches TDC, if the mixture is to be completely ignited as the piston passes TDC. This measurement is given in degrees (of crankshaft rotation) *before* the piston reaches *top dead center* (BTDC). If the ignition timing setting for your engine is six degrees (6°) BTDC, this means that the spark plug must fire at a time when the piston for that cylinder is 6° before top dead center of its compression stroke. However, this only holds true while your engine is at idle speed.

As you accelerate from idle, the speed of your engine (rpm) increases. The increase in rpm means that the pistons are now traveling up and down much faster. Because of this, the spark plugs will have to fire even sooner if the mixture is to be completely ignited as the piston passes TDC. To accomplish this, the distributor incorporates means to advance the timing of the spark as engine speed increases.

The distributor in your car has two means of advancing the ignition timing. One is called centrifugal advance and is actuated by weights in the distributor. The other is called vaccuum advance and is controlled by that large circular housing on the side of the distributor.

In addition, some distributors have a vacuum-retard mechanism which is contained in the same housing on the side of the distributor as the vacuum advance. The function of this mechanism is to retard the timing of the ignition spark under certain engine conditions. This causes more complete burning of the air/fuel mixture in the cylinder and consequently lowers exhaust emissions.

Because these mechanisms change ignition timing, it is necessary to disconnect and plug the one or two vacuum lines from the distributor when setting the basic ignition timing.

If ignition timing is set too far advanced (BTDC), the ignition and expansion of the air/fuel mixture in the cylinder will try to force the piston down the cylinder while it is still traveling upward. This causes engine "ping," a sound which resembles marbles being dropped into an empty tin can. If the ignition timing is too far retarded (after, or ATDC), the piston will have already started down on the power stroke when the air-fuel mixture ignites and expands. This will cause the piston to be forced down only a portion of its travel. This will result in poor engine performance and lack of power.

Ignition timing adjustment is checked with a timing light. This instrument is connected to the No. 1 spark plug of the engine. The timing light flashes every time an electrical current is sent from the distributor, through the No. 1 spark plug wire, to the spark plug. The crankshaft pulley and the front cover of the engine are marked with a timing pointer and a timing scale. When the timing pointer is aligned with the "0" mark on the timing scale, the piston in the No. 1 cylinder is at TDC of its compression stroke. With the engine running, and the timing light aimed at the timing pointer and timing scale, the stroboscopic flashes from the timing light will allow you to check the ignition timing setting

of the engine. The timing light flashes every time the spark plug in the No. 1 cylinder of the engine fires. Since the flash from the timing light makes the crankshaft pulley seem stationary for a moment, you will be able to read the exact position of the piston in the No. 1 cylinder on the timing scale on the front of the engine.

IGNITION TIMING ADJUSTMENT

All 1974 and later engines are equipped with both conventional and "monolithic" timing features. The monolithic system employs a timing receptacle located at the front of all engines, except the 2300 cc engine which has the receptacle in the left rear of the cylinder block. The receptacle is designed to accept an electronic probe which connects to digital read-out equipment. However, since this electronic system requires expensive equipment which few garages and certainly fewer owners will be able to afford, only the con-

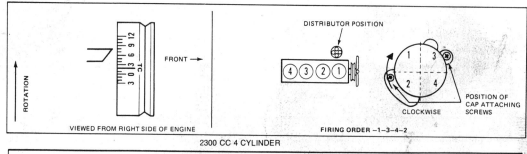

2300 CC 4 CYLINDER

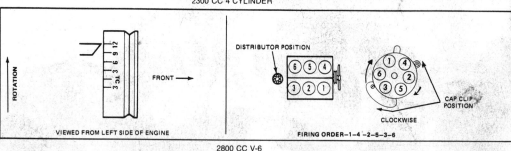

2800 CC V-6

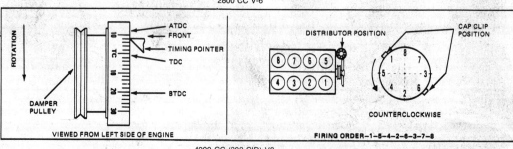

4900 CC (302 CID) V8

Pointer and timing marks locations

ventional "timing light" of ignition timing will be covered here.

Ford recommends that the ignition timing be checked every 12 months or 12,000 miles. The timing adjustment should always follow a breaker point gap and-or dwell angle adjustment and be performed with the engine at normal operating temperature.

Locate the crankshaft damper/pulley and timing pointer at the front of the engine, and clean them with a solvent soaked rag or wire brush so that the marks can be seen. Scribe a mark on the crankshaft damper/pulley and pointer with chalk or luminescent (day glo) paint to highlight the correct timing setting. Disconnect the vacuum hoses(s) at the distributor vacuum capsule and plug it (them) with a pencil, golf tee, or some other small tapered object. Connect a stroboscopic timing light to the No. 1 cylinder spark plug (see firing order illustrations in Chapter 3) and to the battery terminals according to the manufacturer's instructions. On vehicles with solid state ignition (1975 and later) use an inductive timing light only—the kind of light that reads the spark from the high tension lead without disconecting it from the spark plug. Also, if you have solid state ignition, make sure your tachometer is compatible with this type of system, and then connect a tachometer to the engine. On 1974 models equipped with conventional ignition, attach one lead to the distributor primary wire connection at the coil and the other lead to a good ground. On 1975 and later models equipped with solid state (breakerless) ignition, connect one lead to the "TACH TEST" connection atop the ignition coil, and the other wire to a good ground.

Make sure that all of the timing light wires and tachometer wires are well clear of the engine. Start the engine and set the idle speed (if necessary) to the speed specified in

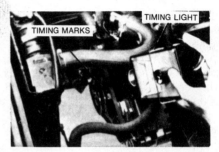

Aiming stroboscopic timing light at pointer and timing marks on crankshaft damper/pulley

the "Tune-Up Specifications" chart, using the idle speed adjusting screws(s). Then, with the engine running, aim the timing light at the pointer and at the marks on the damper/pulley. If the marks made with the chalk or paint coincide when the timing light flashes (at the specified rpm), the engine is timed correctly. If the marks do not coincide, stop the engine. Loosen the distributor locknut and start the engine again. While observing the timing light flashes on the markers, grasp the distributor vacuum capsule—not the distributor cap—and rotate the distributor until the marks do coincide. Then, stop the engine and tighten the distributor locknut, taking care not to disturb the setting. As a final check, start the engine once more to make sure that the timing marks still align.

NOTE: *If necessary, readjust the idle speed to that listed in the tune-up specs. Timing is only correct at the specified rpm.*

Once the engine is timed, reconnect the vacuum hoses(s) to the distributor. Readjust, if necessary, the curb idle to specifications as outlined under "Idle Speed and Mixture Adjustment." Finally, remove the timing light and tachometer from the engine.

Valve Lash

Valve adjustment is a major factor determining how far the intake and exhaust valves will open into the cylinder.

Too large a valve clearance will cause part of the lift of the camshaft to be used in removing the excess clearance. Therefore, the valves will not open far enough. This condition has two effects. First, the valve train components will emit a tapping noise as they take up excessive clearance. Secondly, the less the intake valves open, the smaller the volume of air/fuel mixture that will be admitted to the cylinders; the less the exhaust valves open, the greater the backpressure in the combustion chambers which will prevent

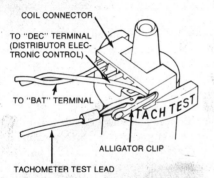

Attaching tachometer lead to coil connector (1975 and later models)

the proper air-fuel mixture from entering the cylinder.

Too small a valve clearance will prevent the valves from fully seating in the cylinder head when they close. When a valve seats on a cylinder head, it does two things. First, it seals the combustion chamber so none of the compressed gases in the cylinder can escape. Secondly, it cools itself by transferring some of the heat it absorbed from the combustion process through the cylinder head and into the engine cooling system. Therefore, if the valve clearance is too small, the engine will run poorly due to loss of compression, and the valves will overheat and warp since they cannot transfer heat unless they are touching the seat in the cylinder head.

NOTE: *While all valve adjustments must be as accurate as possible, it is better to have the adjustment slightly loose than slightly tight as burnt valves may result from overly tight adjustments.*

VALVE LASH ADJUSTMENT

The 2300 cc 4 cylinder engine and the 4900 cc (302 cid) V8 are equipped with hydraulic valve lifters which do not require adjustment. Only the 2800 cc V6 uses mechanical lifters necessitating adjustment.

CAUTION: *Do not run the engine with the hood open until you have carefully inspected the fan for any signs whatsoever of cracking or separation!*

1974–75 2800 cc V6

1. Remove the air cleaner and disconnect the plug wires, marking them or carefully noting their position.
2. Remove the electric choke wire at the choke.
3. Remove the alternator belt, and rotate the alternator toward the right fender.
4. Remove the engine lifting eyes and discard them.
5. Disconnect the vacuum line coming from the Thermactor bypass vacuum control solenoid at the four-way Tee.
6. Remove:
   a. The wiring harness from the attaching bracket on the rear of the left hand rocker arm cover.
   b. The clips attaching the wiring loom to the inside edge of the right hand rocker cover.
   c. Adjustable vacuum hose straps as necessary to reposition the hoses for rocker cover removal. Note locations of straps.

d. Thermactor dump valve, if its position interferes with rocker cover removal.
NOTE: *On 1975 models with the 2800 cc engine, the position of the distributor diaphragm may interfere with the removal of the rocker cover. This can be corrected as follows: Set the ignition timing at TDC. Remove the distributor hold-down bolt and clamp, lift out the distributor and turn it one tooth (20°) clockwise. The diaphragm housing should be pointing toward the rear face of the cylinder block. Reinstall the hold-down bolt and clamp, and reset the timing to the specification given on the underhood tune-up decal.*

7. Remove the rocker cover attaching screws and the rocker covers.
8. The valves are adjusted on this engine with the engine idling. To avoid spillage of oil, it is necessary to install either a set of Valve Rocker Covers (Rotunda Tool Kit T75L-6580-A) or to get a spare set of standard covers and cut the top of each cover off 1¼ inches above the bolt flange to contain the oil spray while permitting access to the valves from above. Install these covers.
9. Reinstall alternator belt and spark plug wires. Start the engine and run it until it reaches operating temperature.
10. Torque rocker arm support bolts to 43–49 ft lbs.
11. With engine idling, adjust valve lash using stepped ("go-no go") type feeler gauges. Adjust intake valves to .014, and exhausts to .016 inches. Adjusting nuts are self locking.
12. Stop engine, remove alternator belt, and then remove the slave type valve covers. Reverse the procedure above for reinstalling valve covers and reconnecting wiring and vacuum hoses.

1976–78 2800 V6

The recommended maintenance interval for valve clearance adjustment is specified in the maintenance interval chart for each model year. Valve clearance should be checked at every tune-up or whenever excessive valve train noise is noticed. The clearance must be checked with the engine at operating temperature (warmed up) and shut off.

1. Remove the air cleaner assembly and disconnect the negative battery cable.
2. Remove the Thermactor air bypass valve and its mounting bracket.
3. Remove the two engine lifting eyes; remove the alternator drive belt, loosen the

alternator mounting bolts and swing the alternator outward toward the fender.

4. Remove the plug wires and remove the rocker covers. See the preceding "Note" on rocker cover removal. If equipped with electric assist choke, disconnect the choke wire at the choke cap. If the wiring harness runs across the valve covers, unclip it and move it aside.

5. When removing the rocker covers, remove or reposition any other wires or hoses which might block the removal of the rocker covers.

6. Torque the rocker arm support bolts to 46 ft lbs.

7. Reconnect the battery cable, place the transmission in Neutral (manual) or Park (automatic), and apply the parking brake.

8. Place your finger on the adjusting screw of the intake valve rocker arm for cylinder No. 5. This way you'll be able to feel exactly when the rocker arm begins to move.

9. Use a remote starter switch to turn the engine over until you can just feel the valve begin to open. Now the cam is in position to adjust the intake and exhaust valves on the No. 1 cylinder.

10. Adjust the No. 1 intake valve so that a 0.014 in. feeler gauge has a slight drag while a 0.015 in. feeler gauge is a tight fit. To decrease lash, turn the adjusting screw clockwise; to increase lash, turn the adjusting screw counterclockwise. There are no lockbolts to tighten as the adjusting screws are selftightening.

CAUTION: *Do not use a step-type, "go-no go" feeler gauge. When checking lash, you must insert the feeler gauge and move it parallel with the crankshaft. Do not move it in and out perpendicular with the crankshaft as this will give an erroneous feel which will result in overtightened valves.*

11. Adjust the exhaust valve the same way so that an 0.018 in. feeler gauge has a slight drag, while a 0.019 in. gauge is a tight fit.

12. The rest of the valves are adjusted in the same way, in their firing order (1-4-2-5-3-6), by positioning the cam according to the chart.

13. Remove all the old gasket material from the cylinder heads and rocker cover gasket surfaces, and disconnect the negative cable from the battery.

14. Remove the spark plug wires and reinstall the rocker arm covers.

15. Reinstall any hoses and wires which were removed previously.

Valve Clearance Adjustment— 2800 cc Engine

Intake valve just opening	Adjust both valves for this cylinder (Intake—0.014 in.; Exhaust—0.018 in.)
5	1
3	4
6	2
1	5
4	3
2	6

16. Reinstall the spark plug wires, the alternator drive belt, and the Thermactor air by-pass valve and it its mounting bracket.

17. Reconnect the battery cable, replace the air cleaner assembly, start the engine, and check for leaks.

Carburetor Adjustments

This section contains only carburetor adjustments as they normally apply to engine tune-up. Descriptions of the carburetor and complete adjustment procedures can be found in Chapter 4, under "Fuel System."

When the engine in your car is running, air/fuel mixture from the carburetor is being drawn into the engine by a partial vacuum which is created by the downward movement of the pistons on the intake stroke of the four-stroke cycle of the engine. The amount of air/fuel mixture which enters the engine is controlled by throttle plate(s) in the bottom of the carburetor. When the engine is not running the throttle plate(s) is (are) closed, almost completely blocking off the bottom of the carburetor from the inside of the engine. The throttle plates are connected, through the throttle linkage, to the gas pedal in the passenger compartment of the car. After you start the engine and put the transmission in gear, you depress the gas pedal to start the car moving. What you actually are doing when you depress the gas pedal is opening the throttle plate in the carburetor to admit more of the air/fuel mixture to the engine. The farther you open the throttle plates in the carburetor, the higher the engine speed becomes.

As previously stated, when the engine is not running, the throttle plates in the carburetor are closed. When the engine is idling, it is necessary to open the throttle plate slightly. To prevent having to keep your foot on the gas pedal when the engine is idling, an idle speed adjusting screw was added to the carburetor. This screw has the same effect as keeping your foot slightly depressed on the gas pedal. The idle speed adjusting screw contacts a lever (the throttle lever) on the outside of the carburetor. When the screw is turned in, it opens the throttle plate on the carburetor, raising the idle speed of the engine. This screw is called the curb idle adjusting screw and the procedures in this section will tell you how to adjust it.

In addition to the curb idle adjusting screw, most engines have a throttle solenoid positioner. Ford has found it necessary to raise the idle speed of these engines to obtain a smooth engine idle. When the ignition key is turned "off," the current to the spark plugs is cut off and the engine normally stops running. However, if an engine has a high operating temperature and a high idle speed, it is possible for the high temperature of the cylinders, instead of the spark plugs, to ignite the air/fuel mixture. When this happens, the engine continues to run after the key is turned off. To solve this problem, a throttle solenoid was added to the carburetor. The solenoid is a cylinder with an adjustable plunger and an electrical lead. When the ignition key is turned to "on," the solenoid plunger extends to contact the carburetor throttle lever and raise the idle speed of the engine. When the ignition key is turned "off," the solenoid is deengergized and the solenoid plunger falls back from the throttle lever. This allows the throttle lever to fall back and rest on the curb idle adjusting screw. This closes the throttle plates far enough so that the engine will not run on.

Since it is difficult for the engine to draw the air/fuel mixture from the carburetor with the small amount of throttle plate opening which is present when the engine is idling, an idle mixture passage is provided in the carburetor. This passage delivers air/fuel mixture to the engine from a hole which is located in the bottom of the carburetor below the throttle plates. This idle mixture passage contains an adjusting screw which restricts the amount of air/fuel mixture which enters the engine at idle. The procedures given in this section will tell how to set the idle mixture adjusting screw(s).

NOTE: *With the electric solenoid disengaged, the carburetor idle speed adjusting screw must make contact with the throttle lever to prevent the throttle plates from jamming in the throttle bore when the engine is turned off.*

IDLE SPEED AND MIXTURE ADJUSTMENTS

The recommended procedure for adjusting the idle mixture on 1975–78 Mustang IIs involves the addition of an artificial enrichment substance (propane), to the air intake at the air cleaner. This method uses special service tools not generally available to the public. The following is an alternate procedure which can be used in place of the factory recommended method on all Mustang IIs.

NOTE: *In order to limit exhaust emissions, plastic caps have been installed on the idle fuel mixture screw(s) which prevent the carburetor from being adjusted to an overly rich idle fuel mixture. Under no circumstances should these limiters be modified or removed. A satisfactory idle should be obtained within the range of the limiter(s).*

Carburetor adjustments—Motorcraft 5200

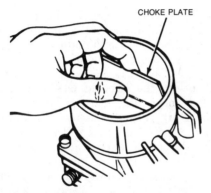

CHOKE PLATE

Typical choke plate in fully open position

Motorcraft 5200, Motorcraft 2150—1975-76

1. Start the engine and run it at idle until it reaches operating temperature (about 10–20 minutes, depending on outside temperatures). Stop the engine.

2. Check the ignition timing as outlined under "Ignition Timing Adjustment."

3. Remove the air cleaner, taking note of the hose locations, and check that the choke plate is in the open position (plate in vertical position). Check the accompanying illustrations to see where the carburetor adjustment locations are. If you cannot reach them with the air cleaner installed, leave it off temporarily.

4. Attach a tachometer to the engine with the positive wire connected to the distributor side of the ignition coil (1974 models), or the "TACH TEST" connection at the coil (1975 and later models), and the negative wire connected to a good ground, such as an engine bolt.

NOTE: *In order to attach an alligator clip to the distributor side (terminal) of the coil (primary connection) on 1974 models, it will be necessary to lift off the connector and slide a female loop type connector (commercially available) down over the terminal threads. Then push down the rubber connector over the loop connector and you have made yourself a little adaptor, to which you can connect the alligator clip of your tachometer.*

5. All idle speed adjustments are made with the headlights off, the air conditioning off (if so equipped), all vacuum hoses connected, the throttle solenoid positioner activated (connected, if so equipped), and the air cleaner on. The only problem here is that on many cars, the adjustments cannot be reached with the air cleaner installed. On these problem cars, you will have to adjust the idle speed approximately 50–100 rpm higher with the air cleaner removed so that the setting is correct when the air cleaner is then installed. Finally, all idle speed adjustments are made in Neutral on cars with manual transmission, and in Drive on cars equipped with automatic transmission.

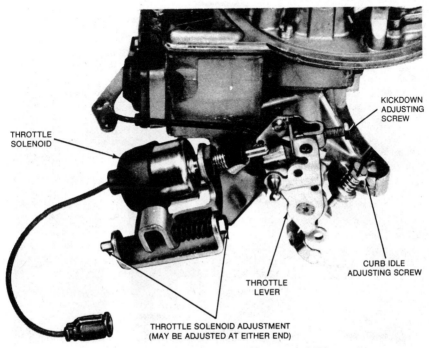

THROTTLE SOLENOID

KICKDOWN ADJUSTING SCREW

CURB IDLE ADJUSTING SCREW

THROTTLE LEVER

THROTTLE SOLENOID ADJUSTMENT (MAY BE ADJUSTED AT EITHER END)

Carburetor adjustments—Motorcraft 2150

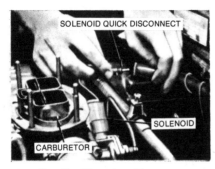

Disconnecting throttle solenoid

NOTE: *Make sure that the parking brake is applied and all four wheels are blocked.*

6a. On cars not equipped with a throttle solenoid positioner, the idle speed is adjusted with the curb idle speed adjusting screw. Start the engine. Turn the curb idle speed adjusting screw inward or outward until the correct idle speed (see "Tune-Up Specifications") is reached, remembering to make the 50–100 rpm allowance if the air cleaner is removed.

b. On cars equipped with a throttle solenoid positioner, the idle speed is adjusted with solenoid adjusting screw (nut), in two stages. Start the engine. The higher speed is adjusted with the solenoid connected. Turn the solenoid adjusting screw (nut) inward or outward until the correct higher idle speed (see "Tune-Up Specifica-

tions") is reached, remembering to make the 50–100 rpm allowance if the air cleaner is removed. After making this adjustment on 302 V8 equipped cars, tighten the solenoid adjusting locknut. The lower idle speed is adjusted with the solenoid lead wire disconnected near the harness (not at the carburetor). Place automatic transmission equipped cars in Neutral for this adjustment. Using the curb idle speed adjusting screw on the carburetor, turn the idle speed adjusting screw inward or outward until the correct lower idle speed (see "Tune-Up Specifications") is reached, remembering again to make the 50–100 rpm allowance if the air cleaner is removed. Finally, reconnect the solenoid, slightly depress the throttle lever and allow the solenoid plunger to fully extend.

7. If removed, install the air cleaner. Recheck the idle speed. If it is not correct, Step 6 will have to be repeated and the approximate corrections made.

8. To adjust the idle mixture, turn the idle mixture screw(s) inward to obtain the smoothest idle possible within the range of the limiter(s).

9. Turn off the engine and disconnect the tachometer.

NOTE: *If any doubt exists as to the proper idle mixture setting for your car, have the exhaust emission level checked at a diag-*

Throttle solenoid positioner—Motorcraft 5200

nostic center or garage with an exhaust (HC/CO) analyzer or an air/fuel ratio meter. Proper CO levels are 0.15% for the 2300 and 0.7% for the 2800 V6.

All Models—1977–78

CAUTION: *Apply the parking brake and block the wheels before starting the engine and performing this procedure.*

NOTE: *Leave all vacuum hoses connected to the air cleaner while temporarily shifting its position to gain access to the adjusting screws. Make sure it is installed when measuring engine speeds. If the engine speed wanders average out the extremes to get the reading.*

1. After taking the safety precautions listed above, run the engine until it is hot and then stop it.

2. Connect a tachometer that is compatible with the Ford "Dura-Spark I" ignition system.

3. On 1978 models only, disconnect the fuel evaporative purge valve signal vacuum hose, *Not By Disconnecting the Hose at the Valve*, but by tracing back from the purge valve to the first connection. Disconnect the valve where specified, and plug the connection and the open end of the hose.

4. Disconnect the evaporative emission purge hose (if so equipped) at the air cleaner and plug the nipple.

5. On 1978 models, disconnect the crankcase ventilation closure hose at the air cleaner and plug the nipple.

6. Remove the idle mixture limiter caps, preferably with a specially designed tool such as Ford Tool T75L-9500-A or equivalent.

7. In 1978 2.3 liter engines with thermactor air pump, if the thermactor dump valve has one or two hoses at the side, disconnect and plug the one or both; if the thermactor dump valve has a hose on top, disconnect and plug that hose and then connect an extra hose between the dump valve vacuum fitting and an intake manifold vacuum fitting.

8. Put the transmission in neutral and run the engine at 2500 rpm for 15 seconds.

9. With air conditioning system off (unless otherwise specified) and transmission in neutral or drive as specified on the emissions decal, adjust the curb idle speed to specification plus the "alternate idle speed change" as specified on the decal.

10. Make sure transmission is in the position specified for the propane enrichment check of mixture (see the emissions sticker).

11. Adjust the idle misture screw(s) rich or lean as necessary to achieve the highest rpm, adjusting the idle speed back to the specified curb idle speed plus the "speed change" specified on the sticker. Go back and forth this way until the best possible mixture adjustment produces exactly the curb idle plus the speed change.

12. If the "speed change" is zero, proceed to the next step. Otherwise, adjust one or both idle mixture screws (if there are two, adjust them both equally) inward until rpm has dropped just to the normal idle speed.

13. Turn the engine off, and, without disturbing mixture screw position(s), install limiter caps. Caps may be soaked in hot water before installation to make them go on more easily.

14. Reroute hoses and remove tachometer.

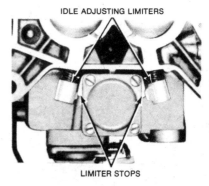

Idle mixture screw limiters for Motorcraft 2150—bottom view

Catalytic Converter Precautions

Many 1975 models, and all 1976 and later models are equipped with a catalytic converter to clean up exhaust emissions after they leave the engine. On these models, lead-free fuel must be used exclusively in order to prevent the converter from being coated with lead particles, rendering it ineffective. However, there are many other precautions which should be taken to prevent a large amount of unburned hydrocarbons from reaching the converter. Should a sufficient amount of HC reach the converter, the unit could overheat, possibly damaging the converter, nearby mechanical components, or cause a fire hazard. Therefore, when working on your car, the following conditions should be avoided:

1. The use of fuel system cleaning agents and additives.

2. Operating the car with an inoperative (closed) choke, or submerged carburetor float.

3. Extended periods of engine run-on (dieseling).

4. Turning off the ignition with the car in motion.

5. Ignition or charging system failure.

6. Misfiring of one or more spark plugs.

7. Disconnecting a spark plug wire while testing for bad wire, plug, or poor compression in one cylinder.

Engine and Engine Rebuilding

ENGINE ELECTRICAL

Ignition System

Two types of ignition systems are used in the Mustang II. A conventional system using breaker points and condenser is used on 1974 models. A breakerless (solid state) ignition system using an armature and magnetic pickup coil assembly in the distributor and a solid state amplifier module located inline between the coil and distributor is installed in all 1975 models as standard equipment.

Both systems employ a distributor which is driven by the camshaft at one half crankshaft rpm, a high voltage rotor, distributor cap and spark plug wiring, and an oil-filled conventional type coil.

The two systems differ in the manner in which they convert electrical primary voltage (12 volt) from the battery into secondary voltage (20,000 volts or greater) to fire the spark

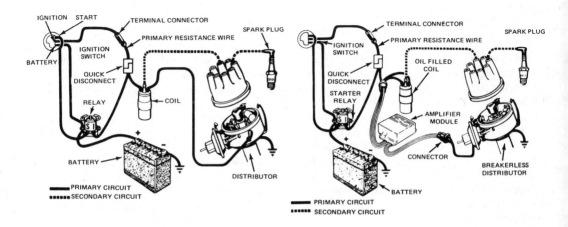

Typical ignition systems

plugs. In the conventional ignition system, the breaker points open and close as the movable breaker arm rides the rotating distributor cam eccentric, thereby opening and closing the current to the ignition coil. When the points open, they interrupt the flow of primary current to the coil, causing a collapse of the magnetic field in the coil and creating a high tension spark which is used to fire the spark plugs. In the breakerless system, a distributor shaft-mounted armature rotates past a magnetic pickup coil assembly causing fluctuations in the magnetic field generated by the pickup coil. These fluctuations in turn, cause the amplifier module to turn the ignition coil current off and on, creating the high tension spark to fire the spark plugs. The amplifier module electronically controls the dwell, which is controlled mechanically in a conventional system by the duration which the points remain closed.

Both the conventional and breakerless ignition systems are equipped with dual advance distributors. The vacuum advance unit governs ignition timing according to engine load, while the centrifugal advance unit governs ignition timing according to engine rpm. Centrifugal advance is controlled by spring-mounted weights contained in the distributor, located under the breaker point mounting plate on conventional systems and under the fixed base plate on breakerless systems. As engine speed increases, centrifugal force moves the weights outward from the distributor shaft advancing the position of the distributor cam (conventional) or armature (breakerless), thereby advancing the ignition timing. Vacuum advance is controlled by a vacuum diaphragm which is mounted on the side of the distributor and attached to the breaker point mounting plate (conventional) or the magnetic pickup coil assembly (breakerless) via the vacuum advance link. Under light acceleration, the engine is operating under a low-load condition, causing the carburetor vacuum to act on the distributor vacuum diaphragm, moving the breaker point mounting plate (conventional) or pickup coil assembly (breakerless) opposite the direction of distributor shaft rotation, thereby advancing the ignition timing.

The distributors on many models also incorporate a vacuum retard mechanism. The retard mechanism is contained in the rear part of the vacuum diaphragm chamber. When the engine is operating under high-vacuum conditions (deceleration or idle), intake manifold vacuum is applied to the retard mechanism. The retard mechanism moves the breaker point mounting plate (conventional) or pickup coil assembly (breakerless) in the direction of distributor rotation, thereby retarding the ignition timing. Ignition retard, under these conditions, reduces exhaust emissions of hydrocarbons, although it does reduce engine efficiency somewhat.

Ford Motor Company Solid-State Ignition

BASIC OPERATING PRINCIPLES

In mid 1974, Ford Motor Company introduced in selected models its new Solid-State Ignition System. In 1975, it became standard equipment in all cars in the Ford lineup. This system was designed primarily to provide a hotter spark necessary to fire the leaner fuel/air mixtures required by today's emission control standards.

The Ford Solid-State Ignition is a pulse-triggered, transistor controlled breakerless ignition system. With the ignition switch "on", the primary circuit is on and the ignition coil is energized. When the armature spokes approach the magnetic pick-up coil assembly, they induce a voltage which tells the amplifier to turn the coil primary current off. A timing circuit in the amplifier module will turn the current on again after the coil field has collapsed. When the current is on, it flows from the battery through the ignition switch, the primary windings of the ignition coil, and through the amplifier module circuits to ground. When the current is off, the magnetic field built up in the ignition coil is allowed to collapse, inducing a high voltage into the secondary windings of the coil. High voltage is produced each time the field is thus built up and collapsed.

Although the systems are basically the same, Ford refers to their solid-state ignition in several different ways. 1974–76 systems are referred to simply as Breakerless systems. In 1977, Ford named their ignition system Dura-Spark I and Dura-Spark II. Dura-Spark II is the version used in all states except California. Dura-Spark I is the system used in California V8's only. Basically, the only difference between the two is that the coil charging currents are higher in the California cars. This is necessary to fire the leaner fuel/air mixtures required by California's stricter emission laws. The difference in coils alters some of the test values.

Ford has used several different types of wiring harness on their solid-state ignition systems, due to internal circuitry changes in the electronic module. Wire continuity and color have not been changed, but the arrangement of the terminals in the connectors is different for each year. Schematics of the different years are included here, but keep in mind that the wiring in all diagrams has been simplified and as a result, the routing of your wiring may not match the wiring in the diagram. However, the wire colors and terminal connections are the same.

Wire color-coding is critical to servicing the Ford Solid-State Ignition. Battery current reaches the electronic module through either the *white* or *red* wire, depending on whether the engine is cranking or running. When the engine is cranking, battery current is flowing through the *white* wire. When the engine is running, battery current flows through the *red* wire. All distributor signals flow through the *orange* and *purple* wires. The *green* wire carries primary current from the coil to the module. The *black* wire is a ground between the distributor and the module. Up until 1975, a *blue* wire provides transient voltage protection. In 1976, the *blue* wire was dropped when a zener diode was added to the module. The *orange* and *purple* wires which run from the stator to the module must *always* be connected to the same color wire at the module. If these connections are crossed, polarity will be reversed and the system will be thrown out of phase. Some replacement wiring harnesses were sold with the wiring crossed, which complicates the problem considerably. As previously noted, the *black* wire is the gound wire. The screw which grounds the black wire also, of course, grounds the entire primary circuit. If this screw is loose, dirty, or corroded, a seemingly incomprehensible ignition problem will develop. Several other cautions should be noted here. Keep in mind that on vehicles equipped with catalytic converters, any test that requires removal of a spark plug wire while the engine is running should be kept to a thirty second maximum. Any longer than this may damage the converter. In the event you are testing spark plug wires, do not pierce them. Test the wires at their terminals only.

TROUBLESHOOTING THE FORD SOLID-STATE IGNITION SYSTEM

This system, which at first appears to be extremely complicated, is actually quite simple to diagnose and repair. Diagnosis does, however, require the use of a voltmeter and an ohmmeter. You will also need several jumper wires with both blade ends and alligator clips.

NOTE: *Ford has substantially altered their 1978 electronic ignition test procedure. Due to the sensitive nature of the system and the complexity of the test procedures, it is recommended that you refer to your dealer if you suspect a problem in your 1978 electronic ignition system. The system can, of course, be tested by substituting known good components (module, stator, etc.)*

The symptoms of a defective component within the solid state system are exactly the same as those you would encounter in a conventional system. Some of these symptoms are:

- Hard or no starting
- Rough Idle
- Poor fuel economy
- Engine misses while under load or while accelerating

If you suspect a problem in your ignition system, first perform a spark intensity test to pinpoint the problem. Using insulated pliers, hold the end of one of the spark plug leads about ½ in. away from the engine block or other good ground, and crank the engine. If you have a nice, fat spark, then your problem is not in the ignition system. If you have no spark or a very weak spark, then proceed to the following tests.

Stator Test

To test the stator (also known as the magnetic pickup assembly), you will need an ohmmeter. Run the engine until it reaches operating temperature, then turn the ignition switch to the "off" position. Disconnect the wire harness from the distributor. Connect the ohmmeter between the orange and purple wires. Resistance should be between 400 and 800 ohms. Next, connect the ohmmeter between the black wire and a good ground on the engine. Operate the vacuum advance, either by hand or with an external vacuum source. Resistance should be zero ohms. Finally, connect the ohmmeter between the orange wire and ground, and then the purple wire and ground. Resistance should be over 70,000 ohms in both cases. If any of your ohmmeter readings differ from the above specifications, then the stator is defective and must be replaced as a unit.

If the stator is good, then either the electronic module or the wiring connections must be checked next. Because of its complicated electronic nature, the module itself cannot be checked, except by substitution. If you have access to a module which you know to be good, then perform a substitution test at this time. If this cures the problem, then the original module is faulty and must be replaced. If it does not cure the problem or if you cannot locate a known-good module, then disconnect the two wiring harnesses from the module, and, using a voltmeter, check the following circuits:

NOTE: *Make no tests at the module side of the connectors.*

1. Starting circuit—Connect the voltmeter leads to ground and to the corresponding female socket of the white male lead from the module (you will need a jumper wire with a blade end). Crank the engine over. The voltage should be between 8 and 12 volts.

2. Running circuit—Turn the ignition switch to the "on" position. Connect the voltmeter leads to ground and the corresponding female socket of the red male lead from the module. Voltage should be battery voltage plus or minus 0.1 volts.

3. Coil circuit—Leave the ignition switch "on". Connect the voltmeter leads to ground and to the corresponding female socket of the green male lead from the module. Voltage should be battery voltage plus or minus 0.1 volts.

If any of the preceding readings are incorrect, inspect and repair any loose, broken, frayed or dirty connections. If this doesn't solve the problem, perform a battery source test.

Battery Source Test

To make this test, *do not* disconnect the coil. Connect the voltmeter leads to the BAT terminal at the coil and a good ground. Connect a jumper wire from the DEC terminal at the coil to a good ground. Make sure all lights and accessories are off. Turn the ignition to the "on" position. Check the voltage. If the voltage is below 4.9 volts (11 volts for Dura-Spark I), then check the primary wiring for

broken strands, cracked or frayed wires, or loose or dirty terminals. Repair or replace any defects. If, however, the voltage is above 7.9 volts (14 volts for Dura-Spark I), then you have a problem in the resistance wiring and it must be replaced.

It should be noted here that if you do have a problem in your electronic ignition system, most of the time will be a case of loose, dirty or frayed wires. The electronic module, being completely solid-state, is not ordinarily subject to failure. It is possible for the unit to fail, of course, but as a general rule, the source of an ignition system problem will be somewhere else in the circuit.

Distributor

DISTRIBUTOR REMOVAL AND INSTALLATION

1. On all V6 and V8 engines, remove the air cleaner assembly, taking note of the hose locations. On 4 cylinder engines, the distributor can be reached without removing the air cleaner, but access will prove easier if it is removed. Also, on 4 cylinder engines equipped with a Thermactor air pump, remove one mounting bolt and swing the pump to one side, to improve access to the distributor.

2. On models equipped with a conventional ignition system, disconnected the primary wire at the coil. On models equipped with breakerless ignition, disconnect the distributor wiring connector from the vehicle wiring harness.

3. Noting the position of the vacuum line(s) on the distributor diaphragm, disconnect the lines at the diaphragm. Unsnap the two distributor cap retaining clamps and remove the cap. Position the cap and ignition wires to one side.

NOTE: *If it is necessary to disconnect ignition wires from the cap to get enough room to remove the distributor, make sure to label every wire and the cap for easy and accurate reinstallation.*

4. Using chalk or paint, carefully mark the position of the distributor rotor in relation to the distributor housing and mark the position of the distributor housing in relation to the engine block. When this is done, you should have a line on the distributor housing directly in line with the tip of the rotor and another line on the engine block directly in line with the mark on the distributor housing. This is very important because the distributor must be reinstalled in the exact same

1975 Test Sequence

	Test Voltage Between	Should Be	If Not, Conduct
Key On	Socket #4 and Engine Ground	Battery Voltage ± 0.1 Volt	Module Bias Test
	Socket #1 and Engine Ground	Battery Voltage ± 0.1 Volt	Battery Source Test
Cranking	Socket #5 and Engine Ground	8 to 12 volts	Cranking Test
	Jumper #1 to #8 Read #6	more than 6 volts	Starting Circuit Test
	Pin #7 and Pin #8	½ volt minimum AC or any DC volt wiggle	Distributor Hardware Test
	Test Voltage Between	*Should Be*	*If Not, Conduct*
Key Off	Socket #7 and #3 Socket #8 and Engine Ground Socket #7 and Engine Ground Socket #3 and Engine Ground	400 to 800 ohms 0 ohms more than 70,000 ohms	Magnetic Pick-up (Stator) Test
	Socket #4 and Coil Tower Socket #1 and Pin #6	7000 to 13000 ohms 1.0 to 2.0 ohms	Coil Test
	Socket #1 and Engine Ground	more than 4.0 ohms	Short Test
	Socket #4 and Pin #6	1.0 to 2.0 ohms	Resistance Wire Test

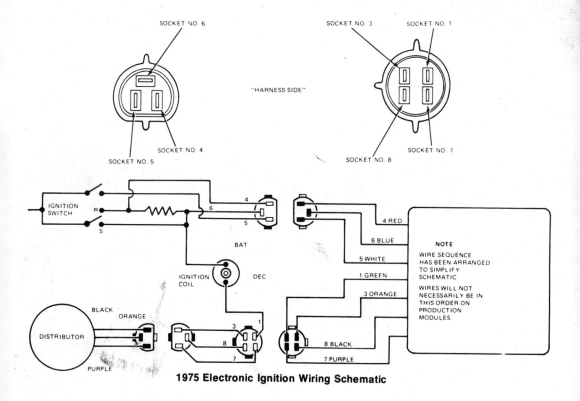

1975 Electronic Ignition Wiring Schematic

1976 Test Sequence

	Test Voltage Between	Should Be	If Not, Conduct
Key On	Socket #4 and Engine Ground	Battery Voltage ± 0.1 Volt	Battery Source Test
	Socket #1 and Engine Ground	Battery Voltage ± 0.1 Volt	Battery Source Test
Cranking	Socket #5 and Engine Ground	8 to 12 volts	Check Supply Circuit (starting) through Ignition Switch
	Jumper #1 to #8 Read #6	more than 6 volts	Starting Circuit Test
	Pin #3 and Pin #8	½ volt minimum AC or any DC volt wiggle	Distributor Hardware Test
	Test Voltage Between	*Should Be*	*If Not, Conduct*
Key Off	Socket #8 and #3 Socket #7 and Engine Ground Socket #8 and Engine Ground Socket #3 and Engine Ground	400 to 800 ohms 0 ohms more than 70,000 ohms more than 70,000 ohms	Magnetic Pick-up (Stator) Test
	Socket #4 and Coil Tower	7000 to 13,000 ohms	Coil Test
	Socket #1 and Engine Ground	more than 4.0 ohms	Short Test

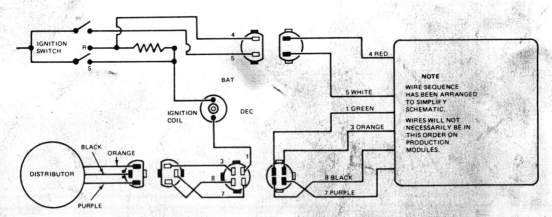

1976 Electronic Ignition Wiring Schematic

1977 Test Sequence

	Test Voltage Between	Should Be	If Not, Conduct
Key On	Socket #4 and Engine Ground	Battery Voltage ± 0.1 volts	Module Bias Test
	Socket #1 and Engine Ground	Battery Voltage ± 0.1 volts	Battery Source Test
Cranking	Socket #5 and Engine Ground	8 to 12 volts	Cranking Test
	Jumper #1 to #8—Read Coil "Bat" Term. & Engine Ground	more than 6 volts	Starting Circuit Test
	Sockets #7 and #3	½ volt minimum wiggle	Distributor Hardware Test

	Test Resistance Between	Should Be	If Not, Conduct
Key Off	Sockets #7 and #3 Socket #8 and Engine Ground Socket #7 and Engine Ground Socket #3 and Engine Ground	400 to 800 ohms 0 ohms more than 70,000 ohms more than 70,000 ohms	Magnetic Pick-up (Stator) Test
	Socket #4 and Coil Tower	7000 to 13,000 ohms	Coil Test
	Socket #1 and Coil "Bat" Term.	1.0 to 2.0 ohms Breakerless & Dura-Spark II	
		0.5 to 1.5 ohms Dura-Spark I	
	Socket #1 and Engine Ground	more than 4 ohms	Short Test
	Socket #4 and Coil "Bat" Term. (Except Dura-Spark I)	1.0 to 2.0 ohms Breakerless	Resistance Wire Test
		0.7 to 1.7 ohms Dura-Spark II	

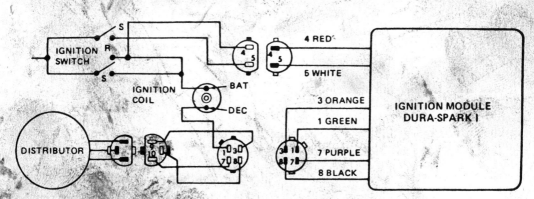

1977 Dura-Spark I Wiring Schematic

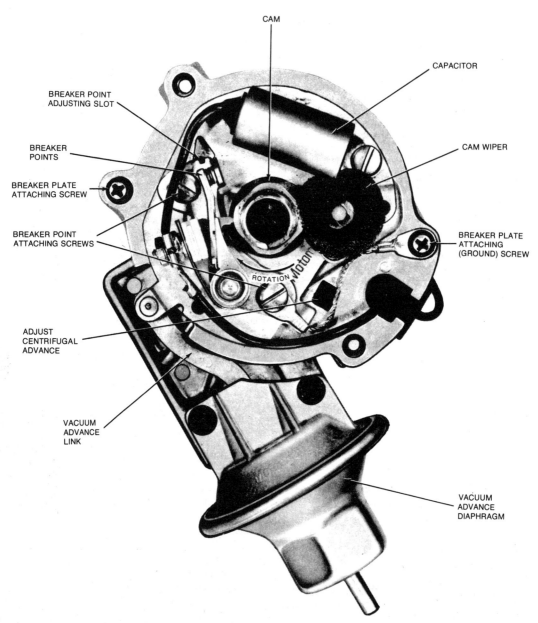

CAM

CAPACITOR

BREAKER POINT
ADJUSTING SLOT

CAM WIPER

BREAKER
POINTS

BREAKER PLATE
ATTACHING SCREW

BREAKER PLATE
ATTACHING
(GROUND) SCREW

BREAKER POINT
ATTACHING SCREWS

ROTATION

ADJUST
CENTRIFUGAL
ADVANCE

VACUUM
ADVANCE
LINK

VACUUM
ADVANCE
DIAPHRAGM

2300cc 4 cylinder conventional distributor—cap and rotor removed

location from which it was removed, if correct ignition timing is to be maintained.

5. Remove the distributor hold-down bolt and clamp. Remove the distributor from the engine. Make sure that the oil pump (intermediate) driveshaft does not come out with the distributor. If it does, remove it from the distributor shaft, coat its lower end with heavy grease, and reinsert it, making sure that it fully engages the oil pump drive.

NOTE: *Do not disturb the engine while the distributor is removed. If you turn the*

engine over with the distributor removed, you will have to retime the engine.

6a. If the engine was cranked (disturbed) with the distributor removed, it will now be necessary to retime the engine. If the distributor has been installed incorrectly and the engine will not start, remove the distributor from the engine and start over again. Hold the distributor close to the engine and install the cap on the distributor in its normal position. Locate the No. 1 spark plug tower on the distributor cap. Scribe a mark on the

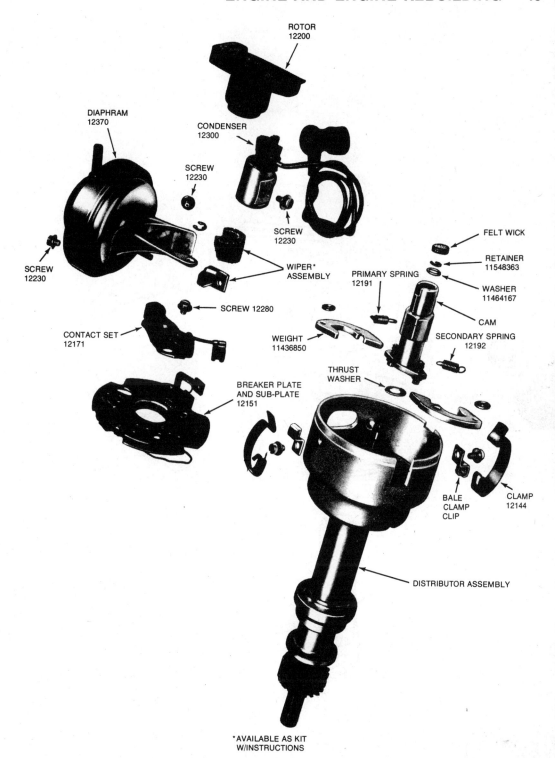

ROTOR
12200

DIAPHRAM
12370

CONDENSER
12300

SCREW
12230

SCREW
12230

SCREW
12230

SCREW
12230

FELT WICK

RETAINER
11548363

WIPER*
ASSEMBLY

PRIMARY SPRING
12191

WASHER
11464167

CAM

SCREW 12280

CONTACT SET
12171

WEIGHT
11436850

SECONDARY SPRING
12192

THRUST
WASHER

BREAKER PLATE
AND SUB-PLATE
12151

BALE
CLAMP
CLIP

CLAMP
12144

DISTRIBUTOR ASSEMBLY

*AVAILABLE AS KIT
W/INSTRUCTIONS

2800cc V6 conventional distributor disassembled

body of the distributor directly below the No. 1 spark plug wire tower on the distributor cap. Remove the distributor cap from the distributor and move the distributor and cap to one side. Remove the No. 1 spark plug and crank the engine over until the No. 1 cylinder is on its compression stroke. To accomplish this, place a wrench on the lower

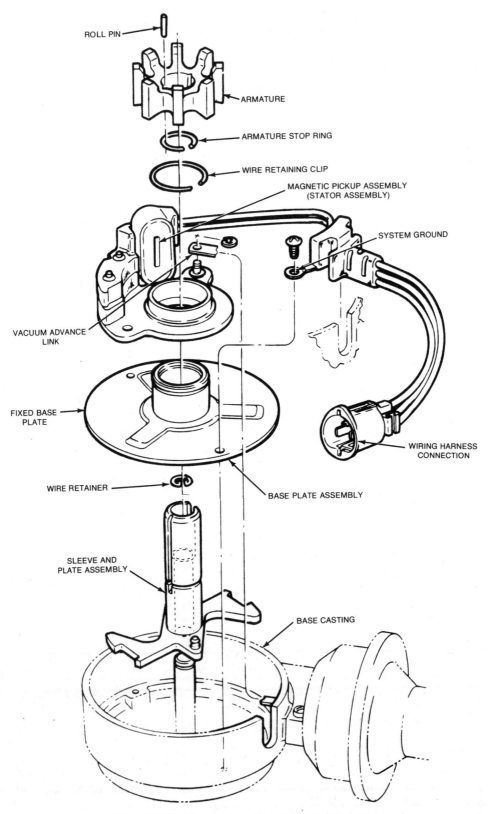

ROLL PIN

ARMATURE

ARMATURE STOP RING

WIRE RETAINING CLIP

MAGNETIC PICKUP ASSEMBLY
(STATOR ASSEMBLY)

SYSTEM GROUND

VACUUM ADVANCE
LINK

FIXED BASE
PLATE

WIRING HARNESS
CONNECTION

WIRE RETAINER

BASE PLATE ASSEMBLY

SLEEVE AND
PLATE ASSEMBLY

BASE CASTING

4900cc (302) V8 breakerless distributor disassembled

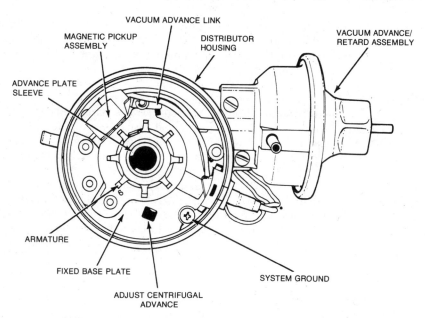

4900cc (302) breakerless distributor—cap and rotor removed

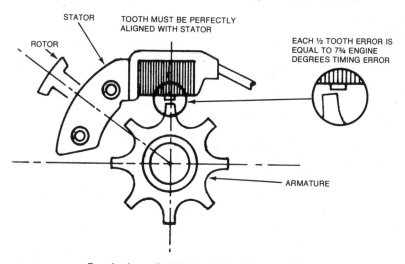

Breakerless distributor static timing position

engine pulley and turn the engine slowly in a clockwise (4 or 6 cylinder) or counterclockwise (V8) direction until the TDC mark on the crankshaft damper aligns with the timing pointer. If you place your finger in the No. 1 spark plug hole, you will feel air escaping as the piston rises in the combustion chamber. On conventional ignition systems, the rotor must be at the No. 1 firing position to install the distributor. On breakerless ignition systems, one of the armature segments must be aligned with the stator as shown in the accompanying illustration to install the distributor. Make sure that the oil pump intermediate shaft properly engages the distributor shaft. It may be necessary to crank

the engine with the starter, after the distributor drive gear is partially engaged, in order to engage the oil pump intermediate shaft. Install, but do not tighten the retaining clamp and bolt. Rotate the distributor to advance the timing to a point where the armature tooth is aligned properly (breakerless ignition) or to a point where the points are just starting to open (conventional ignition). Tighten the clamp.

b. If the engine was not cranked (disturbed) when the distributor was removed, position the distributor in the block with the rotor aligned with the mark previously scribed on the distributor body and the marks on the distributor body and cylinder block in alignment. Install the distributor hold-down bolt and clamp fingertight.

7. Install the distributor cap and wires.

8. On models equipped with conventional ignition, connect the primary wire at the coil. On models equipped with breakerless ignition, connect the distributor wiring connector to the wiring harness.

9. Install the Thermactor air pump mounting bolt, if removed, and adjust the air pump drive belt tension, if necessary, as outlined in Chapter 1.

10. Install the air cleaner, if removed.

11. Check the ignition timing as outlined in Chapter 2.

Firing Order

The firing order illustrations may be found in Chapter 2 under "Ignition Timing."

Charging System

The charging system is composed of the alternator, alternator regulator, charging system warning light, battery, and fuse link wire.

A failure of any component of the charging system can cause the entire system to stop functioning. Because of this, the charging system can be very difficult to troubleshoot when problems occur.

When the ignition key is turned on, current flows from the battery, through the charging system indicator light on the instrument panel, to the voltage regulator, and to the alternator. Since the alternator is not producing any current, the alternator warning light comes on. When the engine is started, the alternator begins to produce current and turns the alternator light off. As the alternator turns and produces current, that current is divided in two ways: part to the battery to charge the battery and power the electrical components of the vehicle, and part is returned to the alternator to enable it to increase its output. In this situation, the alternator is receiving current from the battery and from itself. A voltage regulator is wired into the current supply to the alternator to prevent it from receiving too much current which would cause it to put out too much current. Conversely, if the voltage regulator does not allow the alternator to receive enough current, the battery will not be fully charged and will eventually go dead.

The battery is connected to the alternator at all times, whether the ignition key is turned on or not. If the battery were shorted to ground, the alternator would also be shorted. This would damage the alternator. To prevent this, a fuse link is installed in the wiring between the battery and the alternator. If the battery is shorted, the fuse link is melted, protecting the alternator.

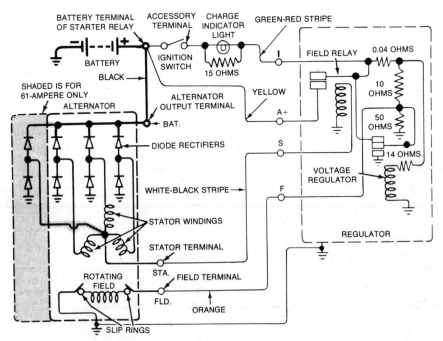

Alternator charging circuit w/indicator light

Since the alternator, the alternator regulator, the charging system warning light, the battery and the fuse link are all interconnected, the failure of one component can cause the others to become inoperative.

ALTERNATOR PRECAUTIONS

Several precautions must be observed with alternator equipped vehicles to avoid damaging the unit. They are as follows:

1. If the battery is removed for any reason, make sure that it is reconnected with the correct polarity. Reversing the battery connections may result in damage to the one-way rectifiers.

2. When utilizing a booster battery as a starting aid, always connect it as follows: positive to positive, and negative (booster battery) to a good ground on the engine of the car being started.

3. Never use a fast charger as a booster to start cars with alternating-current (AC) circuits.

4. When servicing the battery with a fast charger, always disconnect the car battery cables.

5. Never attempt to polarize an alternator.

6. Avoid long soldering times when replacing diodes or transistors. Prolonged heat is damaging to alternators.

7. Do not use test lamps of more than 12 volts (V) for checking diode continuity.

8. Do not short across or ground any of the terminals on the alternator.

9. The polarity of the battery, alternator, and regulator must be matched and considered before making any electrical connections within the system.

10. Never operate the alternator on an open circuit. Make sure that all connections within the circuit are clean and tight.

11. Disconnect the battery terminals when performing any service on the electrical system. This will eliminate the possibility of accidental reversal of polarity.

12. Disconnect the battery ground cable if arc welding is to be done on any part of the car.

ALTERNATOR REPAIR

While internal alternator repairs are possible, they require specialized tools and training. Therefore, it is advisable to replace a defective alternator, or have it repaired by a qualified shop.

REMOVAL AND INSTALLATION

1. Disconnect the negative battery cable from the battery.

2. Disconnect the wires from the rear of the alternator.

3. Loosen the alternator mounting bolts and remove the belt.

Alternator terminal locations

4. Remove the alternator mounting bolts and remove the alternator.

5. To install, position the alternator on the engine and install the attaching bolts.

6. Connect the wires on the rear of the alternator.

7. Position the belt on the alternator.

8. Adjust alternator belt tension as described under "Belt Tension Adjustment" in Chapter 1.

9. Connect the negative battery cable.

VOLTAGE REGULATOR

The voltage regulator is a device which controls the output of the alternator. If the regulator did not limit the voltage output of the alternator, the excessive output could burn out the components of the electrical system. In addition, the regulator compensates for seasonal temperature changes as they affect voltage output.

Three types of regulators are used on Mustang II models. An electromechanical Motorcraft unit is used on most models equipped with conventional ignition. This unit is factory calibrated, permanently sealed, and cannot be adjusted. A transistorized Motorcraft unit is used on most models equipped with solid state ignition. This regulator is equipped with a voltage limiter adjustment screw. The transistorized regulator is identical in appearance to the electromechanical unit, except where the sealed electro-mechanical unit has rivets attaching

Alternator and Regulator Specifications

| | | ALTERNATOR | | | | REGULATOR | | | | | |
| | | | | | | Field Relay | | | Regulator | | |
Year	Model	Part No. or Manufacturer	Field Current @ 12V	Output (amps)	Part No. or Manufacturer	Air Gap (in.)	Point Gap (in.)	Volts to Close	Air Gap (in.)	Point Gap (in.)	Volts @ 75°
'74	All	D3ZF-AA D4ZF-EA D42F-EA D42F-AA	2.9	38	D4AF-AA	Not Adjustable	2.5–4.0		Not Adjustable		13.5–15.3
		D30F-AA D32F-BA	2.9	61	D4AF-AA	Not Adjustable	2.5–4.0		Not Adjustable		13.5–15.3
		D30F-AA D32F-AA D40F-EA D42F-AA D42F-CA	2.9	70	D4TF-AA	Not Adjustable	2.5–4.0		Not Adjustable		13.5–15.3
'75– '76	All	D4ZF-BA	2.9	38	D4AF-AA	Not Adjustable	2.5–4.0		Not Adjustable		13.5–15.3
		D52F-AA D3TF-CA D30F-FA	2.9	42	D4AF-AA	Not Adjustable	2.5–4.0		Not Adjustable		13.5–15.3
		D40F-BA	2.9	55	D4AF-AA	Not Adjustable	2.5–4.0		Not Adjustable		13.5–15.3
		D40F-DA	2.9	61	D4AF-AA	Not Adjustable	2.5–4.0		Not Adjustable		13.5–15.3
		D30F-AA D4ZF-AA D32F-AA D40F-EA	2.9	70	D4TF-AA	Not Adjustable	2.5–4.0		Not Adjustable		13.5–15.3
'77	All	D7AF-AA D7AF-JA	2.9	40	Ford	Not Adjustable	2.5–4.0		Not Adjustable		13.5–15.3
		D7AF-CA D7AF-DA D7AF-LA	2.9	60	Ford	Not Adjustable	2.5–4.0		Not Adjustable		13.5–15.3
		D7AF-BA	2.9	70	Ford	Not Adjustable	2.5–4.0		Not Adjustable		13.5–15.3
'78		D7AF-AA D7AF-BA	2.9	40	Ford	Not Adjustable	2.5–4.0		Not Adjustable		13.5–15.3
		D7AF-CA D7AF-LA D72F-AA	2.9①	50	Ford	Not Adjustable	2.5–4.0		Not Adjustable		13.5–15.3
		D7TF-AA	2.9	65	Ford	Not Adjustable	2.5–4.0		Not Adjustable		13.5–15.3
		D7EF-BA	2.9	70	Ford	Not Adjustable	2.5–4.0		Not Adjustable		13.5–15.3

① Electronic regulator—4.0

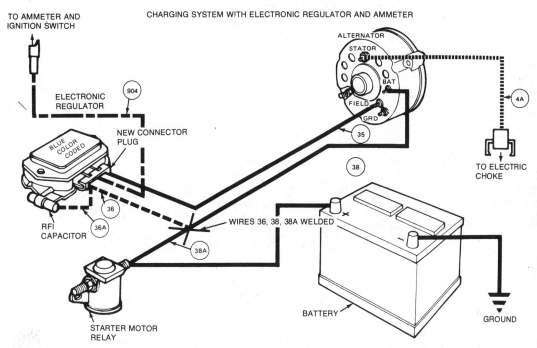

Simplified schematic of electronic regulator type charging system

the regulator cover, the transistorized regulator has phillips head screws.

The electronic regulator is 100% solid state, using only transistors, diodes and resistors, because of a higher (4 amp) field current. It is a compact, flat unit (see illustration). Output is not adjustable. Observe the following additional precautions when working with this regulator:

1. Always use the proper alternator—the higher (4 amp) field current the unit is designed to handle makes for reduced output

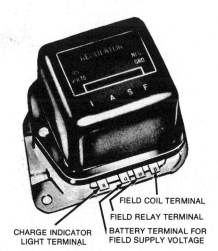

CHARGE INDICATOR
LIGHT TERMINAL

FIELD COIL TERMINAL
FIELD RELAY TERMINAL
BATTERY TERMINAL FOR
FIELD SUPPLY VOLTAGE

Electro-mechanical regulator terminals

when an older type alternator of the wrong design is used. The older alternator with the 3.80 ohm field is the only unit serviced for systems with this type regulator.

2. Make sure to replace the unit with a similar (electronic) unit that is color coded Blue for the ammeter type electrical system *only*. If an attempt is made to Adapt an electro-mechanical unit to the system (the connector plugs are not compatible), the regulator would burn out.

3. Be sure the field terminal connector (it is a push-on type connector) is installed on the "Field" terminal stud at the alternator and *not* the ground stud.

4. Always disconnect the connector plug from the regulator before checking alternator output with test probes or a jumper wire.

5. Always disconnect the connector plug from the regulator before removing the regulator mounting screws. Removing the connector from an ungrounded regulator with the ignition switch on will destroy the regulator.

6. Always disconnect the electric choke wire from the Stator terminal of the alternator before troubleshooting the charging system. Check the choke wire for a ground.

7. *Never* attempt to polarize or test the alternator by grounding the field circuit, as this will destroy the regulator.

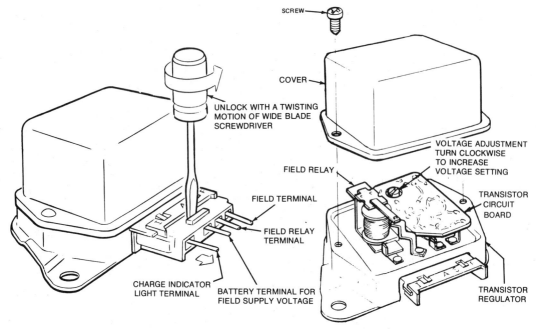

Transistorized regulator adjustment

REMOVAL AND INSTALLATION

1. Remove the battery ground cable. On models with the regulator mounted behind the battery, it is necessary to remove the battery hold-down, and to move the battery.

2. Remove the regulator mounting screws.

3. Disconnect the regulator from the wiring harness.

4. Connect the new regulator to the wiring harness.

5. Mount the regulator to the regulator mounting plate. The radio suppression condenser mounts under one mounting screw; the ground lead under the other mounting screw. Tighten the mounting screws.

6. If the battery was moved to gain access to the regulator, position the battery and install the hold-down. Connect the battery ground cable, and test the system for proper voltage regulation.

TESTING

Autolite (Motorcraft) Electro-Mechanical and Motorcraft Transistor and Electronic Units

Any electro-mechanical regulator that does not perform to specifications must be replaced. A transistorized regulator may be adjusted if not up to specifications as per the test. The accompanying illustration shows

the voltage limiter adjustment screw location beneath the regulator cover.

Before proceeding with the test, make sure that the alternator drive belt tension is properly adjusted, the battery has a good charge (specific gravity of 1.250 or better), and that all charging system electrical connections are clean and tight. A voltmeter is needed for this test. The test is as follows:

1. Connect a voltmeter to the battery with the positive lead to the battery positive terminal and the negative lead to the battery negative terminal. Turn off all electrical equipment. Check and record the voltmeter reading with the engine stopped.

2. Connect a tachometer to the engine with the red (positive) lead to the distributor terminal on the ignition coil and the black (negative) lead to a good ground such as an engine bolt.

3. Place the transmission in Neutral or Park and start the engine. Increase the engine speed to 1,800–2,200 rpm for 2–3 minutes to bring the engine and regulator to operating temperature. Check and record the voltmeter reading. It should now be 1 to 2 volts higher than the first reading. This is the regulated voltage reading. If the reading is less than 1 volt or greater than 2½ volts, the regulator must be replaced (electro-mechanical type) or adjusted (transistorized type).

4. If the reading is between 1 to 2 volts,

turn on the headlights and heater blower to load the alternator. The voltage should not decrease more than ½ volt from the regulated voltage reading in Step 3. If the voltage drop is greater than ½ volt, the regulator should be replaced.

FUSE LINK

The fuse link is a short length of insulated wire contained in the alternator wiring harness, between the alternator and the starter relay. The fuse link is several wire gauge sizes smaller than the other wires in the harness. If a booster battery is connected incorrectly to the car battery or if some component of the charging system is shorted to ground, the fuse link melts and protects the alternator. The fuse link is attached to the starter relay. The insulation on the wire reads: Fuse Link. A melted fuse link can usually be identified by cracked or bubbled insulation. If it is difficult to determine if the fuse link is melted, connect a test light to both ends of the wire. If the fuse link is not melted, the test light will light showing that an open circuit does not exist in the wire.

FUSE LINK REPLACEMENT

Fuse links originally installed in your Mustang II are the color of the circuit being supplied by the fuse link. Service replacements are either green or black, depending on usage. All models have color coded flags molded on the wire or on the terminal insulator to identify the wire gauge of the link. Color identification is as follows: Blue—20 gauge wire, red—18 gauge wire, yellow—17 gauge wire, orange—16 gauge wire, green—14 gauge wire. The procedure for replacement is as follows:

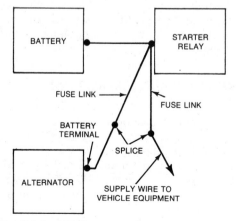

Fuse link installation

1. Disconnect the negative battery cable.
2. Disconnect the eyelet of the fuse link from the starter relay.
3. Cut the other end of the fuse link from the wiring harness at the splice.
4. Connect the eyelet end of a new fuse link to the starter relay.

NOTE: *Use only an original equipment type fuse link. Under no conditions should standard wire be substituted.*

5. Splice the open end of the new fuse link into the wiring harness.
6. Solder the splice with rosin-core solder and wrap the splice with electrical tape. This splice must be soldered.
7. Connect the negative battery cable.
8. Start the engine to check if the new connections complete the circuit.

Starting System

The battery is the first link in the chain of mechanisms which work together to provide cranking of the automobile engine. In most modern cars, the battery is a lead-acid electrochemical device consisting of six two-volt (2 V) subsections connected in series so the unit is capable of producing approximately 12 V of electrical pressure. Each subsection, or cell, consists of a series of positive and negative plates held a short distance apart in a solution of sulfuric acid and water. The two types of plates are of dissimilar metals. This causes a chemical reaction to be set up, and it is this reaction which produces current flow from the battery when its positive and negative terminals are connected to an electrical appliance such as a lamp or motor. The continued transfer of electrons would eventually convert the sulfuric acid in the electrolyte to water, and make the two plates identical in chemical composition. As electrical energy is removed from the battery, its voltage output tends to drop. Thus, measuring battery voltage and battery electrolyte composition are two ways of checking the ability of the unit to supply power. During the starting of the engine, electrical energy is removed from the battery. However, if the charging circuit is in good condition and the operating conditions are normal, the power removed from the battery will be replaced by the alternator which will force electrons back through the battery, reversing the normal flow, and restoring the battery to its original chemical state.

The battery and starting motor are linked

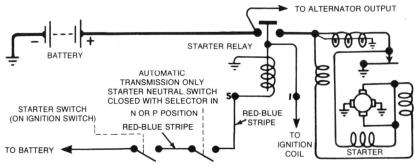

Positive engagement starter circuit

by very heavy electrical cables designed to minimize resistance to the flow of current. Generally, the major power supply cable which leaves the battery goes directly to the starter, while other electrical system needs are supplied by a smaller cable. During starter operation, power flows from the battery to the starter and is grounded through the car's frame and the battery's negative ground strap.

The starting motor is a specially designed, direct current electric motor capable of producing a very great amount of power for its size. One thing which allows the motor to produce a great deal of power is its tremendous rotating speed. It drives the engine through a tiny pinion gear (attached to the starter's armature), which drives the very large flywheel ring gear at a greatly reduced speed. Another factor allowing it to produce so much power is that only intermittent operation is required of it. Thus, little allowance for air circulation is required, and the windings can be built into a very small space.

The starter solenoid is a magnetic device which employs the small current supplied by the starting switch circuit of the ignition switch. This magnetic action moves a plunger which mechanically engages the starter.

Ford starters employ a separate relay, mounted away from the starter, to switch the motor and solenoid current on and off. The relay thus replaces the solenoid electrical switch, but does not eliminate the need for a solenoid mounted on the starter used to mechanically engage the starter drive gears. The relay is used to reduce the amount of current the starting switch must carry.

The starting switch circuit consists of the starting switch contained within the ignition switch, a transmission neutral safety switch or clutch pedal switch which prevents the car from being started in any gear but Neutral or Park (automatic only), and the wiring neces-

sary to connect these in series with the starter solenoid or relay.

A pinion, which is a small gear, is mounted to a one-way drive clutch. This clutch is splined to the starter armature shaft. When the ignition switch is moved to the "start" position, the solenoid plunger slides the pinion toward the flywheel ring gear via a collar and spring. If the teeth on the pinion and flywheel match properly, the pinion will engage the flywheel immediately. If the gear teeth butt one another, the spring will be compressed and will force the gears to mesh as soon as the starter turns far enough to allow them to do so. As the solenoid plunger reaches the end of its travel, it closes the contacts that connect the battery and starter and then the engine is cranked.

As soon as the engine starts, the flywheel ring gear begins turning fast enough to drive the pinion at an extremely high rate of speed. At this point, the one-way clutch begins allowing the pinion to spin faster than the starter shaft so that the starter will not operate at excessive speed. When the ignition switch is released from the starter position, the solenoid is deenergized, and a spring contained within the solenoid assembly pulls the gear out of mesh and interrupts the current flow to the starter. All Mustang II models use the positive engagement starter which utilizes the remote starter relay.

REMOVAL AND INSTALLATION

1. Disconnect the negative battery cable.
2. Raise the car on a hoist and remove the four bolts retaining the crossmember beneath the bellhousing.
3. On V6 and V8 models to 1976, and all later models, remove the flex coupling clamping screw at its attachment point to the steering gear.
4. On all models, remove the three nuts

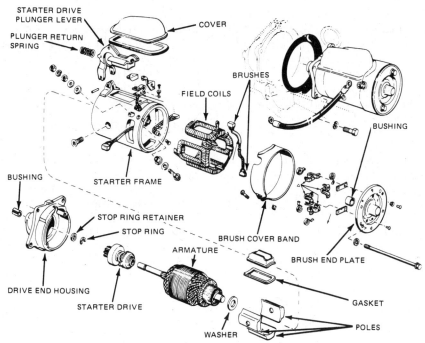

STARTER DRIVE PLUNGER LEVER — COVER

PLUNGER RETURN SPRING

BRUSHES

FIELD COILS

BUSHING

BUSHING

STARTER FRAME

STOP RING RETAINER

STOP RING

BRUSH COVER BAND

ARMATURE

BRUSH END PLATE

DRIVE END HOUSING

STARTER DRIVE

GASKET

WASHER

POLES

Positive engagement starter disassembled

and bolts retaining the steering gear to the crossmember.

5. Disconnect the steering gear from the flex coupling and pull the steering gear downward to gain access to the starter motor.

6. Disconnect the starter cable from the starter.

7. Remove the three starter motor attaching bolts and remove the starter.

8. Reverse the above procedure to install, making sure to torque the attaching bolts to 15–20 ft lbs.

STARTER OVERHAUL

Brush Replacement

1974–77

Replace the starter brushes when they are worn to ¼ in. Always install a complete set of new brushes.

1. Loosen and remove the brush cover band, gasket, and starter drive plunger lever cover. Remove the brushes from their holders.

2. Remove the two through-bolts from the starter frame.

3. Remove the drive end housing and the plunger lever return spring.

4. Remove the starter drive plunger lever pivot pin and lever, and remove the armature.

5. Remove the brush end plate.

6. Remove the ground brush retaining screws from the frame and remove the brushes.

7. Cut the insulated brush leads from the field coils as close to the field connection point as possible.

8. Clean and inspect the starter motor.

9. Replace the brush end plate if the insulator between the field brush holder and the end plate is cracked or broken.

10. Position the new insulated field brushes lead on the field coil connection. Position and crimp the clip provided with the brushes to hold the brush lead to the connection. Solder the lead, clip, and connection together using rosin core solder. Use a 300 watt iron.

11. Install the ground brush leads to the frame with the retaining screws.

12. Clean the commutator with 00 or 000 sandpaper.

13. Position the brush end plate to the starter frame with the end plate boss in the frame slot.

14. Install the armature in the starter frame.

15. Install the starter drive gear plunger lever to the frame and starter drive assembly and install the pivot pin.

16. Partially fill the drive end housing bearing bore with grease (approximately ¼ full). Position the return spring on the

plunger lever and the drive end housing to the starter frame. Install the throughbolts and tighten to specified torque (55–75 in. lbs). Be sure that the stop ring retainer is seated properly in the drive end housing.

17. Install the commutator brushes in the brush holders. Center the brush springs on the brushes.

18. Position the plunger lever cover and the brush cover band, with its gasket, on the starter. Tighten the band retaining screw.

19. Connect the starter to a battery to check its operation.

1978

1. Remove the through bolts and remove the brush end plate and insulator assembly.

2. Remove the brushes from the plastic holder and lift the holder out, noting its location with respect to the end terminal.

3. Remove the two screws which attach the ground brushes to the frame.

4. Cut the positive brush leads from the field coils as close to the field connection point as possible.

5. Position the new ground brushes to the starter frame and install the retaining screws.

6. Check the plastic brush holder for cracks or broken mounting pads, and replace it if necessary. Then, install it and insert the brushes into it. Install brush springs. Note that positive brush leads should be posi-

tioned in their respective slots in the brush holder to prevent possible grounding.

7. Install the brush end plate. Be certain the end plate insulator is positioned properly on the end plate.

8. Install the two through bolts and torque to 55–75 in. lbs.

Starter Drive Replacement

1. Remove the starter from the engine.
2. On 1974–77 starters, remove the brush cover band.
3. Remove the starter drive plunger lever cover.
4. Loosen the thru-bolts just enough to allow removal of the drive end housing and the starter drive plunger lever return spring.
5. Remove the pivot pin which attaches the starter drive plunger lever to the starter frame and remove the lever.
6. Remove the stop ring retainer and stop-ring from the armature shaft.
7. Remove the starter drive from the armature shaft.
8. Inspect the teeth on the starter drive. If they are excessively worn, inspect the teeth on the ring gear of the flywheel. If the teeth on the flywheel are excessively worn, the flywheel should be replaced.
9. Apply a thin coat of white grease to the armature shaft, in the area in which the starter drive operates.

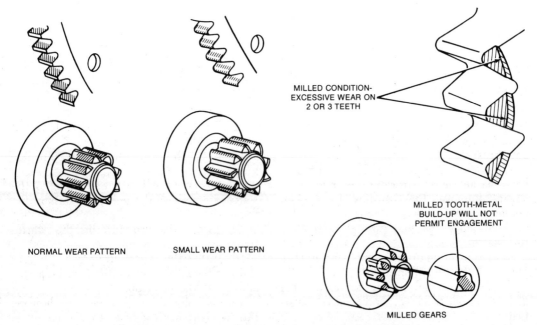

NORMAL WEAR PATTERN

SMALL WEAR PATTERN

MILLED CONDITION-
EXCESSIVE WEAR ON
2 OR 3 TEETH

MILLED TOOTH-METAL
BUILD-UP WILL NOT
PERMIT ENGAGEMENT

MILLED GEARS

Starter drive pinion and flywheel ring gear teeth inspection

10. Install the starter drive on the armature shaft and install a new stop-ring.

11. Position the starter drive plunger lever on the starter frame and install the pivot pin. *Make sure that the plunger lever is properly engaged with the starter drive.*

12. Install a new stop ring retainer on the armature shaft.

13. Fill the drive end housing bearing bore ¼ full with grease.

14. Position the starter drive plunger lever return spring and the drive end housing to the starter frame.

15. Tighten the starter thru-bolts to 55–75 in. lbs.

16. Install the starter drive plunger lever cover and, on 1974–77 models, the brush cover band on the starter.

17. Install the starter.

BATTERY REMOVAL AND INSTALLATION

1. Loosen the battery cable bolts and spread the ends of the battery cable terminals.

2. Disconnect the negative battery cable first.

3. Disconnect the positive battery cable.

4. Remove the battery hold-down.

5. Wearing heavy gloves, remove the battery from under the hood. *Be careful not to tip the battery and spill acid on yourself or the car during removal.*

6. To install, wearing heavy gloves, place the battery in its holder under the hood. *Use care not to spill the acid.*

7. Install the battery hold-down.

8. Install the positive battery cable first.

9. Install the negative battery cable.

10. Apply a *light* coating of grease to the cable ends.

ENGINE MECHANICAL

Design

Three engines are available in the Mustang II: a 2300 cc four-cylinder and a 2800 cc V6 engine on 1974–78 models, and a 4900 cc (302 cid) V8 on 1975–78 models. All three are water-cooled, cast iron units of bore-in block design, but that is where the similarity ends.

The 2300 cc four-cylinder engine is a new design based on the German-built 2000 cc Pinto engine. Featuring a belt-driven overhead camshaft, this engine maintains proper valve clearances using a set of hydraulic valve adjusters to eliminate periodic valve clearance adjustments. The oil pump, fuel pump and distributor are operated by an auxiliary shaft which, along with the camshaft, is

Battery and Starter Specifications

All cars use 12 volt, negative ground electrical systems

Year	Model	Battery Amp Hour Capacity	STARTER						Brush Spring Tension (oz)	Min Brush Length (in.)
			Lock Test			No Load Test				
			Amps	Volts	Torque (ft/lbs)	Amps	Volts	RPM		
'74–'76	All Models①	41, 45, 53	460	5	9.0	70	12	9500	40	¼
	All Models②	41, 45, 53	670	5	15.5	80	12	9500	80	¼
'77	4—140①	41	460	—	9.0	70	12	—	40	¼
	6—170② 8—302	53	670	—	15.5	80	12	—	80	¼
'78	All Models①	45	460	—	9.0	70	12	—	40	¼
	All Models②	—	670	—	15.5	80	12	—	80	¼

① With 4 in. diameter starter
② With 4½ in. diameter starter

driven by a cogged belt. Tension on the belt is maintained by a preloaded and locked idler pulley bearing on the outside of the belt. The engine uses five main bearings and four camshaft bearings. All main, connecting rod, camshaft, and auxiliary shaft bearings are replaceable.

The 2800 cc V6 engine is an enlarged version of the German 2600 cc unit which was first used to power the Capri. It is a remarkably compact powerplant with the cylinder banks at a 60 degree inclination. The 2800 V6 is an overhead valve engine, using mechanical tappets and pushrods, and shaft-mounted rocker arms. Four main bearings support the crankshaft. The distributor and oil pump are driven by an eccentric at the front of the camshaft. The connecting rods are forged steel with replaceable insert bearings. The intake manifold is made from weight saving aluminum and has individual passages to the cylinder head ports.

The 4900 cc V8 engine, or the 302 cid V8 as it is better known, is new to the Mustang II in 1975, but has been with us for a few years appearing in many Ford cars. The basic design goes back to 1962 when its predecessor, the 221 cid V8, first was offered in the then new intermediate Ford Fairlane. This engine was the first of the thinwall casting small block Ford V8s. Over the years it grew in size and is still growing. The 302 cubic inch displacement was first used in 1968. The engine is an overhead valve design using hydraulic lifters and pushrods. Five main bearings support the crankshaft. The distributor and oil pump are gear-driven by a worm gear on the camshaft. The engine uses a traditional timing chain and sprockets. The individual rocker arms are stud-mounted.

Engine Removal and Installation

Before setting out to remove your engine, and tying up both yourself and your car for a length of time, there are a few preliminary steps that should be taken. Jot down those engine and transmission numbers (see Chapter 1) and make a trip to your parts dealer to order all the gaskets, hoses, belts, filters, etc. (i.e., exhaust manifold-to-head pipe flange gasket(s)) which are in need of replacement. This will help avoid last minute or weekend parts dashes that can tie up a car

even longer. Also, have enough oil, antifreeze, transmission fluid, etc. (see "Capacities" chart) on hand for the job.

If the car is still running, have the engine, engine compartment, and underbody steam cleaned, or at least hosed off at a do-it-yourself car wash. The less dirt, the better. Have all of the necessary tools together. These should include a sturdy hydraulic jack and a pair of jackstands of sufficient capacity, a chain/pulley engine hoist of sufficient test strength, a wooden block and a small jack to support the oil pan or transmission, a can of penetrating fluid to help loosen rusty nuts and bolts, a few jars or plastic containers to store and identify used engine hardware, and a punch or bottle of brush paint to match-mark adjacent parts to aid reassembly. Once you have all of your parts, tools, and fluids together, proceed with the task.

CAUTION: *Do not operate the engine with the hood open before inspecting the fan for possible cracks or separation.*

ENGINE REMOVAL—2300 CC

1. Raise the hood and fasten it up.
2. Drain the coolant from the radiator and the oil from the crankcase.
3. Remove the air cleaner and the exhaust manifold shroud.
4. Disconnect the ground cable at the battery and at the cylinder head.
5. Remove the radiator upper and lower hoses and disconnect automatic transmission oil cooler lines.
6. Remove the radiator and fan.
7. Disconnect the heater hose from the water pump and carburetor choke fitting.
8. Disconnect the alternator wires from the alternator, starter cable from the starter, and the accelerator cable from the carburetor. With air conditioning, remove the compressor from the mounting bracket, and position it out of the way, leaving the refrigerant lines attached.
9. Disconnect the flexible fuel line at the fuel pump line and plug the fuel line.
10. Disconnect the coil primary wire at the coil. Disconnect the oil pressure and the water temperature sending unit wires at the sending units.
11. Remove the starter.
12. Raise the vehicle. Remove the flywheel or converter housing upper attaching bolts.
13. Disconnect the headpipe at the ex-

General Engine Specifications

Year	Engine Displacement Cu In. (cc)	Carburetor Type	Horsepower @ rpm	Torque @ rpm (ft lbs)	Bore x Stroke (in.)	Compression Ratio	Oil Pressure @ rpm (psi)
'74	4—140 (2300)	Motorcraft 5200 2bbl	88 @ 5000	116 @ 2600	3.781 x 3.126	8.4 : 1	50 @ 2050
	6—170 (2800)	Motorcraft 5200 2bbl	105 @ 4600	140 @ 3200	3.660 x 2.700	8.2 : 1	40–55 @ 1500
'75–'76	4—140 (2300)	Motorcraft 5200 2bbl	88 @ 5000	116 @ 2600	3.781 x 3.126	8.4 : 1②	50 @ 2050
	6—170 (2800)	Motorcraft 2150 2bbl	105 @ 4600	140 @ 3200	3.660 x 2.700	8.2 : 1②	40–55 @ 1500
	8—302 (4900)	Motorcraft② 2150 2bbl	140 @ 4200	234 @ 2200	4.000 x 3.000	8.0 : 1	40–60 @ 2050
'77	4—140 (2300)	Motorcraft 5200 2bbl	89 @ 4800	120 @ 3000	3.781 x 3.126	9.0 : 1	50 @ 2000
	6—170 (2800)	Motorcraft 2150 2bbl	93 @ 4200	140 @ 2600	3.660 x 2.700	8.7 : 1	40–55 @ 1500
	8—302 (4900)	Motorcraft③ 2150 2bbl	129 @ 3400④	242 @ 2000⑤	4.000 x 3.000	8.4 : 1	40–60 @ 2000
'78	4—140 (2300)	Motorcraft 5200 2bbl	88 @ 4800	118 @ 2800	3.781 x 3.126	9.0 : 1	50 @ 2000
	6—170 (2800)	Motorcraft 2150 2bbl	90 @ 4200	143 @ 2200	3.660 x 2.700	8.7 : 1	40–55 @ 1500
	8—302 (4900)	Motorcraft③ 2150 2bbl	139 @ 3600⑥	250 @ 1600⑦	4.000 x 3.000	8.4 : 1	40–60 @ 2000

① 1976—8.7 : 1
② 1976—9.0 : 1
③ Use Motorcraft 2700UU carburetor in California
④ Applies to manual transmission equipped cars; Automatic—139 @ 3600
⑤ Applies to manual transmission equipped cars; Automatic—247 @ 1800
⑥ California—133 @ 3600
⑦ California—243 @ 1600

haust manifold. Disconnect the engine right and left mount at the underbody bracket. Remove the flywheel or converter housing cover.

With automatic transmission, disconnect the converter from the flywheel. Remove the converter housing lower attaching bolts.

With manual transmission, remove the flywheel housing lower attaching bolts.

14. Lower the vehicle. Support the transmission and the flywheel or converter housing with a jack.

15. Attach the engine lifting device to the existing lifting brackets.

Valve Specifications

Year	Engine Displacement Cu In. (cc)	Seat Angle (deg)	Face Angle (deg)	Spring Test Pressure (lbs @ in.)	Spring Installed Height (in.)	Stem To Guide Clearance (in.)		Stem Diameter (in.)	
						Intake	Exhaust	Intake	Exhaust
'74	4—140 (2300)	45	46	75 @ 1.560	$1\frac{53}{64}$	.0010–.0027	.0015–.0022	.3419	.3415
	6—170 (2800)	45	44	64 @ 1.585	$1\frac{29}{32}$	.0008–.0025	.0018–.0035	.3162	.3153
'75–'76	4—140 (2300)	45	46	75 @ 1.560	$1\frac{9}{16}$	.0006–.0023	.0015–.0032	.3424	.3415
	6—170 (2800)	45	46	64 @ 1.590	$1\frac{19}{32}$	.0008–.0025	.0018–.0035	.3162	.3153
	8—302 (4900)	45	46	80 @ 1.690	$1\frac{11}{16}$	.0007–.0027	.0015–.0032	.3420	.3415
'77	4—140 (2300)	45	44	75 @ 1.560	$1\frac{9}{16}$	.0010–.0027	.0013–.0032	.3416–.3423	.3411–.3418
	6—170 (2800)	45	44	64 @ 1.585	$1\frac{19}{32}$	.0008–.0025	.0018–.0035	.3199–.3167	.3149–.3156
	8—302 (4900)	45	44	80 @ 1.690	$1\frac{11}{16}$	.0010–.0027	.0015–.0032	.3416–.3423	.3411–.3418
'78	4—140 (2300)	45	44	75 @ 1.560	$1\frac{9}{16}$	.0010–.0027	.0015–.0032	.3416–.3423	.3411–.3418
	6—170 (2800)	45	44	64 @ 1.585	$1\frac{9}{16}$	.0008–.0025	.0018–.0035	.3159–.3167	.3149–.3156
	8—302 (4900)	45	44	80 @ 1.690①	$1\frac{11}{16}$	.0010–.0027	.0015–.0032	.3416–.3423	.3411–.3418

① Applies to intake only—Exhaust: 80 @ 1.60

16. Carefully lift the engine out of the engine compartment.

ENGINE INSTALLATION—2300 CC

1. Carefully lower the engine into the engine compartment.
2. Make sure that the studs on the exhaust manifold are aligned with the holes in the headpipe.

With automatic transmission, start the converter pilot into the crankshaft.

With manual transmission, start the transmission main drive gear into the clutch disc. It maybe necessary to adjust the position of the transmission in relation to the engine if the input shaft will not enter the clutch disc. If the engine hangs up after the shaft enters, turn the crankshaft slowly clockwise, with the transmission in gear, until the shaft splines mesh with the clutch disc splines.

3. Install the flywheel or converter housing upper attaching bolts. Remove the engine lifting sling hooks.

Crankshaft and Connecting Rod Specifications
All measurements are given in inches

Year	Engine Displacement Cu In. (cc)	CRANKSHAFT				CONNECTING ROD		
		Main Brg Journal Dia	Main Brg Oil Clearance	Shaft End-Play	Thrust on No.	Journal Diameter	Oil Clearance	Side Clearance
'74	4—140 (2300)	2.3982–2.3990	.0008–.0015	.004–.012	3	2.0465–2.0472	.0006–.0027	.0008–.0026
	6—170 (2800)	2.2433–2.2441	.0006–.0019	.003–.011	3	2.0464–2.0472	.0006–.0022	.004–.011
'75–'76	4—140 (2300)	2.3982–2.3990	.0008–.0026	.004–.008	3	2.0465–2.0472	.0008–.0024	.0008–.0026①
	6—170 (2800)	2.2433–2.2437	.0006–.0019	.004–.008	3	2.0464–2.0472	.0006–.0022	.004–.011
	8—302 (4900)	2.2482–2.2486	.0005–.0024	.004–.008	3	2.1228–2.1236	.0008–.0026	.010–.020
'77	4—140 (2300)	2.3982–2.2441	.0008–.0026	.004–.012	3	2.0465–2.0472	.0008–.0026	.0035–.0105
	6—170 (2800)	2.2433–2.2441	.0008–.0019	.004–.012	3	2.1252–2.1260	.0006–.0022	.004–.014
	8—302 (4900)	2.2482–2.2490	.0005–.0015①	.004–.012	3	2.1228–2.1236	.0007–.0024	.010–.023
'78	4—140 (2300)	2.3990–2.3982	.0008–.0026	.004–.012	3	2.0464–2.0672	.0008–.0026	.0035–.0105
	6—170 (2800)	2.2633–2.2441	.0008–.0019	.004–.012	3	2.1252–2.1260	.0006–.0022	.004–.014
	8—302 (4900)	2.2482–2.2490	.0005–.0015①	.004–.012	3	2.1228–2.1236		.010–.023

① Applies to all bearings but No. 1—No. 1—.0001–.0015.

4. Remove the jack from the transmission. Raise the vehicle.

5. Install the flywheel or converter housing lower attaching bolts.

With automatic transmission, attach the converter to the flywheel.

6. Install the flywheel or converter housing dust cover.

7. Install the engine left and right mount to the underbody bracket.

8. Remove the plug from the fuel line and connect the flexible fuel line to the fuel pump line. Install the exhaust manifold-to-headpipe nuts.

9. Lower the vehicle. Connect the oil pressure and engine temperature sending unit wires. Connect the coil primary wire. Connect the accelerator cable.

10. Install the starter motor. Connect the starter cable. Connect the alternator wires. Connect the heater hose at the water pump and carburetor choke fitting.

Piston Clearance

Year	Engine No. Cyl Displacement (cu in.)	Piston to Bore Clearance (in.)
'74–'76	4—140	.0013–.0021
	6—170	.0010–.0021
	8—302	.0018–.0026
'77–'78	4—140 (2300)	.0014–.0022
	6—170 (2800)	.0011–.0019
	8—302 (4900)	.0018–.0026

① '75–'76—.0020–.0040

Ring Side Clearance
All measurements are given in inches

Year	Engine	Top Compression	Bottom Compression	Oil Control
'74–'78	4—140	.0020–.0040	.0020–.0033 ①	Snug—.006
	6—170	.0020–.0033	.0020–.0033	Snug—.006
	8—302	.0020–.0040	.0020–.0040	Snug—.006

① '75–'78—.0020–.0040

Ring Gap
All measurements are given in inches

Year	Engine No. Cyl Displacement (cu in.)	Top Compression	Bottom Compression	Oil Control
'74–'78	4—140	.010–.020	.010–.020	.015–.055
	6—170	.015–.023	.015–.023	.015–.055
	8—302	.010–.020	.010–.020	.015–.055

Torque Specifications
All readings in ft lbs

Year	Engine Displacement Cu In. (cc)	Cylinder Head Bolts	Rod Bearing Bolts	Main Bearing Bolts	Crankshaft Pulley Bolt	Flywheel-to-Crankshaft Bolts	MANIFOLDS	
							Intake	Exhaust
'74–'76	4—140 (2300)	80–90①	30–36②	80–90①	80–114	54–65	14–21	16–23③
	6—170 (2800)	65–80④	21–25	65–75	92–103	47–51	15–18⑤	14–18⑥
	8—302 (4900)	65–72⑦	19–24	60–70	70–90	75–85	23–25	12–16⑧
'77–'78	4—140 (2300)	80–90①	30–36	80–90	100–120	54–64	14–21⑨	16–23
	6—170 (2800)	65–80④	21–25	65–75	92–103	47–51	15–18⑩⑫	20–30
	8—302 (4900)	65–72⑦	19–24	60–70	70–90	75–85	20–35⑪	18–24

① 1975 and later—Torque in two steps: 1—To 60 ft lbs
   2—To 80–90 ft lbs
② 1975–76—Torque in two steps: 1—To 25–30 ft lbs
   2—To 30–36 ft lbs
③ 1975–76—Torque in two steps: 1—To 5–7 ft lbs
   2—To 16–23 ft lbs
④ 1975 and later—Torque in three steps: 1—To 29–40 ft lbs
   2—To 40–51 ft lbs
   3—To 65–80 ft lbs
⑤ 1975–76—Torque in four steps: 1—To 3–6 ft lbs
   2—To 6–11 ft lbs
   3—To 11–16 ft lbs
   4—To 15–18 ft lbs
   When completed, start engine and then retorque to 15–18 ft lbs
⑥ 1975–76—16–23 ft lbs
⑦ 1975–76—Torque in two steps: 1—55–65 ft lbs
   2—65–72 ft lbs
⑧ 1975–76—18–24 ft lbs
⑨ Torque in sequence, in two steps: 1—To 5–7 ft lbs
   2—To 14–21 ft lbs
⑩ Torque in sequence, in four steps: 1—To 3–6 ft lbs
   2—To 6–11 ft lbs
   3—To 11–15 ft lbs
   4—To 15–18 ft lbs
⑪ Retorque hot
⑫ If attached by stud—10–12

11. Install the pulley, fan, and drive belt. Adjust the drive belt tension. With air conditioning, install the compressor on the mounting bracket, and adjust the belt tension. Install the radiator. Connect the radiator upper and lower hoses. Fill and bleed the cooling system. Fill the crankcase with the proper type and quantity of motor oil.

12. Connect the battery ground cable.

13. Operate the engine at fast idle and check all gaskets and hose connections for leaks.

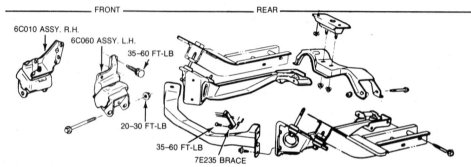

Engine front and rear supports—2300cc 4 cylinder

With an automatic transmission, adjust the transmission control linkage, as necessary.

14. Install the air cleaner and connect the PCV hose.

ENGINE REMOVAL—2800 CC V6, 4900 CC (302) V8

1. Disconnect the battery, drain the cooling system and remove the hood.

2. Remove the air cleaner and intake duct assembly.

3. Disconnect the upper and lower hoses at the radiator.

4. Remove the fan shroud attaching bolts and position the shroud over the fan. Remove the radiator and shroud.

5. Remove the alternator and bracket. Position the alternator out of the way. Disconnect the alternator ground wire from the cylinder block.

6. Disconnect the heater hoses at the block and water pump.

7. Remove the ground wires from the cylinder block.

8. Disconnect the fuel line at the fuel pump. Plug the fuel tank line.

9. Disconnect the accelerator cable or linkage at the carburetor and intake manifold. Disconnect the automatic transmission downshift linkage.

10. Disconnect the engine wire loom at the ignition coil. Disconnect the brake booster vacuum line.

11. Raise the vehicle on a hoist.

12. Disconnect the headpipes at the exhaust manifolds.

13. Disconnect the starter cable and remove the starter.

14. Remove the engine front support through-bolts.

15. With automatic transmission, remove the converter inspection cover and disconnect the flywheel from the converter.

Remove the downshift rod.

Remove the converter housing-to-engine block bolts and the adapter plate-to-converter housing bolt.

With manual transmission, remove the

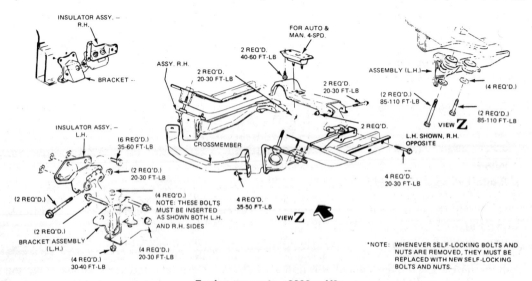

Engine supports—2800cc V6

clutch linkage and remove the bellhousing-to-engine block bolts.

16. Lower the vehicle.

17. Attach an engine lifting device to the lifting brackets at the exhaust manifolds.

18. Position a jack under the transmission.

19. Raise the engine slightly and carefully pull it from the transmission. Carefully lift the engine out of the engine compartment so that the rear cover plate is not bent or parts damaged.

ENGINE INSTALLATION—2800 CC V6, 4900 CC (302) V8

1. Lower the engine carefully into the engine compartment. Make sure that the exhaust manifolds are properly aligned with the headpipes.

2. With manual transmission, start the transmission main driveshaft into the clutch disc. It may be necessary to adjust the position of the transmission in relation to the engine if the input shaft will not enter the clutch disc. If the engine hangs up after the shaft enters, turn the crankshaft slowly, with the transmission in gear, until the shaft splines mesh with the clutch disc splines.

TOOL T53L-300-A

TOOL T70P-6000

Removing or installing engine—V6 shown

With automatic transmission, start the converter pilot into the crankshaft.

3. Install the bellhousing or converter housing upper bolts, making sure that the dowels in the cylinder block engage the fly

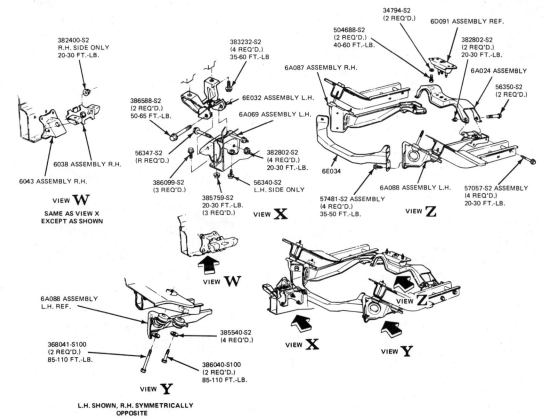

Engine front and rear supports—4900cc (302) V8

wheel housing. Remove the jack from under the transmission.

4. Remove the lifting device from the engine.

5. With automatic transmission, position the downshift rod on the transmission and engine.

6. Raise the vehicle on a hoist.

7. With automatic transmission, position the transmission linkage bracket and install the remaining converter housing bolts. Install the adapter plate-to-converter housing bolts. Install the converter-to-flywheel nuts and install the inspection cover. Connect the downshift rod on the transmission.

On manual transmission cars, install the lower bellhousing bolts and connect the clutch linkage to the engine block.

8. Install the starter and connect the cable.

9. Connect the muffler inlet pipes at the exhaust manifolds.

10. Install the engine front support through-bolts.

11. Lower the vehicle.

12. Install the ground wire. Install the engine wire loom and connect it to the ignition coil, then install the water temperature sending unit and oil pressure sending unit. Connect the brake booster vacuum line.

13. Install the accelerator linkage and connect the automatic transmission downshift rod. Connect the vacuum lines. Connect the fuel tank line at the fuel pump.

14. Connect the ground wire at the cylinder block. Install the heater hoses at the water pump and cylinder block.

15. Install the alternator and bracket. Connect the alternator ground wire to the cylinder block. Install the drive belt and adjust the belt tension.

16. Position the fan shroud over the fan. Install the radiator and connect the upper and lower radiator hoses. Install the fan shroud attaching bolts.

17. Fill and bleed the cooling system. Fill the crankcase with oil. Adjust the automatic transmission downshift linkage. Connect the battery.

18. Operate the engine at fast idle until it reaches normal operating temperature and check all gaskets and hose connections for leaks. Adjust the ignition timing and idle speed.

19. Install the air cleaner and intake duct. Install and adjust the hood.

Cylinder Head

REMOVAL AND INSTALLATION

2300 cc

NOTE: *The cylinder head bolts have a special 12-sided head requiring a special tool for removal and installation.*

1. Drain the cooling system.

2. Remove the air cleaner and the valve rocker cover.

3. Remove the intake and exhaust manifolds. The intake manifold, decel valve and carburetor can be removed as an assembly.

4. Remove the camshaft drive belt cover.

5. Loosen the drive belt tensioner and remove the drive belt.

6. Remove the water outlet from the cylinder head.

7. Remove the cylinder head bolts evenly and remove the cylinder head.

8. Clean the cylinder head and block surfaces thoroughly. Position a new cylinder head gasket on the block.

9. Position the cylinder head and camshaft assembly on the block. Install the bolts finger-tight, then torque according to specifications.

NOTE: *If difficulty in positioning the head on the block is encountered, guide pins may be fabricated by cutting the heads off two extra cylinder head bolts.*

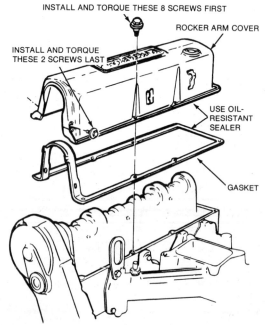

INSTALL AND TORQUE THESE 8 SCREWS FIRST

ROCKER ARM COVER

INSTALL AND TORQUE THESE 2 SCREWS LAST

USE OIL-RESISTANT SEALER

GASKET

Installing valve rocker arm cover—2300cc four

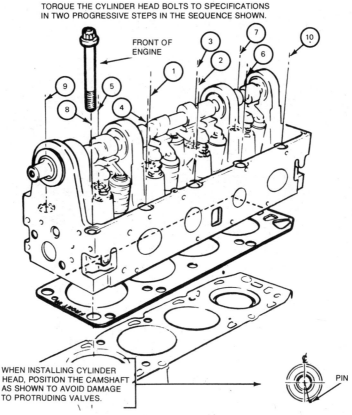

TORQUE THE CYLINDER HEAD BOLTS TO SPECIFICATIONS
IN TWO PROGRESSIVE STEPS IN THE SEQUENCE SHOWN.

FRONT OF
ENGINE

WHEN INSTALLING CYLINDER
HEAD, POSITION THE CAMSHAFT
AS SHOWN TO AVOID DAMAGE
TO PROTRUDING VALVES.

PIN

Installing cylinder head—2300cc four

10. Set the crankshaft at TDC and be sure that the camshaft drive gear and distributor are positioned correctly.

11. Install the camshaft drive belt and release the tensioner. Rotate the crankshaft two full turns to remove all slack from the belt. The timing marks should again be aligned. Tighten the tensioner lockbolt and pivot bolt.

12. Install the camshaft drive belt cover.

13. Apply sealer to the water outlet and new gasket, and install.

14. Install the intake and exhaust manifolds.

15. Adjust the valve clearance.

16. Install a new valve cover gasket and install the valve cover.

17. Install the air cleaner and crankcase ventilation hose.

18. Refill the cooling system.

2800 cc V6

1. Remove the air cleaner assembly and disconnect the battery and accelerator linkage. Drain the cooling system.

2. Remove the distributor cap with the spark plug wires attached. Remove the distributor vacuum line and distributor. Remove the hose from the water pump to the water outlet which is on the carburetor.

3. Remove the valve covers, fuel line and filter, carburetor, and the intake manifold.

4. Remove the rocker arm shaft and oil baffles. Remove the pushrods, keeping them in the proper sequence for installation.

5. Remove the exhaust manifold, referring to the appropriate procedures.

6. Remove the cylinder head retaining bolts and remove the cylinder heads and gaskets.

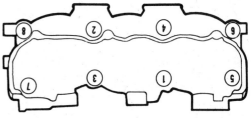

Cylinder head bolt torque sequence—V6

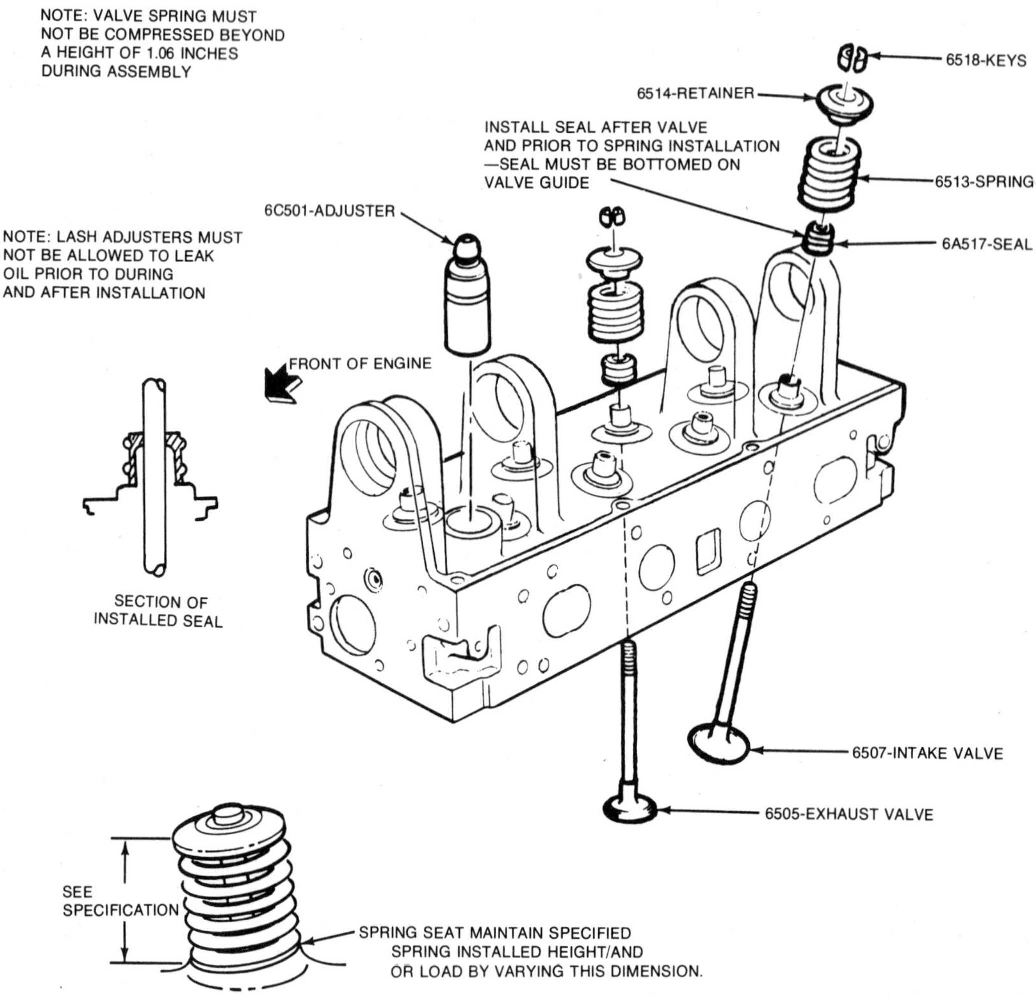

NOTE: VALVE SPRING MUST NOT BE COMPRESSED BEYOND A HEIGHT OF 1.06 INCHES DURING ASSEMBLY

6518-KEYS

6514-RETAINER

INSTALL SEAL AFTER VALVE AND PRIOR TO SPRING INSTALLATION —SEAL MUST BE BOTTOMED ON VALVE GUIDE

6513-SPRING

6C501-ADJUSTER

6A517-SEAL

NOTE: LASH ADJUSTERS MUST NOT BE ALLOWED TO LEAK OIL PRIOR TO DURING AND AFTER INSTALLATION

FRONT OF ENGINE

SECTION OF INSTALLED SEAL

6507-INTAKE VALVE

6505-EXHAUST VALVE

SEE SPECIFICATION

SPRING SEAT MAINTAIN SPECIFIED SPRING INSTALLED HEIGHT/AND OR LOAD BY VARYING THIS DIMENSION.

Installing valves, springs, retainers and lash adjusters—2300cc four

CAUTION: *Do not lay the cylinder head flat on its surface.*

7. Remove all gasket material and carbon from the engine block and cylinder heads.

8. Place the head gaskets on the engine block.

NOTE: *The left and right gaskets are not interchangeable.*

9. Install guide studs in the engine block. Install the cylinder head assemblies on the engine block one at a time. Tighten the cylinder head bolts in sequence, and in steps, to 65–80 lbs.

10. Install the intake and exhaust manifolds.

11. Install the pushrods in the proper sequence. Install the oil baffles and the rocker arm shaft assemblies. Adjust the valve clearances.

12. Install the valve covers with new gaskets.

13. Install the distributor and set the ignition timing.

14. Install the carburetor and the distributor cap with the spark plug wires.

15. Connect the accelerator linkage, fuel line, with fuel filter installed, and distributor vacuum line to the carburetor. Fill the cooling system.

4900 cc (302) V8

1. Drain the cooling system.

2. Remove the intake manifold and the carburetor as an assembly, following the procedures under "Intake Manifold Removal."

3. Disconnect the spark plug wires, marking them as to placement. Position them out of the way of the cylinder head. Remove the spark plugs.

4. Disconnect the resonator or muffler inlet pipe(s) at the exhaust manifold(s).

5. Disconnect the battery ground cable at the cylinder head (if applicable).

6. Remove the rocker arm covers.

7. On cars with air conditioning, remove the mounting bolts and the drive belt, and position the compressor out of the way of the cylinder head. Remove the compressor upper mounting bracket from the cylinder head.

CAUTION: *If the compressor refrigerant lines do not have enough slack to permit repositioning of the compressor without first disconnecting the refrigerant lines, the air conditioning system will have to be evacuated by a trained air conditioning serviceman. Under no circumstances should an untrained person attempt to disconnect the air conditioning refrigerant lines.*

8. In order to remove the left cylinder head, on cars equipped with power steering, it may be necessary to remove the steering pump and bracket, remove the drive belt, and wire or tie the pump out of the way, but in such a way as to prevent the loss of its fluid.

9. In order to remove the right head it may be necessary to remove the alternator mounting bracket bolt and spacer, the ignition coil, and the air cleaner inlet duct from the right cylinder head.

10. In order to remove the left cylinder head on a car equipped with a Thermactor exhaust emission control system, disconnect the hose from the air manifold on the left cylinder head.

11. If the right cylinder head is to be removed on a car equipped with a Thermactor exhaust emission control system, remove the Thermactor air pump and its mounting bracket. Disconnect the hose from the air manifold on the right cylinder head.

12. Loosen the rocker arm stud nuts enough to rotate the rocker arms to the side, in order to facilitate the removal of the pushrods. Remove the pushrods in sequence, so that they may be installed in their original positions. Remove the exhaust valve stem caps.

13. Remove the cylinder head attaching bolts, noting their positions. Lift the cylinder head off the block. Remove and discard the old cylinder head gasket.

Installation is as follows:

1. Clean all surfaces where gaskets are to be installed. These include the cylinder head, intake manifold, rocker arm (valve) cover, and the cylinder block surfaces. If the head was removed because of a blown head gasket, check the flatness of the cylinder head and engine block surfaces. The method for this checking is outlined in the "Engine Rebuilding" section under "Cylinder Head Reconditioning."

2. Position the new cylinder head gasket over the cylinder dowels on the block. Coat the head bolts with water-resistant sealer. Position new gaskets on the muffler inlet pipes at the exhaust manifold flange.

3. Position the cylinder head to the block, and install the head bolts, each in its original position. On all engines on which the exhaust manifold has been removed from the head to facilitate removal, it is necessary to properly guide the exhaust manifold studs into the muffler inlet pipe flange when installing the head.

4. Step-torque the cylinder head retaining bolts first to 50 ft lbs, then to 60 ft lbs, and finally to the torque specification listed in the "Torque Specifications" chart. Tighten the exhaust manifold-to-cylinder head attaching bolts to specifications.

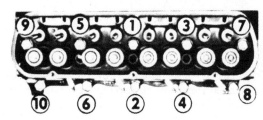

Cylinder head bolt torque sequence—V8

5. Tighten the nuts on the exhaust manifold studs at the muffler inlet flanges to 18 ft lbs.

6. Clean and inspect the pushrods one at a time. Clean the oil passage within each pushrod with a suitable solvent and blow the passage out with compressed air. Check the ends of the pushrods for nicks, grooves, roughness, or excessive wear. Visually inspect the pushrods for straightness, and replace any bent ones. Do not attempt to straighten pushrods.

7. Install the pushrods in their original positions. Apply Lubriplate® or a similar product to the valve stem tips and to the pushrod guides in the cylinder head. Install the exhaust valve stem caps.

8. Apply Lubriplate or a similar product to the fulcrum seats and sockets. Turn the rocker arms to their proper position and

tighten the stud nuts enough to hold the rocker arms in position. Make sure that the lower ends of the pushrods have remained properly seated in the valve lifters.

9. Perform a preliminary valve adjustment. Refer to the following section.

10. Apply a coat of oil-resistant sealer to the upper side of a new valve cover gasket. Position the gasket on the valve cover with the cemented side of the gasket facing the valve cover.

11. Install the valve covers. Tighten the bolts to 3–5 ft lbs.

12. Install the intake manifold and carburetor, following the procedure under "Intake Manifold Installation."

13. Refer to Steps 6–11 (inclusive) of the "Removal" procedure and reverse the procedures if applicable to your car.

14. Refer to the "Belt Tension Adjustment" procedure in Chapter 1 and adjust all drive belts which were removed.

15. Refill the cooling system.

16. Connect the battery ground cable at the cylinder head (if applicable).

17. Install the spark plugs and connect the spark plug wires.

18. Start the engine and check for leaks.

19. With the engine running, check and adjust the carburetor idle speed and mixture as explained in Chapter 2.

20. With the engine running, listen for abnormal valve noises or irregular idle and correct them.

PRELIMINARY VALVE ADJUSTMENT
2800 cc V6—1974–75

1. Remove the rocker arm covers. Make sure that the rocker arm stand bolts are tight.

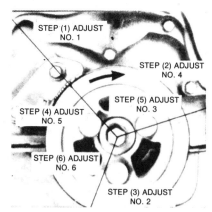

Position of crankshaft for preliminary valve adjustment—2800cc V6

2. The valves are adjusted by positioning each piston in succession at TDC on the compression stroke in the firing order sequence, 1-4-2-5-3-6.

3. Rotate the crankshaft clockwise, as viewed from the front of the vehicle, until the No. 1 piston is on TDC at the end of the compression stroke.

4. With the crankshaft in the correct position, set the valve lash to 0.014 in. on the intake valve and 0.016 on the exhaust valve using a step-type feeler gauge (go and no go). Adjust the clearance by turning the adjusting nuts on the rockers. The adjusting nuts are self-locking.

5. Adjust the valves in the remaining cylinders following the firing order. This can be done by rotating the crankshaft in increments of ⅓ of a revolution (120 degrees) after adjusting the valves in each cylinder. This brings the next piston in the sequence to TDC.

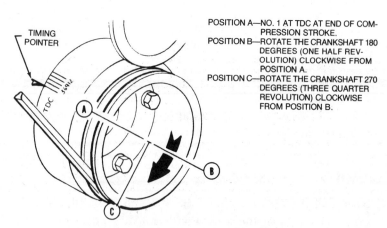

Position of crankshaft for preliminary valve adjustment—4900cc (302) V8

2800 cc V6—1976–78

See the appropriate Valve Adjustment procedure located in the Tune-Up Chapter for engines built in 1976 and later years.

4900 cc 302 V8

1. Crank the engine until the No. 1 cylinder is at TDC of the compression stroke and the timing pointer is aligned with the mark on the crankshaft damper.
2. Scribe a mark on the damper at this point.
3. Scribe two additional marks on the damper (see illustration).
4. With the timing pointer aligned with mark "A" on the damper, tighten the following valves to the specified torque:
No. 1, 7, and 8 Intake; No. 1, 5, and 4 Exhaust.
5. Rotate the crankshaft 180° to point "B" and tighten the following valves:
No. 5 and 4 Intake; No. 2 and 6 Exhaust.
6. Rotate the crankshaft 270° to point "C" and tighten the following valves:
No. 2, 3, and 6 Intake; No. 7, 3, and 8 Exhaust.
7. Rocker arm specifications are: tighten nut until it contacts the rocker shoulder, then torque to 18–20 ft lbs.

Rocker Arms

REMOVAL AND INSTALLATION

2300 cc Four

1. Remove the valve cover and associated parts as required.
2. Rotate the camshaft so that the basic circle of the cam is against the cam follower you intend to remove.
3. Remove the retaining spring from the cam follower, if so equipped.
4. Using special tool T74P-6565-B or a valve spring compressor tool for a 2300 cc engine, collapse the lash adjuster and/or depress the valve spring, as necessary, and slide the cam follower over the lash adjuster and out from under the camshaft.
5. Install the cam follower in the reverse order of removal. Make sure that the last adjuster is collapsed and released before rotating the camshaft.

4900 cc (302) V8

The 302 V8 is equipped with individual stud-mounted rocker arms. Use the following procedure to remove the rocker arms:
1. On the right cylinder head, disconnect the choke heat chamber air hose.

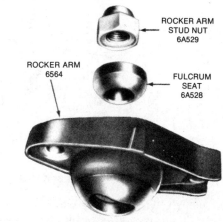

Rocker arm and related parts—V8

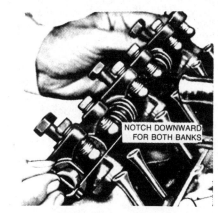

Installing rocker arm shaft assembly—V6

2. Remove the air cleaner and inlet duct assembly, the choke heat tube, PCV valve and hose, and the EGR hoses. Remove the Thermactor by-pass valve and air supply hoses.
3. Label and disconnect the spark plug wires at the plugs. Remove the plug wires from the harness.
4. Remove the valve cover attaching bolts and remove the covers.
5. Remove the valve rocker arm stud nut, fulcrum seat, and then the rocker arm.
6. Reverse the above procedure to install, taking care to adjust the valve lash as outlined under "Preliminary Valve Adjustment."

Rocker Arm Shaft Assembly
REMOVAL AND INSTALLATION
2800 cc V6

1. Remove any emission control equipment as necessary to remove the rocker cov-

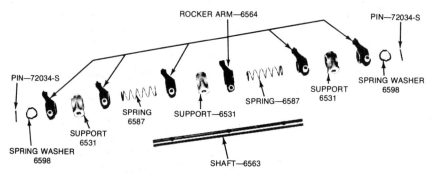

Rocker arm shaft assembly disassembled—V6

er(s), remove the spark plug wires, remove the throttle linkage to the carburetor as necessary, and remove the valve rocker cover(s).

NOTE: *If problems are encountered in rocker cover removal because of distributor diaphragm interference, see the "Note" in Chapter 2 under "Valve Lash Adjustment—1974-75 2800 V6."*

2. Remove the rocker arm shaft stand retaining bolts; loosen them each two turns at a time in sequence. Lift off the rocker arm and shaft assembly and the oil baffle.

3. Before installing the rocker shaft assemblies, back off the adjusting screws on the rockers a few turns. Install the rocker shafts

in the reverse order of removal; tighten the rocker shaft stand retaining bolts two turns at a time in sequence until they are tight.

Intake Manifold
REMOVAL AND INSTALLATION
2300 cc Four

1. Drain the cooling system.

2. Remove the air cleaner and disconnect the throttle shaft at the carburetor throttle lever.

3. Disconnect the fuel line and vacuum line from the carburetor. Disconnect the car-

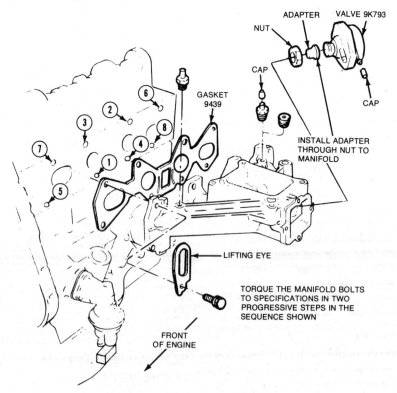

Installing intake manifold—2300cc four

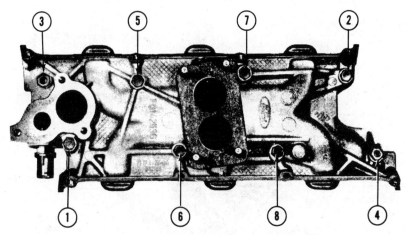

Intake manifold torque sequence—2800cc V6

buretor solenoid wire at the quick-disconnect.

4. Remove the choke thermostatic spring
and water housing.

5. Disconnect the water outlet hose and
crankcase ventilation hose from the intake
manifold.

6. Disconnect the decel valve-to-car-
buretor hose at the carburetor.

7. Remove the intake manifold attaching
bolts and remove the manifold.

8. Remove all gasket material.

9. If the intake manifold is to be replaced, transfer all necessary components to
the new manifold. Loosen the union fitting
on the manifold and remove the decel valve
from the intake manifold. Remove the decel
valve adaptor from the manifold by inserting
a large allen wrench into the adaptor and
turning the adaptor out of the manifold.

10. Clean the cylinder head and intake
manifold mating surfaces thoroughly.

11. Carefully coat the mating surfaces
with sealer and position a new gasket on the
studs. Install the manifold and torque the
nuts alternately and evenly.

12. Further installation is the reverse of
removal.

2800 cc V6

1. Remove the air cleaner assembly and
disconnect the battery.

2. Disconnect the throttle cables.

3. Drain the cooling system. Disconnect
and remove the hose from the water outlet to
the radiator and the hoses and line from the
water outlet to the water pump.

4. Remove the distributor cap and spark
plug wires as an assembly. Disconnect the
distributor wire and the vacuum line.

5. Mark the position of the distributor
and remove it.

6. Remove the fuel line and filter between the fuel pump and the carburetor and
then remove the rocker arm covers.

7. Remove the intake manifold bolts and
nuts. Tap the manifold lightly with a plastic
hammer to break the gasket seal, and then
lift off the manifold.

8. Remove all the gasket material and
dirt from the manifold and cylinder heads.

9. Apply sealing compound to the joining
surfaces. Place the manifold gasket in place.
(Make sure that the tap on the right bank of
the cylinder head gasket fits into the cutout
of the manifold gasket.)

10. Install the intake manifold. Tighten
the attaching bolts until they are hand-tight,
and then tighten them, in sequence, to the
proper torque.

NOTE: *Tightening bolt No. 7 with a
torque wrench will require an attachment
called a "crow's foot."*

11. Install the distributor so that the rotor
is pointing to the mark made previously.

12. Connect the distributor wire and vacuum line.

13. Install the carburetor, fuel line, fuel
filter, and the rocker arm covers.

14. Install the distributor cap and wires.

15. Install and adjust the carburetor linkage.

16. Install the air cleaner assembly and air
cleaner tube to the carburetor. Connect the
battery.

17. Adjust the ignition timing.

4900 cc (302) V8

1. Drain the cooling system.

2. Disconnect the upper radiator hose and

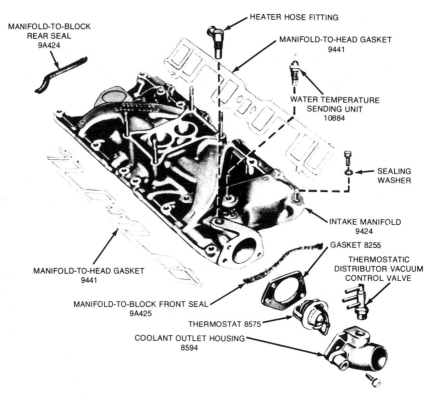

MANIFOLD-TO-BLOCK
REAR SEAL
9A424

HEATER HOSE FITTING

MANIFOLD-TO-HEAD GASKET
9441

WATER TEMPERATURE
SENDING UNIT
10884

SEALING
WASHER

INTAKE MANIFOLD
9424

GASKET 8255

THERMOSTATIC
DISTRIBUTOR VACUUM
CONTROL VALVE

MANIFOLD-TO-HEAD GASKET
9441

MANIFOLD-TO-BLOCK FRONT SEAL
9A425

THERMOSTAT 8575

COOLANT OUTLET HOUSING
8594

Intake manifold and related parts—4900cc (302) V8

water pump by-pass hose from the thermo-stat housing. Disconnect the water tempera-ture sending unit wire. Remove the heater hose from the automatic choke housing and disconnect the hose from the intake mani-fold.

3. Remove the air cleaner. Disconnect the automatic choke heat chamber air inlet hose at the inlet tube near the right valve cover. Remove the crankcase ventilation hose and intake duct assembly. Disconnect the Thermactor air hose from the check valve at the rear of the intake manifold and loosen the hose clamp at the bracket. Remove the air hose and Thermactor air by-pass valve from the bracket and position it to one side.

4. Remove all carburetor linkage and au-tomatic transmission kick-down linkage which attaches to the manifold. Disconnect the fuel line, choke heat tube, and any vac-uum lines from the carburetor or intake man-ifold, marking them for installation.

5. Disconnect the distributor vacuum hoses from the distributor. Remove the dis-tributor cap and mark the relative position of the rotor on the distributor housing. Discon-nect the spark plug wires at the spark plugs and the primary and secondary wires from

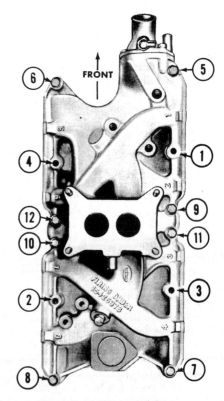

FRONT

Torque sequence—4900cc (302) V8

the coil. Remove the distributor hold-down bolt and remove the distributor.

6. If equipped with air conditioning, remove the bracket retaining the compressor to the intake manifold.

7. Remove the manifold attaching bolts. Lift off the intake manifold and carburetor as an assembly.

NOTE: *If it is necessary to pry the manifold to loosen it from the engine, be careful not to damage any gasket sealing surfaces.*

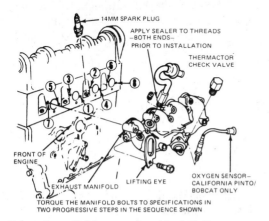

Exhaust manifold removal and installation— 1977-78 2300 cc four

Always discard all old gaskets and attaching bolt sealing washers.

8. Clean all gasket surfaces and firmly cement new gaskets in place, using nonhardening sealer. Make sure that the gaskets interlock with the seal tabs, and that the gasket holes align with those in the cylinder heads.

9. Reverse the above procedure to install, taking care to run a finger around the seal area on the installed manifold to make sure that the seals did not slip out during installation. Finally, torque the intake manifold bolts to 23–25 ft lbs in the proper sequence, and recheck the torque after the engine is warm.

Exhaust Manifold

REMOVAL AND INSTALLATION

1974-76 2300 cc Four

1. Remove the air cleaner. Remove the heat shroud from the exhaust manifold.

2. Place a block of wood under the exhaust pipe, and then disconnect it from the manifold.

3. Remove the attaching nuts and remove the manifold from the head. Clean the mating surfaces.

4. Install a light coat of graphite grease on

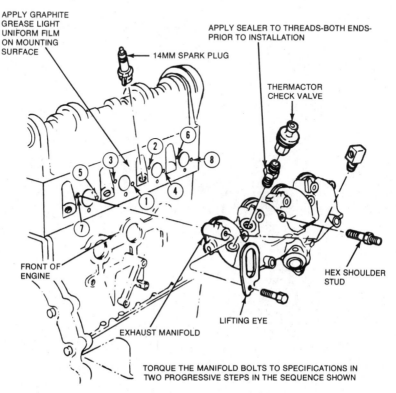

Installing exhaust manifold—2300cc four

the exhaust manifold mating surface and position the manifold on the cylinder head.

5. Install the attaching nuts and tighten them to the proper torque.

6. Connect the exhaust pipe to the manifold and remove the wood support from under the pipe.

7. Install the air cleaner.

1977–78 2300 cc Four

See the illustration below for special procedures to be followed in exhaust manifold removal and installation. Note especially the sequence in which bolts are to be torqued.

2800 cc V6

1. Remove the air cleaner.

2. Remove the four attaching nuts from the exhaust manifold shroud (right-side only).

3. Disconnect the attaching nuts from the muffler inlet pipe.

4. Remove the exhaust manifold attaching nuts and remove the manifold.

5. These manifolds do not use gaskets. When installing the manifold, smear a light coat of graphite grease on the mating surfaces.

6. Position the manifold on the studs and install the bolts hand-tight then torque them evenly to the proper torque.

7. Install a new inlet pipe gasket and the attaching nuts.

8. Position the exhaust manifold shroud on the manifold and install the attaching nuts (right-side).

9. Install the air cleaner.

4900 cc (302) V8

1. On the right exhaust manifold, remove the air cleaner and intake duct assembly.

2. Disconnect the automatic choke heat chamber air inlet hose from the inlet tube near the right valve cover. Remove the automatic choke heat tube.

3. Remove the nuts or bolts retaining the heat stove to the exhaust manifold and remove the stove.

4. Disconnect the exhaust manifold(s) from the muffler inlet pipe(s).

5. Remove the manifold retaining bolts and washers and the manifold(s).

6. Reverse the above procedure to install, using new inlet pipe gaskets. Torque the exhaust manifold retaining bolts to 12–16 ft lbs, in sequence from the centermost bolt outward. Start the engine and check for exhaust leaks.

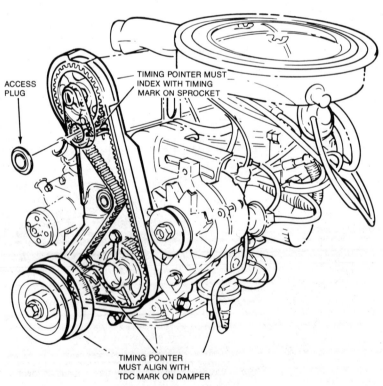

ACCESS PLUG

TIMING POINTER MUST INDEX WITH TIMING MARK ON SPROCKET

TIMING POINTER MUST ALIGN WITH TDC MARK ON DAMPER

Cam timing check—2300cc four

Camshaft, Auxiliary Shaft and Timing Belt—2300 CC

Should the camshaft drive belt jump timing by a tooth or two, the engine might still run, but very poorly. To visually check for correct timing of the camshaft, auxiliary shaft and the crankshaft, follow this procedure.

There is an access plug provided in the cam drive belt cover so that the camshaft timing can be checked without removing the drive belt cover. Remove the access plug, turn the crankshaft until the timing marks on the crankshaft indicate TDC. Then, observe that the sprocket is aligned with the pointer on the inner belt cover. As an additional check, make sure that the distributor rotor is aligned with the No. 1 cylinder firing position on the distributor.

NOTE: *Never turn the crankshaft of an overhead cam engine in the opposite direction of normal rotation. Backward rotation of the crankshaft may cause the timing belt to slip and alter the cam timing.*

TIMING BELT REPLACEMENT
2300 cc Four

1. Remove the camshaft drive belt cover.
2. Remove the distributor cap from the distributor and position it out of the way.
3. Turn the engine clockwise until:
   a. The timing pointer is aligned with the "0" mark on the crankshaft pulley.
   b. The pointer on the camshaft sprocket is aligned with the ball in the belt guide plate.
   c. The distributor rotor is aligned with the timing mark on the upper lip of the distributor housing.
4. Loosen the drive belt tensioner bolt and move the tensioner as far left as possible. Tighten the tensioner adjustment bolt.
5. Remove the belt from the pulleys.
6. Preconditions should be as in Step 3. Install the belt on the three sprockets, making sure that the cogs in the belt engage the slots in the sprockets.
7. Loosen the tensioner adjustment bolt

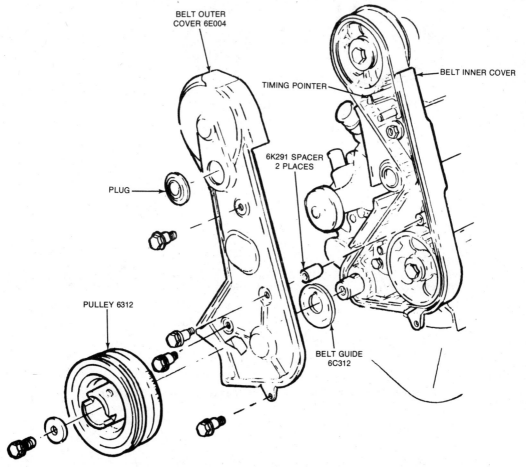

Installing timing belt outer cover, crankshaft belt guide and pulley—2300cc four

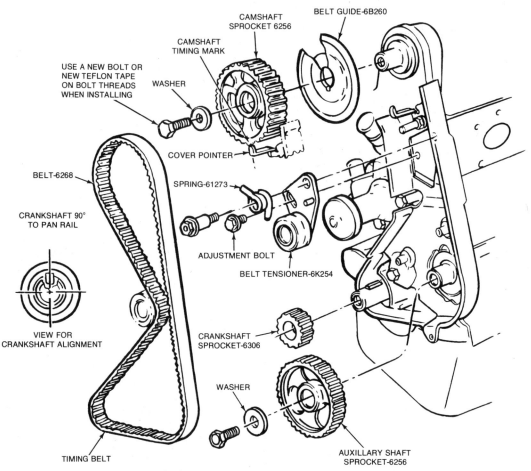

USE A NEW BOLT OR NEW TEFLON TAPE ON BOLT THREADS WHEN INSTALLING

CAMSHAFT TIMING MARK

CAMSHAFT SPROCKET 6256

BELT GUIDE-6B260

WASHER

COVER POINTER

BELT-6268

SPRING-61273

ADJUSTMENT BOLT

BELT TENSIONER-6K254

CRANKSHAFT 90° TO PAN RAIL

VIEW FOR CRANKSHAFT ALIGNMENT

CRANKSHAFT SPROCKET-6306

WASHER

TIMING BELT

AUXILLARY SHAFT SPROCKET-6256

NOTE: IF TIMING RELATIONSHIP BETWEEN CRANKSHAFT, CAMSHAFT AND AUXILIARY SHAFT IS DISTURBED, CHECK AND ADJUST INITIAL IGNITION TIMING AND CURB IDLE SPEED AFTER REASSEMBLY.

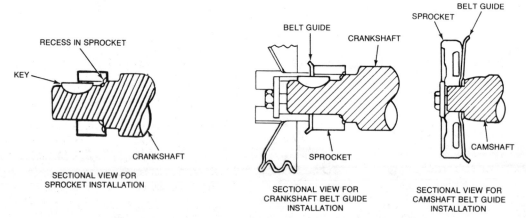

RECESS IN SPROCKET

KEY

CRANKSHAFT

SECTIONAL VIEW FOR SPROCKET INSTALLATION

BELT GUIDE

CRANKSHAFT

SPROCKET

SECTIONAL VIEW FOR CRANKSHAFT BELT GUIDE INSTALLATION

BELT GUIDE

SPROCKET

CAMSHAFT

SECTIONAL VIEW FOR CAMSHAFT BELT GUIDE INSTALLATION

Installing cam drive belt, sprockets and tensioner—2300cc four

and allow the full spring pressure of the tensioner to force the tensioner against the belt.

8. Turn the crankshaft pulley clockwise two complete turns to remove all slack from the belt.

9. Continue to turn the pulley until the marks described in Step 3 are aligned. If the belt has slipped, remove the belt and repeat the installation procedure.

10. Position the drive belt tensioner so there is no free-play in the drive belt and tighten the tensioner adjustment bolt. Be careful not to overtighten the belt.

CAMSHAFT AND SPROCKET REPLACEMENT

2300 cc Four

1. Remove the rocker arm cover and the rocker arms.

2. Remove the timing belt cover.

3. Remove the camshaft sprocket bolt and washer, then slide the sprocket and belt guide from the camshaft.

4. Remove the camshaft retaining plate from the rear of the cylinder head.

5. Carefully remove the camshaft from the front of the head.

6. Coat the valve stems with Lubriplate. Coat the camshaft with oil prior to installation.

7. Reverse the above procedure to install, taking care to use a new camshaft sprocket bolt. If a new bolt is not available, use Teflon® tape on the threads of the old bolt. Use the accompanying illustration as an assembly guide.

AUXILIARY SHAFT AND SPROCKET REPLACEMENT

2300 cc Four

1. Remove the camshaft drive belt cover.

2. Remove the drive belt. Remove the auxiliary shaft sprocket. A puller may be necessary to remove the sprocket.

3. Remove the distributor and fuel pump.

4. Remove the auxiliary shaft cover and thrust plate.

5. Withdraw the auxiliary shaft from the block.

NOTE: *The distributor drive gear and the fuel pump eccentric on the auxiliary shaft must not be allowed to touch the auxiliary shaft bearings during removal and installa-*

tion. Completely coat the shaft with oil before sliding it into place.

6. Slide the auxiliary shaft into the housing and insert the thrust plate to hold the shaft.

7. Install a new gasket and auxiliary shaft cover.

8. Fit a new gasket into the fuel pump and install the pump.

9. Insert the distributor and install the auxiliary shaft sprocket.

10. Align the timing marks and install the drive belt.

11. Install the drive belt cover.

12. Check the ignition timing.

Timing Case and Camshaft—V6

FRONT COVER REMOVAL AND INSTALLATION

2800 cc V6

1. Remove the oil pan. Refer to "Engine Lubrication."

2. Remove the radiator and any other necessary parts to allow clearance.

3. Remove the alternator and drive belts. Remove the water pump and water lines.

4. Remove the fan.

5. Remove the crankshaft pulley with a puller and, if necessary, remove the guide sleeves from the cylinder block.

Removing or installing guide sleeves—2800cc V6

TOOL T72C-6150
Aligning front cover—2300cc four

BELT TENSIONER
ADJUSTING TOOL
T74P-6254-A

Adjusting belt tension—2300cc four

6. Remove the front cover retaining bolts and remove the front cover. If the front cover plate gasket needs replacement, remove the two screws and the plate to replace the gasket.

7. To install, reverse the procedures, cleaning all surfaces of gasket material and installing new gaskets and sealing compound.

NOTE: *If the guide sleeves were removed, install them with new seal rings but do not use sealing compound.*

CAMSHAFT AND TIMING GEAR REMOVAL AND INSTALLATION

2800 cc V6

1. Drain the cooling system.
2. Remove the radiator.
3. Remove the distributor cap with the spark plug wires attached. Remove the distributor vacuum line, distributor, alternator, rocker arm covers, fuel line and filter, carburetor, and intake manifold.
4. Remove the rocker arm and shaft assemblies. Lift out the pushrods and mark them so that they can be replaced in the same location.

5. Remove the oil pan. (See "Engine Lubrication.")

6. Remove the timing gear cover.

7. Remove the camshaft gear retaining bolt and slide the gear off the camshaft. Remove the camshaft thrust plate.

8. Remove the valve lifters from the engine block with a magnet. Lifters should be identified to permit installation in the same location.

9. Carefully pull the camshaft from the engine block, avoiding damage to the camshaft bearings. Remove the key and spacer ring.

10. Coat the camshaft with a moly cam lubricant or SAE 90 gear oil.

11. Install the camshaft, carefully avoiding damage to the bearings.

NOTE: *When installing the camshaft, do not push it hard into the engine. There is an oil plug at the rear of the engine block called the "bore plug." If the camshaft is installed too far into the engine or forced into the engine, it could push this plug out, resulting in oil leaking on the clutch and pressure plate and causing serious damage.*

12. Install the spacer ring with the worn

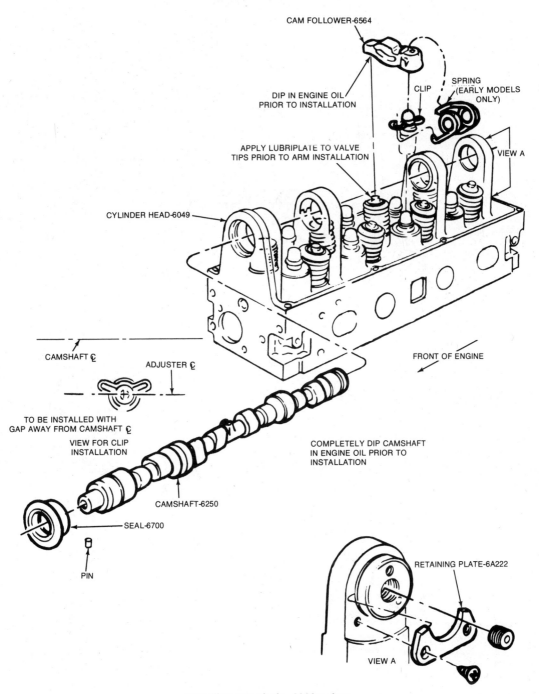

CAM FOLLOWER-6564

DIP IN ENGINE OIL PRIOR TO INSTALLATION

CLIP

SPRING (EARLY MODELS ONLY)

APPLY LUBRIPLATE TO VALVE TIPS PRIOR TO ARM INSTALLATION

VIEW A

CYLINDER HEAD-6049

CAMSHAFT ℄

ADJUSTER ℄

FRONT OF ENGINE

TO BE INSTALLED WITH GAP AWAY FROM CAMSHAFT ℄

VIEW FOR CLIP INSTALLATION

COMPLETELY DIP CAMSHAFT IN ENGINE OIL PRIOR TO INSTALLATION

CAMSHAFT-6250

SEAL-6700

PIN

RETAINING PLATE-6A222

VIEW A

Installing camshaft—2300cc four

side toward the engine. Insert the camshaft key. Install the thrust plate.

13. Install the camshaft timing gear and align the timing marks. Install the retaining washer and bolt.

14. Install the valve lifters.

15. Install the timing cover.

16. Install the belt drive pulley and secure it with the washer and retaining bolt.

17. Install the oil pan.

18. Install the pushrods in the same locations from which they were removed. Install the intake manifold.

19. Install the oil baffles and rocker arm

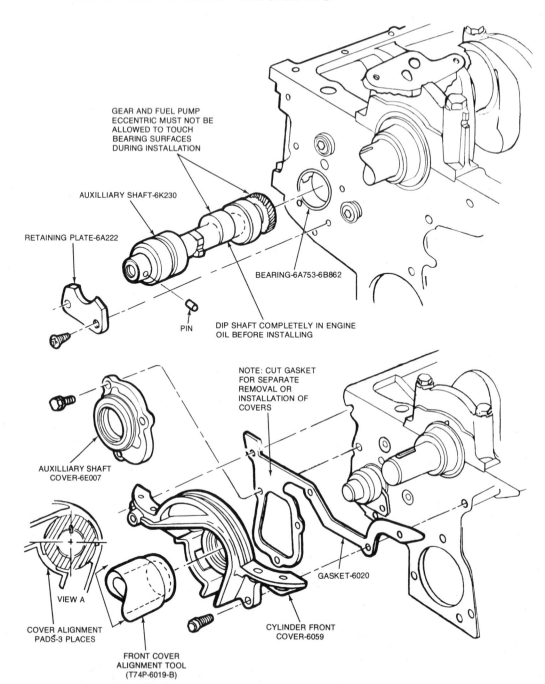

GEAR AND FUEL PUMP
ECCENTRIC MUST NOT BE
ALLOWED TO TOUCH
BEARING SURFACES
DURING INSTALLATION

AUXILLIARY SHAFT-6K230

RETAINING PLATE-6A222

BEARING-6A753-6B862

PIN

DIP SHAFT COMPLETELY IN ENGINE
OIL BEFORE INSTALLING

NOTE: CUT GASKET
FOR SEPARATE
REMOVAL OR
INSTALLATION OF
COVERS

AUXILLIARY SHAFT
COVER-6E007

VIEW A

GASKET-6020

COVER ALIGNMENT
PADS-3 PLACES

CYLINDER FRONT
COVER-6059

FRONT COVER
ALIGNMENT TOOL
(T74P-6019-B)

Installing auxiliary shaft, bearings and cylinder front cover—2300cc four

shaft assemblies. Adjust the valves to the cold setting.

20. Install the carburetor, fuel line and filter, alternator, distributor cap, and wires.

21. Fill the cooling system.

22. Install the rocker arm covers but not permanently. Run the engine, check for leaks, and set the ignition timing.

23. Set the valves at their hot setting. Install the valve covers permanently.

Timing Chain and Cover—4900 CC (302) V8

REMOVAL AND INSTALLATION

1. Drain the cooling system and the crankcase. Disconnect the negative battery cable.

2. If your car is equipped with a fan shroud, remove the shroud retaining bolts and position the shroud to the rear. On all

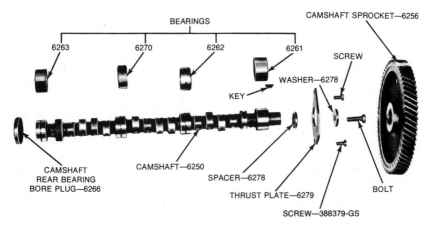

Camshaft and related parts—2800cc V6

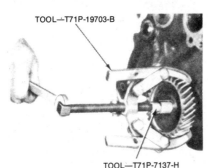

Removing crankshaft gear—2800cc V6

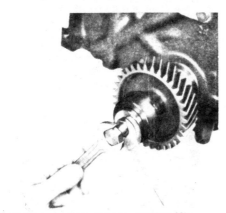

Installing crankshaft gear—2800cc V6

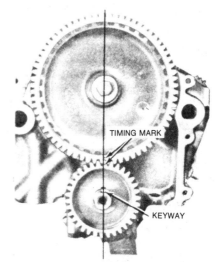

Aligning timing gears—2800cc V6

applications, remove the bolts attaching the spacer to the water pump and remove the fan and spacer (or fan drive clutch) from the water pump shaft. Remove the fan shroud, if so equipped.

3. On models so equipped, remove the air conditioner drive belt and idler pulley bracket. On all models, remove the alternator and alternator drive belt. On models so equipped, remove the power steering pump and drive belt. Remove the Thermactor air pump and drive belt.

4. Remove the water pump pulley.

5. Disconnect the radiator hose, heater hose, and the water pump by-pass hose from the water pump.

6. Remove the crankshaft pulley from the crankshaft vibration damper. After removing the damper retaining screw and washer, install a universal gear puller on the damper and pull it off.

7. Disconnect the fuel pump outlet line at the fuel pump. Remove the fuel pump retaining bolts and position the pump to one side with the flexible fuel line still attached.

8. Remove the engine oil level dipstick.

9. Remove the bolts attaching the oil pan to the cylinder front cover. Using a thin-bladed knife, cut the oil pan gasket flush with

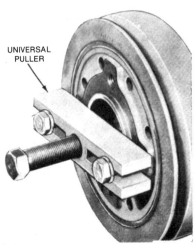

UNIVERSAL
PULLER

Removing the crankshaft damper—4900cc (302) V8

the cylinder block face prior to separating the cover from the cylinder block. Then remove the cylinder front cover and water pump as an assembly.

NOTE: *If the front cover is to be replaced, transfer the water pump and dipstick tube from the old cover.*

10. Discard the old cylinder front cover gasket, and remove the crankshaft front oil slinger.

11. Check the timing chain deflection as follows. With a socket wrench of the proper size on the crankshaft pulley bolt, gently rotate the crankshaft in a clockwise direction until all slack is removed from the left-side of the timing chain. Scribe a mark on the engine block parallel to the present position of the left-side of the chain. Turn the crankshaft in a counterclockwise direction to remove all the slack from the right-side of the chain. Force the left-side of the chain outward with the fingers and measure the distance between the reference point and the present position of the chain. If the distance exceeds $1/2$ in., replace the chain and sprockets.

12. Turn the engine over in the normal direction of rotation until the timing marks (see illustration) are positioned "dot-to-dot."

13. Remove the camshaft sprocket capscrew, washers and the fuel pump eccentric. Slide both sprockets and the timing chain forward, and remove them as an assembly.

To install:

1. Position the sprockets and timing chain on the camshaft and crankshaft simultaneously, on a centerline.

2. Install the fuel pump eccentric, washers and camshaft sprocket capscrew. Tighten the capscrew to 30–35 ft lbs. Install the front oil slinger.

3. Clean the cylinder front covers, oil

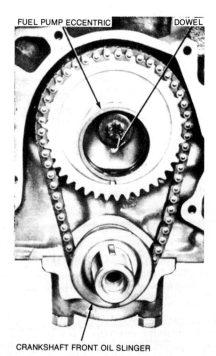

FUEL PUMP ECCENTRIC   DOWEL

CRANKSHAFT FRONT OIL SLINGER

Oil slinger and fuel pump eccentric installed —4900cc (302) V8

TIMING MARKS

Timing mark alignment—4900cc (302) V8

pan and cylinder block mating surfaces to remove all old gasket material.

4. Replace the oil seal as outlined under "Timing Chain Cover Oil Seal Replacement."

5. Lubricate the timing chain with engine oil.

6. Coat the gasket surface of the oil pan with oil-resistant sealer. Cut and position the required sections of a new gasket on the oil pan and apply oil-resistant sealer at the corners. Install the oil pan seal as required. Coat the gasket surfaces of the block and front cover with oil-resistant sealer, and position the new gasket on the block.

7. Place the cylinder front cover on the block, taking care to avoid seal damage or gasket mislocation.

8. Install the front cover, using a crankshaft-to-cover alignment tool. To align the holes in the block with those in the cover, it may be necessary to insert two phillips head screwdrivers in two of the bolt holes and force the cover downward, compressing the new pan gasket. Then, with the attaching bolts coated with oil for ease of installation, install the bolts, tightening them diagonally, in rotation, to a final torque of 12–15 ft lbs. Remove the alignment tool.

9. Apply white grease to the rubbing surface of the vibration damper inner hub to prevent damage to the seal. Apply a light coating of graphite and engine oil to the front of the crankshaft for damper installation. Then, align the vibration damper keyway with that of the camshaft. Install the vibration damper on the crankshaft and install the capscrew and washer. Tighten the screw to 70–90 ft lbs. Install the crankshaft pulley.

10. Using a new gasket, install the fuel

TOOL—T52L-6306-AEE, OR 6306-AJ

Installing crankshaft damper—4900cc (302) V8

pump to the block. Connect the fuel outlet line.

11. Install the dipstick.

12. Connect the radiator hose, heater hose, and the water pump by-pass hose at the water pump.

13. Install the Thermactor air pump and drive belt. On models so equipped, install the power steering pump and drive belt. On all models, install the alternator and drive belt. On models so equipped, install the air conditioner idler pulley and drive belt.

14. Position the fan shroud over the water pump pulley, if so equipped. Install the fan and spacer (or fan clutch drive). Install the fan shroud retaining bolts, if so equipped.

15. Adjust all drive belts as outlined in Chapter 1.

16. Fill the crankcase and cooling system. Connect the battery cable. Bleed the cooling system.

17. Start the engine and operate it at a fast idle. Check for coolant and oil leaks.

18. Adjust the ignition timing.

TIMING CHAIN COVER OIL SEAL REPLACEMET
4900 cc (302) V8, 2800 cc V6

It is a recommended practice to replace the cover seal any time the front cover is removed.

1. With the cover removed from the car, drive the old seal from the rear of the cover with a pin-punch. Clean out the recess in the cover.

2. Coat the new seal with grease and drive it into the cover until it is fully seated. Check the seal after installation to be sure that the spring is properly positioned in the seal.

CAMSHAFT REMOVAL AND INSTALLATION
4900 cc (302) V8

1. Drain the cooling system. Disconnect the radiator hoses and the transmission cooler lines, if equipped with automatic transmission. If equipped with a fan shroud, remove the retaining bolts. Remove the radiator. If equipped with air conditioning, remove the bolts securing the air conditioning condenser and position the condenser to one side.

CAUTION: *Do not disconnect the refrigerant lines.*

2. Remove the intake manifold as outlined

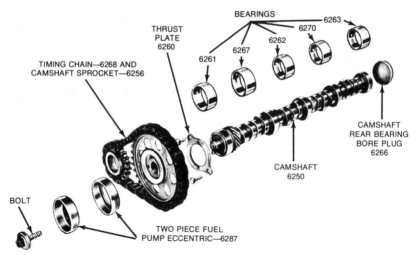

Camshaft and related parts—4900cc (302) V8

under "Intake Manifold Removal and Installation."

3. Remove the cylinder front cover, timing chain and sprockets as outlined under "Timing Chain and Cover Removal and Installation."

4. Remove the crankcase ventilation valve and hoses. Remove the valve covers. Loosen the valve rocker arm stud nuts and rotate the rocker arms to one side (away from the pushrods).

5. Lift out the pushrods, keeping them in order so that they may be installed in their original positions. Using a magnet, remove the valve lifters, also keeping them in order. If the lifters become stuck in their bores, use a clawtype tool to remove them.

6. Remove the camshaft thrust plate and remove the camshaft by carefully pulling it to the front of the engine. Take care not to damage the camshaft lobes or the cam bearing journals while removing the cam from the engine.

7. Prior to installing the camshaft, coat the cam lobes with white grease, and the bearing journals and all valve parts with heavy engine oil.

8. Reverse the above procedure to install, taking care to perform a preliminary valve adjustment, as outlined under "Preliminary Valve Adjustment," before starting the engine. Exercise care to follow all of the recommended torque settings and tightening sequences.

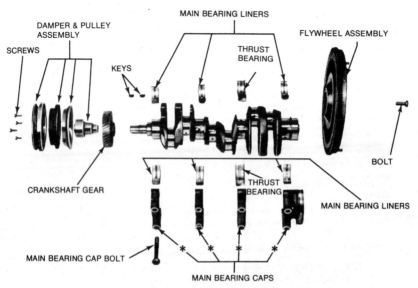

Crankshaft and related parts—2800cc V8

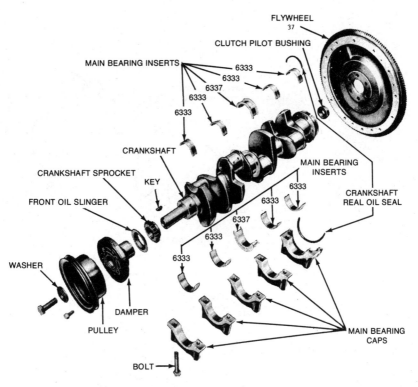

Crankshaft and related parts—4900cc (302) V8

Pistons and Connecting Rods
PISTON AND RING REPLACEMENT

1. Drain the cooling system and the crankcase.

2. Remove the cylinder head and manifolds.

3. Remove the oil pan and oil pump.

4. Turn the crankshaft until the piston to be removed is at the bottom of its stroke.

5. Place a cloth on the head of the piston to be removed and, using a ridge reamer, remove the deposits from the upper end of the cylinder bore.

NOTE: *Never remove more than 1/32 in. from the ring travel area when removing the ridges.*

6. Mark all connecting rod bearing caps so that they may be returned to their original location in the engine.

7. Remove the connecting rod caps.

8. Push the connecting rod and piston out through the top of the cylinder with the handle end of a hammer. Use care not to damage the cylinder wall or crankshaft journal.

9. Using an internal micrometer, measure bores both across thrust faces of cylinder

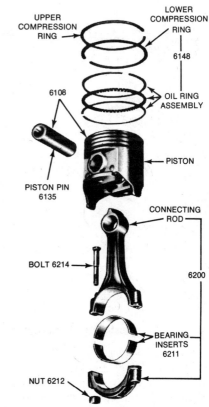

Typical piston and related parts

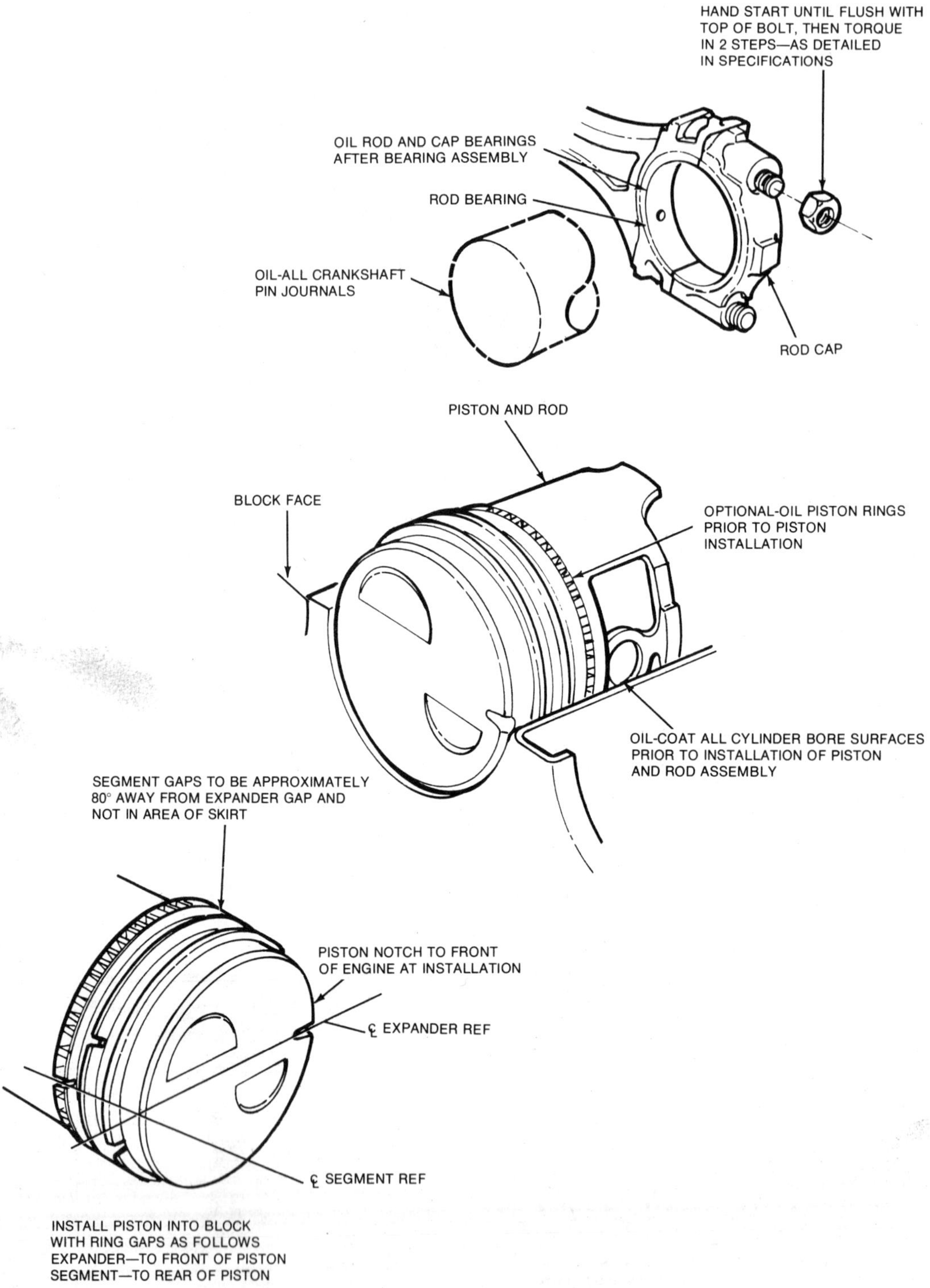

HAND START UNTIL FLUSH WITH
TOP OF BOLT, THEN TORQUE
IN 2 STEPS—AS DETAILED
IN SPECIFICATIONS

OIL ROD AND CAP BEARINGS
AFTER BEARING ASSEMBLY

ROD BEARING

OIL-ALL CRANKSHAFT
PIN JOURNALS

ROD CAP

PISTON AND ROD

BLOCK FACE

OPTIONAL-OIL PISTON RINGS
PRIOR TO PISTON
INSTALLATION

OIL-COAT ALL CYLINDER BORE SURFACES
PRIOR TO INSTALLATION OF PISTON
AND ROD ASSEMBLY

SEGMENT GAPS TO BE APPROXIMATELY
80° AWAY FROM EXPANDER GAP AND
NOT IN AREA OF SKIRT

PISTON NOTCH TO FRONT
OF ENGINE AT INSTALLATION

¢ EXPANDER REF

¢ SEGMENT REF

INSTALL PISTON INTO BLOCK
WITH RING GAPS AS FOLLOWS
EXPANDER—TO FRONT OF PISTON
SEGMENT—TO REAR OF PISTON

Installing pistons, rings and connecting rods—2300cc four

and parallel to axis of crankshaft at a minimum of four locations equally spaced. The bore must not be out of round by more than 0.005 in. and it must not "taper" more than 0.010 in. "Taper" is the difference in wear between two bore measurements in any cylinder.

10. If cylinder bore is in satisfactory condi-

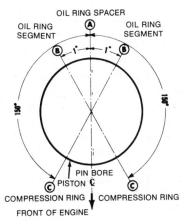

Piston ring spacing

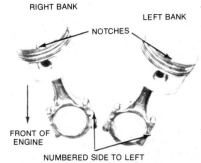

Correct piston and rod position—2800cc V6

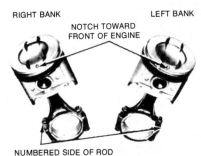

Correct piston and rod position—4900cc (302) V8

tion, place each ring in a bore in turn and square it in bore with head of piston. Measure ring gap. If ring gap is greater than limit, get a new ring. If ring gap is less than limit, file end of ring to obtain correct gap.

11. Check ring side clearance by installing rings on piston, and inserting feeler gauge of correct dimension between ring and lower land. The gauge should slide freely around ring circumference without binding. Any wear will form a step on lower land. Replace any pistons having high steps. Before checking ring side clearance be sure that the ring grooves are clean and free of carbon, sludge, or grit.

12. Space ring gaps at equidistant inter-

vals around piston circumference. Be sure to install piston in its original bore. Install short lengths of rubber tubing over connecting rod bolts to prevent damage to rod journal. Install a ring compressor over rings on piston. Lower piston, and rod assembly into bore until ring compressor contacts block. Using wooden handle of a hammer, push piston into bore while guiding rod into journal.

NOTE: *The arrows or notches on pistons must point forward.*

ENGINE LUBRICATION

Oil Pan

REMOVAL AND INSTALLATION

2300 cc Four

1. Drain the crankcase.
2. Remove the oil dipstick.
3. Disconnect the steering shaft connection from the rack and pinion.
4. Disconnect the rack and pinion from the crossmember and move it forward to provide clearance.
5. Remove the flywheel housing inspection cover.
6. Remove the oil pan attaching bolts and remove the pan.
7. Clean the gasket mounting surfaces of the block and pan.
8. Coat both the engine block and pan gasket with oil-resistant sealer and position the gasket on the block.
9. Coat the oil pan front oil seal and the cylinder front cover with oil-resistant sealer and position the seal on the front cover, making sure that the ends of the seal contact the pan gasket.
10. Coat the rear oil pan seal with oil-resistant sealer and install it on the rear main bearing cap.
11. Position the pan on the block and tighten the bolts, diagonally and in rotation, a few turns at a time to a final figure of 4–6 ft lbs.
12. Reverse steps 1–5 to complete the installation.

2800 cc V6 and 4900 cc V8

1. Remove the dipstick. Remove the bolts attaching the fan shroud to the radiator. Position the shroud over the fan. Disconnect the battery ground cable at the battery. Loosen the alternator bracket and adjusting bolts.

2. Raise the vehicle on a hoist; disconnect automatic transmission cooler lines.

3. Drain the crankcase.

4. Remove the splash shield. Remove the starter.

5. Remove the engine front support nuts (V6 only).

6. Raise the engine and place wood blocks between the engine front supports and the chassis brackets (V6 only).

7. Remove the oil pan attaching bolts and remove the oil pan.

8. Clean the gasket surfaces of the block and the oil pan. The oil pan has a two-piece gasket.

9. Coat the block surface and the oil pan gasket with sealer. Position the oil pan gaskets on the cylinder block.

10. Position the oil pan front seal on the cylinder front cover. Be sure that the tabs on the seal are over the oil pan gasket.

11. Place the end seals in position flush with the cylinder block oil pan rail, if previously removed. Position the oil pan rear seal on the rear main bearing cap. Be sure that the tabs on the seal are over the oil pan gasket.

12. Position the oil pan centered on the cylinder block. Install two bolts at both ends (front and rear) of the oil pan, then install the remaining bolts and tighten them to 5–7 ft lbs, starting with the bolt at the left front corner (looking from the rear) on the leading edge of the oil pan and working around the circumference of the pan.

13. Replace the converter housing or clutch cover.

14. Raise the engine and remove the wood blocks from between the engine supports and chassis brackets. Lower the engine and install the engine support nuts (V6 only).

15. Replace the starter and splash shield. Reconnect the automatic transmission cooler lines.

16. Lower the vehicle.

17. Install the alternator.

18. Connect the battery ground wire.

19. Install the fan shroud.

20. Install the dipstick. Fill the crankcase with oil. Start the engine and check for leaks.

Rear Main Oil Seal

REPLACEMENT

2300 cc Four

1. Remove the oil pan and oil pump, if required.

2. Loosen all the main bearing cap bolts, thereby lowering the crankshaft slightly but not more than $1/32$ in.

3. Remove the rear main bearing cap, and remove the oil seal from the bearing cap and the cylinder block. Install a small sheet metal screw in one end of the cylinder block half of the seal, and pull on the screw to remove the seal. Remove the oil seal retaining pin from the bearing cap if so equipped.

4. Clean the seal grooves in the cap and block with a brush and solvent. Dry the area thoroughly. No solvent should come in contact with the seal.

5. Dip the seal halves in clean engine oil.

6. Carefully install the upper seal (block half) into its groove with the undercut side of the seal toward the front of the engine, by rotating it on the seal journal of the crankshaft until about $3/8$ in. protrudes below the parting surface. Be sure that no rubber has been shaved off. Wipe all oil from the mating surface of the bearing cap and cylinder block.

7. Tighten the bearing cap bolts to specifications.

8. Install the lower seal in the rear main bearing cap with the undercut side of the seal toward the front of the engine. Allow the seal to protrude about $3/8$ in. above the parting surface to mate with the upper seal when the cap is installed.

NOTE: *Install the seals so that the locating tab faces the rear of the engine.*

9. Apply a *small* amount of sealer to the mating surface of the bearing cap. No sealer compound should come in contact with the rubber seals when the bearing cap is installed and tightened.

10. Install the oil pump (if removed) and oil pan. Fill the crankcase with oil, and operate the engine, checking for leaks.

2800 cc V6

1. Remove the transmission. Remove the clutch pressure plate and clutch disc, if so equipped.

2. Remove the flywheel, flywheel housing and rear plate.

3. Punch two holes in the crankshaft rear oil seal on opposite sides of the crankshaft just above the bearing cap-to-cylinder block split line. Install a sheet metal screw in each of the holes and pry the crankshaft rear main oil seal from the block.

NOTE: *Use extreme caution not to scratch the crankshaft oil seal surface.*

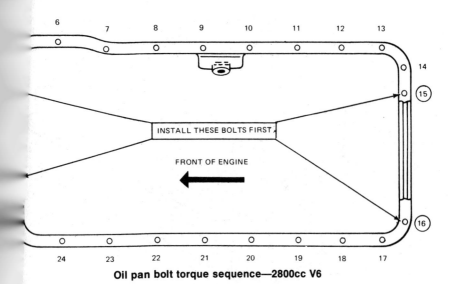

Oil pan bolt torque sequence—2800cc V6

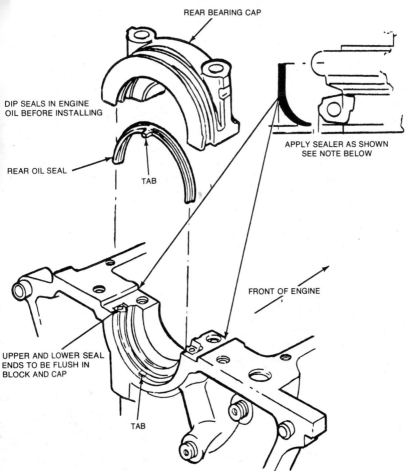

Sealer note: Clean the area where sealer is to be applied before installing the seals. Use Ford spot remover B7A-19521-A or equivalent. After the seals are in place, apply a $1/16$ inch bead of C3AZ-19562-A or -B sealer as shown. Sealer must not contact seals.

Sealer application—2300cc four

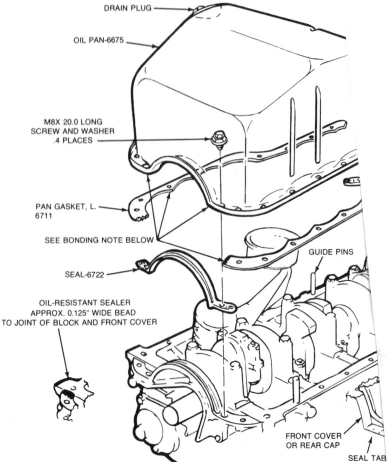

1. Apply gasket adhesive evenly to oil pan flange
and to pan side gaskets. Allow adhesive to dry pas
wet stage, then install gaskets to oil pan.
2. Apply sealer to joint of block and front cover.
Install seals to front cover and rear bearing cap and
press seal tabs firmly into block. *Be sure to instal
the rear seal before the rear main bearing cap sealer
has cured.*
3. Position 2 guide pins and install the oil pan.
Secure the pan with the four M6 bolts shown above.
4. Remove the guide pins and install and torque the
eighteen M6 bolts, beginning at hole A and working
clockwise around the pan.

Oil pan installation—2300cc four

Clean the oil seal recess in the cylinder
block and main bearing cap.

4. Coat the seal and all of the seal mounting surfaces with oil and install the seal in the
recess, driving it in place with an oil seal installation tool.

5. Install the clutch and/or transmission in
the reverse order of removal.

4900 cc (302) V8

1. Remove the oil pan and, if required,
the oil pump.

Sealer application—2800cc V6

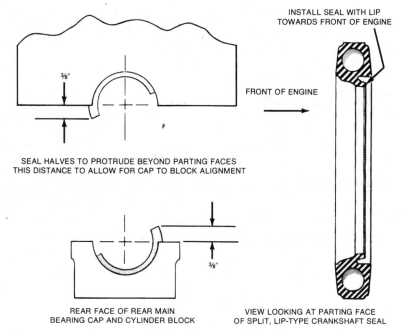

INSTALL SEAL WITH LIP
TOWARDS FRONT OF ENGINE

FRONT OF ENGINE

3/8"

SEAL HALVES TO PROTRUDE BEYOND PARTING FACES
THIS DISTANCE TO ALLOW FOR CAP TO BLOCK ALIGNMENT

3/8"

REAR FACE OF REAR MAIN
BEARING CAP AND CYLINDER BLOCK

VIEW LOOKING AT PARTING FACE
OF SPLIT, LIP-TYPE CRANKSHAFT SEAL

Installing rear main oil seal—4 cylinder and V8

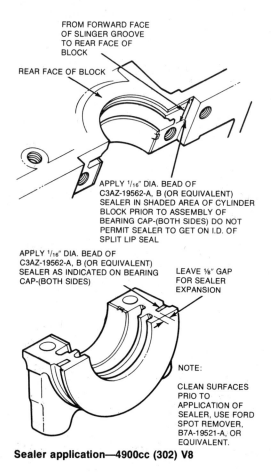

FROM FORWARD FACE
OF SLINGER GROOVE
TO REAR FACE OF
BLOCK

REAR FACE OF BLOCK

APPLY 1/16" DIA. BEAD OF
C3AZ-19562-A, B (OR EQUIVALENT)
SEALER IN SHADED AREA OF CYLINDER
BLOCK PRIOR TO ASSEMBLY OF
BEARING CAP-(BOTH SIDES) DO NOT
PERMIT SEALER TO GET ON I.D. OF
SPLIT LIP SEAL

APPLY 1/16" DIA. BEAD OF
C3AZ-19562-A, B (OR EQUIVALENT)
SEALER AS INDICATED ON BEARING
CAP-(BOTH SIDES)

LEAVE 1/8" GAP
FOR SEALER
EXPANSION

NOTE:

CLEAN SURFACES
PRIO TO
APPLICATION OF
SEALER, USE FORD
SPOT REMOVER,
B7A-19521-A, OR
EQUIVALENT.

Sealer application—4900cc (302) V8

2. Loosen all main bearing caps, allowing the crankshaft to lower slightly.

NOTE: *The crankshaft should not be allowed to drop more than 1/32 in.*

3. Remove the rear main bearing cap and the seal from the cap and block.

4. Carefully clean the seal grooves in the cap and block with solvent.

5. Soak the new seal halves in clean engine oil.

6. Install the upper half of the seal in the block with the undercut side of the seal toward the front of the engine. Slide the seal around the crankshaft journal until 3/8 in. protrudes beyond the base of the block.

7. Repeat the above procedure on the lower seal, allowing an equal length of the seal to protrude beyond the opposite end of the bearing cap.

8. Install the rear bearing cap and torque all main bearings to specifications. Apply sealer only to the rear of the seals.

9. Dip the bearing cap side seals in oil, then immediately install them. Do not use any sealer on the side seals. Tap the seals into place and do not clip the protruding ends.

10. Install the oil pump and pan. Fill the crankcase with oil, start the engine, and check for leaks.

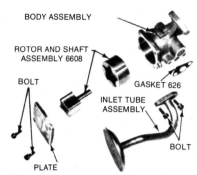

Oil pump disassembled—2800cc V6

Oil Pump
REMOVAL AND INSTALLATION
All Models

The oil pump is mounted on the bottom of the engine block and is enclosed by the oil pan. To remove the oil pump, first remove the oil pan according to the applicable procedure. Then, remove the oil pump attaching bolts and pump. When installing the oil pump, always use a new gasket and prime the pump by filling the inlet or outlet port with motor oil.

NOTE: *The oil pump installed in the 2300 cc engine cannot be disassembled for repairs. If the pump does not operate properly, it must be replaced as a unit.*

ENGINE COOLING

All three Mustang II engines are water-cooled. A solution of water and antifreeze passes from the radiator, through the lower radiator hose, past the water pump, through the cooling passages of the engine, past the thermostat, through the upper radiator hose and back into the radiator. As the hot coolant passes through the radiator, outside air is drawn through the radiator cooling fins by the engine fan and heat is exchanged, prior to the coolant's recirculation through the engine. Heat is supplied to car's interior by by-passing a portion of the coolant through the heater core.

When the engine is cold, the thermostat, which is located in a housing between the top of the engine and the upper radiator hose, is closed and prevents the coolant from passing to the radiator. This causes the coolant in the engine to heat quickly, shortening the time

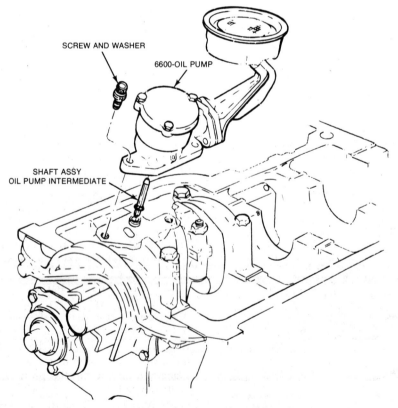

Oil pump installation—2300cc four

needed for the engine to reach its normal operating temperature. When the coolant reaches a predetermined temperature, the thermostat opens and the normal cooling cycle begins.

If your car is equipped with an automatic transmission, the bottom section of the radiator contains an automatic transmission oil cooler. Oil from the transmission is transported by a pair of metal hydraulic lines to and from the radiator's lower section, where it is cooled.

COOLING SYSTEM PRECAUTIONS

Use great care when removing the radiator cap from an overheated engine. The coolant in the engine is *very hot* and under *great pressure* when the engine overheats. Place several heavy rags over the radiator cap and release it very slowly. As soon as steam starts to come out of the cap or radiator overflow hose, *stop* and wait until the steam stops.

Never put cold water into a hot engine without having the engine running. If the engine is very hot, let it cool off first or use warm water, but in all cases, the engine must be running when water is added. Failure to heed this precaution may result in a cracked engine block.

Radiator

REMOVAL AND INSTALLATION

1. Drain the cooling system.
2. Disconnect the upper and lower hoses at the radiator.

3. On cars with automatic transmissions, disconnect the oil cooler lines at the radiator.
4. On vehicles with a fan shroud, remove the shroud retaining screws and position the shroud out of the way.
5. Remove the radiator attaching bolts and lift out the radiator.
6. If a new radiator is to be installed, transfer the petcock from the old radiator to the new one. On cars with automatic transmissions, transfer the oil cooler line fittings from the old radiator to the new one.
7. Position the radiator and install, but do not tighten, the radiator support bolts. On cars with automatic transmissions, connect the oil cooler lines. Then tighten the radiator support bolts.
8. On vehicles with a fan shroud, reinstall the shroud.
9. Connect the radiator hoses. Close the radiator petcock. Then fill and bleed the cooling system.
10. Start the engine and bring to operating temperature. Check for leaks.
11. On cars with automatic transmissions, check the cooler lines for leaks and interference. Check the transmission fluid level.

Water Pump

REMOVAL AND INSTALLATION

2300 cc Four, 2800 cc V6

1. Drain the cooling system.
2. Disconnect the lower radiator hose and heater hose from the water pump.

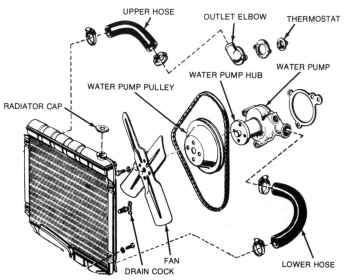

Radiator and related parts—302 V8

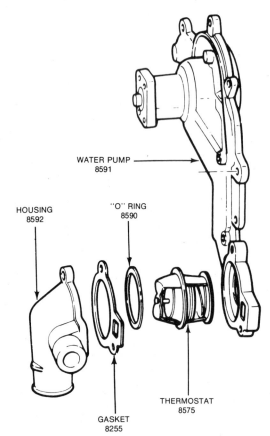

WATER PUMP
8591

HOUSING
8592

"O" RING
8590

THERMOSTAT
8575

GASKET
8255

Water pump and thermostat installation—2800cc V6

3. Loosen the alternator retaining and adjusting bolt, and remove the drive belt.

4. Remove the fan and water pump pulley. On 2300 cc engines, remove the camshaft drive belt cover.

5. Remove the water pump retaining bolts and remove the pump from the engine.

6. Clean all mating surfaces and install the pump with a new gasket coated with sealer. If a new pump is being installed, transfer the heater hose fitting from the old pump.

7. Reverse the removal steps to install the pump. Refill the cooling system.

4900 cc (302)V8

1. Drain the cooling system.

2. If equipped with a fan shroud, remove the shroud attaching bolts and position the shroud over the fan.

3. Remove the fan and spacer from the water pump shaft. Remove the shroud, if so equipped.

4. Remove the air conditioning drive belt and idler pulley, if so equipped. Remove the alternator, power steering, and Thermactor drive belts, if so equipped. Remove the power steering pump attaching bolts, if so equipped, and position it to one side (leaving it connected).

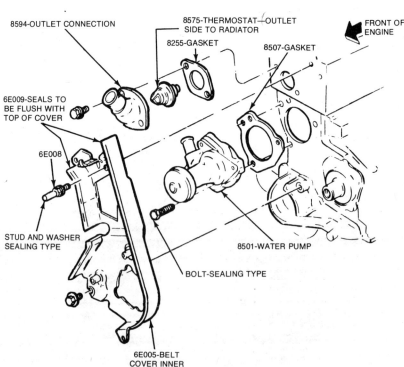

8594-OUTLET CONNECTION

8575-THERMOSTAT—OUTLET
SIDE TO RADIATOR

8255-GASKET

8507-GASKET

FRONT OF
ENGINE

6E009-SEALS TO
BE FLUSH WITH
TOP OF COVER

6E008

STUD AND WASHER
SEALING TYPE

8501-WATER PUMP

BOLT-SEALING TYPE

6E005-BELT
COVER INNER

Installing water pump, thermostat and inner timing belt cover—2300cc four

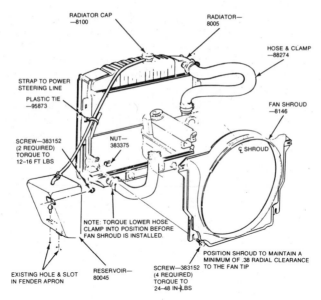

Constant Full cooling system—302 V8

5. Remove all accessory brackets which attach to the water pump. Remove the water pump pulley.

6. Disconnect the lower radiator hose, heater hose, and the water pump by-pass hose at the water pump.

7. Remove the bolts attaching the water pump to the front cover. Remove the pump and gasket. Discard the old gasket.

8. Remove all old gasket material from the mating surfaces of the front cover and water pump.

9. Coat both sides of a new gasket with water-resistant sealer and place it on the front cover. Install the water pump and tighten the attaching bolts diagonally, in rotation, to 12–115 ft lbs.

10. Connect the lower radiator hose, heater hose, and water pump by-pass hose at the water pump.

11. Install all accessory brackets attaching to the water pump. Install the pump pulley on the pump shaft.

12. Install the power steering pump and drive belt, if so equipped. Install the alternator, air conditioning, and Thermactor drive belts, if so equipped. Install the air conditioning idler pulley bracket, if so equipped. Adjust the drive belt tension of all accessory drive belts as outlined in Chapter 1.

13. Position the fan shroud, if so equipped, over the water pump pulley. Install the spacer and fan. Install the shroud attaching bolts, if so equipped.

14. Fill and bleed the cooling system. Operate the engine until normal running temperature is reached. Check for leaks and check the coolant level.

Thermostat
REMOVAL AND INSTALLATION

1. Drain the cooling system so that the level of coolant in the engine is below the thermostat housing.

2. Remove the thermostat housing attaching bolts. On the 2300 cc Four, the housing is located at the upper front part of the cylinder head. On the 2800 cc V6, the housing is located at the bottom of the water pump, connected to the lower radiator hose.

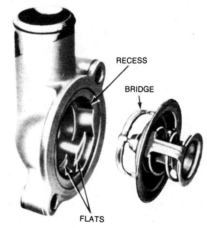

Thermostat installation—4900cc (302) V8

On the 4900 cc (302) V8, the housing is located at the front of the intake manifold.

3. Remove the housing, thermostat, and discard the old gasket. On 302 V8 engines, twist the thermostat to remove it.

4. Clean the gasket mating surfaces and the thermostat housing. Test the operation of the thermostat as outlined under "Cooling System Troubleshooting."

5. Using a good thermostat and new gasket, and O-ring (V6), install the thermostat in the housing. On 302 V8 engines, twist the thermostat so that it fits into the recess in the housing. Coat the gasket with water-resistant sealer.

6. Install the housing and tighten the attaching bolts to 12–15 ft lbs.

7. Refill the cooling system.

ENGINE REBUILDING

Most procedures involved in rebuilding an engine are fairly standard, regardless of the type of engine involved. This section is a guide to accepted rebuilding procedures. Examples of standard rebuilding practices are illustrated and should be used along with specific details concerning your particular engine, found earlier in this chapter.

The procedures given here are those used by any competent rebuilder. Obviously some of the procedures cannot be performed by the do-it-yourself mechanic, but are provided so that you will be familiar with the services that should be offered by rebuilding or machine shops. As an example, in most instances, it is more profitable for the home mechanic to remove the cylinder heads, buy the necessary parts (new valves, seals, keepers, keys, etc.) and deliver these to a machine shop for the necessary work. In this way you will save the money to remove and install the cylinder head and the mark-up on parts.

On the other hand, most of the work involved in rebuilding the lower end is well within the scope of the do-it-yourself mechanic. Only work such as hot-tanking, actually boring the block or Magnafluxing (invisible crack detection) need be sent to a machine shop.

Tools

The tools required for basic engine rebuilding should, with a few exceptions, be those included in a mechanic's tool kit. An accurate torque wrench, and a dial indicator (reading in thousandths) mounted on a universal base should be available. Special tools, where required, are available from the major tool suppliers. The services of a competent automotive machine shop must also be readily available.

Precautions

Aluminum has become increasingly popular for use in engines, due to its low weight and excellent heat transfer characteristics. The following precautions must be observed when handling aluminum (or any other) engine parts:
—Never hot-tank aluminum parts.
—Remove all aluminum parts (identification tags, etc.) from engine parts before hot-tanking (otherwise they will be removed during the process).

—Always coat threads lightly with engine oil or anti-seize compounds before installation, to prevent seizure.
—Never over-torque bolts or spark plugs in aluminum threads. Should stripping occur, threads can be restored using any of a number of thread repair kits available (see next section).

Inspection Techniques

Magnaflux and Zyglo are inspection techniques used to locate material flaws, such as stress cracks. Magnaflux is a magnetic process, applicable only to ferrous materials. The Zyglo process coats the matrial with a fluorescent dye penetrant, and any material may be tested using Zyglo. Specific checks of suspected surface cracks may be made at lower cost and more readily using spot check dye. The dye is sprayed onto the suspected area, wiped off, and the area is then sprayed with a developer. Cracks then will show up brightly.

Overhaul

The section is divided into two parts. The first, Cylinder Head Reconditioning, assumes that the cylinder head is removed from the engine, all manifolds are removed, and the cylinder head is on a workbench. The camshaft should be removed from overhead cam cylinder heads. The second section, Cylinder Block Reconditioning, covers the block, pistons, connecting rods and crankshaft. It is assumed that the engine is mounted on a work stand, and the cylinder head and all accessories are removed.

Procedures are identified as follows:
Unmarked—Basic procedures that must be performed in order to successfully complete the rebuilding process.
Starred (*)—Procedures that should be performed to ensure maximum performance and engine life.
Double starred (**)—Procedures that may be performed to increase engine performance and reliability.

When assembling the engine, any parts that will be in frictional contact must be pre-lubricated, to provide protection on initial start-up. Any product specifically formulated for this purpose may be used. NOTE: *Do not use engine oil. Where semi-permanent* (locked but removable) installation of bolts or nuts is desired, threads should be cleaned and located with Loctite ® or a similar product (non-hardening).

Repairing Damaged Threads

Several methods of repairing damaged threads are available. Heli-Coil® (shown here), Keenserts® and Microdot® are among the most widely used. All involve basically the same principle—drilling out stripped threads, tapping the hole and installing a pre-wound insert—making welding, plugging and oversize fasteners unnecessary.

Two types of thread repair inserts are usually supplied—a standard type for most Inch Coarse, Inch Fine, Metric Coarse and Metric Fine thread sizes and a spark plug type to fit most spark plug port sizes. Consult the individual manufacturer's catalog to determine exact applications. Typical thread repair kits will contain a selection of pre-wound threaded inserts, a tap (corresponding to the outside diameter threads of the insert) and an installation tool. Spark plug inserts usually differ because they require a tap equipped with pilot threads and a combined reamer/tap section. Most manufacturers also supply blister-packed thread repair inserts separately in addition to a master kit containing a variety of taps and inserts plus installation tools.

Before effecting a repair to a threaded hole, remove any snapped, broken or damaged bolts or studs. Penetrating oil can be used to free frozen threads; the offending item can be removed with locking pliers or with a screw or stud extractor. After the hole is clear, the thread can be repaired, as follows:

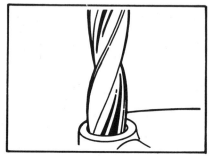

Drill out the damaged threads with specified drill. Drill completely through the hole or to the bottom of a blind hole

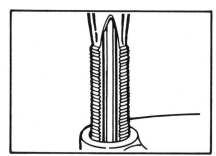

With the tap supplied, tap the hole to receive the thread insert. Keep the tap well oiled and back it out frequently to avoid clogging the threads

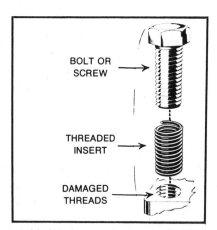

Damaged bolt holes can be repaired with thread repair inserts

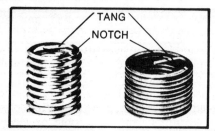

Standard thread repair insert (left) and spark plug thread insert (right)

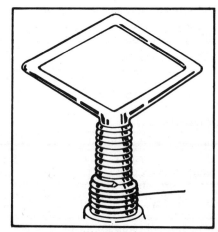

Screw the threaded insert onto the installation tool until the tang engages the slot. Screw the insert into the tapped hole until it is ¼–½ turn below the top surface. After installation break off the tang with a hammer and punch

Standard Torque Specifications and Fastener Markings

The Newton-metre has been designated the world standard for measuring torque and will gradually replace the foot-pound and kilogram-meter. In the absence of specific torques, the following chart can be used as a guide to the maximum safe torque of a particular size/grade of fastener.

- There is no torque difference for fine or coarse threads.
- Torque values are based on clean, dry threads. Reduce the value by 10% if threads are oiled prior to assembly.
- The torque required for aluminum components or fasteners is considerably less.

U. S. BOLTS

SAE Grade Number	1 or 2			5			6 or 7		

Bolt Markings

Manufacturer's marks may vary—number of lines always 2 less than the grade number.

Usage	Frequent			Frequent			Infrequent		
Bolt Size (inches)—(Thread)	Maximum Torque			Maximum Torque			Maximum Torque		
	Ft-Lb	kgm	Nm	Ft-Lb	kgm	Nm	Ft-Lb	kgm	Nm
¼—20	5	0.7	6.8	8	1.1	10.8	10	1.4	13.5
—28	6	0.8	8.1	10	1.4	13.6			
⁵⁄₁₆—18	11	1.5	14.9	17	2.3	23.0	19	2.6	25.8
—24	13	1.8	17.6	19	2.6	25.7			
³⁄₈—16	18	2.5	24.4	31	4.3	42.0	34	4.7	46.0
—24	20	2.75	27.1	35	4.8	47.5			
⁷⁄₁₆—14	28	3.8	37.0	49	6.8	66.4	55	7.6	74.5
—20	30	4.2	40.7	55	7.6	74.5			
½—13	39	5.4	52.8	75	10.4	101.7	85	11.75	115.2
—20	41	5.7	55.6	85	11.7	115.2			
⁹⁄₁₆—12	51	7.0	69.2	110	15.2	149.1	120	16.6	162.7
—18	55	7.6	74.5	120	16.6	162.7			
⁵⁄₈—11	83	11.5	112.5	150	20.7	203.3	167	23.0	226.5
—18	95	13.1	128.8	170	23.5	230.5			
¾—10	105	14.5	142.3	270	37.3	366.0	280	38.7	379.6
—16	115	15.9	155.9	295	40.8	400.0			
⁷⁄₈— 9	160	22.1	216.9	395	54.6	535.5	440	60.9	596.5
—14	175	24.2	237.2	435	60.1	589.7			
1— 8	236	32.5	318.6	590	81.6	799.9	660	91.3	894.8
—14	250	34.6	338.9	660	91.3	849.8			

METRIC BOLTS

NOTE: *Metric bolts are marked with a number indicating the relative strength of the bolt. These numbers have nothing to do with size.*

Description	Torque ft-lbs (Nm)			
Thread size x pitch (mm)	Head mark—4		Head mark—7	
6 x 1.0	2.2–2.9	(3.0–3.9)	3.6–5.8	(4.9–7.8)
8 x 1.25	5.8–8.7	(7.9–12)	9.4–14	(13–19)
10 x 1.25	12–17	(16–23)	20–29	(27–39)
12 x 1.25	21–32	(29–43)	35–53	(47–72)
14 x 1.5	35–52	(48–70)	57–85	(77–110)
16 x 1.5	51–77	(67–100)	90–120	(130–160)
18 x 1.5	74–110	(100–150)	130–170	(180–230)
20 x 1.5	110–140	(150–190)	190–240	(160–320)
22 x 1.5	150–190	(200–260)	250–320	(340–430)
24 x 1.5	190–240	(260–320)	310–410	(420–550)

NOTE: *This engine rebuilding section is a guide to accepted rebuilding procedures. Typical examples of standard rebuilding procedures are illustrated. Use these procedures along with the detailed instructions earlier in this chapter, concerning your particular engine.*

Cylinder Head Reconditioning

Procedure	Method
Remove the cylinder head:	See the engine service procedures earlier in this chapter for details concerning specific engines.
Identify the valves:	Invert the cylinder head, and number the valve faces front to rear, using a permanent felt-tip marker.
Remove the rocker arms (OHV engines only):	Remove the rocker arms with shaft(s) or balls and nuts. Wire the sets of rockers, balls and nuts together, and identify according to the corresponding valve.
Remove the camshaft (OHC engines only):	See the engine service procedures earlier in this chapter for details concerning specific engines.
Remove the valves and springs:	Using an appropriate valve spring compressor (depending on the configuration of the cylinder head), compress the valve springs. Lift out the keepers with needlenose pliers, release the compressor, and remove the valve, spring, and spring retainer. See the engine service procedures earlier in this chapter for details concerning specific engines.

Cylinder Head Reconditioning

Procedure	Method

Check the valve stem-to-guide clearance:

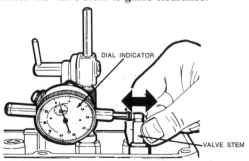

Check the valve stem-to-guide clearance

Clean the valve stem with lacquer thinner or a similar solvent to remove all gum and varnish. Clean the valve guides using solvent and an expanding wire-type valve guide cleaner. Mount a dial indicator so that the stem is at 90° to the valve stem, as close to the valve guide as possible. Move the valve off its seat, and measure the valve guide-to-stem clearance by rocking the stem back and forth to actuate the dial indicator. Measure the valve stems using a micrometer, and compare to specifications, to determine whether stem or guide wear is responsible for excessive clearance.
NOTE: *Consult the Specifications tables earlier in this chapter.*

De-carbon the cylinder head and valves:

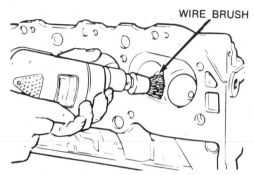

Remove the carbon from the cylinder head with a wire brush and electric drill

Chip carbon away from the valve heads, combustion chambers, and ports, using a chisel made of hardwood. Remove the remaining deposits with a stiff wire brush.
NOTE: *Be sure that the deposits are actually removed, rather than burnished.*

Hot-tank the cylinder head (cast iron heads only):
CAUTION: *Do not hot-tank aluminum parts.*

Have the cylinder head hot-tanked to remove grease, corrosion, and scale from the water passages.
NOTE: *In the case of overhead cam cylinder heads, consult the operator to determine whether the camshaft bearings will be damaged by the caustic solution.*

Degrease the remaining cylinder head parts:

Clean the remaining cylinder head parts in an engine cleaning solvent. Do not remove the protective coating from the springs.

Check the cylinder head for warpage:

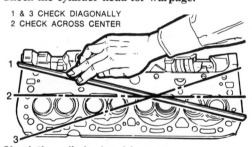

Check the cylinder head for warpage

Place a straight-edge across the gasket surface of the cylinder head. Using feeler gauges, determine the clearance at the center of the straight-edge. If warpage exceeds .003″ in a 6″ span, or .006″ over the total length, the cylinder head must be resurfaced.
NOTE: *If warpage exceeds the manufacturer's maximum tolerance for material removal, the cylinder head must be replaced.* When milling the cylinder heads of V-type engines, the intake manifold mounting position is altered, and must be corrected by milling the manifold flange a proportionate amount.

Cylinder Head Reconditioning

Procedure	Method
*Knurl the valve guides: 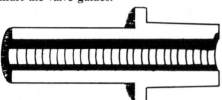 **Cut-away view of a knurled valve guide**	*Valve guides which are not excessively worn or distorted may, in some cases, be knurled rather than replaced. Knurling is a process in which metal is displaced and raised, thereby reducing clearance. Knurling also provides excellent oil control. The possibility of knurling rather than replacing valve guides should be discussed with a machinist.
Replace the valve guides: NOTE: *Valve guides should only be replaced if damaged or if an oversize valve stem is not available.* 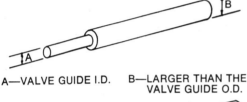 A—VALVE GUIDE I.D. B—LARGER THAN THE VALVE GUIDE O.D. 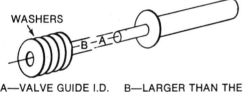 A—VALVE GUIDE I.D. B—LARGER THAN THE VALVE GUIDE O.D. **Valve guide installation tool using washers for installation**	See the engine service procedures earlier in this chapter for details concerning specific engines. Depending on the type of cylinder head, valve guides may be pressed, hammered, or shrunk in. In cases where the guides are shrunk into the head, replacement should be left to an equipped machine shop. In other cases, the guides are replaced using a stepped drift (see illustration). Determine the height above the boss that the guide must extend, and obtain a stack of washers, their I.D. similar to the guide's O.D., of that height. Place the stack of washers on the guide, and insert the guide into the boss. NOTE: *Valve guides are often tapered or beveled for installation.* Using the stepped installation tool (see illustration), press or tap the guides into position. Ream the guides according to the size of the valve stem.
Replace valve seat inserts:	Replacement of valve seat inserts which are worn beyond resurfacing or broken, if feasible, must be done by a machine shop.
Resurface (grind) the valve face: 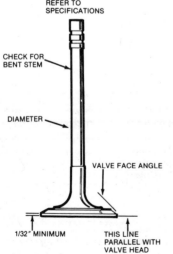 FOR DIMENSIONS, REFER TO SPECIFICATIONS CHECK FOR BENT STEM DIAMETER VALVE FACE ANGLE 1/32″ MINIMUM THIS LINE PARALLEL WITH VALVE HEAD **Critical valve dimensions**	Using a valve grinder, resurface the valves according to specifications given earlier in this chapter. CAUTION: *Valve face angle is not always identical to valve seat angle.* A minimum margin of 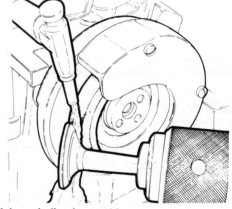 **Valve grinding by machine**

Cylinder Head Reconditioning

Procedure	Method
	$1/32''$ should remain after grinding the valve. The valve stem top should also be squared and resurfaced, by placing the stem in the V-block of the grinder, and turning it while pressing lightly against the grinding wheel. NOTE: *Do not grind sodium filled exhaust valves on a machine. These should be hand lapped.*

Procedure	Method
Resurface the valve seats using reamers or grinder: 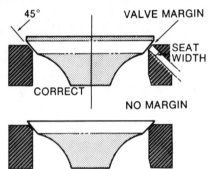 **Valve seat width and centering**  **Reaming the valve seat with a hand reamer**	Select a reamer of the correct seat angle, slightly larger than the diameter of the valve seat, and assemble it with a pilot of the correct size. Install the pilot into the valve guide, and using steady pressure, turn the reamer clockwise. CAUTION: *Do not turn the reamer counterclockwise.* Remove only as much material as necessary to clean the seat. Check the concentricity of the seat (following). If the dye method is not used, coat the valve face with Prussian blue dye, install and rotate it on the valve seat. Using the dye marked area as a centering guide, center and narrow the valve seat to specifications with correction cutters. NOTE: *When no specifications are available, minimum seat width for exhaust valves should be $5/64''$, intake valves $1/16''$.* After making correction cuts, check the position of the valve seat on the valve face using Prussian blue dye.
	To resurface the seat with a power grinder, select a pilot of the correct size and coarse stone of the proper angle. Lubricate the pilot and move the stone on and off the valve seat at 2 cycles per second, until all flaws are gone. Finish the seat with a fine stone. If necessary the seat can be corrected or narrowed using correction stones.

Procedure	Method
Check the valve seat concentricity:  **Check the valve seat concentricity with a dial gauge**	Coat the valve face with Prussian blue dye, install the valve, and rotate it on the valve seat. If the entire seat becomes coated, and the valve is known to be concentric, the seat is concentric. *Install the dial gauge pilot into the guide, and rest of the arm on the valve seat. Zero the gauge, and rotate the arm around the seat. Run-out should not exceed .002''.

Cylinder Head Reconditioning

Procedure	Method
*Lap the valves: NOTE: *Valve lapping is done to ensure efficient sealing of resurfaced valves and seats.*	*Invert the cylinder head, lightly lubricate the valve stems, and install the valves in the head as numbered. Coat valve seats with fine grinding compound, and attach the lapping tool suction cup to a valve head. NOTE: *Moisten the suction cup.* Rotate the tool between the palms, changing position and lifting the tool often to prevent grooving. Lap the valve until a smooth, polished seat is evident. Remove the valve and tool, and rinse away all traces of grinding compound.

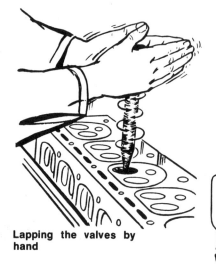

Lapping the valves by hand

Home-made valve lapping tool

HAND DRILL

ROD

SUCTION CUP

| | **Fasten a suction cup to a piece of drill rod, and mount the rod in a hand drill. Proceed as above, using the hand drill as a lapping tool.
 CAUTION: *Due to the higher speeds involved when using the hand drill, care must be exercised to avoid grooving the seat.* Lift the tool and change direction of rotation often. |

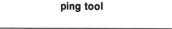

Check the valve springs:

NOT MORE THAN 5/64''

CLOSED COIL END DOWNWARD

Check the valve spring free length and squareness

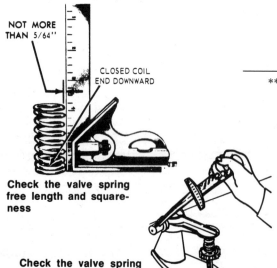

Check the valve spring test pressure

Place the spring on a flat surface next to a square. Measure the height of the spring, and rotate it against the edge of the square to measure distortion. If spring height varies (by comparison) by more than $1/16''$ or if distortion exceeds $1/16''$, replace the spring.

**In addition to evaluating the spring as above, test the spring pressure at the installed and compressed (installed height minus valve lift) height using a valve spring tester. Springs used on small displacement engines (up to 3 liters) should be $\mp$ 1 lb of all other springs in either position. A tolerance of $\mp$ 5 lbs is permissible on larger engines.

Cylinder Head Reconditioning

Procedure	Method

*Install valve stem seals:

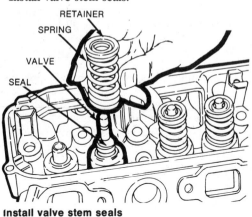

RETAINER
SPRING
VALVE
SEAL

Install valve stem seals

* Due to the pressure differential that exists at the ends of the intake valve guides (atmospheric pressure above, manifold vacuum below), oil is drawn through the valve guides into the intake port. This has been alleviated somewhat since the addition of positive crankcase ventilation, which lowers the pressure above the guides. Several types of valve stem seals are available to rocker arms and balls, and install them on the the stem and guide boss, while others require that the boss be machined. Recently, Teflon guide seals have become popular. Consult a parts supplier or machinist concerning availability and suggested usages.

NOTE: *When installing seals, ensure that a small amount of oil is able to pass the seal to lubricate the valve guides; otherwise, excessive wear may result.*

Install the valves:

See the engine service procedures earlier in this chapter for details concerning specific engines.

Lubricate the valve stems, and install the valves in the cylinder head as numbered. Lubricate and position the seals (if used) and the valve springs. Install the spring retainers, compress the springs, and insert the keys using needle-nose pliers or a tool designed for this purpose.

NOTE: *Retain the keys with wheel bearing grease during installation.*

Check valve spring installed height:

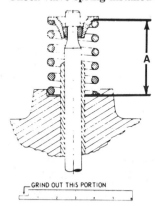

A

Measure the valve spring installed height (A) with a modified steel rule

GRIND OUT THIS PORTION

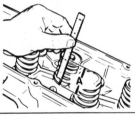

A

Valve spring installed height (A)

Measure the distance between the spring pad and the lower edge of the spring retainer, and compare to specifications. If the installed height is incorrect, add shim washers between the spring pad and the spring.

CAUTION: *Use only washers designed for this purpose.*

Install the camshaft (OHC engines only) and check end-play:

See the engine service procedures earlier in this chapter for details concerning specific engines.

Cylinder Head Reconditioning

Procedure	Method

Inspect the rocker arms, balls, studs, and nuts (OHV engines only):

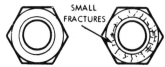

SMALL FRACTURES

Stress cracks in the rocker nuts

Visually inspect the rocker arms, balls, studs, and nuts for cracks, galling, burning, scoring, or wear. If all parts are intact, liberally lubricate the rocker arms and balls, and install them on the cylinder head. If wear is noted on a rocker arm at the point of valve contact, grind it smooth and square, removing as little material as possible. Replace the rocker arm if excessively worn. If a rocker stud shows signs of wear, it must be replaced (see below). If a rocker nut shows stress cracks, replace it. If an exhaust ball is galled or burned, substitute the intake ball from the same cylinder (if it is intact), and install a new intake ball.

NOTE: *Avoid using new rocker balls on exhaust valves.*

Replacing rocker studs (OHV engines only):

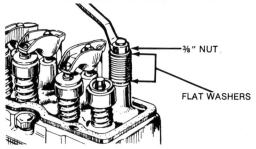

AS STUB BEGINS TO PULL UP, IT WILL BE NECESSARY TO REMOVE THE NUT AND ADD MORE WASHERS

⅜″ NUT

FLAT WASHERS

Extracting a pressed-in rocker stud

In order to remove a threaded stud, lock two nuts on the stud, and unscrew the stud using the lower nut. Coat the lower threads of the new stud with Loctite, and install.

Two alternative methods are available for replacing pressed in studs. Remove the damaged stud using a stack of washers and a nut (see illustration). In the first, the boss is reamed .005–.006″ oversize, and an oversize stud pressed in. Control the stud extension over the boss using washers, in the same manner as valve guides. Before installing the stud, coat it with white lead and grease. To retain the stud more positively drill a hole through the stud and boss, and install a roll pin. In the second method, the boss is tapped, and a threaded stud installed.

Ream the stud bore for oversize rocker studs

Inspect the rocker shaft(s) and rocker arms (OHV engines only)

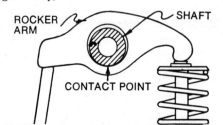

ROCKER ARM

SHAFT

CONTACT POINT

Check the rocker arm-to-rocker shaft contact area

Remove rocker arms, springs and washers from rocker shaft.

NOTE: *Lay out parts in the order as they are removed.* Inspect rocker arms for pitting or wear on the valve contact point, or excessive bushing wear. Bushings need only be replaced if wear is excessive, because the rocker arm normally contacts the shaft at one point only. Grind the valve contact point of rocker arm smooth if necessary, removing as little material as possible. If excessive material must be removed to smooth and square the arm, it should be replaced. Clean out all oil holes and passages in rocker shaft. If shaft is grooved or worn, replace it. Lubricate and assemble the rocker shaft.

Cylinder Head Reconditioning

Procedure	Method
Inspect the pushrods (OHV engines only):	Remove the pushrods, and, if hollow, clean out the oil passages using fine wire. Roll each pushrod over a piece of clean glass. If a distinct clicking sound is heard as the pushrod rolls, the rod is bent, and must be replaced.
	*The length of all pushrods must be equal. Measure the length of the pushrods, compare to specifications, and replace as necessary.
Inspect the valve lifters (OHV engines only): 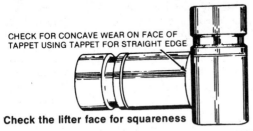 CHECK FOR CONCAVE WEAR ON FACE OF TAPPET USING TAPPET FOR STRAIGHT EDGE **Check the lifter face for squareness**	Remove lifters from their bores, and remove gum and varnish, using solvent. Clean walls of lifter bores. Check lifters for concave wear as illustrated. If face is worn concave, replace lifter, and carefully inspect the camshaft. Lightly lubricate lifter and insert it into its bore. If play is excessive, an oversize lifter must be installed (where possible). Consult a machinist concerning feasibility. If play is satisfactory, remove, lubricate, and reinstall the lifter.
*Testing hydraulic lifter leak down (OHV engines only):	Submerge lifter in a container of kerosene. Chuck a used pushrod or its equivalent into a drill press. Position container of kerosene so pushrod acts on the lifter plunger. Pump lifter with the drill press, until resistance increases. Pump several more times to bleed any air out of lifter. Apply very firm, constant pressure to the lifter, and observe rate at which fluid bleeds out of lifter. If the fluid bleeds very quickly (less than 15 seconds), lifter is defective. If the time exceeds 60 seconds, lifter is sticking. In either case, recondition or replace lifter. If lifter is operating properly (leak down time 15–60 seconds), lubricate and install it.

Cylinder Block Reconditioning

Procedure	Method
Checking the main bearing clearance: 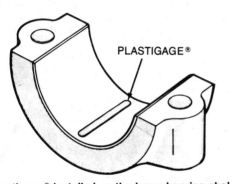 PLASTIGAGE® **Plastigage® installed on the lower bearing shell**	Invert engine, and remove cap from the bearing to be checked. Using a clean, dry rag, thoroughly clean all oil from crankshaft journal and bearing insert. NOTE: *Plastigage® is soluble in oil; therefore, oil on the journal or bearing could result in erroneous readings.* Place a piece of Plastigage along the full length of journal, reinstall cap, and torque to specifications. NOTE: *Specifications are given in the engine specifications earlier in this chapter.* Remove bearing cap, and determine bearing clearance by comparing width of Plastigage to the scale on Plastigage envelope. Journal taper is determined by comparing width of the Plastigage strip near its ends. Rotate crankshaft 90° and retest, to determine journal eccentricity. NOTE: *Do not rotate crankshaft with Plastigage*

Cylinder Block Reconditioning

Procedure	Method

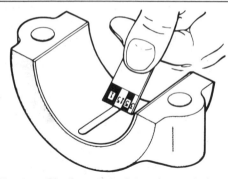

Measure Plastigage® to determine main bearing clearance

installed. If bearing insert and journal appear intact, and are within tolerances, no further main bearing service is required. If bearing or journal appear defective, cause of failure should be determined before replacement.

* Remove crankshaft from block (see below). Measure the main bearing journals at each end tiwce (90° apart) using a micrometer, to determine diameter, journal taper and eccentricity. If journals are within tolerances, reinstall bearing caps at their specified torque. Using a telescope gauge and micrometer, measure bearing I.D. parallel to piston axis and at 30° on each side of piston axis. Subtract journal O.D. from bearing I.D. to determine oil clearance. If crankshaft journals appear defective, or do not meet tolerances, there is no need to measure bearings; for the crankshaft will require grinding and/or undersize bearings will be required. If bearing appears defective, cause for failure should be determined prior to replacement.

Check the connecting rod bearing clearance:

Connecting rod bearing clearance is checked in the same manner as main bearing clearance, using Plastigage. Before removing the crankshaft, connecting rod side clearance also should be measured and recorded.

* Checking connecting rod bearing clearance, using a micrometer, is identical to checking main bearing clearance. If no other service is required, the piston and rod assemblies need not be removed.

Remove the crankshaft:

Using a punch, mark the corresponding main bearing caps and saddles according to position (i.e., one punch on the front main cap and saddle, two on the second, three on the third, etc.). Using number stamps, identify the corresponding connecting rods and caps, according to cylinder (if no numbers are present). Remove the main and connecting rod caps, and place sleeves of plastic tubing or vacuum hose over the connecting rod bolts, to protect the journals as the crankshaft is removed. Lift the crankshaft out of the block.

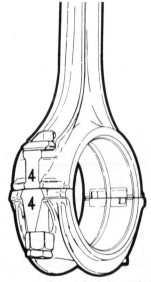

Match the connecting rod to the cylinder with a number stamp

Match the connecting rod and cap with scribe marks

Cylinder Block Reconditioning

Procedure	Method
Remove the ridge from the top of the cylinder: 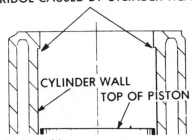 RIDGE CAUSED BY CYLINDER WEAR — CYLINDER WALL — TOP OF PISTON **Cylinder bore ridge**	In order to facilitate removal of the piston and connecting rod, the ridge at the top of the cylinder (unworn area; see illustration) must be removed. Place the piston at the bottom of the bore, and cover it with a rag. Cut the ridge away using a ridge reamer, exercising extreme care to avoid cutting too deeply. Remove the rag, and remove cuttings that remain on the piston. **CAUTION:** *If the ridge is not removed, and new rings are installed, damage to rings will result.*
Remove the piston and connecting rod: 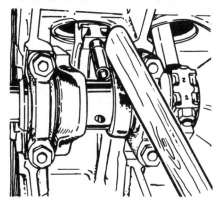 **Push the piston out with a hammer handle**	Invert the engine, and push the pistons and connecting rods out of the cylinders. If necessary, tap the connecting rod boss with a wooden hammer handle, to force the piston out. **CAUTION:** *Do not attempt to force the piston past the cylinder ridge* (see above).
Service the crankshaft:	Ensure that all oil holes and passages in the crankshaft are open and free of sludge. If necessary, have the crankshaft ground to the largest possible undersize.
	** Have the crankshaft Magnafluxed, to locate stress cracks. Consult a machinist concerning additional service procedures, such as surface hardening (e.g., nitriding, Tuftriding) to improve wear characteristics, cross drilling and chamfering the oil holes to improve lubrication, and balancing.
Removing freeze plugs:	Drill a small hole in the middle of the freeze plugs. Thread a large sheet metal screw into the hole and remove the plug with a slide hammer.
Remove the oil gallery plugs:	Threaded plugs should be removed using an appropriate (usually square) wrench. To remove soft, pressed in plugs, drill a hole in the plug, and thread in a sheet metal screw. Pull the plug out by the screw using pliers.
Hot-tank the block: **NOTE:** *Do not hot-tank aluminum parts.*	Have the block hot-tanked to remove grease, corrosion, and scale from the water jackets. **NOTE:** *Consult the operator to determine whether the camshaft bearings will be damaged during the hot-tank process.*

Cylinder Block Reconditioning

Procedure	Method

Check the block for cracks:	Visually inspect the block for cracks or chips. The most common locations are as follows:
	    Adjacent to freeze plugs.
	    Between the cylinders and water jackets.
	    Adjacent to the main bearing saddles.
	    At the extreme bottom of the cylinders.
	Check only suspected cracks using spot check dye (see introduction). If a crack is located, consult a machinist concerning possible repairs.

	** Magnaflux the block to locate hidden cracks. If cracks are located, consult a machinist about feasibility of repair.
Install the oil gallery plugs and freeze plugs:	Coat freeze plugs with sealer and tap into position using a piece of pipe, slightly smaller than the plug, as a driver. To ensure retention, stake the edges of the plugs. Coat threaded oil gallery plugs with sealer and install. Drive replacement soft plugs into block using a large drift as driver.
	* Rather than reinstalling lead plugs, drill and tap the holes, and install threaded plugs.
Check the bore diameter and surface:	Visually inspect the cylinder bores for roughness, scoring, or scuffing. If evident, the cylinder bore must be bored or honed oversize to eliminate imperfections, and the smallest possible oversize piston used. The new pistons should be given to the machinist with the block, so that the cylinders can be bored or honed exactly to the piston size (plus clearance). If no flaws are evident, measure the bore diameter using a telescope gauge and micrometer, or dial gauge, parallel and perpendicular to the engine centerline, at the top (below the ridge) and bottom of the bore. Subtract the bottom measurements from the top to determine taper, and the parallel to the centerline measurements from the perpendicular measurements to determine eccentricity. If the measurements are not within specifications, the cylinder must be bored or honed, and an oversize piston installed. If the measurements are within specifications the cylinder may be used as is, with only finish honing (see below).

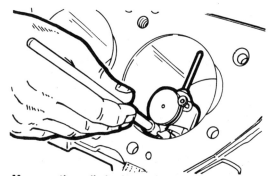

Measure the cylinder bore with a dial gauge

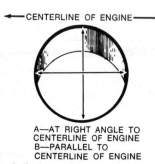

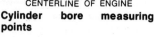

A—AT RIGHT ANGLE TO CENTERLINE OF ENGINE
B—PARALLEL TO CENTERLINE OF ENGINE

Cylinder bore measuring points

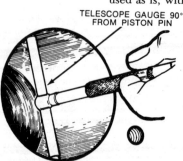

Measure the cylinder bore with a telescope gauge

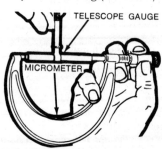

Measure the telescope gauge with a micrometer to determine the cylinder bore

Cylinder Block Reconditioning

Procedure	Method
	NOTE: *Prior to submitting the block for boring, perform the following operation(s).*
Check the cylinder block bearing alignment: 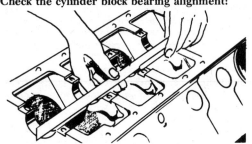 **Check the main bearing saddle alignment**	Remove the upper bearing inserts. Place a straightedge in the bearing saddles along the centerline of the crankshaft. If clearance exists between the straightedge and the center saddle, the block must be alignbored.
*Check the deck height:	The deck height is the distance from the crankshaft centerline to the block deck. To measure, invert the engine, and install the crankshaft, retaining it with the center main cap. Measure the distance from the crankshaft journal to the block deck, parallel to the cylinder centerline. Measure the diameter of the end (front and rear) main journals, parallel to the centerline of the cylinders, divide the diameter in half, and subtract it from the previous measurement. The results of the front and rear measurements should be identical. If the difference exceeds .005″, the deck height should be corrected. NOTE: *Block deck height and warpage should be corrected at the same time.*
Check the block deck for warpage:	Using a straightedge and feeler gauges, check the block deck for warpage in the same manner that the cylinder head is checked (see Cylinder Head Reconditioning). If warpage exceeds specifications, have the deck resurfaced. NOTE: *In certain cases a specification for total material removal (Cylinder head and block deck) is provided. This specification must not be exceeded.*
Clean and inspect the pistons and connecting rods: 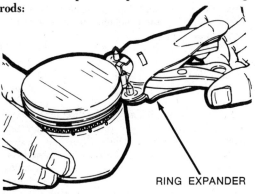 RING EXPANDER **Remove the piston rings**	Using a ring expander, remove the rings from the piston. Remove the retaining rings (if so equipped) and remove piston pin. NOTE: *If the piston pin must be pressed out, determine the proper method and use the proper tools; otherwise the piston will distort.* Clean the ring grooves using an appropriate tool, exercising care to avoid cutting too deeply. Thoroughly clean all carbon and varnish from the piston with solvent. CAUTION: *Do not use a wire brush or caustic solvent on pistons.* Inspect the pistons for scuffing, scoring, cracks, pitting, or excessive ring groove wear. If wear is evident, the piston must be replaced. Check the connecting rod length by measuring the rod from the inside of the large end to the

Cylinder Block Reconditioning

Procedure	Method

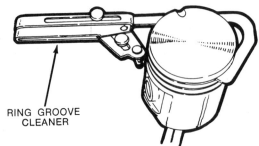

RING GROOVE
CLEANER

Clean the piston ring grooves

inside of the small end using calipers (see illustration). All connecting rods should be equal length. Replace any rod that differs from the others in the engine.

* Have the connecting rod alignment checked in an alignment fixture by a machinist. Replace any twisted or bent rods.

* Magnaflux the connecting rods to locate stress cracks. If cracks are found, replace the connecting rod.

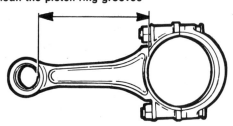

Check the connecting rod length (arrow)

Fit the pistons to the cylinders:

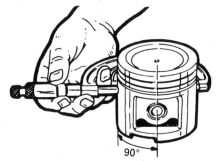

90°

Measure the piston prior to fitting

Using a telescope gauge and micrometer, or a dial gauge, measure the cylinder bore diameter perpendicular to the piston pin, 2½″ below the deck. Measure the piston perpendicular to its pin on the skirt. The difference between the two measurements is the piston clearance. If the clearance is within specifications or slightly below (after boring or honing), finish honing is all that is required. If the clearance is excessive, try to obtain a slightly larger piston to bring clearance within specifications. Where this is not possible, obtain the first oversize piston, and hone (or if necessary, bore) the cylinder to size.

Assemble the pistons and connecting rods:

Install the piston pin lock-rings (if used)

Inspect piston pin, connecting rod small end bushing, and piston bore for galling, scoring, or excessive wear. If evident, replace defective part(s). Measure the I.D. of the piston boss and connecting rod small end, and the O.D. of the piston pin. If within specifications, assemble piston pin and rod.
CAUTION: *If piston pin must be pressed in, determine the proper method and use the proper tools; otherwise the piston will distort.*
Install the lock rings; ensure that they seat properly. If the parts are not within specifications, determine the service method for the type of engine. In some cases, piston and pin are serviced as an assembly when either is defective. Others specify reaming the piston and connecting rods for an oversize pin. If the connecting rod bushing is worn, it may in many cases be replaced. Reaming the piston and replacing the rod bushing are machine shop operations.

Cylinder Block Reconditioning

Procedure	Method

Clean and inspect the camshaft:

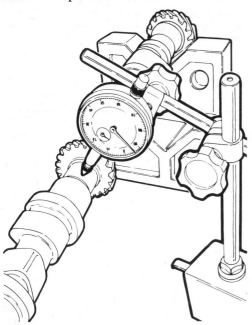

Check the camshaft for straightness

Degrease the camshaft, using solvent, and clean out all oil holes. Visually inspect cam lobes and bearing journals for excessive wear. If a lobe is questionable, check all lobes as indicated below. If a journal or lobe is worn, the camshaft must be reground or replaced.

NOTE: *If a journal is worn, there is a good chance that the bushings are worn.* If lobes and journals appear intact, place the front and rear journals in V-blocks, and rest a dial indicator on the center journal. Rotate the camshaft to check straightness. If deviation exceeds .001″, replace the camshaft.

*Check the camshaft lobes with a micrometer, by measuring the lobes from the nose to base and again at 90° (see illustration). The lift is determined by subtracting the second measurement from the first. If all exhaust lobes and all intake lobes are not identical, the camshaft must be reground or replaced.

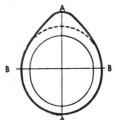

Camshaft lobe measurement

Replace the camshaft bearings (OHV engines only):

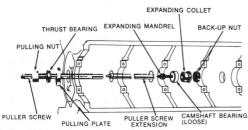

Camshaft bearing removal and installation tool (OHV engines only)

If excessive wear is indicated, or if the engine is being completely rebuilt, camshaft bearings should be replaced as follows: Drive the camshaft rear plug from the block. Assemble the removal puller with its shoulder on the bearing to be removed. Gradually tighten the puller nut until bearing is removed. Remove remaining bearings, leaving the front and rear for last. To remove front and rear bearings, reverse position of the tool, so as to pull the bearings in toward the center of the block. Leave the tool in this position, pilot the new front and rear bearings on the installer, and pull them into position: Return the tool to its original position and pull remaining bearings into position.

NOTE: *Ensure that oil holes align when installing bearings.* Replace camshaft rear plug, and stake it into position to aid retention.

Finish hone the cylinders:

Chuck a flexible drive hone into a power drill, and insert it into the cylinder. Start the hone, and move it up and down in the cylinder at a rate which will produce approximately a 60° cross-hatch pattern.

NOTE: *Do not extend the hone below the cylin-*

Cylinder Block Reconditioning

Procedure	Method

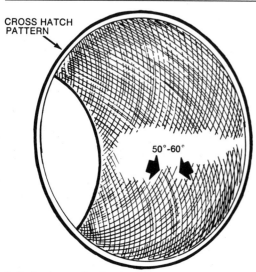

CROSS HATCH PATTERN

50°-60°

Cylinder bore after honing

der bore. After developing the pattern, remove the hone and recheck piston fit. Wash the cylinders with a detergent and water solution to remove abrasive dust, dry, and wipe several times with a rag soaked in engine oil.

Check piston ring end-gap:

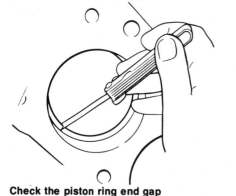

Check the piston ring end gap

Compress the piston rings to be used in a cylinder, one at a time, into that cylinder, and press them approximately 1″ below the deck with an inverted piston. Using feeler gauges, measure the ring end-gap, and compare to specifications. Pull the ring out of the cylinder and file the ends with a fine file to obtain proper clearance.
CAUTION: *If inadequate ring end-gap is utilized, ring breakage will result.*

Install the piston rings:

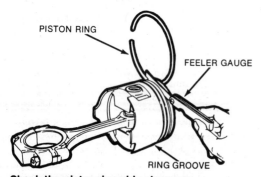

PISTON RING

FEELER GAUGE

RING GROOVE

Check the piston ring side clearance

Inspect the ring grooves in the piston for excessive wear or taper. If necessary, recut the grooves(s) for use with an overwidth ring or a standard ring and spacer. If the groove is worn uniformly, overwidth rings, or standard rings and spacers may be installed without recutting. Roll the outside of the ring around the groove to check for burrs or deposits. If any are found, remove with a fine file. Hold the ring in the groove, and measure side clearance. If necessary, correct as indicated above.
NOTE: *Always install any additional spacers above the piston ring.*
The ring groove must be deep enough to allow the ring to seat below the lands (see illustration). In many cases, a "go-no-go" depth gauge will be provided with the piston rings. Shallow grooves may be corrected by recutting, while deep grooves require some type of filler or expander behind the piston. Consult the piston ring sup-

Cylinder Block Reconditioning

Procedure	Method
	plier concerning the suggested method. Install the rings on the piston, lowest ring first, using a ring expander. NOTE: *Position the ring as specified by the manufacturer.* Consult the engine service procedures earlier in this chapter for details concerning specific engines.
Install the camshaft (OHV engines only):	Liberally lubricate the camshaft lobes and journals, and install the camshaft. CAUTION: *Exercise extreme care to avoid damaging the bearings when inserting the camshaft.* Install and tighten the camshaft thrust plate retaining bolts. See the engine service procedures earlier in this chapter for details concerning specific engines.
Check camshaft end-play (OHV engines only): 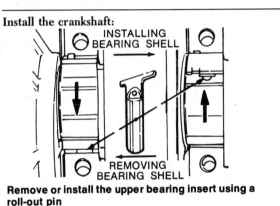 **Check the camshaft end-play with a feeler gauge** DIAL INDICATOR CAMSHAFT **Check the camshaft end-play with a dial indicator**	Using feeler gauges, determine whether the clearance between the camshaft boss (or gear) and backing plate is within specifications. Install shims behind the thrust plate, or reposition the camshaft gear and retest endplay. In some cases, adjustment is by replacing the thrust plate. See the engine service procedures earlier in this chapter for details concerning specific engines. * Mount a dial indicator stand so that the stem of the dial indicator rests on the nose of the camshaft, parallel to the camshaft axis. Push the camshaft as far in as possible and zero the gauge. Move the camshaft outward to determine the amount of camshaft endplay. If the endplay is not within tolerance, install shims behind the thrust plate, or reposition the camshaft gear and retest. See the engine service procedures earlier in this chapter for details concerning specific engines.
Install the rear main seal:	See the engine service procedures earlier in this chapter for details concerning specific engines.
Install the crankshaft: INSTALLING BEARING SHELL REMOVING BEARING SHELL **Remove or install the upper bearing insert using a roll-out pin**	Thoroughly clean the main bearing saddles and caps. Place the upper halves of the bearing inserts on the saddles and press into position. NOTE: *Ensure that the oil holes align.* Press the corresponding bearing inserts into the main bearing caps. Lubricate the upper main bearings, and lay the crankshaft in position. Place a strip of Plastigage on each of the crankshaft journals, install the main caps, and torque to specifications. Remove the main caps, and compare the Plastigage to the scale on the Plastigage envelope. If clearances are within tolerances, remove the Plastigage, turn the crankshaft 90°, wipe off all oil and retest. If all clearances are correct, re-

Cylinder Block Reconditioning

Procedure	Method

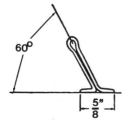

Home-made bearing roll-out pin

move all Plastigage, thoroughly lubricate the main caps and bearing journals, and install the main caps. If clearances are not within tolerance, the upper bearing inserts may be removed, without removing the crankshaft, using a bearing roll out pin (see illustration). Roll in a bearing that will provide proper clearance, and retest. Torque all main caps, excluding the thrust bearing cap, to specifications. Tighten the thrust bearing cap finger tight. To properly align the thrust bearing, pry the crankshaft the extent of its axial travel several times, the last movement held toward the front of the engine, and torque the thrust bearing cap to specifications. Determine the crankshaft end-play (see below), and bring within tolerance with thrust washers.

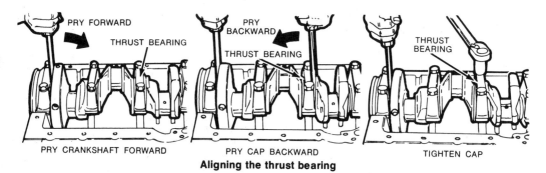

Aligning the thrust bearing

Measure crankshaft end-play:

Mount a dial indicator stand on the front of the block, with the dial indicator stem resting on the nose of the crankshaft, parallel to the crankshaft axis. Pry the crankshaft the extent of its travel rearward, and zero the indicator. Pry the crankshaft forward and record crankshaft end-play.
NOTE: *Crankshaft end-play also may be measured at the thrust bearing, using feeler gauges (see illustration).*

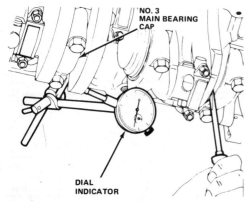

Check the crankshaft end-play with a dial indicator

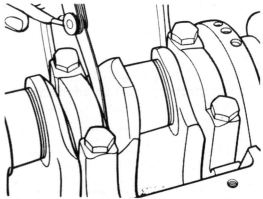

Check the crankshaft end-play with a feeler gauge

Cylinder Block Reconditioning

Procedure	Method

Install the pistons:

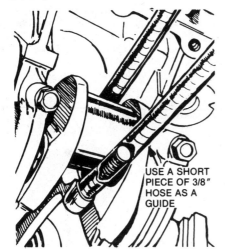

USE A SHORT
PIECE OF 3/8"
HOSE AS A
GUIDE

Use lengths of vacuum hose or rubber tubing to protect the crankshaft journals and cylinder walls during piston installation

RING COMPRESSOR

Install the piston using a ring compressor

Press the upper connecting rod bearing halves into the connecting rods, and the lower halves into the connecting rod caps. Position the piston ring gaps according to specifications (see car section), and lubricate the pistons. Install a ring compresser on a piston, and press two long (8") pieces of plastic tubing over the rod bolts. Using the tubes as a guide, press the pistons into the bores and onto the crankshaft with a wooden hammer handle. After seating the rod on the crankshaft journal, remove the tubes and install the cap finger tight. Install the remaining pistons in the same manner. Invert the engine and check the bearing clearance at two points (90° apart) on each journal with Plastigage.

NOTE: *Do not turn the crankshaft with Plastigage installed.* If clearance is within tolerances, remove *all* Plastigage, thoroughly lubricate the journals, and torque the rod caps to specifications. If clearance is not within specifications, install different thickness bearing inserts and recheck.

CAUTION: *Never shim or file the connecting rods or caps.* Always install plastic tube sleeves over the rod bolts when the caps are not installed, to protect the crankshaft journals.

Check connecting rod side clearance:

Check the connecting rod side clearance with a feeler gauge

Determine the clearance between the sides of the connecting rods and the crankshaft, using feeler gauges. If clearance is below the minimum tolerance, the rod may be machined to provide adequate clearance. If clearance is excessive, substitute an unworn rod, and recheck. If clearance is still outside specifications, the crankshaft must be welded and reground, or replaced.

Inspect the timing chain (or belt):

Visually inspect the timing chain for broken or loose links, and replace the chain if any are found. If the chain will flex sideways, it must be replaced. Install the timing chain as specified. Be sure the timing belt is not stretched, frayed or broken.

NOTE: *If the original timing chain is to be reused, install it in its original position.*

Cylinder Block Reconditioning

Procedure	Method
Check timing gear backlash and runout (OHV engines):	Mount a dial indicator with its stem resting on a tooth of the camshaft gear (as illustrated). Rotate the gear until all slack is removed, and zero the indicator. Rotate the gear in the opposite direction until slack is removed, and record gear backlash. Mount the indicator with its stem resting on the edge of the camshaft gear, parallel to the axis of the camshaft. Zero the indicator, and turn the camshaft gear one full turn, recording the runout. If either backlash or runout exceed specifications, replace the worn gear(s).

Check the camshaft gear backlash

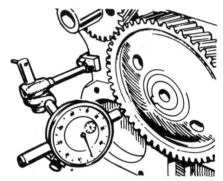

Check the camshaft gear run-out

Completing the Rebuilding Process

Following the above procedures, complete the rebuilding process as follows:

Fill the oil pump with oil, to prevent cavitating (sucking air) on initial engine start up. Install the oil pump and the pickup tube on the engine. Coat the oil pan gasket as necessary, and install the gasket and the oil pan. Mount the flywheel and the crankshaft vibration damper or pulley on the crankshaft. NOTE: *Always use new bolts when installing the flywheel.* Inspect the clutch shaft pilot bushing in the crankshaft. If the bushing is excessively worn, remove it with an expanding puller and a slide hammer, and tap a new bushing into place.

Position the engine, cylinder head side up. Lubricate the lifters, and install them into their bores. Install the cylinder head, and torque it as specified. Insert the pushrods (where applicable), and install the rocker shaft(s) (if so equipped) or position the rocker arms on the pushrods. Adjust the valves.

Install the intake and exhaust manifolds, the carburetor(s), the distributor and spark plugs. Adjust the point gap and the static ignition timing. Mount all accessories and install the engine in the car. Fill the radiator with coolant, and the crankcase with high quality engine oil.

Break-in Procedure

Start the engine, and allow it to run at low speed for a few minutes, while checking for leaks. Stop the engine, check the oil level, and fill as necessary. Restart the engine, and fill the cooling system to capacity. Check the point dwell angle and adjust the ignition timing and the valves. Run the engine at low to medium speed (800–2500 rpm) for approximately ½ hour, and retorque the cylinder head bolts. Road test the car, and check again for leaks.

Follow the manufacturer's recommended engine break-in procedure and maintenance schedule for new engines.

Emission Controls and Fuel System

EMISSION CONTROLS

There are three basic sources of automotive pollution in the modern internal combustion engine. They are the crankcase with its accompanying blowby vapors, the fuel system with its evaporation of unburned gasoline, and the combustion chambers with their resulting exhaust emissions. Pollution arising from the incomplete combustion of fuel generally falls into three categories: hydrocarbons (HC), carbon monoxide (CO), and oxides of nitrogen (NO$_x$).

Positive Crankcase Ventilation System

All Mustang II models are equipped with a closed positive crankcase ventilation (PCV) system to control crankcase blow-by vapors. The system consists of a PCV valve and oil separator mounted behind the distributor (4 cylinder) or mounted on top of the valve cover (V6 and V8), a non-ventilated oil filler cap, and a pair of hoses supplying filtered intake air to the valve cover and delivering the crankcase vapors to the intake manifold or carburetor spacer.

The system functions as follows:

When the engine is running, a small portion of the gases which are formed in the

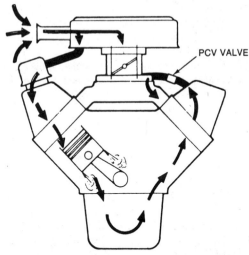

Positive crankcase ventilation system operation —V8 shown

combustion chamber leak by the piston rings and enter the crankcase. Since these gases are under pressure, they tend to escape from the crankcase and enter the atmosphere. If these gases are allowed to remain in the crankcase for any period of time, they contaminate the engine oil and cause sludge to build up in the crankcase. If the gases are allowed to escape into the atmosphere, they pollute the air, with burned hydrocarbons. The job of the crankcase emission control equipment is to recycle these gases back into the engine combustion chamber where they are reburned.

The crankcase (blow-by) gases are recycled in the following way: as the engine is running, clean, filtered air is drawn through the air filter and into the crankcase. As the air passes through the crankcase, it picks up the combustion gases and carries them out of the crankcase, through the oil separator, through the PCV valve, and into the induction system. As they enter the intake manifold, they are drawn into the combustion chamber where they are reburned.

The most critical component in the system is the PCV valve. This valve controls the amount of gases which are recycled into the combustion chamber. At low engine speeds, the valve is partially closed, limiting the flow of the gases into the intake manifold. As engine speed increases, the valve opens to admit greater quantities of the gases into the intake manifold. If the valve should become blocked or plugged, the gases will be prevented from escaping from the crankcase by the normal route. Since these gases are under pressure, they will find their own way out of the crankcase. This route is usually a weak oil seal or gasket in the engine. As the gas escapes by the gasket, it also creates an oil leak. Besides causing oil leaks, a clogged PCV valve also allows these gases to remain in the crankcase for an extended period of time, promoting the formation of sludge in the engine.

Fuel Evaporative Control System

All Mustang II models are equipped with a fuel evaporative control system to prevent the evaporation of unburned gasoline. The system consists of a special vacuum/pressure relief filler cap, an expansion area at the top of the fuel tank, a foam-filled vapor separator mounted on top of the fuel tank, a carbon canister which stores fuel vapors and hoses which connect this equipment. The carburetor fuel bowl vapors are retained within the fuel bowl until the engine is started, at which point they are vented into the engine for burning.

The system functions as follows:

Changes in atmospheric temperature cause the gasoline in the fuel tank to expand or contract. If this expansion and consequent vaporization takes place in a conventional

fuel tank, the fuel vapors escape through the filler cap or vent hose and pollute the atmosphere. The fuel evaporative emission control system prevents this by routing the gasoline vapors to the engine where they are burned.

As the gasoline in the fuel tank of a parked car begins to expand due to heat, the vapor which forms moves to the top of the fuel tank. The fuel tanks on all Mustang II models are designed with an area representing 10–20% of the total fuel tank volume above the level of the fuel tank filler tube where these gases may collect. The gases then travel upward into the vapor separator which prevents liquid gasoline from escaping from the fuel tank.

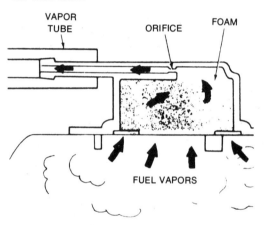

Fuel vapors entering vapor separator

The fuel vapor is then drawn through the vapor separator outlet hose and into the charcoal canister in the engine compartment. The vapor enters the canister, passes through a charcoal filter, and then exits through the canister's grated bottom. As the vapor passes through the charcoal, it is cleansed of hydrocarbons, so that the air which passes out of the bottom of the canister is free of pollutants.

When the engine is started, vacuum from the carburetor draws fresh air into the canister. As the entering air passes through the charcoal, it picks up hydrocarbons which were deposited there by the fuel vapors. This mixture of hydrocarbons and fesh air is then carried through a hose to the air cleaner. In the carburetor, it combines with the incoming air/fuel mixture and enters the combustion chambers of the engine where it is burned.

There still remains the problem of allowing air into the fuel tank to replace the gasoline

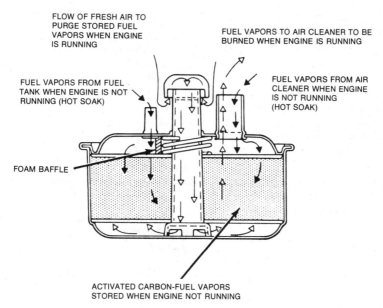

FLOW OF FRESH AIR TO
PURGE STORED FUEL
VAPORS WHEN ENGINE
IS RUNNING

FUEL VAPORS TO AIR CLEANER TO BE
BURNED WHEN ENGINE IS RUNNING

FUEL VAPORS FROM FUEL
TANK WHEN ENGINE IS NOT
RUNNING (HOT SOAK)

FUEL VAPORS FROM AIR
CLEANER WHEN ENGINE
IS NOT RUNNING
(HOT SOAK)

FOAM BAFFLE

ACTIVATED CARBON-FUEL VAPORS
STORED WHEN ENGINE NOT RUNNING

Cross-section of charcoal canister

displaced during normal use and the problem of relieving excess pressure from the tank should it reach a dangerous level. The special filler cap performs this task. Under normal circumstances, the filler cap functions as a check valve, allowing air to enter the tank to replace the fuel which is consumed, while preventing vapors from escaping from the cap. In case of severe pressure within the tank, the filler cap valve opens, venting the vapors to the atmosphere.

Improved Combustion System

All Mustang II models, regardless of other exhaust emission control equipment, are equipped with the Improved Combustion (IMCO) System for controlling emissions arising from the incomplete combusion of fuel. The IMCO system incorporates a number of modifications in the distributor spark control system, the fuel system, and the internal design of the engine.

Internal engine modifications include the following: elimination of surface irregularities and crevices as well as a low surface area-to-volume ratio in the combustion chambers, a high-velocity intake manifold combined with short exhaust ports, selective valve timing and a higher temperature and capacity cooling system.

Modifications to the fuel system include the following: recalibrated carburetors to achieve a leaner air/fuel mixture, more precise calibration of the choke mechanism, the installation of idle mixture limiter caps, a fuel deceleration valve, and a heated air intake system. Some models employ the 2700VV carburetor, introduced in 1977. This carburetor has a venturi valve which effectively varies the size of the carburetor venturi so that the velocity of the air passing through the venturi is almost constant. This provides more consistent atomization and mixing of fuel at all rpms and eliminates some of the complex auxiliary circuits (such as the idle circuit) required to enable an ordinary carburetor to deliver a good mixture under a wide variety of conditions. Fuel/air ratios, however, are more constant with the variable venturi carburetor, contributing to effective emission control without adverse effects on driveability.

Modifications to the distributor spark control system include the following: a modified centrifugal advance curve, the use of dual diaphragm distributors in many applications, a ported vacuum switch on some models, and a spark delay valve in most applications.

HEATED AIR INTAKE SYSTEM

The heated air intake portion of the air cleaner consists of a bimetal switch, vacuum motor, and a spring-loaded temperature control door in the snorkel of the air cleaner. The temperature control door is located between the end of the air cleaner snorkel which draws in air from the engine compartment and the duct which carries heated air up from the exhaust manifold. When underhood temperature is below 90° F, the temperature control door blocks off underhood air from entering the air cleaner and allows only heated air from the exhaust manifold to be drawn into the air cleaner. When underhood temperature rises above 130° F, the temperature control door blocks off heated air from the exhaust manifold and allows only underhood air to be drawn into the air cleaner.

By controlling the temperature of the engine intake air this way, exhaust emissions are lowered and fuel economy is improved. In addition, throttle plate icing is reduced, and cold weather driveability is improved from the necessary leaner mixtures.

DUAL DIAPHRAGM DISTRIBUTORS

Dual diaphragm distributors are installed in most 1974 Mustang II models equipped with the 2800 cc V6, all 1975–76 models equipped with the 2800 cc V6 or 4900 cc (302 cid) V8, and 1975–76 models sold in California equipped with a 2300 cc Four and manual transmission. All 1977 and 1978 models employ the dual diaphragm distributor.

The dual distributor diaphragm is a two-chambered housing which is mounted on the side of the distributor. The outer side of the housing is a distributor vacuum advance mechanism, connected to the carburetor by a vacuum hose. The purpose of the vacuum advance is to advance ignition timing according to the conditions under which the engine is operating. This device has been used on automobiles for many years now and its chief advantage is economical engine operation. The second side of the dual diaphragm is the side that has been added to help control engine exhaust emissions at idle and during deceleration.

The inner side of the dual diaphragm is connected by a vacuum hose to the intake manifold. When the engine is idling or decelerating, intake manifold vacuum is high and carburetor vacuum is low. Under these conditions, intake manifold vacuum, applied to the inner side of the dual diaphragm, retards ignition timing to promote more complete combustion of the air fuel mixture in the engine combustion chamgers.

PORTED VACUUM SWITCH (DISTRIBUTOR VACUUM CONTROL VALVE)

A ported vacuum switch is used in all 2300 cc Mustang II models equipped with air conditioning, and in most V6 and V8 installations.

The distributor vacuum control valve is a temperature-sensitive valve which screws into the water jacket of the engine. Three vacuum lines are attached to the vacuum control valve: one which runs from the carburetor to the control valve, one which runs from the control valve to the distributor vacuum advance (outer) chamber, and one which runs from the intake manifold to the distributor vacuum control valve.

During normal engine operation, vacuum from the carburetor passes through the top nipple on the distributor control valve, through the valve to the second nipple on the valve, and out the second nipple on the valve to the distributor vacuum advance chamber. When the engine is idling however, carburetor vacuum is very low, so that there is

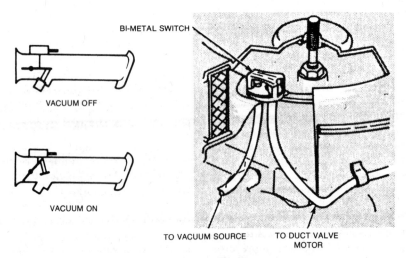

BI-METAL SWITCH

VACUUM OFF

VACUUM ON

TO VACUUM SOURCE   TO DUCT VALVE MOTOR

Vacuum-operated duct and valve assembly

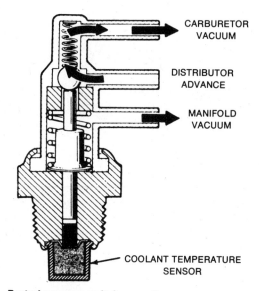

Ported-vacuum switch operation

little, if any, vacuum in the passageways described above.

If the engine should begin to overheat while idling, a check ball inside the distributor vacuum control which normally blocks off the third nipple of the valve intake manifold vacuum) moves upward to block off the first nipple (carburetor vacuum). This applies intake manifold vacuum (third nipple) to the distributor vacuum advance chamber (second nipple). Since intake manifold vacuum is very high while the engine is idling, ignition timing is advanced by the application of intake manifold vacuum to the distributor vacuum advance chamber. This raises the engine idle speed and helps to cool the engine.

SPARK DELAY VALVE (SDV) SYSTEM

The spark delay valve is a plastic, spring-loaded color coded valve which is installed in the vacuum line to the distributor advance diaphragm on most 1974–76 models.

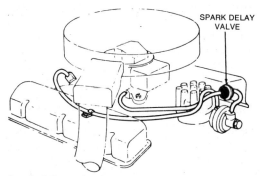

Spark delay valve installation—V8 shown

Under heavy throttle application, the valve will close, blocking normal carburetor vacuum to the distributor. After the designated period of closed time, the valve opens, restoring the carburetor vacuum to the distributor. The following chart outlines the spark delay valve applications.

NOTE: *The black side of the valve always faces the vacuum source, the carburetor.*

Valve Color	ID #	Time Delay Min.	(seconds) Max.
Black/Gray	1	1	4
Black/Brown	2	2	5
Black/White	5	4	12
Black/Yellow	10	5.8	14
Black/Blue	15	7	16
Black/Green	20	9	20
Black/Orange	30	13	24
Black/Red	40	15	28

FUEL DECELERATION VALVE

All 2300 cc and 2800 cc engines equipped with manual transmissions use a deceleration valve to control emissions during deceleration. The valve works as follows:

The deceleration valve is a vacuum-actuated valve attached to the intake manifold of the engine. A hose connects the deceleration valve to the carburetor.

Since the throttle valve(s) in the base of the carburetor are closed during deceleration, very little air/fuel mixture from the carburetor enters the intake manifold during deceleration. This causes engine speed to drop very rapidly. This rapid closing of the throttle plates also causes a high-vacuum condition in the intake manifold. This high-vacuum condition opens the deceleration valve and draws a metered air/fuel mixture from the carburetor, through the connecting hose to the deceleration valve through the deceleration valve and into the intake manifold. This additional air/fuel mixture then enters the combustion chamber and is burned. Due to this additional mixture, engine speed drops gradually instead of rapidly. This helps to lower engine exhaust emissions during deceleration.

As engine speed gradually decreases, intake manifold vacuum drops and the valve closes. The engine then operates on the normal idle mixture from the carburetor.

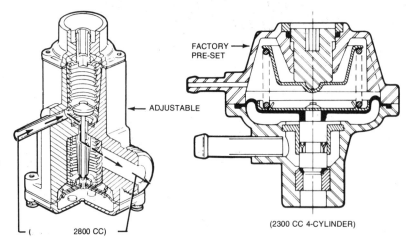

FACTORY PRE-SET

ADJUSTABLE

(2800 CC)

(2300 CC 4-CYLINDER)

Fuel deceleration valves

On 2300 cc engines, the deceleration valve used is present at the factory and cannot be adjusted. If this valve does not perform properly, replace it with a new unit.

On 2800 cc engines, a large, white nylon adjusting screw in the top of the deceleration valve determines the amount of spring pressure that is applied to the poppet valve inside the deceleration valve. The amount of spring pressure determines how much vacuum is required to open the deceleration valve and how long it will remain open. This adjustment is critical. If too much spring pressure is exerted, the deceleration valve will not open and engine emissions will be high during deceleration. If too little spring pressure is exerted, the deceleration valve will open too soon and stay open too long; it may even remain open at all times. This will result in very high engine idle speeds and excessive fuel consumption. If the diaphragm in the deceleration valve becomes ruptured, additional air will be admitted into the intake manifold. This will cause a lean air/fuel mixture, rough engine idle, and poor throttle response.

A/C MODULATED DECEL VALVE

On 1977 vehicles with the V6 engine, the deceleration valve is tied into the air conditioner. The system cannot operate unless the air conditioner is on.

ELECTRIC ASSISTED CHOKE

With this system, the choke is equipped with an electric heater and a temperature sensitive bimetallic disc. The electric heater opens the choke more rapidly when operat-

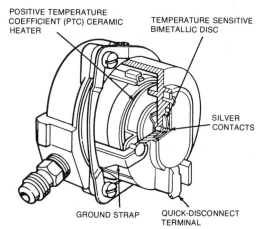

POSITIVE TEMPERATURE COEFFICIENT (PTC) CERAMIC HEATER

TEMPERATURE SENSITIVE BIMETALLIC DISC

SILVER CONTACTS

GROUND STRAP

QUICK-DISCONNECT TERMINAL

Electric assisted choke

ing conditions permit. Power is supplied to the choke only when the center terminal of the alternator is hot (alternator is charging) and when the temperature as measured by the bimetallic disc is over 60 degrees.

ELECTRIC PORTED VACUUM SWITCH

This type of Ported Vacuum Switch is used on some 1977 engines equipped with both a Thermactor air pump and a catalytic converter, and is used to provide an electric signal to other components which is based on engine temperature.

DISTRIBUTOR VACUUM VENT VALVE

Some 1978 engines are equipped with this valve, which controls vacuum advance as well as continually purging the vacuum advance line of fuel from the carburetor. When spark port vacuum is applied to the valve,

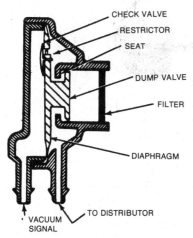

Cross section of distributor vacuum vent valve

vacuum begins to pull air at a controlled rate out of the vacuum advance diaphragm, and to purge the vacuum line of fuel. Heavy acceleration brings applied vacuum down to the point where the valve quickly relieves vacuum to the vacuum advance diaphragm to reduce emissions and to prevent the fuel from migrating to the vacuum diaphragm.

COLD START SPARK ADVANCE

This system is used to apply spark port vacuum to the vacuum advance diaphragm on some 1978 engines when the engine is cold (water temperature is below 125 degrees). The system employs its own ported vacuum switch which routes vacuum through a Distributor Retard Control Valve at lower temperatures. This valve has the function of allowing maximum vacuum to effect the vacuum advance diaphragm on the distributor and then trapping this vacuum, thus keeping the advance diaphragm in maximum advance position even when manifold vacuum drops. As temperatures rise above 125 degrees, the vacuum is ported either directly or through a Spark Delay Valve to provide a vacuum signal to the diaphragm which varies with engine operating conditions.

COLD START SPARK HOLD

Used on some 1978 engines, this system is able to provide either full intake manifold vacuum to the distributor vacuum advance diaphragm, or to apply it through a restrictor, which delays its application. When temperatures are below 128 degrees F., full vacuum is immediately applied for better driveability.

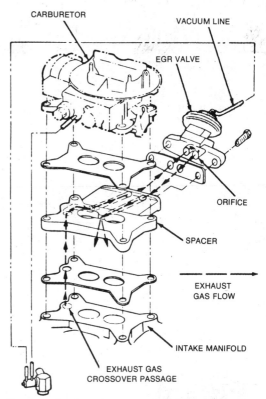

Routing of exhaust gasses through spacer

Exhaust Gas Recirculation System

All Mustang II models are equipped with an exhaust gas recirculation (EGR) system to control oxides of nitrogen. The system dilutes the air/fuel mixture in the manifold with a small amount (approx. 10%) of exhaust gases. The exhaust gases are relatively oxygen-free. Therefore, the 10% exhaust gas mixture cannot burn, tending to dilute the fuel mixture with a noncombustible inert gas. In addition, the gases absorb some of the heat of burning. This tends to lower peak combustion temperature in the cylinders resulting in lower emissions of NO_x.

On four-cylinder engines, the exhaust gases are carried in a tube from the exhaust manifold to the carburetor spacer. On V6 and V8 engines, the exhaust gases are diverted from the manifold crossover passage to the spacer. The EGR valve, which is located at the rear of the spacer, diverts a small amount of these gases into the intake charge. The valve consists of a vacuum diaphragm with an attached plunger which meters the amount of exhaust gases entering the mixture. The valve is controlled by a vacuum line from the carburetor which passes through a ported

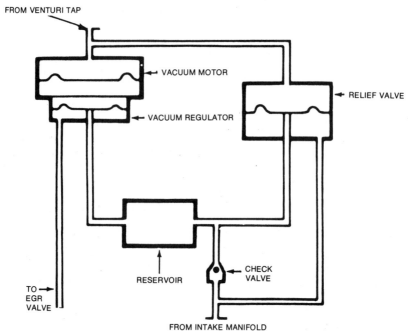

FROM VENTURI TAP

VACUUM MOTOR

RELIEF VALVE

VACUUM REGULATOR

TO EGR VALVE

RESERVOIR

CHECK VALVE

FROM INTAKE MANIFOLD

Typical venturi vacuum amplifier schematic

vacuum switch (on all models except the 1974 2800 V6). The EGR ported vacuum switch blocks vacuum (and therefore exhaust gases) from the EGR valve when the engine is cold to improve driveability. The EGR/PVS is calibrated for different engine chassis combinations and may be identified by the color code on top of the valve (the valve is installed in the heater hose connection). Calibration is as follows: green—60° F, black—85° F, plain—125° F. At the calibrated temperature, the EGR/PVS admits vacuum to the EGR valve diaphragm, permitting exhaust gases to dilute the combustion chamber mixture.

VENTURI VACUUM AMPLIFIER SYSTEM

All Mustang II models, except those 1975–76 models equipped with a 302 V8 and automatic transmission sold in California, use a venturi vacuum amplifier. The amplifier is used to boost a relatively weak venturi vacuum signal in the throat of the carburetor into a strong intake manifold vacuum signal to operate the EGR valve. This device improves driveability by more closely matching a venturi airflow and EGR flow.

The amplifier features a vacuum reservoir and check valve to maintain an adequate vacuum supply regardless of variations in engine manifold vacuum. Also used in conjunction with the amplifier, is a relief valve, which

will cancel the output EGR vacuum signal whenever the venturi vacuum signal is equal to, or greater than, the intake manifold vacuum. Thus, the EGR valve may close at or near wide-open throttle acceleration, when maximum power is needed.

EGR BACKPRESSURE TRANSDUCER

Some 1977 and 1978 EGR systems incorporate a backpressure transducer which is connected to an adapter between the EGR valve and the intake manifold. The transducer modulates the flow of exhaust gas through the EGR valve, using exhaust backpressure as an input signal, and varying amounts of manifold vacuum to the EGR valve diaphragm as an output signal.

In some models, the transducer may be an integral part of the EGR valve assembly.

EGR/CSC SYSTEM

The Exhaust Gas Recirculation and Coolant Spark Control system provides full (undelayed) spark advance to the distributor and prevents vacuum from going to the EGR valve. As coolant temperature reaches the EGR PVS opening temperature, the EGR PVS switches vacuum to the EGR valve. Vacuum is also supplied to the distributor through the Spark Delay Valve. The purpose of this system is to improve cold engine driveability.

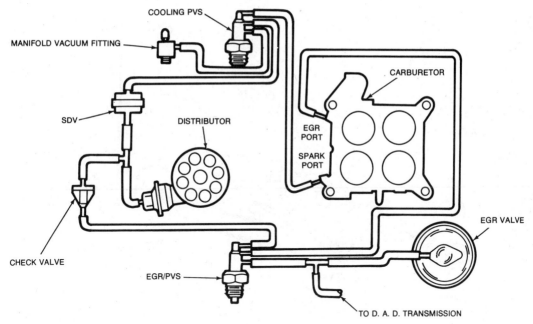

Diagram of the EGR/CSC system

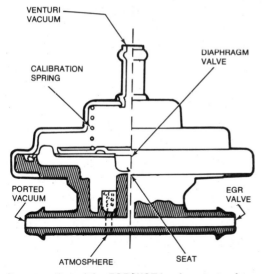

Cross section of the EGR/WOT load control valve

WIDE OPEN THROTTLE LOAD CONTROL VALVE

Some EGR systems also incorporate this system, which dumps vacuum to the diaphragm of the EGR valve when full throttle is used. A carburetor venturi vacuum signal provided to the WOT valve signals it (at very low vacuum levels) to divert EGR vacuum to the atmosphere and let the EGR valve close.

Thermactor Air Injection System

All models, except those 1974 2300 cc models sold outside of California, are equipped with a Thermactor Air Injection System to reduce exhaust emissions of HC and CO.

The Thermactor emission control system makes use of a belt-driven air pump to inject fresh air into the hot exhaust stream through the engine exhaust ports. The result is the extended burning of those fumes which were not completely ignited in the combustion chamber, and the subsequent reduction of some of the hydrocarbon and carbon monoxide content of the exhaust emissions into harmless carbon dioxide and water.

The 1974 system and the one used in later models differ slightly. The 1974 system is composed of the following components:

1. Air supply pump (belt-driven).
2. Air by-pass valve.
3. Check valves.
4. Air manifolds (internal or external).
5. Air supply tubes (on external manifolds only).

Air for the Thermactor system is cleaned by means of a centrifugal filter fan mounted on the air pump driveshaft. The air filter does not require a replaceable element.

To prevent excessive pressure, the air pump is equipped with a pressure relief valve which uses a replaceable plastic plug to control the pressure setting.

The Thermactor air pump has sealed bearings which are lubricated for the life of the unit, and pre-set rotor vane and bearing clearances, which do not require any periodic adjustments.

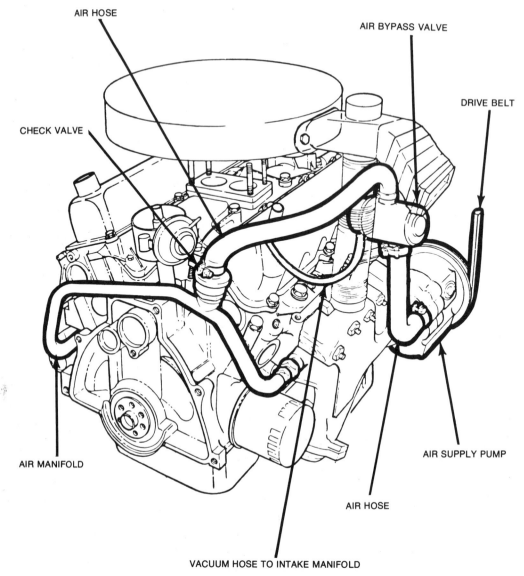

Thermactor system operation—1974 V6

The air supply from the pump is controlled by the air by-pass valve, sometimes called a dump valve. During deceleration, the air by-pass valve opens, momentarily diverting the air supply through a silencer and into the atmosphere, thus preventing backfires within the exhaust system.

A check valve is incorporated in the air inlet side of the air manifolds. Its purpose is to prevent exhaust gases from backing up into the Thermactor system. This valve is especially important in the event of drive belt failure, and during deceleration, when the air by-pass valve is dumping the air supply.

The air manifolds and air supply tubes channel the air from the Thermactor air pump into the exhaust ports of each cylinder, thus completing the cycle of the Thermactor system.

The 1975–78 system operates in a similar fashion to the 1974 system. Modifications are needed to make the air pump compatible with the catalytic reactors (converters) used in most 1975 and later cars. The changes include the following:

1. Internal manifolds (drilled passages) on all models.

2. Redesigned, full-round bore air pump.

3. Revised by-pass air valve system which

dumps air at wide-open throttle, low ambient temperature, and at excessive coolant temperature (on 302 V8 models).

4. A new Thermactor by-pass control valve.

Catalytic Reactor (Converter) System

All 1975 models, except those equipped with a 2300 cc Four or 4900 cc (302) V8 sold outside of California, are equipped with a catalytic reactor system. A single converter is used on 2300 cc installations in California and on 2800 cc V6 installations in the 49 states. Dual converters (one in each exhaust pipe) are used on all V6 and V8 installations sold in California. All 1976 and later Mustang IIs are equipped with catalytic converters and must be run on unleaded fuel.

Catalytic reactors convert noxious emissions of hydrocarbons (HC) and carbon monoxide (CO) into harmless carbon dioxide and water. The reaction takes place inside the reactor(s) at great heat using platinum or palladium metals as the catalyst. The units are installed in the exhaust system, ahead of the mufflers. They are designed, if the engine is properly tuned, to last 50,000 miles before replacement.

Component Service

POSITIVE CRANKCASE VENTILATION SYSTEM

1. Remove the PCV system components, filler cap, PCV valve, hoses, tubes, fittings, etc. from the engine.

2. Soak the rubber ventilation hose(s) in a low volatility petroleum base solvent.

3. Clean the rubber ventilation hose(s) by passing a suitable cleaning brush through them.

4. Thoroughly wash the rubber hoses in a low volatility petroleum base solvent and dry with compressed air.

5. Thoroughly wash the crankcase breather cap, if so equipped, in a low volatility petroleum base solvent and shake dry. Do not dry with compressed air; damage to the filtering media may result.

6. Thoroughly clean tubes, fittings, connections to assure unobstructed flow of emission gases.

7. Install new PCV valve and re-install previously removed hoses, tubes, fittings, etc. to their proper location.

8. Replace any system component that

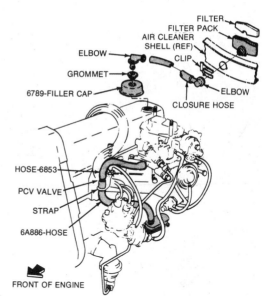

Positive crankcase ventilation components— 2300cc four

shows signs of damage, wear or deterioration as required.

9. Replace any hose or tube that cannot be cleaned satisfactorily.

FUEL EVAPORATIVE CONTROL SYSTEM

The only servicing of the evaporative control system is the periodic replacement of the carbon canister. To remove the canister, loosen and remove the mounting bolts from the mounting bracket, disconnect the purge hose from the air cleaner, and the feed hose from the fuel tank. The canister cannot be cleaned.

EXHAUST GAS RECIRCULATION SYSTEM

EGR Valve Cleaning

NOTE: *Those vehicles requiring use of unleaded gas only do not require periodic cleaning of EGR system parts because of the reduced tendency for carbon deposits to form when there is no lead present.*

Remove the EGR valve for cleaning. Do not strike or pry on the valve diaphragm housing or supports as this may damage the valve operating mechanism and/or change the valve calibration. Check orifice hole in the EGR valve body for deposits. A small hand drill of no more than 0.060 in. diameter may be used to clean the hole if plugged. Extreme care must be taken to avoid enlarging the hole or damaging the surface of the orifice plate.

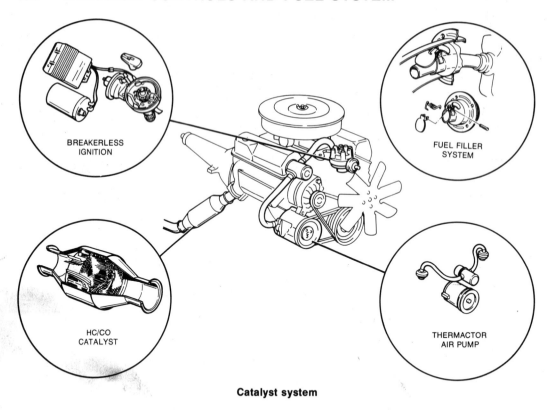

BREAKERLESS
IGNITION

FUEL FILLER
SYSTEM

HC/CO
CATALYST

THERMACTOR
AIR PUMP

Catalyst system

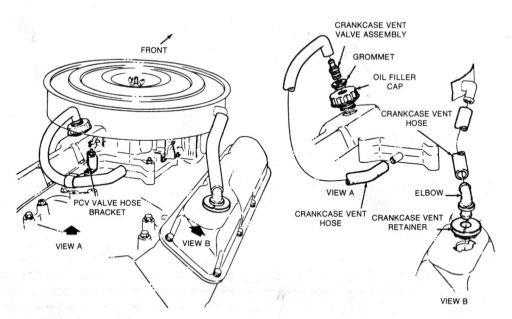

FRONT

PCV VALVE HOSE
BRACKET

VIEW A

VIEW B

CRANKCASE VENT
VALVE ASSEMBLY

GROMMET

OIL FILLER
CAP

CRANKCASE VENT
HOSE

VIEW A

ELBOW

CRANKCASE VENT
HOSE

CRANKCASE VENT
RETAINER

VIEW B

Positive crankcase ventilation components—302 V8

VALVES WHICH CANNOT BE DISASSEMBLED

Valves which are riveted or otherwise permanently assembled should be replaced if highly contaminated; they cannot be cleaned.

VALVES WHICH CAN BE DISASSEMBLED

Separate the diaphragm section from the main mounting body. Clean the valve plates, stem, and the mounting plate, using a small power driven rotary type wire brush. Take

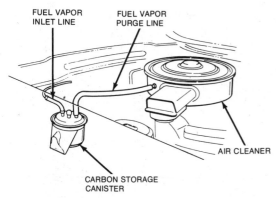

Charcoal canister location

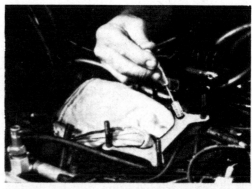

Cleaning EGR entry port in intake manifold

Cleaning EGR valve orifice

Cleaning EGR spacer exhaust passages

care not to damage the parts. Remove deposits between stem and valve disc by using a steel blade or shim approximately 0.028 inch thick in a sawing motion around the stem shoulder at both sides of the disc.

The poppet must wobble and move axially before re-assembly.

Clean the cavity and passages in the main body of the valve with a power driven rotary wire brush. If the orifice plate has a hole less than 0.450 in., it must be removed for cleaning. Remove all loosened debris using shop compressed air. Reassemble the diaphragm section on the main body using a new gasket between them. Torque the attaching screws to specification. Clean the orifice plate and

the counterbore in the valve body. Re-install the orifice plate using a small amount of contact cement to retain the plate in place during assembly of the valve to the carburetor spacer. Apply cement only to outer edges of the orifice plate to avoid restriction of the orifice.

EGR Supply Passages and Carburetor Spacer Cleaning

Remove the carburetor and carburetor spacer on engines so equipped. Clean the supply tube with a small power driven rotary type wire brush or blast cleaning equipment. Clean the exhaust gas passages in the spacer

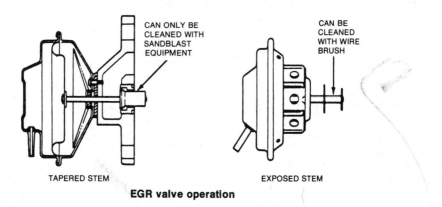

EGR valve operation

using a suitable wire brush and/or scraper. The machined holes in the spacer can be cleaned by using a suitable round wire brush. Hard encrusted material should be probed loose first, then brushed out.

EGR Exhaust Gas Channel Cleaning

Clean the exhaust gas channel, where applicable, in the intake manifold, using a suitable carbon scraper. Clean the exhaust gas entry port in the intake manifold by hand passing a suitable drill bit thru the holes to auger out the deposits. Do not use a wire brush. The manifold riser bore(s) should be suitably plugged during the above action to prevent any of the residue from entering the induction system.

Component Adjustments

FUEL DECELERATION VALVE

1974 2800 V6

1. Set the engine ignition timing to specification. See Chapter 2 for the procedure. Attach a tachometer to the engine.

2. Disconnect the air/fuel hose which runs from the carburetor to the deceleration valve at the carburetor and then plug the hose.

3. Connect a vacuum gauge to the engine. This can be done by removing a vacuum hose from the intake manifold and connecting the vacuum gauge to the fitting for the hose you remove.

4. Start the engine and adjust the carburetor idle mixture screw to obtain the highest reading possible on the vacuum gauge. See Chapter 2 for idle mixture screw locations.

NOTE: *Although this step calls for the carburetor to be adjusted to produce the highest possible reading on the vacuum gauge, the reading must not exceed 18.5 in. Hg for cars with a dual diaphragm (two vacuum hoses running to the distributor) distributor or 19.5 in. Hg for cars with a single diaphragm (one vacuum hose running to the distributor) distributor. If engine vacuum exceeds these values, it must be reduced or the deceleration valve will not function properly. If the vacuum is too high, and the ignition timing is set to specifications, readjust the carburetor idle mixture adjusting screw to obtain 18.5 or 19.5 in. Hg.*

5. Adjust the engine idle speed to specification. See Chapter 2.

6. Unplug the hose which was discon-

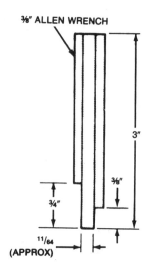

ADJUSTING TOOL

Dimensions for deceleration valve adjusting tool

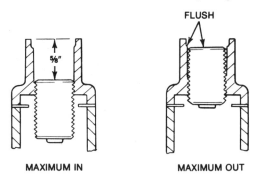

MAXIMUM IN · · · · · · MAXIMUM OUT

Deceleration valve adjustments—2800cc V6

nected in Step 2 and disconnect the vacuum gauge from the engine. Reconnect the vacuum hose which was removed to facilitate installation of the vacuum gauge.

7. Attach the air/fuel hose to the carburetor and then, using a tee fitting, connect the vacuum gauge into the air/fuel line between the carburetor and the deceleration valve.

8. Have a friend raise the speed of the engine to 3,000 rpm and hold it at that for five seconds.

9. Have your friend quickly release the gas pedal while you observe the vacuum gauge and your watch. As soon as the gas pedal is released, the vacuum gauge should show a reading. A reading should hold on the gauge for two seconds and then the needle on the gauge should return to zero. If everything works out that way, your deceleration

valve is working properly. If not proceed to Step 10.

10. If the reading on the gauge remained for more than two seconds, you must turn the adjusting screw on the top of the deceleration valve "in." If the reading remained for less than two seconds, the adjusting screw must be turned OUTWARD. Before you can adjust the valve, however, you must fabricate an adjusting tool by grinding a ⅜ in. allen wrench, or piece of hex rod, to the dimensions shown in the illustration.

11. Insert the tool into the deceleration valve nylon adjusting screw and turn in or out as required. If you have the new style valve, with the hidden adjusting screw, you must first pry the gray cover off the top of the deceleration valve to uncover the adjusting screw.

12. After adjusting the valve repeat Steps 8, 9, and 10 to check the operation of the valve. If you are unable to adjust the valve to bring it within specifications, the valve must be overhauled or replaced.

Component Replacement

PCV VALVE

On V6 and V8 models, disconnect the ventilation hose at the valve cover and pull out the PCV valve from its grommet. On four-cylinder models, disconnect the ventilation hose at the valve cover and pull out the PCV valve from the flame trap on the driver's side of the engine block. Clean out all of the passageways in the hoses and fittings with a kerosene-soaked rag. Install a new PCV valve and connect the ventilation hoses.

PORTED VACUUM SWITCH (DISTRIBUTOR VACUUM CONTROL VALVE)

1. Drain about one gallon of coolant out of the radiator.
2. Tag the vacuum hoses that attach to the control valve and disconnect them.
3. Unscrew and remove the control valve.
4. Install the new control valve.
5. Connect the vacuum hoses.
6. Fill the cooling system.

HEATED AIR INTAKE SYSTEM

1. Disconnect the vacuum hose at the vacuum motor.
2. Remove the hex head cap screws that secure the air intake duct and valve assembly to the air cleaner.

3. Remove the duct and valve assembly from the engine.
4. Position the duct and valve assembly to the air cleaner and heat stove tube. Install the attaching cap screws.
5. Connect the vacuum line at the vacuum motor.

SPARK DELAY VALVE

1. Locate the spark delay valve in the distributor vacuum line and disconnect it from the line.
2. Install a new spark delay valve in the line, making sure that the black end of the valve is connected to the line from the carburetor and the color coded end is connected to the line from the spark delay valve to the distributor.

FUEL DECELERATION VALVE

Removal

1. Disconnect the air/fuel hose from the deceleration valve.
2. Loosen the union nut which attaches the deceleration valve to the intake manifold and remove the valve.

POPPET VALVE REPLACEMENT

1. Loosen the four screws which hold the top cover on the deceleration valve while holding the cover in place with your hand.
   CAUTION: *The top cover is springloaded and could fly off if it is not held in place while the attaching screws are removed.*
2. Remove the top cover attaching screws and gradually release the spring pressure from the cover.
3. Remove the cover and its gasket.
4. Turn the valve over to remove the poppet valve and spring.
5. Install a new poppet valve in the housing and install the spring, gasket, and cover.

DIAPHRAGM REPLACEMENT

1. Remove the four screws which attach the bottom cover to the deceleration valve and remove the cover.
2. Remove the diaphragm and spring retainer.
3. Install a new diaphragm and spring retainer in the bottom of the housing.
4. Install the bottom cover on the deceleration valve.

Installation

1. Position the deceleration valve on the intake manifold and tighten the union nut.

2. Connect the air/fuel hose to the valve.

3. Test and adjust the deceleration valve as required.

THERMACTOR AIR PUMP

1. Disconnect the air outlet hose at the air pump.

2. Loosen the pump belt tension adjuster.

3. Disengage the drive belt.

4. Remove the mounting bolt and air pump.

5. To install, position the air pump on the mounting bracket and install the mounting bolt.

6. Place drive belt in pulleys and attach the adjusting arm to the air pump.

7. Adjust the drive belt tension to specifications and tighten the adjusting arm and mounting bolts.

8. Connect the air outlet hose to the air pump.

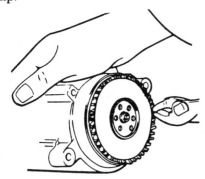

Thermactor air pump filter fan removal

THERMACTOR AIR PUMP FILTER FAN

1. Loosen the air pump adjusting arm bolt and mounting bracket bolt to relieve drive belt tension.

2. Remove drive pulley attaching bolts and pull drive pulley off the air pump shaft.

3. Pry the outer disc loose; then, pull off the centrifugal filter fan with slip-joint pliers.

CAUTION: *Do not attempt to remove the metal drive hub.*

4. Install a new filter fan by drawing it into position, using the pulley and bolts as an installer. Draw the fan evenly by alternately tightening the bolts, making certain that the outer edge of the fan slips into the housing.

NOTE: *A slight interference with the housing bore is normal. After a new fan is installed, it may squeal upon initial operation, until its outer diameter sealing lip has worn in, which may require 20 to 30 miles of operation.*

THERMACTOR CHECK VALVE

1. Disconnect the air supply hose at the valve. (Use a 1¼ in. crowfoot wrench, the valve has a standard, righthand pipe thread.)

2. Clean the threads on the air manifold adaptor with a wire brush. Do not blow compressed air through the check valve in either direction.

3. Install the check valve and tighten.

4. Connect the air supply hose.

THERMACTOR AIR BY-PASS VALVE

1. Disconnect the air and vacuum hoses at the air by-pass valve body.

2. Position the air by-pass valve and connect the respective hoses.

FUEL SYSTEM

A single-action, diaphragm-type mechanical fuel pump located on the lower left-side of the engine is used on all models. On the 2300 cc Four, the pump is operated by a lever running on an eccentric on the auxiliary shaft. On the 2800 cc V6, the pump is operated by a pushrod running on an eccentric on the auxiliary shaft. On the 4900 cc (302) V8, the pump is operated by a lever running directly on the camshaft eccentric.

All of the fuel pumps are permanently sealed and must be replaced when defective.

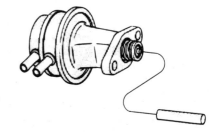

Fuel pump—2800cc V6

Fuel pump—302 V8, 2300cc unit similar

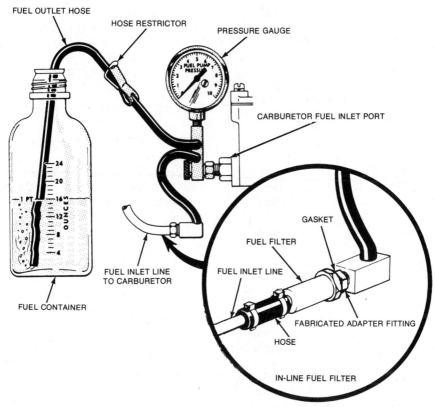

Typical fuel pump pressure and capacity test equipment

Fuel Pump

REMOVAL AND INSTALLATION

1. Disconnect the fuel lines from the fuel pump and plug the inlet line from the gas tank to prevent gas leakage.

2. Remove the fuel pump retaining screws and remove the pump.

3. Remove the fuel pump actuating rod, if so equipped.

4. Clean all gasket mounting surfaces.

5. Install the fuel pump actuating rod, if so equipped.

6. Apply oil-resistant sealer to both sides of a new gasket, position the pump on the engine and install the retaining screws.

NOTE: *Make sure that the pushrod or auxiliary shaft fuel pump rocker arm is riding on the camshaft eccentric.*

7. Connect the fuel lines to the fuel pump, start the engine and check for leaks.

TESTING AND ADJUSTMENT

No adjustments may be made to the fuel pump. Before removing and replacing the old fuel pump, the following test may be made while the pump is still installed on the engine.

CAUTION: *To avoid accidental ignition of fuel during the test, first remove the coil high-tension wire from the distributor and the coil.*

1. If a fuel pressure gauge is available, connect the gauge to the engine and operate the engine until the pressure stops rising. Stop the engine and take the reading. If the reading is within the specifications given in the "Tune-Up Specifications" chart in Chapter 2, the malfunction is not in the fuel pump. Also check the pressure drop after the engine is stopped. A large pressure drop below the minimum specification indicates leaky valves. If the pump proves to be satisfactory, check the tank and inlet line.

2. If a fuel pressure gauge is not available, disconnect the fuel line at the pump outlet, place a vessel beneath the pump outlet, and crank the engine. A good pump will force the fuel out of the outlet in steady spurts. A worn diaphragm spring may not provide proper pumping action.

3. As a further test, disconnect and plug

the fuel line from the tank at the pump, and hold your thumb over the pump inlet. If the pump is functioning properly, a suction should be felt on your thumb. No suction indicates that the pump diaphragm is leaking, or that the diaphragm linkage is worn.

4. Check the crankcase for gasoline. A ruptured diaphragm may leak fuel into the engine.

Electric Choke

All Mustang II models use an electrically assisted choke to reduce exhaust emissions of carbon monoxide during warmup. The system consists of a choke cap, a thermostatic spring, a bimetal sensing disc (switch) and a ceramic positive temperature coefficient (PTC) heater.

The choke is powered from the center tap of the alternator, so that current is constantly applied to the temperature sensing disc. The system is grounded through the carburetor body. At temperatures below approximately 60°F, the switch is open and no current is supplied to the ceramic heater, thereby resulting in normal unassisted thermostatic spring choking action. When the temperature rises above about 60°F, the temperature sensing disc closes and current is supplied to

the heater, which in turn, acts on the thermostatic spring. Once the heater starts, it causes the thermostatic spring to pull the choke plate(s) open within 1½ minutes, which is sooner than it would open if nonassisted.

ELECTRIC CHOKE OPERATIONAL TEST

1. Detach the electrical lead from the choke cap. Hook up a test light between the wire terminal and ground. Start the engine and operate it at idle. The test lamp should light. If not, the lead between the alternator and choke is defective and requires repair.

2. Tape the bulb end of a thermometer to the metallic portion of the choke housing. It is necessary to get the temperature warmer than 80 degrees F.; run the engine for a short time (with the choke lead connected) if the temperature is too low. When the temperature is high enough, disconnect the lead from the choke housing and connect the test lamp between the wire terminal and the choke housing terminal. With the engine running, the test lamp should light, indicating that current is flowing through the choke. If no current flows through the choke under these conditions, connect an ohmmeter between the terminal on the choke housing and the electric choke ground strap. If there is conti-

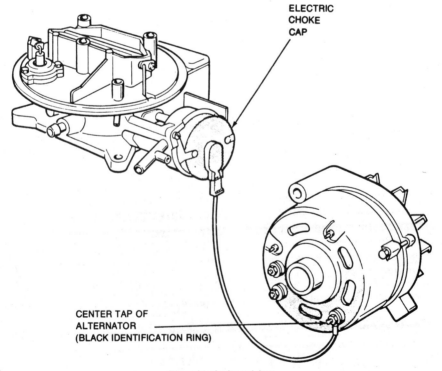

ELECTRIC
CHOKE
CAP

CENTER TAP OF
ALTERNATOR
(BLACK IDENTIFICATION RING)

Electric choke wiring

nuity, check for defects in the electrical supply or ground circuits and repair. If there is no continuity, replace the choke unit.

3. If the choke gets current, but does not behave properly (gradually open when energized) make sure the bimetallic spring is connected to the tang on the choke lever.

4. If the complaint is poor engine operation shortly after cold start (as if the choke opens too rapidly in cooler weather), allow the engine to get overnight cold in an atmosphere of 55 degrees F. or less, or employ a choke testing system that will bring the choke housing down to that temperature. Then, repeat the amperage test described in test 2 above (test lamp wired electrically in series with the choke). If the choke passes electrical current under these conditions, the thermostatic switch is defective and the unit must be replaced.

Carburetors

Two different carburetors are used on Mustang II models. A two-barrel Motorcraft (Holley/Weber) 5200 unit is used on all 1974 models and on the 1975–76 2300 cc four. Another two-barrel Motorcraft 2150 carburetor is used on all 1975–76 V6 and V8 models, and on 1977 and 1978 49 states models. 1977–78 California cars use a 2700 VV carburetor.

In accordance with Federal emissions regulations, all carburetors are equipped with idle mixture screw limiter caps. These caps are installed to prevent tampering with the carburetor fuel mixture screws so that the engine cannot be adjusted to a richer idle mixture.

Most models are equipped with a throttle solenoid positioner. The purpose of a throttle solenoid is to prevent the engine from running on (dieseling) after the ignition is turned off. Dieseling is a common occurrence with many cars using emission control systems that require a leaner fuel mixture, a higher operating temperature, and a higher curb idle speed. The throttle solenoid prevents running-on and dieseling by closing the throttle plate(s) after the key is turned off, thereby shutting off the air and gas to the overheated combustion chambers.

THROTTLE SOLENOID (ANTI-DIESELING SOLENOID) TEST

1. Turn the ignition key on and open the throttle. The solenoid plunger should extend (solenoid energize).

2. Turn the ignition off. The plunger should retract, allowing the throttle to close.

NOTE: *With the antidieseling solenoid deenergized, the carburetor idle speed adjusting screw must make contact with the throttle shaft to prevent the throttle plates from jamming in the throttle bore when the engine is turned off.*

3. If the solenoid is functioning properly and the engine is still dieseling, check for one of the following:

a. High idle or engine shut off speed;
b. Engine timing not set to specification;
c. Binding throttle linkage;
d. Too low an octane fuel being used.

Correct any of these problems as necessary.

4. If the solenoid fails to function as outlined in Steps 1–2, disconnect the solenoid leads; the solenoid should deenergize. If it does not, it is jammed and must be replaced.

5. Connect the solenoid to a 12 V power source and to ground. Open the throttle so that the plunger can extend. If it does not, the solenoid is defective.

6. If the solenoid is functioning correctly and no other source of trouble can be found, the fault probably lies in the wiring between the solenoid and the ignition switch or in the ignition switch itself. Remember to reconnect the solenoid when finished testing.

CARBURETOR REMOVAL AND INSTALLATION

1. Remove the air cleaner.

2. Disconnect the throttle cable or rod at the throttle lever. Disconnect the distributor vacuum line, exhaust gas recirculation line, inline fuel filter, choke heat tube and the positive crankcase ventilation hose at the carburetor.

3. Disconnect the throttle solenoid (if so equipped) and electric choke assist at their connectors.

4. Remove the carburetor retaining nuts. Lift off the carburetor carefully, taking care not to spill any fuel. Remove the carburetor mounting gasket and discard it. Remove the carburetor mounting spacer, if so equipped, from the intake manifold.

5. Prior to installation, clean the gasket mounting surfaces of the intake manifold, spacer (if so equipped), and carburetor. When using a spacer, use two new gaskets, sandwiching the spacer between the gaskets.

If a spacer is not used, only one new carburetor mounting gasket is required.

6. Place the new gasket(s) and spacer (if so equipped) on the carburetor mounting studs. Position the carburetor on top of the gasket and hand-tighten the retaining nuts. Then tighten the nuts in a criss-cross pattern to 10–15 ft lbs.

7. Connect the throttle linkage, the distributor vacuum line, exhaust gas recirculation line, inline fuel filter, choke heat tube, positive crankcase ventilation hose, throttle solenoid (if so equipped) and electric-choke assist.

8. Adjust the curb idle speed, the idle fuel mixture and the accelerator pump stroke (Motorcraft 2150 only).

OVERHAUL—MOTORCRAFT 5200

Disassembly

BOWL COVER

1. Remove the fuel inlet filter plug and filter screen assembly.

2. Remove the bowl cover screws and lockwashers.

3. Remove the retainer clips from the choke rod and carefully remove the bowl cover. Remove the choke rod seal.

4. Remove the float hinge pin, foat and inlet needle.

5. Remove the inlet needle seat and gasket.

6. Remove the three power valve vacuum diaphragm screws, washers, and diaphragm.

AUTOMATIC CHOKE

1. Remove the choke water housing attaching screw and washer. Note the position of the water hose connections for reassembly in correct relationship to the hoses on the vehicle. Remove the water cover and gasket.

2. Remove the choke thermostatic spring housing retaining ring attaching screws. Remove the ring housing and electric heater assembly.

3. Remove the choke housing assembly

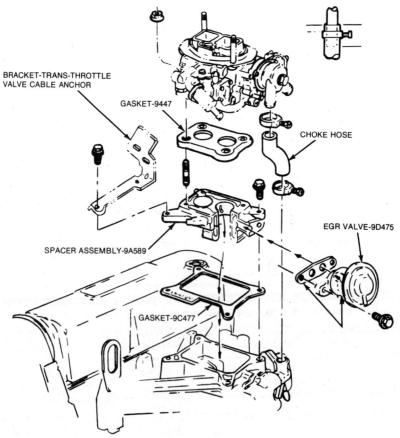

BRACKET-TRANS-THROTTLE
VALVE CABLE ANCHOR

GASKET-9447

CHOKE HOSE

EGR VALVE-9D475

SPACER ASSEMBLY-9A589

GASKET-9C477

Carburetor installation—2300cc four

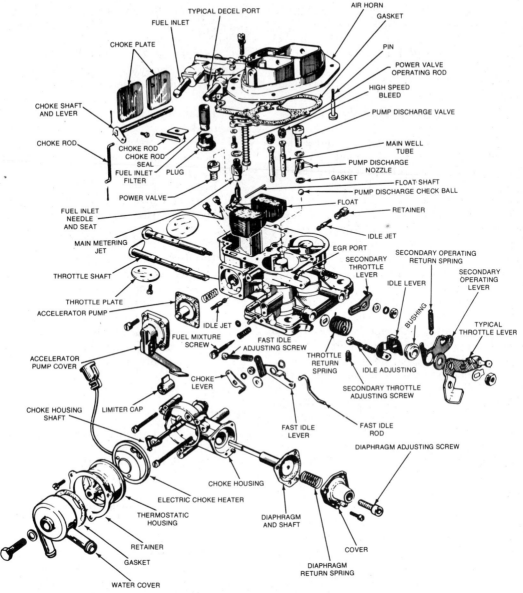

Exploded view—Motorcraft 5200-2V

screws. Note that the long screw goes in the long leg of the assembly. Slip the housing aweay from the main body and disengage the fast idle rod. Remove the O-ring from the vacuum passage.

4. Remove the choke shaft nut and lock-washer, choke lever and fast idle cam.

5. Remove the fast idle lever attaching screw, fast idle lever and spacer. Remove the screw and spring from the lever.

6. Remove the choke diaphragm cover screws and cover, return spring, diaphragm and rod assembly.

ACCELERATOR PUMP

1. Remove the four pump cover screws and pump cover assembly. Remove the pump diaphragm assembly and pump return spring.

2. Remove the pump discharge screw assembly and pump discharge nozzle and two gaskets. Remove the two pump discharge check balls.

MAIN BODY

1. Remove the primary high speed bleed and main well tube.

2. Remove the secondary high speed bleed and main well tube. Note the size of the air bleed plugs and main well tubes so that they can be installed in the correct position.

3. Remove the primary and secondary main metering jets. Note the different size jets so that they may be installed in the correct position.

4. Remove the power valve and gasket. Remove the primary and secondary idle jet retainers and idle jets located on the sides of the carburetor body.

5. Turn the limiter cap in to the stop. Remove the idle limiter cap. Count the turns required to lightly seat the idle adjustment needle. Count to the nearest 1/16 turn. Remove the idle needle and spring.

6. Remove the secondary operating lever return spring.

7. Remove the primary lever and flat washer. Remove the transmission downshift lever and bushing assembly (2800 cc V6 engines only). Remove the secondary operating lever assembly and lever bushing.

8. Remove the idle adjusting lever spring and shat washer. Note how the primary throttle return spring is hooked over the idle adjusting lever and the carburetor body.

9. Remove the idle speed screw and spring from the idle adjusting lever.

10. Remove the secondary throttle lever nut, lockwasher, flat washer and secondary throttle lever. Remove the secondary idle adjusting screw.

Assembly

MAIN BODY

1. Install the secondary idle adjusting screw, secondary throttle lever, flat washer, lockwasher and nut.

2. Install the idle speed screw and spring in the idle adjusting lever.

3. Install the washer, primary throttle return spring and idle adjusting lever and lever bushing. Install the secondary operating lever assembly. On 2800 cc V6 engines, install the transmission lever and bushing assembly.

4. Install the flat washer and primary throttle lever. Install the lockwasher and nut. Attach the secondary operating lever return spring.

5. Install the idle mixture adjusting needle and spring. Turn it in until it lightly bottoms. Back out the screw the exact number of turns recorded at disassembly. Install a new

limiter cap on the idle mixture needle with the stop tab on the cap against the lean side of the stop on the carburetor body.

6. Install the idle jet and retainer assemblies on each side of the carburetor body. Check carefully for the correct primary and secondary sizes.

7. Install the power valve gasket and power valve.

8. Install the primary and secondary main jets. Be sure that the correct sizes are installed.

9. Install the primary and secondary main well tubes and high speed bleeds. Be sure that the correct sizes are installed.

ACCELERATOR PUMP ASSEMBLY

1. Install the pump discharge check balls (2) screw. Install the pump discharge nozzle with a gasket on top and bottom. Install the pump discharge screw.

2. Install the pump return spring and pump diaphragm assembly. Start the four pump cover screws. Hold the pump operating lever partially open to align the diaphragm gasket. Tighten the four cover screws evenly.

AUTOMATIC CHOKE

1. Install the diaphragm adjusting screw. Initially adjust the screw so that the threads are flush with the inside of the cover.

2. Install the choke diaphragm and rod assembly. Install the diaphragm return spring and cover. Install the cover screws and lockwashers.

3. Install the fast idle adjusting screw and spring to the fast idle arm. Install the flat spacer, fast idle arm and attaching screw.

4. Install the choke shaft into the housing and position the fast idle cam on the housing post.

5. Install the choke lever, lockwasher and nut.

6. Install the O-ring on the vacuum passage. Install the fast idle rod with the end with one tab in the fast idle adjusting lever and the end with two tabs in the primary throttle lever.

7. Position the choke housing against the main carburetor body and install the long attaching screw in the long leg of the housing. Install the other screws.

8. Adjust choke plate pulldown, as outlined later in this chapter.

9. Install the electric choke heater, thermostatic housing, retaining ring and at-

taching screws. Index the housing as per the "Specifications" chart and tighten the screws.

10. Install the choke water housing gasket, water housing lockwasher and attaching bolt. Position the housing as it will be when installed on the vehicle and tighten the attaching bolt.

BOWL COVER

1. Install the inlet needle seat and gasket.

2. Install the power valve vacuum diaphragm. Depress the spring and install the screws and washers finger-tight. Hold the stem so that the diaphragm is horizontal and tighten the screws evenly.

3. Install the float needle clip on the float tab and position the float and needle. Install the float shaft.

4. Hold the bowl cover in an inverted position and adjust the dry float setting.

5. Hold the cover in its normal position and adjust the float drop.

6. Install the choke rod seal and seal plug. Install the choke rod through the seal and hook it into the choke lever. Install the retaining clip.

7. Install the bowl cover gasket.

8. Install the choke link into the choke lever. Install the retaining clip.

9. Install the five bowl screws and torque them evenly.

10. Install the fuel filter screen, open end in. Install the filter screen plug.

OVERHAUL—MOTORCRAFT 2150

Disassembly

To facilitate working on the carburetor, and to prevent damage to the throttle plates, install carburetor legs on the base. If legs are unavailable, install 4 bolts (about 2¼ in. long of the correct diameter) and 8 nuts on the carburetor base.

Use a separate container for the component parts of the various assemblies to facilitate cleaning, inspection and assembly.

The following is a step-by-step sequence of operations for completely overhauling the carburetor. However certain components of the carburetor can be serviced without a complete disassembly of the entire unit. For a complete carburetor overhaul, follow all of the steps. To partially overhaul a carburetor or to install a new gasket kit, follow only the applicable steps.

AIR HORN

1. Remove the air cleaner anchor screw.

2. Remove the automatic choke control rod retainer.

3. Remove the air horn attaching screws, lockwashers and the carburetor identification tag. Remove the air horn and air horn gasket.

4. Remove the choke control rod by loosening the screws which secure the choke shaft lever to the choke shaft. Remove the rod from the air horn. Slide the plastic dust seal out of the air horn.

5. If it is necessary to remove the choke plate, remove the staking marks on the choke plate attaching screws and remove the screws. Remove the choke plate by sliding it out of the shaft from the top of the air horn. Remove any burrs around screw holes prior to removing the choke shaft. Slide the choke shaft out of the air horn.

IDLE DECEL METERING ASSEMBLY (2800 CC V6 ONLY)

1. Invert the air horn assembly and remove the three attaching screws from the decel metering assembly.

2. Remove the meter assembly and gasket from the air horn.

3. To install, using a new gasket, position the decel assembly to the bottom of the air horn.

4. Install and torque the attaching screws evenly. After assembly, use compressed air to make sure that all passages in the decel metering assembly are open.

CHOKE PULLDOWN DIAPHRAGM ASSEMBLY

1. Disconnect the choke pulldown link by removing the rod retainer and pulling the rod out of the diaphragm link slot.

2. Remove the two screws from the attaching bracket. Disconnect the vacuum supply tube and remove the pulldown diaphragm.

3. To install, position the choke pulldown diaphragm mounting bracket against the main body casting and install the two attaching screws.

4. Connect the vacuum supply tube to the correct vacuum base tube connection.

5. Insert the choke pulldown control rod through the slot in the diaphragm link. Install the retainer clip over the end of the rod in the slot.

6. Perform an automatic choke pulldown clearance and fast idle cam index setting ad-

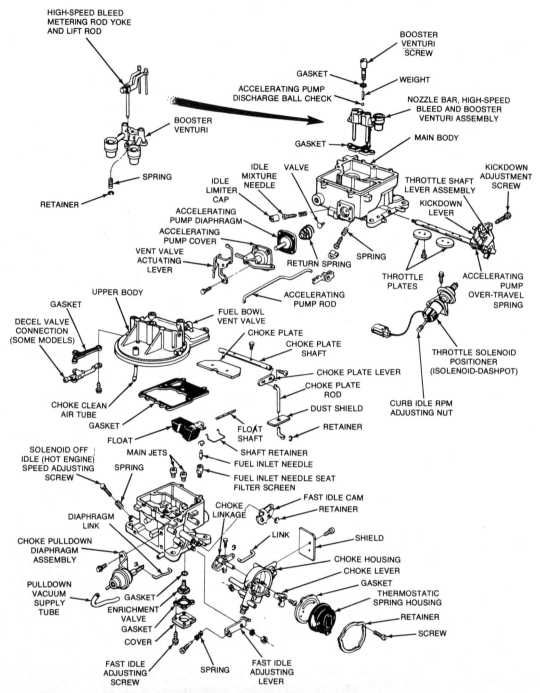

Exploded view—Motorcraft 2150-2V

justments as described at the end of this chapter.

AUTOMATIC CHOKE

1. Remove the fast idle cam retainer.

2. Remove the thermostatic choke spring housing retaining screws and remove the clamp, housing and gasket.

3. Remove the choke housing assembly retaining screws. If the air horn was not previously removed, remove the choke control rod retainer. Remove the choke housing assembly, gasket and the fast idle cam rod from the fast idle cam lever.

4. Remove the choke lever retaining screw and washer. Disconnect the choke

control rod from the choke lever. Remove the choke lever and fast idle cam lever from the choke housing.

MAIN BODY

1. With the use of a screwdriver, pry the float shaft retainer from the fuel inlet seat. Remove the float, float shaft retainer and fuel inlet needle assembly. Remove the retainer and float shaft from the float lever.

2. Remove the fuel inlet needle, seat, filter screen, and main jets with a jet wrench.

3. Remove the booster venturi screw (accelerator pump discharge), air distribution plate, booster venturi ad metering rod assembly and gasket. Invert the main body. Let the accelerating pump discharge weight and ball and the mechanical high speed bleed lift rod and spring fall into your hand.

4. Remove the accelerator pump operating rod from the overtravel lever to the retainer. To release the operating rod from the overtravel lever retainer, press upward on the part of the retainer which snaps over the rod. Disengage the rod from the retainer and from the overtravel lever. Remove the rod and retaincr.

5. Remove the accelerating pump cover attaching screws. Remove the accelerating pump cover, diaphragm assembly and spring.

6. If it is necessary to remove the Elastomer (power) valve, grasp it firmly and pull it out. If the Elastomer valve tip broke off during removal, be sure to remove the tip from the fuel bowl. An Elastomer valve must be replaced whenever it has been removed from the carubretor, as it will dry out and crack.

7. Invert the main body and remove the enrichment valve with a box wrench or socket wrench. Remove the enrichment valve gasket. Discard the gasket.

8. Remove the idle fuel mixture adjusting screws (needles) and the springs. Remove the limiters from the adjusting screws.

9. If necessary remove the nut and washer securing the fast idle adjusting lever assembly to the throttle shaft and remove the lever assembly. If necessary, remove the idle screw and the retainer from the fast idle adjusting lever.

10. Remove the anti-stall dashpot, solenoid, or solenoid-dashpot (if so equipped).

11. If it is necessary to remove the throttle plates, lightly scribe the throttle plates along the throttle shaft, and mark each plate and its corresponding bore with a number or letter for proper installation.

12. Slide the throttle shaft out of the main body, making sure that you catch the mechanical high speed bleed actuator located on the throttle shaft between the throttle plates.

Clean and inspect the carburetor components.

Assembly

Make sure that all holes in new gaskets have been properly punched and that no foreign material has adhered to the gaskets. Make sure that the accelerating pump diaphragm is not torn or cut.

MAIN BODY

1. Slide the throttle shaft assembly into the main body until it begins to enter the high speed bleed cam slot in the body.

2. Holding the cam by the edge of the point, hold it in the slot and rotate the throttle shaft until it will pass through the cam. Rotate the shaft clockwise until the throttle lever clear the boss for the TSP "Off" idle speed screw. Continue inserting the shaft into proper position, rotating as necessary to properly position the cam.

3 Refer to the lines scribed on the throttle plates and install the throttle plates in their proper location with the screws snug, but not tight. Always use new screws when installing throttle plates.

4. Close the throttle plates. Invert the main body, and hold it up to the light. Little or no light should show between the throttle plates and the throttle bores. Tap the plates lightly with a screwdriver handle to seat them. Hold the throttle plates closed and tighten and stake the attaching screws. Stake hardened screws by crimping the exposed threads with diagonal cutters.

5. If necessary, install the fast idle screw on the fast idle adjusting lever.

6. Install the anti-stall dashpot, solenoid, or solenoid-dashpot (if so equipped).

7. Place the fast idle adjusting lever assembly on the throttle shaft and install the retaining washer and nut.

8. If the Elastomer power valve was removed, lubricate the tip of a new Elastomer valve and insert the tip into the accelerator pump cavity center hole. Using a pair of needlenose pliers, reach into the fuel bowl and grasp the valve tip. Pull the valve in until it seats in the pump cavity wall and cut off the

tip forward of the retaining shoulder. Remove the tip from the bowl.

9. Install the accelerating pump diaphragm return spring on the boss in the chamber. Insert the diaphragm assembly into position on the main body. Install the cover screws.

10. Insert the accelerating pump operating rod retainer over the specified hole in the overtravel lever. Insert the operating rod through the retainer and the hole in the overtravel lever and snap the retainer down over the rod.

11. Invert the main body. Install the enrichment valve and new gasket with a wrench. Tighten the valve securely.

12. Install the idle mixture adjusting screws (needles) and springs. Turn the needles in gently with your fingers until they just touch the seat, then back them off 1½ turns for a preliminary idle fuel mixture adjustment. Do not install the idle mixture limiters at this time. Install the enrichment valve cover and new gasket. The cover must be installed with the limiter stops on the cover in position to provide a positive stop for the tabs on the idle mixture adjusting screw limiters.

13. Install the main jets and the fuel inlet seat, filter screen, baffle and new gasket. Be sure that the correct jets are installed.

14. Install the fuel inlet needle assembly in the fuel inlet seat.

15. Slide the float shaft into the float lever. Position the float shaft retainer on the float shaft.

16. Insert the float assembly into the fuel bowl and hook the float lever tab under the fuel inlet needle assembly. Insert the float shaft into its guides at the sides of the fuel bowl.

17. With a screwdriver, position the float shaft retainer in the groove on the fuel needle inlet seat. Check the float setting.

18. Drop the accelerating pump discharge ball and weight into the passage in the main body.

19. Position the new booster assembly gasket and the booster venturi assembly in the main body. Install the air distribution plate and the accelerator pump discharge screw. Tighten screw.

AUTOMATIC CHOKE

1. Position the fast idle cam lever on the thermostatic choke shaft and lever assembly. The bottom of the fast idle cam lever adjusting screw must rest against the tang on the choke lever. Insert the choke lever into the rear of the choke housing. Position the choke lever so that the hole in the lever is to the leftside of the choke housing.

2. Install the fast idle cam rod on the fast idle cam lever. Place the fast idle cam on the fast idle cam rod and install the retainer. Place the choke housing vacuum pickup port to main body gasket on the choke housing flange.

3. Position the choke housing on the main body and at the same time, install the fast idle cam on the hub on the main body. Position the gasket and install the choke housing attaching screws. Install the fast idle cam retainer. Install the thermostatic spring housing.

AIR HORN

1. If the choke plate shaft was removed, position the shaft in the air horn, then install the choke plate rod on the end of the choke shaft.

2. If the choke plate was removed, insert the choke plate into the choke plate shaft. Install the choke plate screws snug, but not tight. Check for proper plate fit, binding in the air horn and free rotation of the shaft by moving the plate from the closed position to the open position. If necessary, remove the choke plate and grind or file the plate edge where it is binding or scraping on the air horn wall. If the choke plate and shaft moves freely, tighten the choke plate screws while holding the choke in the fully closed position.

3. Position the main body gasket and the choke rod plastic seal on the main body. Position the air horn on the main body and gasket so that the choke plate rod fits through the seal and the opening in the main body. Insert the end of the choke plate rod into the automatic choke lever. Install the air horn attaching screws and the carburetor identification tag. Tighten the attaching screws. Install the choke plate rod retainer. Install the air cleaner anchor screw. Tighten the air cleaner anchor screw to the specified torque.

Perform all automatic choke adjustments and other carburetor functions to specifications.

OVERHAUL—MOTORCRAFT 2700 VV CARBURETOR

This type of carburetor must be supported at the right points during overhaul work to protect the throttle plates. Utilize a carburetor stand or use four ⁵/₁₆ in. x 2½ in. bolts in-

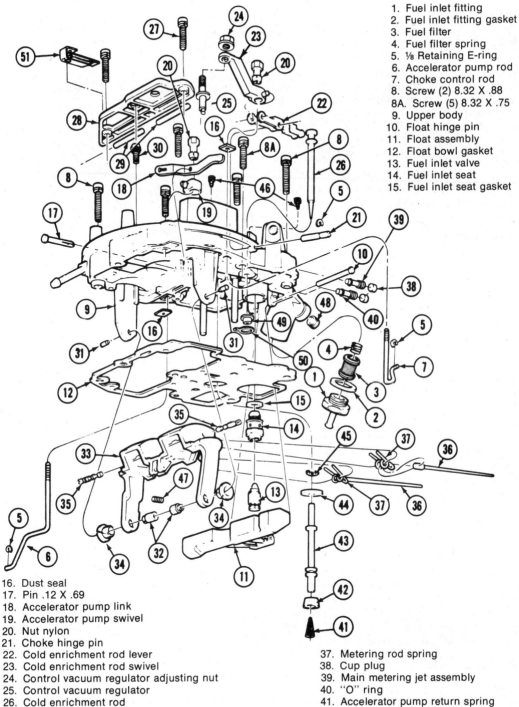

1. Fuel inlet fitting
2. Fuel inlet fitting gasket
3. Fuel filter
4. Fuel filter spring
5. ⅛ Retaining E-ring
6. Accelerator pump rod
7. Choke control rod
8. Screw (2) 8.32 X .88
8A. Screw (5) 8.32 X .75
9. Upper body
10. Float hinge pin
11. Float assembly
12. Float bowl gasket
13. Fuel inlet valve
14. Fuel inlet seat
15. Fuel inlet seat gasket

16. Dust seal
17. Pin .12 X .69
18. Accelerator pump link
19. Accelerator pump swivel
20. Nut nylon
21. Choke hinge pin
22. Cold enrichment rod lever
23. Cold enrichment rod swivel
24. Control vacuum regulator adjusting nut
25. Control vacuum regulator
26. Cold enrichment rod
27. Screw (2) 8.32 X .75
28. Venturi valve cover plate
29. Roller bearing
30. Venturi air bypass screw
31. Venturi valve pivot plug
32. Venturi valve pivot pin
33. Venturi valve
34. Venturi valve pivot pin bushing
35. Metering rod pivot pin
36. Metering rod

37. Metering rod spring
38. Cup plug
39. Main metering jet assembly
40. "O" ring
41. Accelerator pump return spring
42. Accelerator pump cup
43. Accelerator pump plunger
44. Internal vent valve
45. ³/₁₆ Retaining E-ring
46. Idle trim screw
47. Venturi valve limiter adjusting screw
48. Pipe plug
49. Cold enrichment rod seal
50. Seal retainer
51. Hot idle compensator

Exploded view of upper body

stalled in the mounting holes in the throttle body as legs, installing nuts both above and below the throttle body.

A complete procedure is supplied below. It is often possible to service a specific area of the carburetor without performing a complete overhaul or a complete disassembly. You may follow just those steps specific to the type of work you have to do, if necessary.

Make sure to lay out parts in the order of disassembly, grouped by their function in the complete unit. Some sort of large tray with divided compartments would be useful for keeping track of parts.

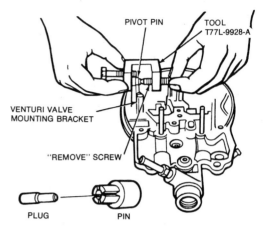

Pressing out tapered pins

Disassembly

UPPER BODY

1. Remove fuel inlet fitting, filter, gasket, and filter spring. Remove the E rings on the accelerator pump and choke control rods, and disengage both. Remove the air cleaner stud.

2. Remove the seven upper body retaining screws, noting the position of the two longer screws. Remove the upper body, and invert it and place it on a clean work surface.

3. Remove the float hinge pin, and then remove the float assembly.

4. Remove the float bowl gasket.

5. Remove the fuel inlet valve, seat, and gasket.

6. Remove the accelerator pump rod and dust seal. Then remove the accelerator pump link retaining pin and link. Remove the accelerator pump swivel and adjusting nut.

7. Remove the choke control rod. Then, remove the dust seal by carefully lifting the seal retainer and then sliding the seal out.

8. Remove the E ring on the choke hinge pin and slide the pin out of the casting.

9. Remove the following parts as a single assembly: the cold enrichment rod adjusting nut, lever, adjusting swivel, control vacuum regulator, and adjusting nut. Then, disassemble these parts as required for cleaning or replacement.

10. Slide the cold enrichment rod out of the upper body casting and its seal.

11. Remove the venturi valve cover plate screws, the cover plate, and the roller bearings.

12. Remove the venturi air bypass screw.

13. Using a special tool such as T77P-9928-A, press the tapered plugs out of the venturi valve pivot pins. See the illustration. Then, push the venturi pivot pins out and slide the venturi valve to the rear until it is free of the casting. Remove the venturi valve pivot pin bushings.

14. Remove the metering rod pivot pins (on the outboard sides of the venturi valve) and the metering rods and springs. As you remove the metering rods, label them "Throttle" and "Choke" (referring to which side each came from) for proper reassembly.

15. *BLOCK THE VENTURI VALVE WIDE OPEN IN ORDER TO PERFORM THIS STEP WITHOUT PARTS DAMAGE.* Then, using Tool T77L-9533-B, remove the cup plugs recessed in the upper body casting.

16. *THE MAIN JET SETTING (POSITION IN THE CARBURETOR BODY) HAS A CRITICAL EFFECT ON CARBURETOR FUNCTION. MAKE SURE TO FOLLOW THE FIRST PART OF THIS STEP CAREFULLY SO THAT THESE PARTS MAY BE REINSTALLED IN THEIR ORIGINAL POSITION.* Using a jet wrench (T77L-9533-A or equivalent), note the position of each main jet and then turn it slowly clockwise until it bottoms in the casting. Record the number of turns required to the nearest ¼ turn for each jet.

17. Then back each jet out (turn counterclockwise) to remove it, and remove the O rings. Label the jets "Throttle" and "Choke" according to which side of the carburetor body the came from.

18. Remove the accelerator pump plunger assembly. Disassemble it as required to clean it and replace defective parts.

19. Remove: the idle trim screws: the venturi valve limiter adjusting screw (from the throttle side of the venturi valve); the ⅛ in. pipe plug from the fuel inlet boss.

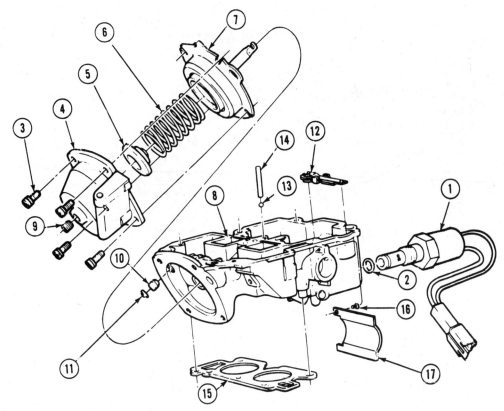

1. Cranking enrichment solenoid
2. "O" ring seal
3. Screw, (4) 8-32 X .56
4. Venturi valve diaphragm cover
5. Venturi valve diaphragm spring guide
6. Venturi valve diaphragm spring
7 Venturi valve diaphragm assembly
8. Main body
9. Venturi valve adjusting screw
10. Wide open stop screw
11. Plug expansion
12. Cranking fuel control assembly
13. Accelerator pump check ball
14. Accelerator pump check ball weight
15. Throttle body gasket
16. Screw, 6-32 X .38
17. Choke heat shield

Exploded view of main body

MAIN BODY

1. Remove the cranking enrichment solenoid and its Q ring.

2. Remove the venturi valve diaphragm cover by removing the screws and then lightly tapping the cover to loosen it (do not pry it). Remove the spring guide and spring. Then, carefully loosen the diaphragm and slide it out of the main body.

3. Remove the venturi valve diaphragm adjusting screw.

4. Center punch the access hole cover plug of the venturi valve wide open stop screw until it is loose, and then remove it and remove the stop screw.

5. Inspect the cranking fuel control for physical damage. *Do not remove it* if it is in good condition; if it is damaged, it, of course, may be removed. To remove it, bend the bi-metal of the unit enough to expose the discharge port and then use jet plug removal Tool T77L-9533-B or equivalent to extract it.

6. Invert the main body and place it on a clean work surface, *COVERING THE BOTTOM WITH YOUR HAND SO THAT YOU WILL CATCH THE ACCELERATOR PUMP CHECK BALL AND WEIGHT.*

7. Remove the five throttle body retaining screws, and remove the throttle body and gasket.

8. Remove the choke heat shield screw and shield.

THROTTLE BODY

1. Remove the throttle return control device sol-a-dash, solenoid, dashpot, and

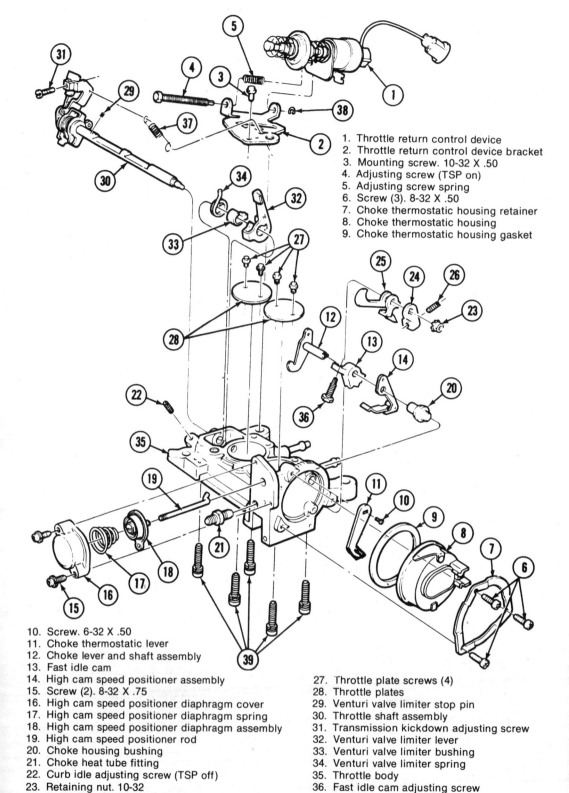

1. Throttle return control device
2. Throttle return control device bracket
3. Mounting screw. 10-32 X .50
4. Adjusting screw (TSP on)
5. Adjusting screw spring
6. Screw (3). 8-32 X .50
7. Choke thermostatic housing retainer
8. Choke thermostatic housing
9. Choke thermostatic housing gasket
10. Screw. 6-32 X .50
11. Choke thermostatic lever
12. Choke lever and shaft assembly
13. Fast idle cam
14. High cam speed positioner assembly
15. Screw (2). 8-32 X .75
16. High cam speed positioner diaphragm cover
17. High cam speed positioner diaphragm spring
18. High cam speed positioner diaphragm assembly
19. High cam speed positioner rod
20. Choke housing bushing
21. Choke heat tube fitting
22. Curb idle adjusting screw (TSP off)
23. Retaining nut. 10-32
24. Fast idle adjusting lever
25. Fast idle lever
26. Fast idle adjusting screw
27. Throttle plate screws (4)
28. Throttle plates
29. Venturi valve limiter stop pin
30. Throttle shaft assembly
31. Transmission kickdown adjusting screw
32. Venturi valve limiter lever
33. Venturi valve limiter bushing
34. Venturi valve limiter spring
35. Throttle body
36. Fast idle cam adjusting screw
37. Transmission kickdown lever return spring
38. $3/16$ retaining E-ring
39. Screw (5) 8-32 X .75

Exploded view of throttle body

bracket, and disengage the transmission kick-down return spring. Note that on 1977 models, this involves removing an adjusting screw spring (5) which is not used on 1978 models.

2. Remove the choke housing screws, retainer ring, housing, and gasket.

3. Remove the choke thermostatic lever screw and the lever.

4. Slide the choke shaft and lever (assembled) out of the casting and remove the fast idle cam.

5. Remove the high cam speed positioner assembly, and then remove the high cam speed positioner cover screws, cover, and return spring.

6. Disassemble if necessary and then remove the high cam speed positioner diaphragm and rod.

7. Inspect the choke housing bushing. If it is badly worn, it must be pressed out. To do this, first file or grind off the stake areas, and then support the casting very carefully while pressing it out.

8. Remove the choke heat tube fitting.

9. Remove the (T.S.P. Off) idle speed adjusting screw.

10. Remove the throttle shaft retaining nut, fast idle adjusting lever, fast idle lever, and fast idle adjusting screw.

11. Inspect the throttle plates to see if they need to be removed for cleaning or parts replacement. If so, lightly scribe a line along the throttle shaft and mark the plates "T" or "C" (throttle or choke side of the throttle body). Then, file off the staking marks on the throttle plate screws, and remove *and discard* the screws. Remove the throttle plates.

12. Remove the throttle shaft assembly by driving the limiter lever stop pin down until it is flush with the shaft. Then, slide the throttle shaft assembly out of the casting and remove the transmission kickdown adjusting screw.

13. Remove the venturi valve limiter lever and bushing, and disassemble if inspection reveals a need to do so for cleaning or parts replacement.

Assembly

THROTTLE BODY

1. Support the throttle shaft securely, and drive the venturi valve limiter stop pin out of the shaft, and discard it.

2. Position the venturi valve limiter assembly in the throttle body and slide the throttle shaft into place. Then, position the throttle plates according to letter and scribe marks made on them before disassembly, and install new fastening screws *just snugly* (not tight). Finally, close the throttles, tap the throttle plates lightly to properly center them, and then tighten the screws and stake them.

3. Drive a new venturi valve limiter stop pin into the shaft, leaving about ⅛ in. exposed.

4. Install the fast idle lever, the fast idle adjusting lever, the throttle shaft retaining nut, and the fast idle adjusting screw.

5. Install the (T.S.P. Off idle) adjusting screw.

6. If the choke housing bushing was removed, carefully press it into the body and stake it into place. *Make sure the casting is properly supported throughout this operation.*

7. Install the cam speed positioner assembly and the fast idle cam. Slide the high speed cam positioner diaphragm and rod into position and engage the rod.

8. Slide the choke shaft and lever assembly into the casting and install the choke thermostatic lever and screw.

9. Place the high cam speed positioner (H.C.S.P.) in the corner of the specified cam step, counting the highest step as the first. Then, place the fast idle lever in the corner of the H.C.S.P. Hold the throttle closed firmly to maintain these positions.

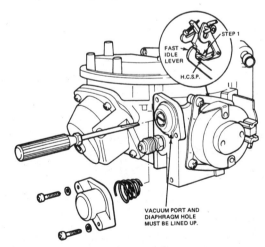

High cam speed positioner adjustment

10. Adjust the diaphragm assembly clockwise until it is lightly bottomed on the casting, and then rotate it counterclockwise ½ to 1½ turns, until the vacuum port and diaphragm hole line up.

11. Install the diaphragm spring, cover, and screws.

12. Install the choke thermostatic gasket, housing, retainer, and attaching screws.

13. Install the throttle return control device and bracket.

14. Install the choke heat tube fitting.

MAIN BODY

1. Put the throttle body gasket into position on the main body, and assemble the main body onto the throttle body.

2. Drop the accelerator pump check ball and weight into the pump discharge channel.

3. If the cranking fuel control has been removed, replace the assembly. Place the control assembly on top of its cavity and tap it lightly with a brass drift and small hammer, alternating from side to side to avoid cocking it, until it is seated.

NOTE: *Do not install the venturi valve wide open stop screw and plug at this time.*

4. Slide the venturi valve diaphragm into the main body. Install the valve diaphragm spring, spring guide, and, cover, and retaining screws.

5. Install the venturi valve diaphragm adjusting screw (final adjustment is made with the unit on the car).

6. Place the cranking enrichment solenoid O ring seal (coated with soapy water) onto the solenoid and then install the assembly.

7. Install the choke heat shield and attaching screw.

UPPER BODY

1. Install the ⅛ in. pipe plug into the fuel inlet boss.

2. Install the venturi valve limiter screw in the venturi valve.

3. Install the idel trim screws.

4. Coat the main metering jet O ring seals with soapy water, and install them onto the main metering jets. Then, using the special jet wrench used during disassembly, install each main jet into the casting and turn it just until it bottoms. Then, back each jet out just the number of turns recorded during the disassembly procedure.

5. Using the special jet plug puller (T77L-9533-C or equivalent), install the jet plugs by tapping each lightly until the tool bottoms on the face of the casting.

6. Install the metering rods, metering rod springs, and metering rod pivot pins onto the venturi valve.

7. Install the venturi valve, carefully guiding the metering rods into the main metering jets. Press down onto the metering rods and release to make sure they spring back, indicating springs are properly assembled.

8. Install the venturi valve pivot pin bushings and pivot pins.

9. Using Special Tool T77P-9928-A or equivalent, carefully press the tapered plugs into the venturi valve pivot pins.

10. Install the venturi air bypass screw. Turn it clockwise four turns to provide proper clearance for installing the cover plate. Then, install the venturi valve cover plate roller bearings, the plate, and the attaching screws.

11. Insert the accelerator pump swivel and adjusting nut into the pump link. Then, install the pump link and retaining pin.

12. Install the accelerator pump operating rod and the dust seal.

13. Install the fuel inlet valve seat gasket, the seat, and the valve.

14. Install the float bowl gasket. Install the float assembly and the hinge pin.

15. Assemble the: accelerator pump return spring; the accelerator pump cup; the accelerator pump plunger; internal vent valve; and the retainer. Then position the assembly in the hole in the upper body.

16. Assemble the upper body to the main body, holding the pump piston assembly with your finger and guiding it into the pump cavity in the main body as you bring the two bodies together. Make sure the venturi valve diaphragm stem engages the venturi valve.

17. Install the fuel filter spring, filter, inlet fitting gasket and inlet fitting.

18. Install the air cleaner stud.

19. Install the choke control rod dust seal and tap it gently to straighten the retainer.

20. Slide the cold enrichment rod into the upper body. Assemble the cold enrichment rod adjusting nut, lever, adjusting swivel, control vacuum regulator, and adjusting nut. Install the assembly.

21. Install the choke hinge pin and E ring.

22. Install the choke control rod. Final adjustment should be made with the carburetor on the car.

23. Engage the accelerator pump operating rod and the choke control rod and install the E ring retainers.

24. Block the throttle plates wide open. Manually move the venturi valve to the wide open position and insert an allen wrench into the hole where the stop screw goes. Apply light closing pressure to the venturi valve

and the air horn wall. If not .73–.77 in., turn the limiter adjusting screw clockwise to increase the gap or counterclockwise to decrease it. Remove the allen wrench, reapply light pressure, and recheck the gap.

25. Install the wide open stop screw and turn it clockwise until it contacts the valve. Again, push the valve to the wide open position and check the gap between the valve and air horn wall. Turn the stop screw until the gap is correct. Install a new expansion plug in the access hole, and reinstall the venturi valve cover and roller bearings.

THERMOSTATIC SPRING HOUSING INDEX MARK

CHOKE HOUSING INDEX MARK

Automatic choke housing adjustment

Automatic Choke Housing Adjustment
All Fixed Venturi Carburetors

By rotating the spring housing of the automatic choke, the reaction of the choke to engine temperature can be controlled. To adjust, remove the air cleaner assembly, loosen the thermostatic spring housing retaining screws and set the spring housing to the specified index mark. The marks are shown in the accompanying illustration. After adjusting the setting, tighten the retaining screws and replace the air cleaner assembly to the carburetor.

CHOKE PLATE PULLDOWN CLEARANCE ADJUSTMENT
Motorcraft 5200

1. Remove the three screws from around the choke water cover which attach the cover to the choke housing.

2. Remove the water housing with the hoses attached.

3. Position the fast idle cam so that the fast idle adjusting screw is contacting the highest step on the cam.

4. Using a screwdriver, push the vacuum diaphragm stem back into the diaphragm housing until it stops. Hold the stem in this position.

5. Insert a $^{15}/_{64}$ in. drill bit into the air

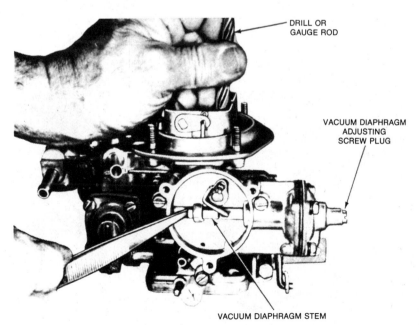

DRILL OR GAUGE ROD

VACUUM DIAPHRAGM ADJUSTING SCREW PLUG

VACUUM DIAPHRAGM STEM

Adjusting choke plate pulldown—Motorcraft 5200

horn of the carburetor and apply light pressure to the choke plate to remove all slack. With the drill bit against the air horn wall, the bottom of the choke plate should just contact the drill bit.

6. If the clearance is incorrect, remove the vacuum diaphragm adjusting screw plug and insert a screwdriver into the exposed hole, then adjust the screw inward or outward as required.

7. Install the choke water housing on the choke housing, making sure that the tab on the end of the coil spring engages the slot in the choke housing shaft.

8. Install the three choke water housing attaching screws and tighten them finger-tight. Adjust the automatic choke housing as described previously.

Motorcraft 2150

1. Remove the air cleaner assembly.

2. Set the throttle on the top step of the fast idle cam.

3. Noting the position of the choke housing cap, loosen the retaining screws and rotate the cap 90 degrees in the rich (closing) direction.

4. Activate the pulldown motor by manually forcing the pulldown control diaphragm link in the direction of applied vacuum or by applying vacuum to the external vacuum tube.

5. Using a drill gauge of the specified diameter, measure the clearance between the choke plate and the center of the air horn wall nearest the fuel bowl.

6. To adjust, reset the diaphragm stop on the end of the choke pulldown diaphragm.

7. After adjusting, reset the choke housing cap to the specified notch. Check and reset fast idle speed, if necessary. Install the air cleaner.

FLOAT LEVEL ADJUSTMENT

Motorcraft 5200

1. Remove the air cleaner.

2. Disconnect the fuel and deceleration valve hoses from the carburetor.

3. Remove the small clip which attaches the choke rod to the choke plate shaft and disconnect the rod from the shaft.

4. Remove the screws which attach the upper body of the carburetor to the main

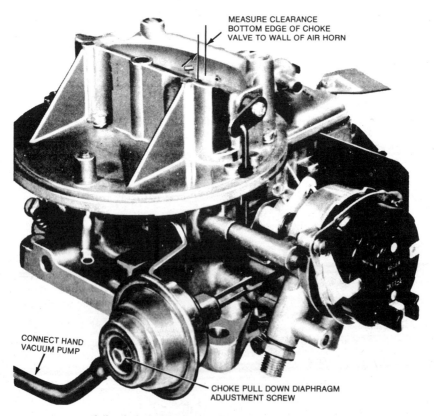

MEASURE CLEARANCE
BOTTOM EDGE OF CHOKE
VALVE TO WALL OF AIR HORN

CONNECT HAND
VACUUM PUMP

CHOKE PULL DOWN DIAPHRAGM
ADJUSTMENT SCREW

Adjusting choke plate pulldown—Motorcraft 2150

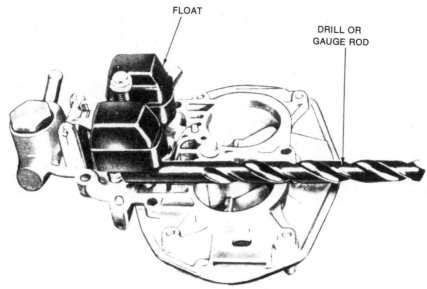

Checking float level—Motorcraft 5200

body of the carburetor and carefully lift the upper body off the main body. Be careful not to tear the upper body gasket.

5. Turn the carburetor upper body upside down and measure the clearance between the bottom of each float and the bottom of the carburetor upper body. The clearance should be 0.420 in. (No. 58 drill bit).

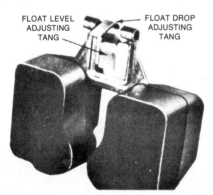

Float level adjustment locations—Motorcraft 5200

6. If the clearance is incorrect, bend the float level adjusting tang to correct.

NOTE: *Both floats must be adjusted to the same clearance.*

7. With the upper body still in the inverted position, measure the clearance between the tang on the rear of the float mounting bracket and the bumper spring on the float pivot pin. The clearance should be 0.020–0.050 in. If the clearance is incorrect, bend the float drop tang to adjust.

8. Position the upper body and gasket of the main body of the carburetor and connect the choke rod to the choke plate lever. Install the choke rod attaching clip in the hole in the rod.

9. Install the upper body attaching screws.

10. Connect the fuel and deceleration valve hoses to the carburetor.

11. Install the air cleaner.

Motorcraft 2150

Dry Adjustment

This preliminary setting of the float level adjustment must be done with the carburetor removed from the engine.

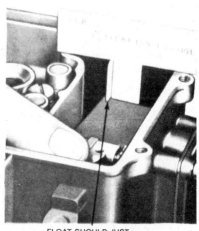

FLOAT SHOULD JUST TOUCH AT THIS POINT

Dry float level check—Motorcraft 2150

1. Remove the air horn and see that the float is raised and the fuel inlet needle is seated. Check the distance between the top surface of the main body (with the gasket removed) and the top surface of the float. Depress the float tab to seat the fuel inlet needle. Take a measurement near the center of the float, at a point $1/8$ in. from the free end. If you are using a prefabricated float gauge, place the gauge in the corner of the enlarged end section of the fuel bowl. The gauge should touch the float near the end, but not on the end radius.

2. If necessary, bend the tab on the end of the float to bring the setting within the specified limits.

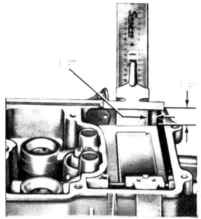

Wet float level check—Motorcraft 2150

Wet Adjustment

1. Bring the engine to its normal operating temperature, park the car on as nearly level a surface as possible, and stop the engine.

2. Remove the air cleaner assembly from the carburetor.

3. Remove the air horn retaining screws and the carburetor identification tag. Leave the air horn and gasket in position on the carburetor main body. Start the engine, let it idle for several minutes, rotate the air horn out of the way, and remove the gasket to provide access to the float assembly.

4. With the engine idling, use a standard depth scale to measure the vertical distance from the top machined surface of the carburetor main body to the level of the fuel in the fuel bowl. This measurement must be made at least $1/4$ in. away from any vertical surface in order to assure an accurate reading.

5. Stop the engine before making any adjustment to the float level. Adjustment is ac-

complished by bending the float tab (which contacts the fuel inlet valve) up or down as required to raise or lower the fuel level. After making an adjustment, start the engine, and allow it to idle for several minutes before repeating the fuel level check. Repeat as necessary until the proper fuel level is attained.

6. Reinstall the air horn with a new gasket and secure it with the screws. Include the installation of the identification tag in its proper location.

7. Check the idle speed, fuel mixture, and dashpot adjustments. Install the air cleaner assembly.

DECHOKE CLEARANCE ADJUSTMENT
Motorcraft 5200

1. Hold the carburetor throttle lever in the wide-open position.

2. Insert a $9/32$ in. drill bit (0.282 in.) into the air horn of the carburetor.

3. Apply light pressure to the choke plate to remove all slack.

4. With the drill bit against the carburetor wall, the bottom of the choke plate should just contact the drill. If it does not, bend the tab on the fast idle lever where it contacts the fast idle cam to correct it.

Motorcraft 2150

1. With the throttle held completely open, move the choke valve to the closed position.

2. Measure the distance between the lower edge of the choke valve and the air horn wall.

3. Adjust by bending the tang on the fast idle speed lever which is located on the throttle shaft.

NOTE: *Final unloader adjustment must be performed on the car and the throttle should be opened by using the accelerator pedal of the car. This is to be sure that full throttle operation is achieved.*

ACCELERATOR PUMP STROKE ADJUSTMENT
Motorcraft 2150

In order to keep the exhaust emission level of the engine within the specified limits, the accelerating pump stroke has been preset at the factory. The additional holes are provided for differing engine-transmission-body applications only. The primary throttle shaft lever (overtravel lever) has 4 holes and the

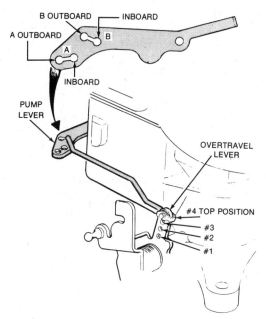

Accelerator pump stroke hole locations—
Motorcraft 2150

accelerating pump link 2 holes to control the pump stroke. The accelerating pump operating rod should be in the overtravel lever hole number listed in the "Carburetor Adjustments" specifications chart, and in the inboard hole (hole closest to the pump plunger) in the accelerating pump link. If the pump stroke has been changed from the specified settings, use the following procedure to correct the stroke.

1. Release the operating rod from the retaining clip by pressing the tab end of the clip toward the rod while pressing the rod away from the clip until it disengages.

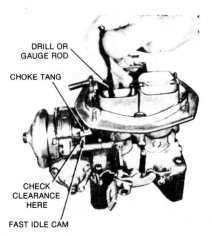

Fast idle cam index clearance—Motorcraft 5200

2. Position the clip over the specified hole (see "Carburetor Adjustments" specifications chart) in the overtravel lever. Press the ends of the clip together and insert the operating rod through the clip and the overtravel lever. Release the clip to engage the rod.

FAST IDLE CAM INDEX SETTING
Motorcraft 5200

1. Insert a drill gauge of the specified diameter between the lower edge of the choke plate and the air horn wall.

2. While holding the fast idle screw on the bottom step of the fast idle cam, measure the clearance between the choke lever tang and the arm on the fast idle cam. The tang and arm should be in light contact.

3. To adjust, bend the choke lever tang up or down as necessary.

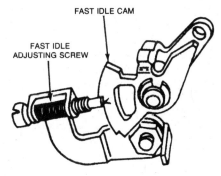

Fast idle cam index setting—Motorcraft 2150

Motorcraft 2150

1. Loosen the choke thremostatic spring housing retaining screws and rotate the housing 90° in the rich direction.

2. Position the fast idle speed screw or lever on the high step of the cam.

3. Depress the choke pulldown diaphragm against the diaphragm stop screw thereby placing the choke in the pulldown position.

4. While holding the choke pulldown diaphragm depressed, slightly open the throttle and allow the fast idle cam to fall.

5. Close the throttle and check the position of the fast idle cam or lever. When the fast idle cam is adjusted correctly, the screw should contact the "V" mark on the cam. Adjustment is accomplished by rotating the fast idle cam adjusting screw as needed.

FAST IDLE SPEED

Motorcraft 2700 VV

1. Run the engine until it reaches normal operating temperature, and then idle it. Place the fast idle lever on the third step of the fast idle cam (see the engine compartment sticker). Disconnect the EGR valve and plug the line.

2. Make sure the high cam speed positioner lever is disengaged.

3. Turn the fast idle screw in or out as necessary to get the specified speed.

FAST IDLE CAM

Motorcraft 2700 VV

1. Remove the choke cap. Place the fast idle lever in the corner of the specified step of the fast idle cam (counting the highest step as the first) with the high cam speed positioner retracted.

2. Hold the throttle lightly closed with a rubber band to maintain cam position, if this adjustment is being performed with the engine off the vehicle.

3. Install a stator cap (Ford Tool T77L-9848-A) and rotate it clockwise until the lever contacts the adjusting screw.

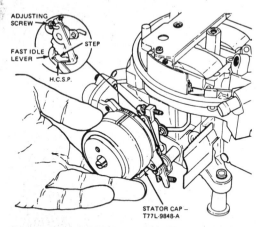

Setting the fast idle cam—2700 VV carburetor

4. Turn the fast idle cam adjusting screw until the index mark on the stator cap lines up with the specified notch (Index) on the choke casting.

5. Remove the stator cap and reinstall the choke cap.

FUEL LEVEL ADJUSTMENT

2700 VV Carburetor

1. Remove the upper body assembly. Remove the upper body gasket and install a new gasket.

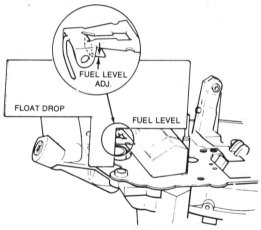

Adjusting fuel level—2700 VV carburetor

2. Fabricate a gauge like the one shown in the illustration. The dimension for fuel level is 1-3/64 in on 1977 carburetors, and 1.040 in. on 1978 models.

3. Invert the upper body and place the gauge on the bare metal surface of the casting. Measure the distance from this bare surface to the bottom of the float (actually the top surface of the float with the assembly in an inverted position).

4. If the dimension is not within $1/32$ either side of the specification, bend the float operating lever away from the inlet needle to decrease the dimension, or toward the needle to increase it.

5. Check float drop and adjust if necessary (see below).

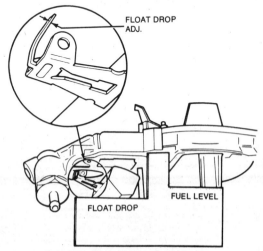

Adjusting float drop—2700 VV carburetor

FLOAT DROP ADJUSTMENT

2700 VV Carburetor

1. Float drop is 1 $15/32$ in. on 1977 models, 1.460 in. on 1978 models. Tolerance is plus

CHILTON'S
FUEL ECONOMY
& TUNE-UP TIPS

Tune-up • Spark Plug Diagnosis • Emission Controls

Fuel System • Cooling System • Tires and Wheels

General Maintenance

CHILTON'S FUEL ECONOMY & TUNE-UP TIPS

Fuel economy is important to everyone, no matter what kind of vehicle you drive. The maintenance-minded motorist can save both money and fuel using these tips and the periodic maintenance and tune-up procedures in this Repair and Tune-Up Guide.

There are more than 130,000,000 cars and trucks registered for private use in the United States. Each travels an average of 10-12,000 miles per year, and, and in total they consume close to 70 billion gallons of fuel each year. This represents nearly ⅔ of the oil imported by the United States each year. The Federal government's goal is to reduce consumption 10% by 1985. A variety of methods are either already in use or under serious consideration, and they all affect you driving and the cars you will drive. In addition to "down-sizing", the auto industry is using or investigating the use of electronic fuel delivery, electronic engine controls and alternative engines for use in smaller and lighter vehicles, among other alternatives to meet the federally mandated Corporate Average Fuel Economy (CAFE) of 27.5 mpg by 1985. The government, for its part, is considering rationing, mandatory driving curtailments and tax increases on motor vehicle fuel in an effort to reduce consumption. The government's goal of a 10% reduction could be realized — and further government regulation avoided — if every private vehicle could use just 1 less gallon of fuel per week.

How Much Can You Save?

Tests have proven that almost anyone can make at least a 10% reduction in fuel consumption through regular maintenance and tune-ups. When a major manufacturer of spark plugs sur-

---

TUNE-UP

1. Check the cylinder compression to be sure the engine will really benefit from a tune-up and that it is capable of producing good fuel economy. A tune-up will be wasted on an engine in poor mechanical condition.

2. Replace spark plugs regularly. New spark plugs alone can increase fuel economy 3%.

3. Be sure the spark plugs are the correct type (heat range) for your vehicle. See the Tune-Up Specifications.

Heat range refers to the spark plug's ability to conduct heat away from the firing end. It must conduct the heat away in an even pattern to avoid becoming a source of pre-ignition, yet it must also operate hot enough to burn off conductive deposits that could cause misfiring.

The heat range is usually indicated by a number on the spark plug, part of the manufacturer's designation for each individual spark plug. The numbers in bold-face indicate the heat range in each manufacturer's identification system.

Periodically, check the spark plugs to be sure they are firing efficiently. They are excellent indicators of the internal condition of your engine.

Manufacturer	Typical Designation
AC	R **45** TS
Bosch (old)	WA **145** T30
Bosch (new)	HR **8** Y
Champion	RBL **15** Y
Fram/Autolite	4**15**
Mopar	P-**62** PR
Motorcraft	BRF-**42**
NGK	BP **5** ES-15
Nippondenso	W **16** EP
Prestolite	14GR **5** 2A

On AC, Bosch (new), Champion, Fram/Autolite, Mopar, Motorcraft and Prestolite, a higher number indicates a hotter plug. On Bosch (old), NGK and Nippondenso, a higher number indicates a colder plug.

4. Make sure the spark plugs are properly gapped. See the Tune-Up Specifications in this book.

5. Be sure the spark plugs are firing efficiently. The illustrations on the next 2 pages show you how to "read" the firing end of the spark plug.

6. Check the ignition timing and set it to specifications. Tests show that almost all cars have incorrect ignition timing by more than 2°.

veyed over 6,000 cars nationwide, they found that a tune-up, on cars that needed one, increased fuel economy over 11%. Replacing worn plugs alone, accounted for a 3% increase. The same test also revealed that 8 out of every 10 vehicles will have some maintenance deficiency that will directly affect fuel economy, emissions or performance. Most of this mileage-robbing neglect could be prevented with regular maintenance.

Modern engines require that all of the functioning systems operate properly for maximum efficiency. A malfunction anywhere wastes fuel. You can keep your vehicle running as efficiently and economically as possible, by being aware of your vehicle's operating and performance characteristics. If your vehicle suddenly develops performance or fuel economy problems it could be due to one or more of the following:

PROBLEM	POSSIBLE CAUSE
Engine Idles Rough	Ignition timing, idle mixture, vacuum leak or something amiss in the emission control system.
Hesitates on Acceleration	Dirty carburetor or fuel filter, improper accelerator pump setting, ignition timing or fouled spark plugs.
Starts Hard or Fails to Start	Worn spark plugs, improperly set automatic choke, ice (or water) in fuel system.
Stalls Frequently	Automatic choke improperly adjusted and possible dirty air filter or fuel filter.
Performs Sluggishly	Worn spark plugs, dirty fuel or air filter, ignition timing or automatic choke out of adjustment.

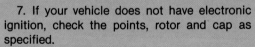

Check spark plug wires on conventional point type ignition for cracks by bending them in a loop around your finger.

Be sure that spark plug wires leading to adjacent cylinders do not run too close together. (Photo courtesy Champion Spark Plug Co.)

7. If your vehicle does not have electronic ignition, check the points, rotor and cap as specified.

8. Check the spark plug wires (used with conventional point-type ignitions) for cracks and burned or broken insulation by bending them in a loop around your finger. Cracked wires decrease fuel efficiency by failing to deliver full voltage to the spark plugs. One misfiring spark plug can cost you as much as 2 mpg.

9. Check the routing of the plug wires. Misfiring can be the result of spark plug leads to adjacent cylinders running parallel to each other and too close together. One wire tends to

pick up voltage from the other causing it to fire "out of time".

10. Check all electrical and ignition circuits for voltage drop and resistance.

11. Check the distributor mechanical and/or vacuum advance mechanisms for proper functioning. The vacuum advance can be checked by twisting the distributor plate in the opposite direction of rotation. It should spring back when released.

12. Check and adjust the valve clearance on engines with mechanical lifters. The clearance should be slightly loose rather than too tight.

SPARK PLUG DIAGNOSIS

Normal

APPEARANCE: This plug is typical of one operating normally. The insulator nose varies from a light tan to grayish color with slight electrode wear. The presence of slight deposits is normal on used plugs and will have no adverse effect on engine performance. The spark plug heat range is correct for the engine and the engine is running normally.

CAUSE: Properly running engine.

RECOMMENDATION: Before reinstalling this plug, the electrodes should be cleaned and filed square. Set the gap to specifications. If the plug has been in service for more than 10-12,000 miles, the entire set should probably be replaced with a fresh set of the same heat range.

Oil Deposits

APPEARANCE: The firing end of the plug is covered with a wet, oily coating.

CAUSE: The problem is poor oil control. On high mileage engines, oil is leaking past the rings or valve guides into the combustion chamber. A common cause is also a plugged PCV valve, and a ruptured fuel pump diaphragm can also cause this condition. Oil fouled plugs such as these are often found in new or recently overhauled engines, before normal oil control is achieved, and can be cleaned and reinstalled.

RECOMMENDATION: A hotter spark plug may temporarily relieve the problem, but the engine is probably in need of work.

Incorrect Heat Range

APPEARANCE: The effects of high temperature on a spark plug are indicated by clean white, often blistered insulator. This can also be accompanied by excessive wear of the electrode, and the absence of deposits.

CAUSE: Check for the correct spark plug heat range. A plug which is too hot for the engine can result in overheating. A car operated mostly at high speeds can require a colder plug. Also check ignition timing, cooling system level, fuel mixture and leaking intake manifold.

RECOMMENDATION: If all ignition and engine adjustments are known to be correct, and no other malfunction exists, install spark plugs one heat range colder.

Carbon Deposits

APPEARANCE: Carbon fouling is easily identified by the presence of dry, soft, black, sooty deposits.

CAUSE: Changing the heat range can often lead to carbon fouling, as can prolonged slow, stop-and-start driving. If the heat range is correct, carbon fouling can be attributed to a rich fuel mixture, sticking choke, clogged air cleaner, worn breaker points, retarded timing or low compression. If only one or two plugs are carbon fouled, check for corroded or cracked wires on the affected plugs. Also look for cracks in the distributor cap between the towers of affected cylinders.

RECOMMENDATION: After the problem is corrected, these plugs can be cleaned and reinstalled if not worn severely.

Photos Courtesy Fram Corporation

MMT Fouled

APPEARANCE: Spark plugs fouled by MMT (Methycyclopentadienyl Maganese Tricarbonyl) have reddish, rusty appearance on the insulator and side electrode.

CAUSE: MMT is an anti-knock additive in gasoline used to replace lead. During the combustion process, the MMT leaves a reddish deposit on the insulator and side electrode.

RECOMMENDATION: No engine malfunction is indicated and the deposits will not affect plug performance any more than lead deposits (see Ash Deposits). MMT fouled plugs can be cleaned, regapped and reinstalled.

High Speed Glazing

APPEARANCE: Glazing appears as shiny coating on the plug, either yellow or tan in color.

CAUSE: During hard, fast acceleration, plug temperatures rise suddenly. Deposits from normal combustion have no chance to fluff-off; instead, they melt on the insulator forming an electrically conductive coating which causes misfiring.

RECOMMENDATION: Glazed plugs are not easily cleaned. They should be replaced with a fresh set of plugs of the correct heat range. If the condition recurs, using plugs with a heat range one step colder may cure the problem.

Ash (Lead) Deposits

APPEARANCE: Ash deposits are characterized by light brown or white colored deposits crusted on the side or center electrodes. In some cases it may give the plug a rusty appearance.

CAUSE: Ash deposits are normally derived from oil or fuel additives burned during normal combustion. Normally they are harmless, though excessive amounts can cause misfiring. If deposits are excessive in short mileage, the valve guides may be worn.

RECOMMENDATION: Ash-fouled plugs can be cleaned, gapped and reinstalled.

Detonation

APPEARANCE: Detonation is usually characterized by a broken plug insulator.

CAUSE: A portion of the fuel charge will begin to burn spontaneously, from the increased heat following ignition. The explosion that results applies extreme pressure to engine components, frequently damaging spark plugs and pistons.

Detonation can result by over-advanced ignition timing, inferior gasoline (low octane) lean air/fuel mixture, poor carburetion, engine lugging or an increase in compression ratio due to combustion chamber deposits or engine modification.

RECOMMENDATION: Replace the plugs after correcting the problem.

EMISSION CONTROLS

13. Be aware of the general condition of the emission control system. It contributes to reduced pollution and should be serviced regularly to maintain efficient engine operation.

14. Check all vacuum lines for dried, cracked or brittle conditions. Something as simple as a leaking vacuum hose can cause poor performance and loss of economy.

15. Avoid tampering with the emission control system. Attempting to improve fuel econ-

FUEL SYSTEM

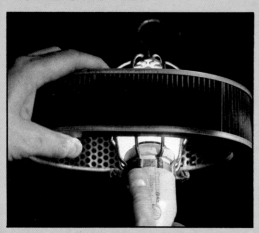

Check the air filter with a light behind it. If you can see light through the filter it can be reused.

Extremely clogged filters should be discarded and replaced with a new one.

18. Replace the air filter regularly. A dirty air filter richens the air/fuel mixture and can increase fuel consumption as much as 10%. Tests show that 1/3 of all vehicles have air filters in need of replacement.

19. Replace the fuel filter at least as often as recommended.

20. Set the idle speed and carburetor mixture to specifications.

21. Check the automatic choke. A sticking or malfunctioning choke wastes gas.

22. During the summer months, adjust the automatic choke for a leaner mixture which will produce faster engine warm-ups.

COOLING SYSTEM

29. Be sure all accessory drive belts are in good condition. Check for cracks or wear.

30. Adjust all accessory drive belts to proper tension.

31. Check all hoses for swollen areas, worn spots, or loose clamps.

32. Check coolant level in the radiator or expansion tank.

33. Be sure the thermostat is operating properly. A stuck thermostat delays engine warm-up and a cold engine uses nearly twice as much fuel as a warm engine.

34. Drain and replace the engine coolant at least as often as recommended. Rust and scale

TIRES & WHEELS

38. Check the tire pressure often with a pencil type gauge. Tests by a major tire manufacturer show that 90% of all vehicles have at least 1 tire improperly inflated. Better mileage can be achieved by over-inflating tires, but never exceed the maximum inflation pressure on the side of the tire.

39. If possible, install radial tires. Radial tires deliver as much as 1/2 mpg more than bias belted tires.

40. Avoid installing super-wide tires. They only create extra rolling resistance and decrease fuel mileage. Stick to the manufacturer's recommendations.

41. Have the wheels properly balanced.

omy by tampering with emission controls is more likely to worsen fuel economy than improve it. Emission control changes on modern engines are not readily reversible.

16. Clean (or replace) the EGR valve and lines as recommended.

17. Be sure that all vacuum lines and hoses are reconnected properly after working under the hood. An unconnected or misrouted vacuum line can wreak havoc with engine performance.

23. Check for fuel leaks at the carburetor, fuel pump, fuel lines and fuel tank. Be sure all lines and connections are tight.

24. Periodically check the tightness of the carburetor and intake manifold attaching nuts and bolts. These are a common place for vacuum leaks to occur.

25. Clean the carburetor periodically and lubricate the linkage.

26. The condition of the tailpipe can be an excellent indicator of proper engine combustion. After a long drive at highway speeds, the inside of the tailpipe should be a light grey in color. Black or soot on the insides indicates an overly rich mixture.

27. Check the fuel pump pressure. The fuel pump may be supplying more fuel than the engine needs.

28. Use the proper grade of gasoline for your engine. Don't try to compensate for knocking or "pinging" by advancing the ignition timing. This practice will only increase plug temperature and the chances of detonation or pre-ignition with relatively little performance gain.

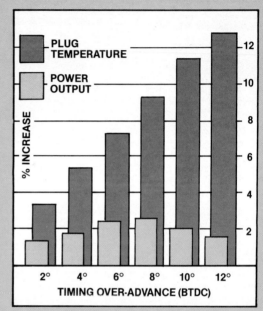

Increasing ignition timing past the specified setting results in a drastic increase in spark plug temperature with increased chance of detonation or preignition. Performance increase is considerably less. (Photo courtesy Champion Spark Plug Co.)

that form in the engine should be flushed out to allow the engine to operate at peak efficiency.

35. Clean the radiator of debris that can decrease cooling efficiency.

36. Install a flex-type or electric cooling fan, if you don't have a clutch type fan. Flex fans use curved plastic blades to push more air at low speeds when more cooling is needed; at high speeds the blades flatten out for less resistance. Electric fans only run when the engine temperature reaches a predetermined level.

37. Check the radiator cap for a worn or cracked gasket. If the cap does not seal properly, the cooling system will not function properly.

42. Be sure the front end is correctly aligned. A misaligned front end actually has wheels going in differed directions. The increased drag can reduce fuel economy by .3 mpg.

43. Correctly adjust the wheel bearings. Wheel bearings that are adjusted too tight increase rolling resistance.

Check tire pressures regularly with a reliable pocket type gauge. Be sure to check the pressure on a cold tire.

GENERAL MAINTENANCE

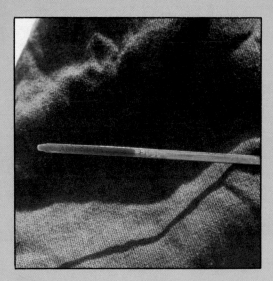

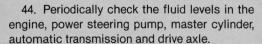

Check the fluid levels (particularly engine oil) on a regular basis. Be sure to check the oil for grit, water or other contamination.

A vacuum gauge is another excellent indicator of internal engine condition and can also be installed in the dash as a mileage indicator.

44. Periodically check the fluid levels in the engine, power steering pump, master cylinder, automatic transmission and drive axle.

45. Change the oil at the recommended interval and change the filter at every oil change. Dirty oil is thick and causes extra friction between moving parts, cutting efficiency and increasing wear. A worn engine requires more frequent tune-ups and gets progressively worse fuel economy. In general, use the lightest viscosity oil for the driving conditions you will encounter.

46. Use the recommended viscosity fluids in the transmission and axle.

47. Be sure the battery is fully charged for fast starts. A slow starting engine wastes fuel.

48. Be sure battery terminals are clean and tight.

49. Check the battery electrolyte level and add distilled water if necessary.

50. Check the exhaust system for crushed pipes, blockages and leaks.

51. Adjust the brakes. Dragging brakes or brakes that are not releasing create increased drag on the engine.

52. Install a vacuum gauge or miles-per-gallon gauge. These gauges visually indicate engine vacuum in the intake manifold. High vacuum = good mileage and low vacuum = poorer mileage. The gauge can also be an excellent indicator of internal engine conditions.

53. Be sure the clutch is properly adjusted. A slipping clutch wastes fuel.

54. Check and periodically lubricate the heat control valve in the exhaust manifold. A sticking or inoperative valve prevents engine warm-up and wastes gas.

55. Keep accurate records to check fuel economy over a period of time. A sudden drop in fuel economy may signal a need for tune-up or other maintenance.

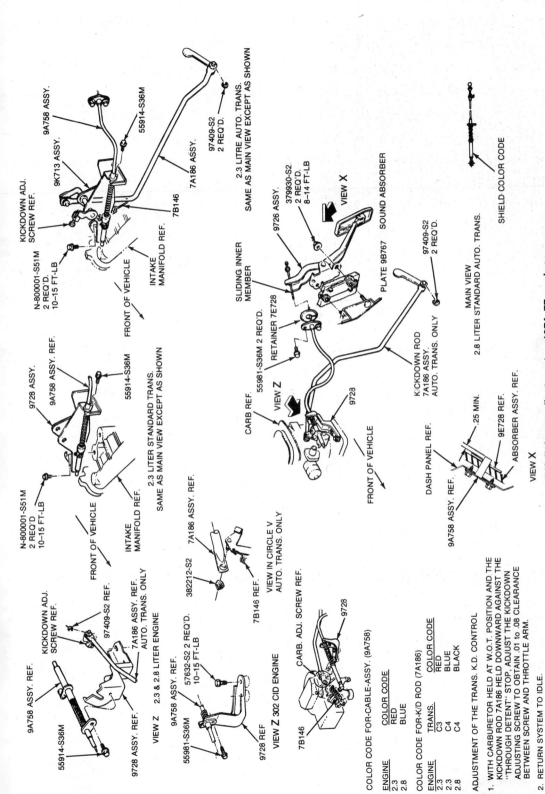

COLOR CODE FOR-CABLE-ASSY. (9A758)

ENGINE	COLOR CODE
2.3	RED
2.8	BLUE

COLOR CODE FOR-K/D ROD (7A186)

ENGINE	TRANS.	COLOR CODE
2.3	C3	RED
2.3	C4	BLUE
2.8	C4	BLACK

ADJUSTMENT OF THE TRANS. K.D. CONTROL

1. WITH CARBURETOR HELD AT W.O.T. POSITION AND THE KICKDOWN ROD 7A186 HELD DOWNWARD AGAINST THE "THROUGH DETENT" STOP, ADJUST THE KICKDOWN ADJUSTING SCREW TO OBTAIN .01 to 08 CLEARANCE BETWEEN SCREW AND THROTTLE ARM.

2. RETURN SYSTEM TO IDLE.

Throttle and downshift linkage adjustments—1974-77 engines

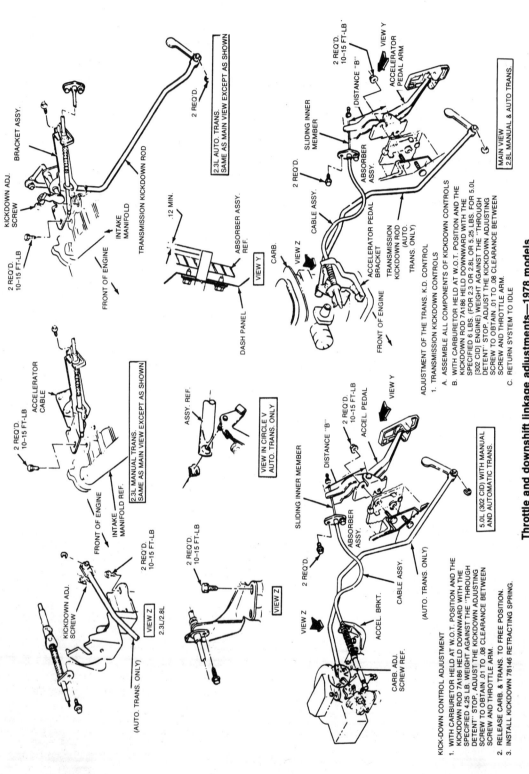

2 REQ'D.

2.3L AUTO. TRANS.
SAME AS MAIN VIEW EXCEPT AS SHOWN

KICKDOWN ADJ.
SCREW

BRACKET ASSY.

2 REQ'D.
10-15 FT-LB

INTAKE
MANIFOLD

TRANSMISSION KICKDOWN ROD

FRONT OF ENGINE

.12 MIN.

ABSORBER ASSY.
REF.

DASH PANEL

VIEW Y

2 REQ'D.
10-15 FT-LB

SLIDING INNER
MEMBER

DISTANCE "B"

VIEW Y

ACCELERATOR
PEDAL ARM

ABSORBER
ASSY.

2 REQ'D.

CABLE ASSY.

VIEW Z

CARB.

ACCELERATOR PEDAL
BRACKET

TRANSMISSION
KICKDOWN ROD
(AUTO.
TRANS. ONLY)

FRONT OF ENGINE

MAIN VIEW
2.8L MANUAL & AUTO TRANS.

ADJUSTMENT OF THE TRANS. K.D. CONTROL

1. TRANSMISSION KICKDOWN CONTROLS

A. ASSEMBLE ALL COMPONENTS OF KICKDOWN CONTROLS
B. WITH CARBURETOR HELD AT W.O.T. POSITION AND THE
   KICKDOWN ROD 7A186 HELD DOWNWARD WITH THE
   SPECIFIED 6 LBS. (FOR 2.3 OR 2.8L OR 5.25 LBS. FOR 5.0L
   [302 CID] ENGINE) WEIGHT AGAINST THE "THROUGH
   DETENT" STOP, ADJUST THE KICKDOWN ADJUSTING
   SCREW TO OBTAIN .01 TO .08 CLEARANCE BETWEEN
   SCREW AND THROTTLE ARM.
C. RETURN SYSTEM TO IDLE.

2 REQ'D.
10-15 FT-LB

ACCELERATOR
CABLE

INTAKE
MANIFOLD REF.

FRONT OF ENGINE

2.3L MANUAL TRANS.
SAME AS MAIN VIEW EXCEPT AS SHOWN

ASSY. REF.

VIEW IN CIRCLE V
AUTO. TRANS. ONLY

KICKDOWN ADJ.
SCREW

VIEW Z
2.3L/2.8L

(AUTO. TRANS. ONLY)

2 REQ'D.
10-15 FT-LB

2 REQ'D.
10-15 FT-LB

VIEW Z

(AUTO. TRANS. ONLY)

CARB. ADJ.
SCREW REF.

SLIDING INNER MEMBER

DISTANCE "B"

2 REQ'D.
10-15 FT-LB

ACCEL. PEDAL

VIEW Y

VIEW Z

ABSORBER
ASSY.

2 REQ'D.

ACCEL. BRKT.

CABLE ASSY.

5.0L (302 CID) WITH MANUAL
AND AUTOMATIC TRANS.

CARB. ADJ.
SCREW REF.

(AUTO. TRANS. ONLY)

KICK-DOWN CONTROL ADJUSTMENT

1. WITH CARBURETOR HELD AT W.O.T. POSITION AND THE
   KICKDOWN ROD 7A186 HELD DOWNWARD WITH THE
   SPECIFIED 4.25 LB. WEIGHT AGAINST THE "THROUGH
   DETENT" STOP, ADJUST THE KICKDOWN ADJUSTING
   SCREW TO OBTAIN .01 TO .08 CLEARANCE BETWEEN
   SCREW AND THROTTLE ARM.
2. RELEASE CARB. & TRANS. TO FREE POSITION.
3. INSTALL KICKDOWN 78146 RETRACTING SPRING.

Throttle and downshift linkage adjustments—1978 models

Carburetor Adjustments

Motorcraft 5200

Year	Float Level Adjust-ment (in.)	Choke Plate Pulldown Clearance Adj (in.)	Automatic Choke Housing Setting	Dechoke Clearance Adjustment (in.)	Fast Idle Cam Index Setting (in.)	Accelerator Pump Stroke Adj (hole number)
'74	0.46	2300—0.280 2800—0.195	Man Trans—1 Rich Auto Trans—Index	0.255	2300—0.158 2800—0.195	#2
'75–'77	0.46	2800—$\frac{3}{8}$ 2300—0.23	All—1 Lean	0.255	2800—0.120–0.130 2300—0.125	#2
'78	$\frac{29}{64}$	6.0 mm	Man Trans—2 Rich Auto Trans—1 Rich	6.0 mm	3.0 mm	#2

Motorcraft 2150

Year	Float Level Adjust-ment (in.)	Choke Plate Pulldown Clearance Adj (in.)	Automatic Choke Housing Setting	Dechoke Clearance Adjustment (in.)	Fast Idle Cam Index Setting (in.)	Accelerator Pump Stroke Adj (hole number)
'75–'77	Dry—$\frac{7}{16}$ Wet—$1\frac{3}{16}$	See Text	All—3 Rich	——	See Text	#2
'78	Dry—$\frac{7}{16}$ Wet—$1\frac{3}{16}$	.110	3 Rich	——	①	#2

① Open throttle slightly, close choke and hold, then release throttle.

or minus $\frac{1}{32}$ in. for 1977 models, and $\frac{1}{16}$ in. on 1978 models. Make a gauge like the one shown in the illustration to the standard dimension. Invert the upper body so that it now is in the upright (normal) position, position the gauge against the bare, cast surface of the upper body measure the vertical distance between the surface and the bottom of the float.

2. If the dimension is not within the tolerance specified above, the setting may be increased by bending the stop tab on the float lever away from the hinge pin, or decreased by bending it toward the hinge pin.

3. Reinstall the upper body using the new gasket.

THROTTLE AND DOWNSHIFT LINKAGE ADJUSTMENT

The throttle and downshift linkage is adjusted as per the illustration. Make sure that there is a 0.01–0.08 in. clearance between the kick-down adjusting screw and the throttle arm.

Chassis Electrical

HEATER

Cars Without Air Conditioning

HEATER ASSEMBLY REMOVAL AND INSTALLATION

1. Drain the cooling system and disconnect the negative battery cable.
2. Disconnect the blower motor ground wire (black) at the engine side of the dash panel.
3. Disconnect the heater hoses at the engine block.
4. Remove the four nuts which attach the heater assembly to the dash, from the engine side of the dash.
5. Working inside the car, remove the glove box.
6. Disconnect the control cables from the heater. Disconnect the motor lead. Remove the radio.
7. Remove the snap-rivet which attaches the forward side of the defroster air duct to the heater assembly. Move the air duct back into the defroster nozzle and disengage it from the tabs on the heater box. Tilt the forward edge of the duct up and forward to disengage it from the nozzle, and remove it from the left-side of the heater assembly.

8. Remove the heater assembly-to-dash panel support bracket mounting screw and remove the heater assembly. At the same time, pull the heater hoses through the dash panel. Then, disconnect the hoses from the heater core in the case.
9. Install in the reverse order of removal.

BLOWER MOTOR REMOVAL AND INSTALLATION

1. Remove the heater assembly.
2. Disconnect the blower motor lead wire from the resistor.
3. Remove the four blower motor mounting plate attaching nuts and remove the motor and wheel.
4. Install in the reverse order.

HEATER CORE REMOVAL AND INSTALLATION

1. Remove the heater assembly.
2. Remove the compression gasket from the cowl air inlet and remove the 11 clips from the case. Separate the case and remove the heater core.
3. Install in the reverse order.

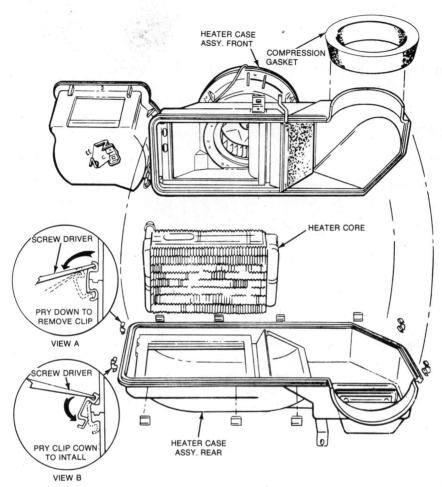

Heater core removal—cars without A/C

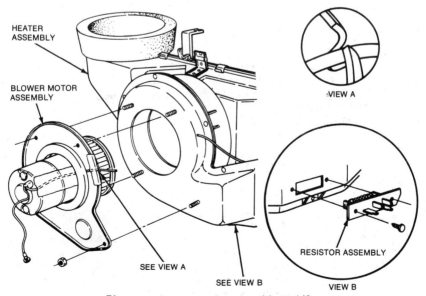

Blower motor removal—cars without A/C

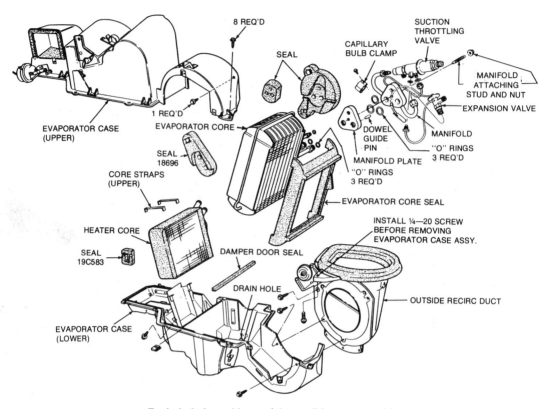

8 REQ'D

SEAL

CAPILLARY
BULB CLAMP

SUCTION
THROTTLING
VALVE

MANIFOLD
ATTACHING
STUD AND NUT

EXPANSION VALVE

1 REQ'D

EVAPORATOR CASE
(UPPER)

EVAPORATOR CORE

DOWEL
GUIDE
PIN

MANIFOLD

"O" RINGS
3 REQ'D

SEAL
18696

MANIFOLD PLATE
"O" RINGS
3 REQ'D

CORE STRAPS
(UPPER)

EVAPORATOR CORE SEAL

INSTALL ¼—20 SCREW
BEFORE REMOVING
EVAPORATOR CASE ASSY.

HEATER CORE

SEAL
19C583

DAMPER DOOR SEAL

DRAIN HOLE

OUTSIDE RECIRC DUCT

EVAPORATOR CASE
(LOWER)

Exploded view of heater/air conditioner assembly

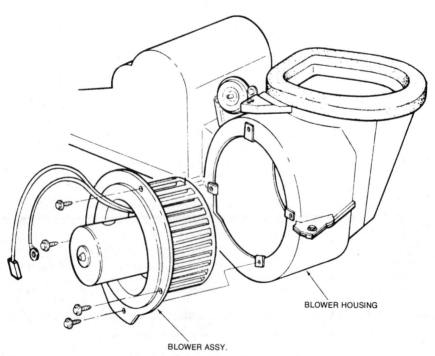

BLOWER HOUSING

BLOWER ASSY.

Blower motor removal—cars with A/C

HEATER

Cars with Air Conditioning

HEATER/AIR CONDITIONER ASSEMBLY REMOVAL AND INSTALLATION

NOTE: *This procedure requires evacuation of the air conditioning refrigerant. Failure to exercise proper safety precautions could cause personal injury.*

1. Drain the engine coolant, discharge the air conditioning system and disconnect the battery.

2. Remove the A/C refrigerant lines and the front half of the refrigerant manifold.

3. Remove the manifold mounting stud with vice-grips to provide clearance when removing the evaporator case assembly.

4. Disconnect the two heater hoses from the core tubes in the engine compartment.

5. Remove the A/C condensate drain hose in the engine compartment.

6. Remove the glove box.

7. Disconnect the vacuum hoses from the evaporator case.

8. Disconnect the temperature control cable from the blend door crank arm.

9. Remove the heat distribution duct. Remove the mode door vacuum motor which is retained to the evaporator case assembly by two nuts and a spring nut.

10. Remove the lower section of the A/C defrost plenum which is retained by three screws and two retaining tabs.

11. Remove the blower motor and wheel from the blower scroll.

12. Install one ¼-20 hex-washer head screw to the mounting tab on the inlet duct to upper cowl bracket to hold the duct in place. Leave this screw in place when installing the case assembly.

13. Remove the three inlet duct-to-evaporator case attaching screws through the blower scroll opening.

14. Remove the one upper case-to-inlet duct attaching screw located under the outside-recirculating motor mounting bracket.

15. Remove the two evaporator-to-upper cowl bracket attaching screws.

16. Remove the four evaporator-to-dash panel attaching nuts in the engine compartment.

17. Rotate the evaporator assembly down and away from the dash panel and out from under the instrument panel.

18. Install the heater/evaporator case in the reverse order of removal. During installation, position the fold-down door of the defrost plenum between the locating tabs on each side of the plenum and tape it in position with two pieces of black tape 1 in. wide by 4 in. long.

BLOWER MOTOR REMOVAL AND INSTALLATION

The blower motor and wheel is integrally located within the scroll portion of the evaporator assembly on the right-side of the evaporator case. To remove the blower motor and wheel, remove the glove box and remove the four screws retaining the blower motor and wheel in the blower scroll. Install the blower motor and wheel in the reverse order of removal.

HEATER CORE REMOVAL AND INSTALLATION

1. Remove the heater/air conditioner assembly from the vehicle.

2. Remove the eight upper-to-lower case attaching screws.

3. Remove the rubber seal from the heater core tubes.

4. Remove the upper half of the evaporator case.

5. Move the rubber seal on the evaporator core forward to clear the case mounting stud and pull the core out of the lower case.

6. Remove the two heater core upper straps.

7. Remove the air deflector mounting screw on the lower case to the left of the heater core, remove the deflector and remove the heater core.

8. Install in the reverse order of removal. Be sure to install new rope sealer around the flange of the lower case before installing the upper half of the case. Install new O-rings on the manifold plate. Dip the new O-rings in refrigerant oil before installing them.

RADIO

REMOVAL AND INSTALLATION

1. Disconnect the negative battery cable at the battery.

2. Pull off the control knobs and discs. Unscrew the control shaft nuts and remove the washers.

3. On models equipped with a Motorola

radio, pull out the ash tray to expose the lower mounting bolt. Remove the bolt.

4. Remove the radio rear support attaching nut or bolt.

5. Lower the radio down from behind the instrument panel.

6. Disconnect the power lead wire, the antenna cable, and the speaker leads. Remove the radio from the car.

7. Reverse the above procedure to install.

WINDSHIELD WIPERS

BLADE REPLACEMENT

See Chapter 1 under "Routine Maintenance."

MOTOR REMOVAL AND INSTALLATION

1. Loosen the two nuts and disconnect the wiper pivot shaft and link assembly from the motor drive arm ball. A link retaining clip is used.

2. Remove the three motor attaching screws and lower the motor away from the left-side of the dash.

3. Disconnect the wiper motor wires and remove the motor.

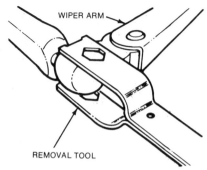

REMOVAL TOOL

Wiper arm removal

4. To install, position the motor under the dash and install the wires. Operate the motor to ensure it is in Park position.

5. Position the motor to the dash and install the retaining screws.

6. Position the wiper pivot shaft and link assembly to the motor drive arm ball and tighten the two nuts. Install the retaining clip.

PIVOT SHAFT AND LINKAGE REMOVAL AND INSTALLATION

1. Remove the windshield wiper arms and blades from the pivot shafts.

2. Loosen the two nuts retaining the

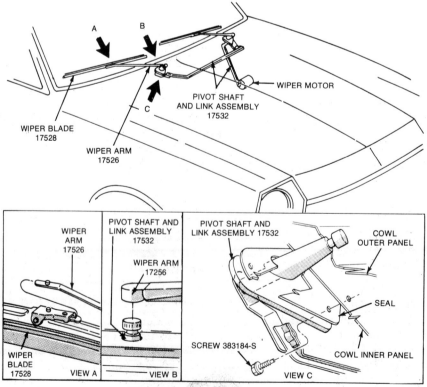

Pivot shaft and link assembly

wiper pivot shaft and link assembly to the motor drive arm ball.

3. Remove the screws attaching each pivot shaft.

4. Remove the pivot shaft and link assembly from under the left-side of the dash.

5. Reverse above procedure to install. Operate the wiper motor before installing the wiper blades to ensure the pivots are in Park.

NOTE: *On a car with air conditioning, the blower motor and housing must be removed to gain access to the wiper pivot and link assembly. After removing the blower motor and housing, follow the previous procedure.*

INSTRUMENT CLUSTER

REMOVAL AND INSTALLATION

1. Disconnect the negative battery cable.

2. Disconnect the speedometer cable underneath the dashboard by pressing on the flat surface of the plastic connector and pulling the cable away from the head.

3. Disconnect the wiring harness to the instrument cluster underneath the dashboard by squeezing the clips on the quick disconnect and pulling apart.

4. Pull off the windshield wiper switch knob (1974–75 only), and remove the bezel nut. To remove the windshield wiper switch knob, use a piece of coat-hanger wire with a bend in one end. Insert the end of the wire in the slot in the base of the knob and pull back to release the knob.

5. Remove the headlight switch as described under "Headlight Switch Removal and Installation."

6. Remove the three upper and four lower attaching screws for the cluster trim cover and remove the cover.

7. Remove the two upper and two lower screws attaching the cluster to the instrument panel.

8. Pull out the cluster far enough to gain access to the tachometer. Disconnect the tachometer.

9. Remove the cluster from the instrument panel.

10. Reverse the above procedure to install.

Ignition Switch
SWITCH REMOVAL AND INSTALLATION

1. To gain access to the switch, remove the steering column shroud and disconnect

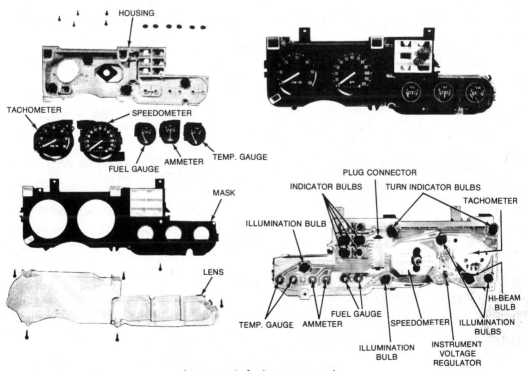

Instrument cluster components

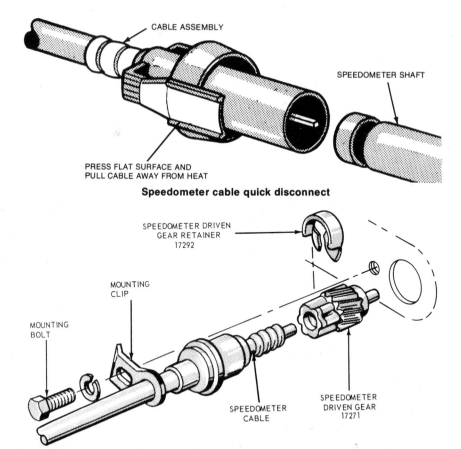

CABLE ASSEMBLY

SPEEDOMETER SHAFT

PRESS FLAT SURFACE AND
PULL CABLE AWAY FROM HEAT

Speedometer cable quick disconnect

SPEEDOMETER DRIVEN
GEAR RETAINER
17292

MOUNTING
CLIP

MOUNTING
BOLT

SPEEDOMETER
CABLE

SPEEDOMETER
DRIVEN GEAR
17271

Speedometer cable to transmission mounting

and lower the steering column from the brake support bracket.

2. Disconnect the negative battery cable.

3. Disconnect the switch wiring at the multiple connector.

4. Remove the two nuts which retain the ignition switch to the steering column.

5. Remove the pin which connects the switch plunger to the actuating rod and remove the switch.

6. When installing the ignition switch, both the switch and the ignition lock must be in the LOCK position. The manual parts can be held in place by turning the ignition lock cylinder to the LOCK position with the transmission in Park (automatic transmission) or Reverse (manual transmission). To hold the switch in the LOCK position, insert a pin in the hole on the top of the switch, after manually moving the switch to the LOCK position.

7. Position the hole in the end of the switch plunger to the hole in the actuator and install the connecting pin.

8. Position the ignition switch on the

steering column, and install, but do not tighten the retaining nuts.

9. Move the switch up and down on the steering column to find the midpoint of the actuating rod lash, then tighten the switch retaining nuts.

10. Remove the locking pin from the switch and install the steering column and shroud.

LOCK CYLINDER REMOVAL AND INSTALLATION

1. Disconnect the negative battery cable.

2. Remove the steering wheel. Refer to Chapter 8. Insert a stiff wire into the hole located in the lock cylinder housing.

3. Place the gearshift lever in Reverse on manual transmission cars and in Park on cars with an automatic transmission, and turn the ignition key to the On position.

4. Depress the wire and remove the lock cylinder and wire.

5. Insert the new cylinder into the housing and turn it to the Off position. This will lock the cylinder into position.

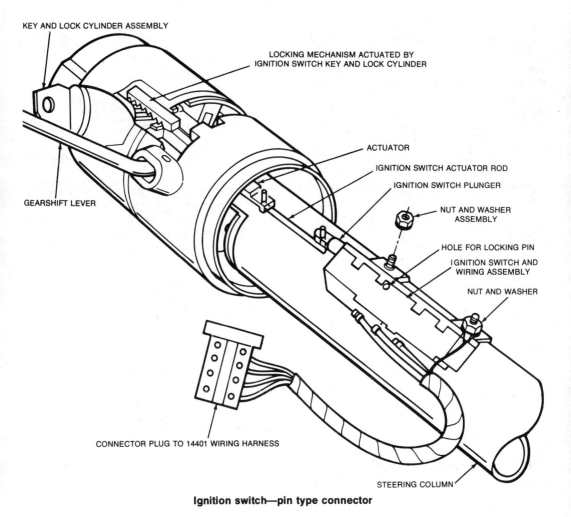

KEY AND LOCK CYLINDER ASSEMBLY

LOCKING MECHANISM ACTUATED BY
IGNITION SWITCH KEY AND LOCK CYLINDER

ACTUATOR

IGNITION SWITCH ACTUATOR ROD

IGNITION SWITCH PLUNGER

NUT AND WASHER
ASSEMBLY

HOLE FOR LOCKING PIN

IGNITION SWITCH AND
WIRING ASSEMBLY

NUT AND WASHER

GEARSHIFT LEVER

CONNECTOR PLUG TO 14401 WIRING HARNESS

STEERING COLUMN

Ignition switch—pin type connector

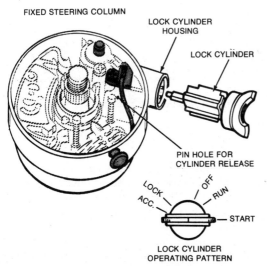

FIXED STEERING COLUMN

LOCK CYLINDER
HOUSING

LOCK CYLINDER

PIN HOLE FOR
CYLINDER RELEASE

LOCK
ACC.
OFF
RUN
START

LOCK CYLINDER
OPERATING PATTERN

Ignition switch lock cylinder removal

6. Reinstall the steering wheel and pad.
7. Connect the negative battery cable.

STARTER INTERLOCK

All 1974 Mustang II models are equipped with a seat belt/starter interlock system. The system consists of a warning light, buzzer, seat sensors, switches in the outboard belt retractors, and an electronic logic module. Basically, the starter will not engage unless the driver and other front seat passenger sit in the seat and pull out the seat belt. Unless the driver or passenger has remained seated and buckled, the sequence must be repeated every time the engine is started. Leaving the belts pulled all the way out also will prevent the engine from being started, as the belts must be retracted and buckled each time the engine is started. In the event of a starter interlock system failure, or to permit the use of a remote starter switch when working under the hood, a starter interlock by-pass switch is located in the engine compartment on the left wheel well, thereby eliminating the need to perform the buckling sequence.

NOTE: *Each time the by-pass switch is operated, the buckling sequence may be eliminated once and once only. The system may not be permanently by-passed.*

Disabling the Starter Interlock System

Cars built after October 29, 1974 are no longer required to have the interlock system. The system may be legally disabled on cars which have it, but the following procedure must be used:

1. Open the hood and locate the override switch and terminal connector attached to it.

2. Remove the number 32 wire(s) which are red with a light blue stripe, and the number 33 wire(s) which are white with pink dots. After cutting these wires, splice them together.

3. To remove the buzzer, remove the terminal connector from the buzzer and tape it to the wiring harness to prevent it from rattling. The buzzer now can be removed and discarded. Federal law requires that the warning light still be operable, so do not disconnect it.

LIGHTING

HEADLIGHT SWITCH REMOVAL AND INSTALLATION

1. Disconnect the battery ground cable.
2. Through the hole in the underside of

Headlight switch

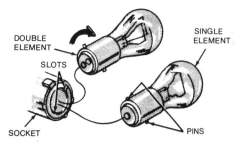

DEPRESS BULB IN SOCKET AND ROTATE COUNTERCLOCKWISE, THEN, PULL BULB FROM SOCKET.

TO INSTALL, INSPECT PINS ON BULB BASE. IF THEY ARE NOT SAME DISTANCE FROM BOTTOM OF BASE, THEY MUST BE INSERTED INTO THE CORRECT SLOT. DETERMINE WHICH SLOT IN SOCKET PINS SHOULD BE INSERTD INTO AND PUSH BULB BASE INTO SOCKET, THEN, ROTATE CLOCKWISE TO ENGAGE PINS, IF BULB WILL NOT ROTATE, PINS ARE IN WRONG SLOTS.

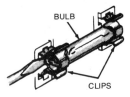

INSERT A SCREWDRIVER UNDER END OF BULB AND PRY BULB OUT OF CLIPS.

TO INTALL, POSITION BULB TO CLIPS AND PRESS INTO PLACE.

PULL BULB STRAIGHT OUT OF SOCKET TO REMOVE.

TO INSTALL, POSITION BULB TO SOCKET AND PUSH STRAIGHT IN UNTIL SEATED.

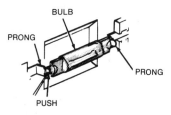

TO REMOVE, PUSH PRONG TOWARD BULB AND LIFT BULB FROM PRONG.

TO INSTALL, ENGAGE ONE END OF THE BULB OVER ONE PRONG, THEN, PUSH OTHER PRONG TOWARD BULB AND ENGAGE BULB END OVER PRONG. DO NOT FORCE BULB END OVER PRONG.

Light bulb replacement

the instrument panel, press the release button with a screwdriver, and remove the knob and shaft assembly.

3. Remove the bezel nut, lower the switch and disconnect the multiple connector.

4. Remove the switch.

5. Install the headlight switch in the reverse order of removal.

HEADLIGHT REMOVAL AND INSTALLATION

1. Remove the headlight door retaining screws and remove the headlight door.

2. Remove the three screws attaching the bulb retainer to the adjusting ring and remove the retainer.

3. Pull the headlight bulb forward and disconnect the three-prong connector plug.

4. To install, connect the three-prong plug to the new headlight. Place the bulb in position, locating the bulb glass tabs in the positioning slots.

5. Position the retainer ring over the bulb and install the attaching screws.

6. Place the headlight door (chrome molding) over the headlight and install the retaining screws.

7. Check the aim of the headlight. Adjust

Light Bulb Specifications

Light Bulb Description	Trade Number
Headlights	6014
Front Park & Turn Signal	1157NA
Front Side Marker	194 ('75–'76—161)
Rear Tail/Stop	1157
Turn Signal	1156
Back-Up Light	1156
License Plate Light	194 (168—'78)
Dome Light	212-2
Rear Side Marker Light	194
Auto Trans Indicator (floor shift)	1445 ('77–'78—1893)
Seat Belt Light	194
Illumination Light	1445
Turn Signal Indicator	194
Hi-Beam Indicator	194
Instrument Illumination Lights	194
Oil Warning	194
Brake System Warning	154 ('77–'78—194)
Door Courtesy Light	214-2
Glove Compartment Light	1816
Luggage Compartment Light	631 ('75–'76—89)
Engine Compartment Light	631 ('75–'76—161)
Courtesy Light-Under Inst Panel	631 ('75–'78—89)
Map Light	212-2 ('75–'78—1816)
Warning Light-Parking Brake	194
Clock Illumination Light (Console)	194
Digital Clock III	194
Rear Window Electric Defrost Ind	Bulb and Wire Assembly
Ash Recept Light-Instr Panel	1892
Door Ajar Light	194
Headlights On Warning	194
Heater	161
Radio	1893
Luggage or Engine Compartment	89
Radio (All RPO)	
Radio Pilot Light	
AM	1893
AM/FM/MPX	1893
AM/FM/MPX/Tape	37 ('77–'78—1893)
Radio Stereo Light	
AM/FM/MPX	1892 ('77–'78—1893)
AM/FM/MPX/Tape	37 ('77–'78—1893)

as necessary using the headlight adjusting screws.

WIRING DIAGRAMS

Wiring diagrams have been left out of this book. As cars have become more complex, and available with longer and longer option lists, wiring diagrams have grown in size and complexity also. It has become virtually impossible to provide a readable reproduction in a reasonable number of pages. Information on ordering wiring diagrams from the vehicle manufacturer can be found in the owners manual.

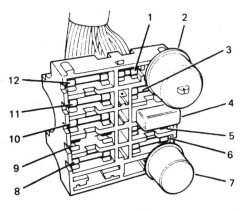

Fuse box

Fuses, Fusible Links, and Circuit Protection Chart

Fuse Position No.	Circuit	Circuit Protection Rating	Location
1	Instrument Panel & Cluster Illumination Clock, Radio, Dial Lights Heater, or A/C Controls, Ash Tray Illumination	4 AMP fuse	Fuse panel located on dash panel directly above the accelerator pedal.
2	Turn Signal Flasher		
3	Oil, Brakes and Seat Belt Indicator Lights, Seat Belt Indicator Lights, Seat Belt Module and Buzzer, Throttle Solenoid Positioner	7.5 AMP fuse	
4	W/S Wiper (2 speed)	6 AMP CB	
5	Windshield Washer Pump; Door Ajar, Parking Brake and Headlights, Indicator Light; Electric Rear Window Defroster Control and Indicator Light; and Anti-Theft Module	15 AMP fuse	
6	Radio/Tape Player	7.5 AMP fuse	
7	Emergency Flasher		
8	Horn & Cigar Lighter	20 AMP fuse	

Fuses, Fusible Links, and
Circuit Protection Chart (cont.)

Fuse Position No.	Circuit	Circuit Protection Rating	Location
9	Courtesy, Dome, Map, Luggage & Glove Compt Lights, Clock Feed, Ignition Key Warning and Headlights "ON" Buzzer, Anti-Theft Trigger and Horn Feed; and Seat Belt Module, Headlights "ON" Indicator Light	15 AMP fuse	
10	Stop Lights & Emergency Lights	15 AMP fuse	
11	Heater-Defroster Air Conditioner	15 AMP fuse 30 AMP fuse (35 AMP—1978)	
12	Back-up Lights	15 AMP fuse	
	Park, Tail Sidemarker, and License Lights; Turn Indicator Light (PRND21)	15 AMP CB	Integral with lighting switch
	Headlights	18 AMP CB	
	Load Circuit	Fuse link	In harness (dealer repair)
	Electric Choke	Fuse link	
	Electric Rear Window Defroster	Fuse link	
	Engine Compartment Light	Fuse link	

Clutch and Transmission

MANUAL TRANSMISSION

The manual transmission installed in the Mustang II is a Ford design, top cover 4-speed. All forward gears are fully synchronized, helically cut and in constant mesh. A floor-mounted shifter is standard on all applications. The shifter is the single sliding rail type, requiring no adjustments.

The clutch is of conventional design, using a single dry disc, diaphragm-type pressure plate, and release (throwout bearing). An 8.5 in. diameter disc is used on all 2300 cc applications, and a 9.5 inch disc on the 2800 cc V6. The 302 V8 available with manual transmission in 1977 and 1978 model years uses a 10 inch clutch.

TRANSMISSION REMOVAL AND INSTALLATION

1. Place the shifter in Neutral.
2. Pull back the carpet, as shown in the accompanying illustration, unscrew the four shifter boot retaining bolts, and remove the boot.
3. Remove the three bolts retaining the shifter to the top of the transmission extension. Remove the shifter from the transmission.
4. Raise the car on a hoist. If a hoist is not available, first raise the front, then the rear of

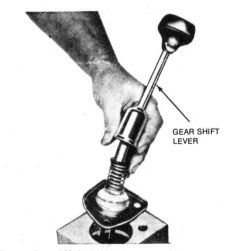

Removing shift lever

the car at least a foot off the ground and install sturdy jackstands beneath each of the four jacking points or adjacent reinforced box members.

5. Matchmark and disconnect the driveshaft at the transmission output shaft flange. Place rags in the extension housing to prevent loss of transmission lubricant.
6. Disconnect the back-up light and seat belt sensing switch leads at the transmission.
7. Remove the speedometer cable bracket attaching screw and lift the cable

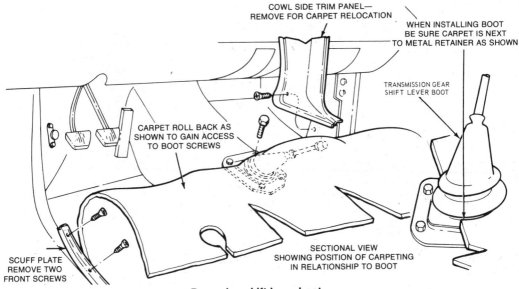

COWL SIDE TRIM PANEL—
REMOVE FOR CARPET RELOCATION

WHEN INSTALLING BOOT
BE SURE CARPET IS NEXT
TO METAL RETAINER AS SHOWN

TRANSMISSION GEAR
SHIFT LEVER BOOT

CARPET ROLL BACK AS
SHOWN TO GAIN ACCESS
TO BOOT SCREWS

SCUFF PLATE
REMOVE TWO
FRONT SCREWS

SECTIONAL VIEW
SHOWING POSITION OF CARPETING
IN RELATIONSHIP TO BOOT

Removing shift lever boot

from the extension housing. Plug the hole to prevent leakage.

8. Support the rear of the engine with a jack cushioned with a wooden block. Remove the bolts attaching the crossmember to the body. Then, remove the two bolts retaining the crossmember to the transmission extension housing and remove the crossmember.

9. Slowly lower the jack and engine until the angle looks right to pull the transmission clear of the engine. There should be no interference between the top of the bellhousing and the transmission tunnel (floor pan). Remove the bolts attaching the transmission to the bell housing.

10. At this point, enlist some support either from a friend or a good transmission jack. The transmission is heavy. Finally, with sufficient support, pull the transmission straight back and off the engine.

11. Prior to installation, intall the clutch release lever and bearing (if removed) in the bellhousing. Also, lube the input shaft splines with a light coating of white grease.

12. Position the transmission input shaft into the flywheel housing.

NOTE: *It may be necessary to place the transmission in gear and rotate the output shaft to align the input shaft and clutch splines.*

13. Install the transmission-to-bell-housing attaching bolts and torque them to 25–36 ft lbs.

14. Raise the engine until the transmission is in its normal position. Install the crossmember.

15. Install the speedometer cable and retaining screw.

16. Connect the driveshaft to the transmission output shaft flange, making sure that the matchmarks align.

17. Fill the transmission (if necessary) to the bottom of the filler plug hole with the specified lubricant (see Chapter 1).

18. Connect the back-up light and seat belt switch leads to the transmission.

19. Lower the car to the ground.

20. After making sure that the shift lever insulator is in a straight downward position on the shift rail, place the shifter in the extension housing so that the forked ends locate in the insulator.

21. Install the three shifter retaining bolts. Install the boot and retaining plate. Position the carpet on the floor and install the step plates and screws (if removed). Install the 2 kick panels, and shifter locknut and shift knob (if removed).

22. Check the shifter for proper operation. Road-test the car.

CLUTCH

The clutch is a system of parts which, when engaged, connects the engine to the transmission. When the clutch is disengaged (clutch pedal pushed in), the turning motion of the engine crankshaft is separated from the transmission. Since the engine does not produce enough torque at idle to turn the rear wheels and start the car in motion, it is

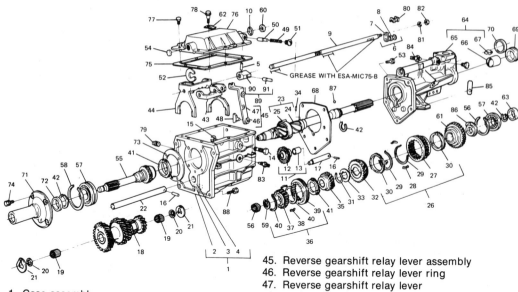

GREASE WITH ESA-MIC75-B

1. Case assembly
2. Case
3. Case magnet
4. Spring nut $^{9}/_{64}$ in.
5. Roll pin $^{3}/_{16}$ in. dia. x $^{13}/_{16}$
6. Gearshift shaft offset lever assembly
7. Gearshift shaft offset lever
8. Gearshift shaft offset lever pin
9. Shifter shaft
10. O-ring
11. Reverse idler slider gear and bushing assembly
12. Reverse idler sliding gear
13. Reverse idler gear bushing
14. Reverse gear selector fork pivot pin
15. Retaining ring $^{7}/_{16}$ in.
16. Spring pin ¼ x 1
17. Reverse idler gear shaft
18. Countershaft gear
19. Countershaft gear bearing roller
20. Flat washer 208/.918
21. Countershaft gear thrust washer
22. Countershaft
23. Output shaft assembly
24. Output shaft
25. 1st and 2nd gear clutch synchronizer hub
26. Output shaft and gear assembly
27. Reverse sliding gear
28. Synchronizer hub insert
29. Synchronizer retaining spring
30. Synchronizer blocking ring
31. 2nd gear retaining snap-ring
32. 2nd gear
33. 2nd gear thrust washer
34. Rolled spring pin ⅛ x ⅜
35. 3rd gear
36. 3rd and 4th gear synchronizer assembly
37. 4th gear clutch synchronizer hub
38. Synchronizer hub insert
39. 3rd and 4th gear clutch hub sleeve
40. Synchronizer retaining spring
41. Synchronizer blocking ring
42. Main drive gear bearing snap-ring
43. 1st and 2nd gearshift fork
44. 3rd and 4th gearshift fork
45. Reverse gearshift relay lever assembly
46. Reverse gearshift relay lever ring
47. Reverse gearshift relay lever
48. Reverse gearshift fork
49. Shifter interlock spring
50. Plunger
51. Round head flat screw M12 x 10
52. Gear selector interlock plate
53. Hex head screw and washer assembly M10 x 30
54. Welch plug ¾ in. dia.
55. Input shaft
56. Mainshaft roller bearing
57. Main drive gear ball bearing assembly
58. Main drive gear bearing snap-ring
59. Retaining ring 1 in.
60. Shifter shaft seal
61. 1st gear
62. Spark control switch wire retaining clip
63. Speedometer drive gear
64. Extension assembly
65. Extension
66. Extension bushing
67. Reverse gearshift lever stop
68. Extension gasket
69. Extension oil seal assembly
70. Extension plug
71. Input shaft gear bearing retainer
72. Input shaft oil seal assembly
73. Input shaft bearing retainer gasket
74. Hex head lockbolt M8 x 20
75. Case cover gasket
76. Case cover
77. Hex head screw M6 x 20
78. Hex head washer shoulder bolt M6 x 32
79. Pipe plug ½ x 14
80. Gearshift damper bushing
81. Lockwasher
82. Hexagon nut
83. Back-up lamp switch assembly
84. Seat belt warning sensor switch assembly
85. Service identification tag
86. 1st gear thrust washer
87. Ball ¼ in. dia.
88. Screw and lock washer assembly M12 x 40
89. Control selector arm assembly
90. Control selector arm
91. Gearshift pin

Exploded view—4-speed transmission

necessary to gradually connect the engine to the rest of the drive train to prevent the engine from stalling on acceleration. It is also much easier to shift the gears within a manual transmission when engine power is disconnected from the transmission.

When the clutch pedal is depressed, a cable attached to the clutch pedal pulls on the clutch release lever. This causes the clutch release bearing, which is attached to the clutch release lever, to press against the release fingers of the pressure plate. This removes the spring pressure of the pressure plate from the clutch disc. Since it was this pressure which was holding the clutch disc against the engine flywheel, the clutch can now move away from the flywheel. If engine power is to be transmitted to the rest of the power train, the clutch must be firmly held against the flywheel (which is attached to, and turns with, the crankshaft). By depressing the clutch pedal you allow the clutch disc to move away from the flywheel, thus isolating engine power from the rest of the drive train.

CLUTCH REMOVAL AND INSTALLATION

2300 cc Four

1. Raise the car and remove the transmission as outlined under "Transmission Removal and Installation."
2. Remove the clutch lever cover and the cable retainer. Disengage the clutch cable from the release lever. Disconnect the cable from the bellhousing.
3. Disconnect the starter cable and remove the starter from the flywheel housing.
4. Remove the bolts retaining the engine rear plate to the front lower part of the flywheel housing.
5. Remove the bolts retaining the flywheel housing to the cylinder block. Slide the housing back far enough to clear the pressure plate and remove the housing.
6. Loosen each of the six pressure plate retaining bolts gradually, in a diagonal pattern, so that the spring tension may be released without distorting the cover. If the same pressure plate is to be reused, matchmark the flywheel and pressure plate for installation.
7. Remove the pressure plate and clutch disc from the flywheel.
8. Inspect all of the clutch components as outlined under "Clutch Component Inspection."

9. To install, position the clutch disc and pressure plate on the flywheel with the three dowel pins aligned. Replace any missing or damaged dowel pins. Install the pressure plate retaining bolts loosely, only tight enough to hold the plate in place. Take care not to contaminate the pressure plate or disc with oil or grease.
10. Align the disc with a centering shaft, dummy shaft, or an old input shaft from an extra transmission. Push the aligning shaft in until it seats in the pilot bearing. Then, tighten the pressure plate retaining bolts diagonally, in sequence, to a final torque of 12–24 ft lbs. If the flywheel starts to rotate, block it by placing a screwdriver in one of the ring gear teeth wedged against a stationary object.
11. Fill the grease groove of the release bearing hub with white grease. Clean all excess from inside the bore of the bearing hub.
12. Reverse Steps 1–5 to install, taking care to torque the flywheel housing-to-engine bolts to 28–38 ft lbs. Adjust clutch free-play.

2800 cc V6

1. Raise the car and remove the transmission as outlined under "Transmission Removal and Installation."
2. Remove the release bearing. Remove the clutch cable retaining clip and clevis pin from the clevis at the release lever connection. Disengage the clevis from the cable.
3. Disconnect the clutch cable from the flywheel housing by removing the nut attaching the cable to the housing, and then pulling the cable toward the front of the car until it clears the housing boss.
4. Disconnect the clutch return spring.
5. Disconnect the starter cable and remove the starter from the flywheel housing.
6. Remove the four bolts retaining #2A crossmember to the body and remove the crossmember.
7. Remove the bolts retaining the engine rear plate to the front lower part of the flywheel housing.
8. Remove the bolts attaching the housing to the cylinder block. Lift off the engine decking shield and set it aside for reinstallation. Move the flywheel housing back far enough to clear the pressure plate and remove the housing.
9. Loosen each of the six pressure plate retaining bolts gradually, in a diagonal pat-

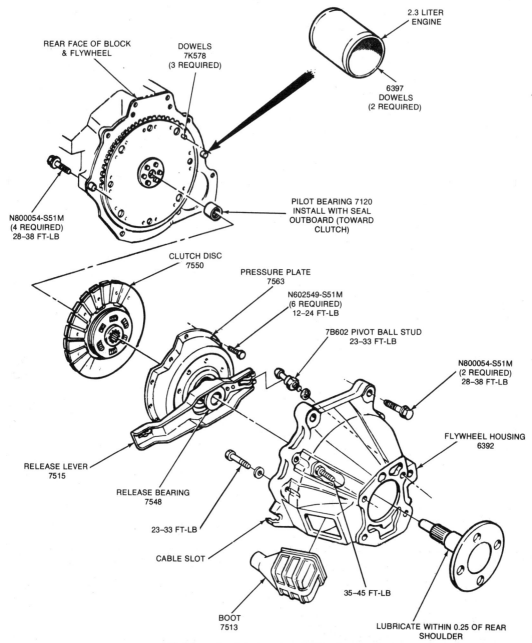

Clutch and related parts—2300cc four

tern, so that the spring tension may be released without distorting the cover. If the same pressure plate is to be reused, matchmark the flywheel and pressure plate for installation.

10. Remove the pressure plate and clutch disc from the flywheel.

11. Inspect all of the clutch components as outlined under "Clutch Component Inspection."

12. To install, position the clutch disc and

pressure plate on the flywheel with the three dowel pins aligned. Replace any missing or damaged dowel pins. Install the pressure plate retaining bolts loosely, only tight enough to hold the plate in place. Take care not to contaminate the pressure plate or disc with oil or grease.

13. Align the disc with a centering shaft, dummy shaft, or an old input shaft from an extra transmission. Push the aligning shaft in until it seats in the pilot bearing. Then,

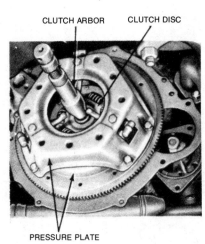

CLUTCH ARBOR   CLUTCH DISC

PRESSURE PLATE

Aligning clutch disc

tighten the pressure plate retaining bolts diagonally, in sequence, to a final torque of 12–24 ft lbs. Block the flywheel, if necessary, with a screwdriver.

14. Fill the grease groove of the release bearing hub with lithium base grease. Clean all excess grease from inside the bore of the bearing hub.

15. Reverse Steps 1–8 to install, taking care to torque the flywheel housing-to-engine bolts to 28–38 ft lbs. Adjust clutch free-play.

302 V8

1. Remove the clutch cable retaining clip and loosen the clutch cable adjusting nut to put some slack in the cable. Raise the vehicle on a hoist or support securely on axle stands.

2. Refer to procedures above and remove the transmission.

3. Remove the clutch lever cover and cable retainer, and then disengage the clutch cable from the release lever.

4. Disconnect the clutch cable from the flywheel housing.

5. Remove the starter electrical cable and starter motor from the clutch housing.

6. Remove the bolts that secure the engine rear plate to the front/lower part of the flywheel housing. Then, remove the bolts that attach the housing to the engine block and move the housing back just far enough to clear the pressure plate and remove it.

7. Pull the clutch release lever through the window in the housing until the retainer spring is disengaged from the pivot and remove it.

8. Loosen the six pressure plate cover attaching bolts *evenly* to release spring tension without distorting the cover. If the pressure plate and cover are to be (or might be) reused, mark the cover and the flywheel so the pressure plate and flywheel can be reinstalled in the same relative positions. Remove the pressure plate and clutch disc from the flywheel.

9. Inspect the clutch components as described under "Clutch Component Inspection."

NOTE: *In the following Step, avoid touching the clutch disc face or contaminating parts with oil or grease.*

10. Install the clutch release lever. Then,

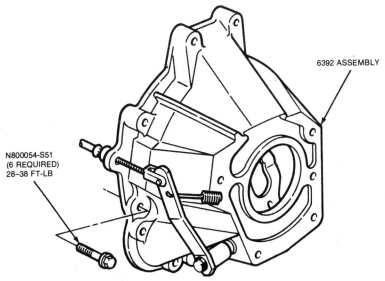

6392 ASSEMBLY

N800054-S51
(6 REQUIRED)
28–38 FT-LB

Clutch housing and release lever assembly

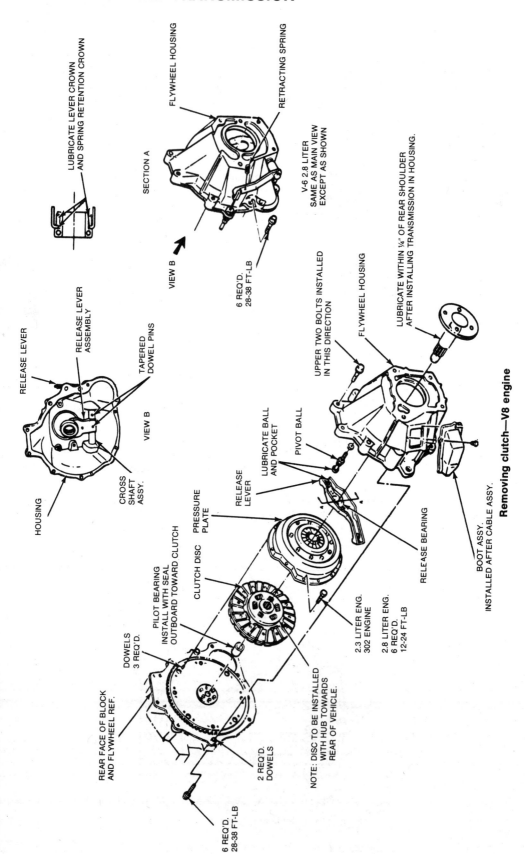

LUBRICATE LEVER CROWN AND SPRING RETENTION CROWN

FLYWHEEL HOUSING

RETRACTING SPRING

SECTION A

V-6 2.8 LITER SAME AS MAIN VIEW EXCEPT AS SHOWN

VIEW B

6 REQ'D. 28-38 FT-LB

LUBRICATE WITHIN ¼" OF REAR SHOULDER AFTER INSTALLING TRANSMISSION IN HOUSING.

UPPER TWO BOLTS INSTALLED IN THIS DIRECTION

FLYWHEEL HOUSING

RELEASE LEVER

RELEASE LEVER ASSEMBLY

TAPERED DOWEL PINS

VIEW B

HOUSING

CROSS SHAFT ASSY.

LUBRICATE BALL AND POCKET

PIVOT BALL

RELEASE LEVER

PRESSURE PLATE

CLUTCH DISC

PILOT BEARING INSTALL WITH SEAL OUTBOARD TOWARD CLUTCH

DOWELS 3 REQ'D.

REAR FACE OF BLOCK AND FLYWHEEL REF.

RELEASE BEARING

BOOT ASSY. INSTALLED AFTER CABLE ASSY.

2.3 LITER ENG. 302 ENGINE

2.8 LITER ENG. 6 REQ'D. 12-24 FT-LB

2 REQ'D. DOWELS

NOTE: DISC TO BE INSTALLED WITH HUB TOWARDS REAR OF VEHICLE.

6 REQ'D. 28-38 FT-LB

Removing clutch—V8 engine

position the clutch disc and pressure plate (assembled) on the flywheel. Make sure the three dowel pins on the flywheel are properly aligned with corresponding holes in the pressure plate. If any of the dowel pins are either damaged or missing, they *must* be replaced. Then, just start the cover attaching bolts.

11. Align the clutch disc using an appropriate alignment tool inserted into the pilot bearing. Then, alternately and evenly tighten the cover bolts to 12–24 ft lbs. Then, remove the alignment tool.

12. Apply a light film of lithium base grease to: the outside diameter of the transmission front bearing retainer; the release lever fork and antirattle spring where they contact the release bearing hub; the release bearing surface which contacts the pressure plate release fingers.

13. Fill the grease groove of the release bearing hub with the same grease used in Step 12. Clean *all* excess grease from the inside bore of the bearing hub. *Failure to do this will cause grease to contaminate the clutch disc and cause slippage.*

14. Position the clutch release bearing onto the release lever.

15. Attach the release lever and bearing to the flywheel housing.

16. Make certain that the flywheel housing and cylinder block mounting surfaces are clean and that dowels are in good condition. *Replace any missing or damaged dowels.*

17. Position the housing on the dowels against the block. Install and alternately and evenly torque housing bolts to 28–38 ft lbs.

18. Install the starter and reconnect starter cable.

19. Install the engine rear plate to the front of the flywheel housing and install bolts.

20. Connect the clutch cable to the flywheel housing and to the release lever. Reinstall the cable retainer.

21. Install the clutch lever cover. Adjust clutch pedal free-play.

CLUTCH COMPONENT INSPECTION

If the clutch disc, pressure plate, and clutch release bearing have a considerable amount of mileage on them, it is probably smart to replace them all at the same time. This will save you the aggravation of having to yank the transmission out again in a few thousand miles if one of them should fail.

Clutch Disc

The coil springs near the center of the disc are supposed to be loose. Do not replace the clutch because the springs are loose.

If the clutch disc is contaminated with oil or any other foreign substance, it must be replaced. However, you must also locate and repair the source of the leak to avoid repeated clutch failure. If the clutch disc is worn, distorted or if the friction material is loose on the disc it must be replaced.

Pressure Plate

If the face of the plate is worn, scored, or burnt, it should be replaced. If the release fingers are excessively worn, the pressure plate must be replaced. Do not clean the pressure plate in any way other than wiping the face with alcohol.

Release Bearing

The bearing is prelubricated and should not be cleaned with solvent. Inspect the rivets and spring clips on the bearing cover; if they are loose, replace the bearing.

Check the face of the bearing; if it is distorted, replace the bearing.

As a general rule, whenever in doubt about the release bearing, replace it. Release bearings are not that expensive and they make very annoying noises when they go bad.

Pilot Bearing

The pilot bearing is a press fit in the end of the crankshaft. Therefore, if it is loose it must be replaced. If the opening in the center of the bearing is worn out of round it should be replaced.

Do not lubricate the pilot bearing with grease.

If it is necessary to replace the bearing, it can be removed with an expanding type slide hammer.

Flywheel

If the flywheel is grooved or burnt, it is necessary to replace the flywheel or have the surface machined by an automotive machine shop.

CLUTCH FREE-PLAY ADJUSTMENT

1. Remove the cable retaining clip at the dash panel.

2. Remove the screw holding the cable attaching bracket on the fender apron.

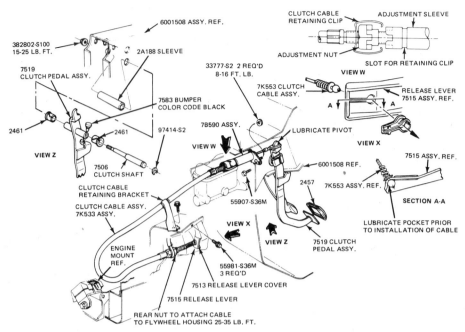

1. With clutch cable installed at both ends · pull clutch cable forward by hand until it stops

2. Then turn adjustment nut until surface A of nut contacts surface B of adjustment sleeve · release hand from cable & then index adjustment nut into next notch of adjustment sleeve.

3. Place retention spring into position · make sure both tabs of spring are installed into slot of adjustment sleeve.

4. Bolt clutch cable bracket to finder apron

Clutch free-play adjustment—2300cc four

3. Pull the cable toward the front of the vehicle until the adjusting nut can be turned. Rotate the nut away from the adjustment sleeve about ¼ in.

4. Release the cable, and then pull the cable again until free movement of the release lever is eliminated.

5. Rotate the adjusting nut toward the adjustment sleeve until contact is made, then index it into the next notch.

6. Reinstall the cable retaining clip and cable attaching bracket, and screw on the fender apron.

AUTOMATIC TRANSMISSION

Two types of automatic transmission are used in the Mustang II. A Ford designed C3 unit is used in all 2300 cc Four applications. An-

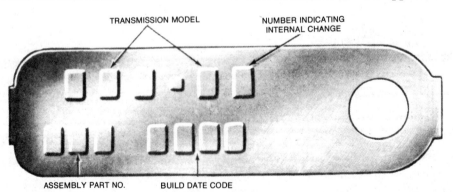

Transmission identification tag—1974–76

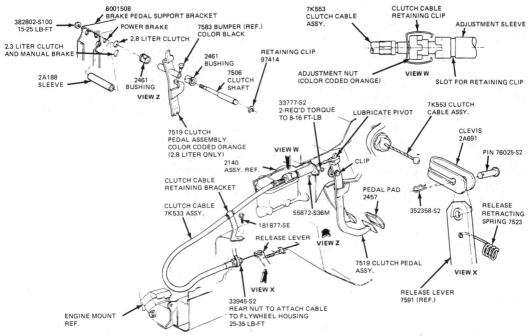

1. Remove clutch cable retaining clip

2. Remove bolt holding cable retaining bracket to fender apron

3. Pull clutch cable forward by hand until it stops

4. Then turn adjustment nut until surface of a nut contacts surface B of adjustment sleeve—release

hand from cable & then index adjustment nut into next notch of adjustment sleeve

5. Place cable retaining clip into position, make sure both tabs of spring are installed into slot of adjustment sleeve

6. Bolt clutch cable bracket to fender apron

Clutch free-play adjustment—2800cc V6 and 302 V8

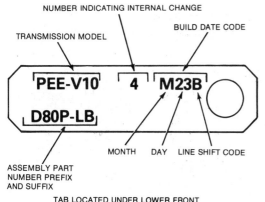

Transmission identification tag—1977–78

other Ford designed C4 unit is installed in the 2800 cc V6 and 302 V8 equipped models.

Both transmissions are 3-speed units capable of providing automatic upshifts and downshifts through three forward gear ratios, and also capable of providing manual selection of First and Second gears.

An identification tag is located under the lower front intermediate servo cover bolt. The tag shows the model prefix and suffix, assembly part numbers, and the built-date code.

While the automatic transmission is a complex unit, there are some adjustments that may be performed by the average do-it-yourselfer. Internal transmission repairs are best referred to a qualified repair shop.

PAN REMOVAL AND FLUID DRAINING

Normal maintenance and lubrication requirements do not include periodic changes of transmission fluid. A change is required only when it is necessary to replace the transmission fluid. At this time the converter, oil cooler core, and cooler lines should be thoroughly flushed out to remove any dirt or deposits that might clog these units later.

When filling a completely dry (no fluid) transmission and converter, install five quarts of transmission fluid and then start the engine. Shift the selector lever through all positions briefly and set at Park position. Check the fluid level and add enough fluid to raise the level to between the marks on the dipstick. Do not overfill the transmission.

The procedure for a partial drain and refill of the transmission fluid is as follows:

1. Raise the car on a hoist or jackstands.

2. Place a drain pan under the transmission pan.

NOTE: *On PEA and PEF models (see identification tag), the fluid is drained by disconnecting the filler tube from the transmission fluid pan.*

3. Loosen the pan attaching bolts to allow the fluid to drain.

4. When the fluid has stopped draining to level of the pan flange, remove the pan bolts starting at the rear and along both sides of the pan, allowing the pan to drop and drain gradually.

5. When all the transmission fluid has drained, remove the pan and the fluid filter and clean them.

6. After completing the transmission repairs or adjustments, install the fluid filter screen, a new pan gasket, and the pan on the tranmission. Tighten the pan attaching bolts to 12–16 ft lbs.

NOTE: *Be sure to use Type "F" transmission fluid. The use of any other type of fluid such as Type "A" suffix "A," or DEXRON will materially affect the service life of the transmission.*

7. Install three quarts of transmission fluid through the filler tube. If the filler tube was removed to drain the transmission, install the filler tube using a new O-ring.

8. Start and run the engine for a few minutes at low idle speed and then at the fast idle speed (about 1,200 rpm) until the normal operating temperature is reached. Do not race the engine.

9. Move the selector lever through all positions and place it at the Park position. Check the fluid level, and add fluid until the level is between the "add" and "full" marks on the dipstick. Do not overfill the transmission.

AUTOMATIC SHIFT LINKAGE ADJUSTMENT

1. Place the transmission selector lever in the Drive position.

2. Raise the vehicle and loosen the manual linkage shift rod at the selector lever.

3. Move the transmission manual lever to

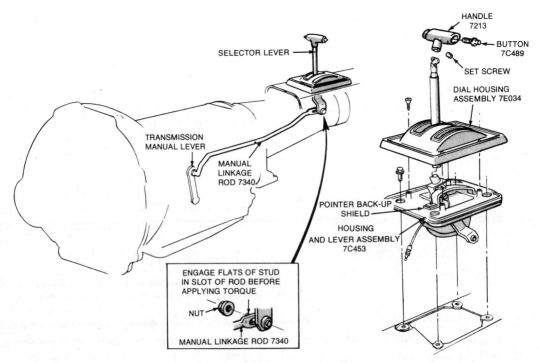

Automatic transmission manual linkage

the Drive position (second detent position from the rear of the transmission).

4. Tighten the nut on the manual linkage shift rod to 10–20 ft lbs.

5. Lower the car and check transmission operation.

NEUTRAL START SWITCH ADJUSTMENT

1. Adjust the shift linkage as outlined under "Automatic Shift Linkage Adjustment."

2. Loosen the two neutral start switch attaching bolts underneath the transmission selector lever on the transmission case.

3. With the lever on the transmission in Neutral, rotate the switch and insert a No. 43 gauge pin into the gauge pin holes of the switch. The gauge pin must be inserted a full $31/_{64}$ in. into the 3 holes of the switch.

4. Torque the two switch attaching bolts to 55–75 in. lbs. Remove the gauge pin from the switch.

5. Check the operation of the switch. The engine should start only with the selector lever in Neutral or Park.

NEUTRAL START SWITCH REPLACEMENT

1. Raise the car, with the transmission in Neutral, and disconnect the downshift linkage.

2. Remove the neutral switch attaching bolts and remove the switch and disconnect the wires.

3. Install the replacement switch and adjust it as described above.

4. Install the downshift outer lever.

5. Connect the downshift linkage rod to the downshift lever.

BAND ADJUSTMENTS
C3 and C4 Transmissions

CAUTION: *The torque figures and numbers of turns given in these procedures must be exactly correct to prevent transmission damage.*

NOTE: *The only band adjustment required on the C3 transmission is on the front band.*

INTERMEDIATE (FRONT) BAND

1. Wipe clean the area around the adjusting screw on the side of the transmission, near the left-front corner of the transmission.

2. Remove the adjusting screw locknut and discard it.

3. Install a new locknut on the adjusting screw but do not tighten it.

4. Tighten the adjusting screw to exactly 10 ft lbs.

5. Back off the adjusting screw exactly 1¾ turns; 1½ turns on the C3.

6. Hold the adjusting screw so that it *does*

Adjusting intermediate (front) band

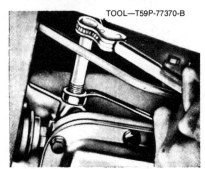

Adjusting low-reverse band (C4 only)

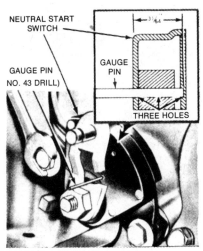

Neutral start switch adjustment

not turn and tighten the adjusting screw locknut to 35–45 ft lbs.

LOW-REVERSE BAND (C4 ONLY)

1. Wipe clean the area around the adjusting screw on the side of the transmission, near the right-rear corner.

2. Remove the adjusting screw locknut and discard it.

3. Install a new locknut on the adjusting screw but do not tighten it.

4. Tighten the adjusting screw to *exactly 10 ft lbs.*

5. Back off the adjusting screw *exactly 3 full turns.*

6. Hold the adjusting screw so that it *does not turn* and tighten the adjusting screw to 35–45 ft lbs.

Drive Train

DRIVELINE

The driveshaft is the means by which the power from the engine and transmission (in the front of the car) is transferred to the differential and rear axles, and finally to the rear wheels.

The driveshaft assembly incorporates two universal joints—ont at each end—and a slip yoke at the front end of the assembly, which fits into the back of the transmission.

All driveshafts are balanced when installed in a car. It is therefore imperative that before applying undercoating to the chassis, the driveshaft and universal joint assembly be completely covered to prevent the accidental application of undercoating to their surfaces, and the subsequent loss of balance.

Driveshaft and U-Joints
REMOVAL

The procedure for removing the driveshaft assembly—complete with universal joint and slip yoke—is as follows:

1. Mark the relationship of the rear driveshaft yoke and the drive pinion flange of the axle. If the original yellow alignment marks are visible, there is no need for new marks. The purpose of this marking is to facilitate in-

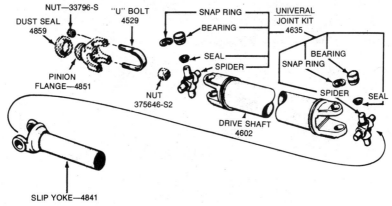

Driveshaft and universal joints disassembled

stallation of the assembly in its exact original position, thereby maintaining proper balance.

2. Remove the four bolts which hold the rear universal joint to the pinion flange. Wrap tape around the loose bearing caps in order to prevent them from falling off the spider.

3. Pull the driveshaft toward the rear of the vehicle until the slip yoke clears the transmission housing and the seal. Plug the hole at the rear of the transmission housing or place a container under the opening to catch any fluid which might leak.

UNIVERSAL JOINT OVERHAUL

1. Position the driveshaft assembly in a sturdy vise.

2. Remove the snap-rings which retain the bearings in the slip yoke (front only) and in the driveshaft (front and rear).

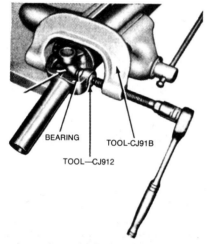

Removing universal joint bearing

3. Using a large punch or an arbor press, drive one of the bearings in toward the center of the universal joint, which will force the opposite bearing out.

4. As each bearing is pressed or punched far enough out of the universal joint assembly that it is accessible, grip it with a pair of pliers, and pull it from the driveshaft yoke. Drive or press the spider in the opposite direction in order to make the opposite bearing accessible, and pull it free with a pair of pliers. Use this procedure to remove all bearings from both universal joints.

5. After removing the bearings, lift the spider from the yoke.

6. Thoroughly clean all dirt and foreign matter from the yoke on both ends of the driveshaft.

NOTE: *When installing new bearings in the yokes, it is advisable to use an arbor press. However, if this tool is not available, the bearings should be driven into position with extreme care, as a heavy jolt on the needle bearings can easily damage or misalign them, greatly shortening their life and hampering their efficiency.*

7. Start a new bearing into the yoke at the rear of the driveshaft.

8. Position a new spider in the rear yoke and press (or drive) the new bearing ¼ in. below the outer surface of the yoke.

9. With the bearing in position, install a new snap-ring.

10. Start a new bearing into the opposite side of the yoke.

11. Press (or drive) the bearing until the opposite bearing—which you have just installed—contacts the inner surface of the snap-ring.

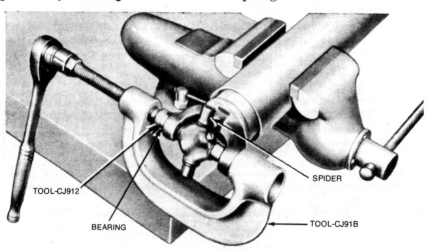

Installing universal joint bearings

12. Install a new snap-ring on the second bearing. It may be necessary to grind the surface of this second snap-ring.

13. Reposition the driveshaft in the vise, so that the front universal joint is accessible.

14. Install the new bearings, new spider, and new snap-rings in the same manner as you did for the rear universal joint.

15. Position the slip yoke on the spider. Install new bearings, nylon thrust bearings, and snap-rings.

16. Check both reassembled joints for freedom of movement. If misalignment of any part is causing a bind, a sharp rap on the side of the yoke with a brass hammer should seat the bearing needles and provide the desired freedom of movement. Care should be exercised to firmly support the shaft end during this operation, as well as to prevent blows to the bearings themselves. Under no circumstances should a driveshaft be installed in a car if there is any binding in the universal joints.

DRIVESHAFT INSTALLATION

1. Carefully inspect the rubber seal on the output shaft and the seal in end of the transmission extension housing. Replace them if they are damaged.

2. Examine the lugs on the axle pinion flange and replace the flange if the lugs are shaved or distorted.

3. Coat the yoke spline with special-purpose lubricant. The Ford part number for this lubricant is B8A-19589-A.

4. Remove the plug from the rear of the transmission housing.

5. Insert the yoke into the transmission housing and onto the transmission output shaft. Make sure that the yoke assembly does not bottom on the output shaft with excessive force.

6. Locate the marks which you made on the rear driveshaft yoke and the pinion flange prior to removal of the driveshaft assembly. Install the driveshaft assembly with the marks properly aligned.

7. Install the U-bolts and nuts which attach the universal joint to the pinion flange. Torque the U-bolt nuts to 8–15 ft lbs.

REAR AXLE ASSEMBLY

The Mustang II uses two basic rear axle assemblies. They are the integral carrier type and the removable carrier type. The integral carrier type is used on most four and six cylinder applications. Although this type has an inspection plate which provides working access to the differential components, it is recommended that the entire axle assembly be removed from the car to perform differential work.

The removable carrier type is used on most 302 V8 models. The carrier assembly may be unbolted from the axle housings to perform differential work.

Procedures for removing the axle shafts and their bearings are the same for both types. In order to remove the axles, the housings need not be removed from the car.

Axle Shaft

SHAFT REMOVAL AND INSTALLATION/BEARING REPLACEMENT

NOTE: *Bearings must be pressed on and off the shaft with an arbor press. Unless you have access to one, it is inadvisable to attempt any repair work on the axle shaft and bearing assemblies.*

Removable Carrier Axle

1. Remove the wheel, tire, and brake drum.

2. Remove the nuts holding the retainer plate to the backing plate. Disconnect the brake line.

3. Remove the retainer and install nuts, finger-tight, to prevent the brake backing plate from being dislodged.

4. Pull out the axle shaft and bearing assembly, using a slide hammer.

NOTE: *If end-play is found to be excessive, the bearing should be replaced. Shimming the bearing is not recommended as this ignores end-play of the bearing itself and could result in improper seating of the bearing.*

5. Using a chisel, nick the bearing retainer in 3 or 4 places. The retainer does not have to be cut, but merely collapsed sufficiently to allow the bearing retainer to be slid from the shaft.

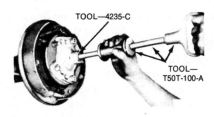

TOOL—4235-C

TOOL—T50T-100-A

Removing axle shaft

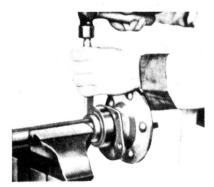

Removing rear wheel bearing retaining ring

6. Press off the bearing and install the new one by pressing it into position.

7. Press on the new retainer.

NOTE: *Do not attempt to press the bearing and the retainer on at the same time.*

8. Assemble the shaft and bearing in the housing, being sure that the bearing is seated properly in the housing.

9. Install the retainer, drum, wheel, and tire. Bleed the brakes.

AXLE SHAFT SEAL REPLACEMENT

1. Remove the axle shaft from the rear axle assembly, following the procedures previously discussed.

2. Using a two-fingered seal puller (slide hammer), remove the seal from the axle housing.

3. Thoroughly clean the recess in the rear axle housing from which the seal was removed.

TOOL 1177
T72P-4245-A
OR
T72P-4245-B

Installing rear wheel bearing oil seal

4. Position a new seal on the housing and drive it into place with a seal installation tool. If this tool is not available, a wood block may be substituted.

NOTE: *Although the right and left-hand seals are identical, there are many different types of seals which have been used on Mustang II rear axle assemblies. It is advis-*

able to have one of the old seals with you when you are purchasing new ones.

5. When the seal is properly installed, install the axle shaft.

Integral Carrier Axle

1. Remove the wheel cover, wheel, and tire from the brake drum. Remove the speed nuts that secure the brake drum to the axle housing flange, and remove the brake drum.

2. Remove the wheel bearing retainer plate attaching nuts, going in through the holes in the axle shaft flange. Then, bolt a slide hammer onto the axle shaft flange, and pull the axle shaft assembly out off the axle housing.

3. Remove the brake backing plate and hang it from the frame rail with a piece of wire.

4. To remove the rear wheel bearing, loosen the inner retainer ring. This is done by using a cold chisel to put several deep nicks in the outer diameter. Then, slide the retaining ring off.

5. The shaft assembly must be placed in a press in such a way as to support the bearing all the way around while pressing squarely downward on the inner end of the axle shaft. HEAT MUST NOT BE USED TO EASE REMOVAL, AS THE SHAFT BEARING JOURNAL WILL BE WEAKENED IF THE SHAFT IS HEATED.

6. Inspect the machined surfaces of the axle shaft and housing for rough spots or any irregularities, as these will keep the oil seal from sealing. Check the axle shaft splines for burrs, wear, or torque damage. Carefully remove any burrs or rough spots, or replace the assembly. Note that if a new axle shaft is used, the seal *must* be replaced. See the procedure below.

7. Position the retainer plate and a new bearing on the shaft, with the retainer plate going on first. The bearing *must* be pressed on when supported even from all sides *by the inner retaining ring only. Do not use heat.* Press the bearing on until it seats firmly on the shaft shoulder.

8. Wipe all lubricant from the inside of the axle housing in the area of the oil seal before installing the hex seal. Seals must be removed and installed with a slide hammer designed especially for this purpose or distortion and leakage will result.

9. Install a new gasket on the housing flange, and install the brake backing plate.

10. *Carefully* slide the axle shaft into the

housing so that the rough forging (un-machined) areas of the shaft will not damage the seal. *The entire length of the shaft (including the splined area) right up to the seal journal, must pass through the seal without touching it.* If the seal is roughened or cut during the procedure, it will leak. You may have to rotate the shaft very slowly to get the splines to engage the center of the differential side gear. Once the splines engage, push the axle in until the bearing bottoms in the housing.

11. Install the bearing retainer plate onto the mounting bolts at the axle housing, install attaching nuts, and torque to 20–40 ft-lbs.

12. Install the brake drum and brake drum retaining nuts. Install wheel, tire, and wheel cover.

Suspension and Steering

FRONT SUSPENSION

The front wheels mount to, and rotate on, the spindles. The spindles are attached to the upper and lower control arms by the upper and lower ball joints. A coil spring is mounted between the upper and lower control arms on both sides of the front suspension. A pair of shock absorbers provide suspension dampening. The shocks are attached to the lower control arms and the tops of the spring housings.

A rod-type stabilizing strut mounts between two rubber pads at the front crossmember and each lower control arm. The strut aids the lower end of the spindle through its cycle of vertical movement and serves to cushion the fore and aft thrust of the suspension. A stabilizer bar is used to control suspension roll.

Coil Spring

REMOVAL AND INSTALLATION

CAUTION: *Extreme care must be exercised when removing or installing coil springs. If possible, safety chain the lower coil of the spring to some stationary component. When a coil spring is released it will suddenly attempt to reach its unloaded* length before it was intalled in a 3,000 lb automobile. If the spring should strike you, it could result in serious injury.

1. Raise the front of the car and place safety stands under the frame.

2. Remove the shock absorber.

3. Disconnect the strut bar from the lower control arm.

4. Place a floor jack under the lower control arm.

5. Remove the nut and bolt which attaches the lower control arm to the front crossmember. Disconnect the stabilizer bar.

6. Carefully lower the jack slowly to relieve the spring pressure from the lower arm.

7. Remove the coil spring and upper insulator.

8. To install, place the upper insulator on the spring and secure it in place with tape.

9. Position the spring on the lower control arm. Make sure that the bottom of the spring properly engages the seat on the lower control arm. The end of the spring must not be more than ½ in. from the end of the depression in the lower control arm.

10. Raise the lower control arm with the floor jack and guide the lower control arm and the top of the spring into place. Install the lower control arm attaching bolt and nut. Tighten the lower control arm attaching bolt to 75–110 ft lbs.

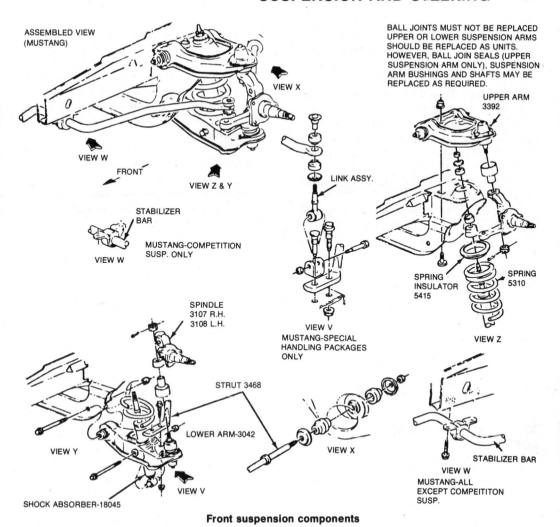

ASSEMBLED VIEW
(MUSTANG)

BALL JOINTS MUST NOT BE REPLACED
UPPER OR LOWER SUSPENSION ARMS
SHOULD BE REPLACED AS UNITS.
HOWEVER, BALL JOIN SEALS (UPPER
SUSPENSION ARM ONLY), SUSPENSION
ARM BUSHINGS AND SHAFTS MAY BE
REPLACED AS REQUIRED.

VIEW X

VIEW W

FRONT

VIEW Z & Y

STABILIZER
BAR

VIEW W

MUSTANG-COMPETITION
SUSP. ONLY

LINK ASSY.

UPPER ARM
3392

SPRING
INSULATOR
5415

SPRING
5310

VIEW Z

SPINDLE
3107 R.H.
3108 L.H.

STRUT 3468

LOWER ARM-3042

VIEW V
MUSTANG-SPECIAL
HANDLING PACKAGES
ONLY

VIEW Y

VIEW X

VIEW V

SHOCK ABSORBER-18045

STABILIZER BAR

VIEW W
MUSTANG-ALL
EXCEPT COMPEITITON
SUSP.

Front suspension components

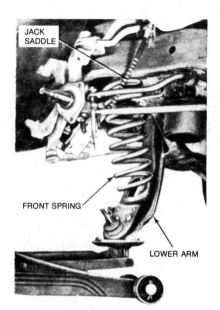

JACK
SADDLE

FRONT SPRING

LOWER ARM

Removing coil spring and lower control arm

11. Install the shock absorber after removing the jack.

12. Attach the strut bar to the lower control arm. Connect the stabilizer bar.

13. Remove the safety stands and lower the vehicle.

Front Shock Absorber

Replace any shock absorber with a damaged or dented body, bent piston rod or fluid leakage. With the shock absorber still installed, rock the suspension up and down and make sure that when you let go the car does not continue to rock up and down. Once removed, you may check the shock absorber by extending and compressing it by hand. Depending on the factory calibrated valving of the shock, the shock should offer substantial resistance in both directions without seizing. The resistance does not have to be exactly even, but it should be close. Also, check the shock for air pockets or areas of no resistance.

REMOVAL AND INSTALLATION

1. Remove the nut, washer, and bushing from the upper end of the shock. If the shaft of the shock absorber turns while you are trying to remove the attaching nut, hold the shaft in place with an adjustable wrench while removing the nut.

2. Raise the front end of the vehicle and install safety stands.

3. Disconnect the bottom of the shock absorber from the lower control arm. It may be necessary to raise the lower arm to remove the bottom bolt.

4. Remove the shock absorber from under the car. Lightly wire brush the shock studs to remove rust and corrosion.

5. Position the new shock absorber on the lower control arm and install the attaching bolts.

6. Remove the safety stands and lower the car.

7. Connect the top of the shock absorber to the upper spring pad.

ADJUSTING ADJUSTABLE SHOCK ABSORBERS

Some Mustangs with competition or Rallye Package suspension incorporate adjustable shock absorbers. These are initially adjusted to the regular (R) control position. To adjust to a different position, first remove the shock from the car, as described above. Then, remove the rubber jounce cushion from the piston rod. This will permit the shock to be fully compressed. Compress the shock fully to engage a dog on the end of the piston with a slot in the base valve.

Rotate the piston rod to the next position until a definite click is heard and movement to a definite detent is noticed. The notch in the upper piston rod head will be lined up with the control rod setting.

To reinstall, pull out the piston rod, install the jounce cushion, and then reinstall the shock.

Upper Ball Joint
INSPECTION

1. Raise the vehicle by placing a floor jack under the lower arm. Do not allow the lower arm to hang freely with the vehicle on a hoist or bumper jack.

2. Have an assistant grasp the bottom of the tire and move the wheel in and out.

3. As the wheel is being moved, observe the upper control arm where the spindle attaches to it. Any movement between the upper part of the spindle and the upper ball joint indicates a bad control arm which must be replaced.

NOTE: *During this check the lower ball joint will be unloaded and may move; this is normal and not an indication of a bad ball joint. Also, do not mistake a loose wheel bearing for a defective ball joint.*

REPLACEMENT

1. Raise the vehicle on a hoist and allow the front wheels to fall to their full down position.

2. Drill a ⅛ in. hole completely through each ball joint attaching rivet.

3. Using a large chisel, cut off the head of each rivet and drive them from the upper arm.

4. Place a jack under the lower arm and lower the vehicle about 6 in.

5. Remove the cotter pin and attaching nut from the ball joint stud.

6. Using a suitable tool, loosen the ball joint stud from the spindle and remove the ball joint from the upper arm.

7. Clean all metal burrs from the upper arm and install the new ball joint, using the service part nuts and bolts to attach the ball joint to the upper arm. Do not attempt to rerivet the ball joint once it has been removed.

8. Have the front end alignment checked.

Lower Ball Joint
INSPECTION

1. Raise the vehicle by placing a floor jack under the lower arm; or, raise the vehicle on a hoist and place a jackstand under the lower arm and lower the vehicle onto it to remove the preload from the lower ball joint.

2. Have an assistant grasp the wheel top and bottom and apply alternate in and out pressure to the top and bottom of the wheel.

3. Radial play of ¼ in. is acceptable measured at the inside of the wheel adjacent to the lower arm.

NOTE: *This radial play is multiplied at the outer circumference of the tire and should be measured only at the inside of the wheel.*

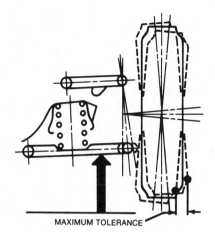

Measuring lower ball joint radial play

REPLACEMENT

1. Raise the vehicle and allow the front wheels to fall to their full down position.

2. Drill a ⅛ in. hole completely through each ball joint attaching rivet.

3. Use a ⅜ in. drill in the pilot hole to drill off the head of the rivet.

4. Drive the rivets from the lower arm.

5. Place a jack under the lower arm and lower the vehicle about 6 in.

6. Remove the lower ball joint stud cotter pin and attaching nut.

7. Using a suitable tool, loosen the ball joint from the spindle and remove the ball joint from the lower arm.

8. Clean all metal burrs from the lower arm and install the new ball joint, using the service part nuts and bolts to attach the ball joint to the lower arm. Do not attempt to rerivet the ball joint once it has been removed.

9. Have the front end alignment checked.

Upper Control Arm
REMOVAL AND INSTALLATION

1. Raise the vehicle and remove the coil spring. See "Front Spring" in this chapter.

2. Remove the tire and wheel, remove the caliper attaching bolts, and position the caliper out of the way with the brake hose attached. Remove the rotor and hub from the spindle.

3. Remove the cotter pin and attaching nut from the ball joint stud.

4. Using a suitable tool, loosen the upper ball joint from the spindle.

5. Remove the upper arm inner shaft attaching bolts and remove the arm and shaft from the chassis as an assembly.

6. Reverse above procedure to install.

7. Have the front end alignment checked.

Lower Control Arm
REMOVAL AND INSTALLATION

1. Raise the car and support it with stands placed in back of the lower arms.

2. Remove the wheel from the hub. Remove the caliper from the rotor and wire it back out of the way. Then, remove the hub and rotor from the spindle.

3. Disconnect the shock absorber and remove it.

4. Remove cotter pins from the upper and lower ball joint stud nuts.

5. Remove two bolts and nuts holding the strut to the lower arm.

6. Loosen the lower ball joint stud nut two turns. Do not remove this nut.

7. Install a spreader tool between the upper and lower ball joint studs.

8. Expand the tool until the tool exerts considerable pressure on the studs. Tap the spindle near the lower stud with a hammer to loosen the stud in the spindle. Do not loosen the stud with tool pressure only.

9. Position the floor jack under the lower arm and remove the lower ball joint stud nut.

10. Lower the floor jack and remove the spring and insulator.

11. Remove the A-arm-to-crossmember attaching parts and remove the arm from the car.

12. Reverse the above procedure to install. If the lower control arm was replaced because of damage, have front end alignment checked.

Front End Alignment

Front end alignment can only be adjusted on a front end alignment machine. This section is included only for reference.

CAMBER, CASTER AND TOE-IN ADJUSTMENT

Position one Ford tool T71P-3000 A at each end of the upper control arm, pivot shaft with the leg of the tools through the holes in the sheet metal (see illustration). Turn the adjusting bolts until they are solidly contacting the sheet metal and loosen the pivot shaft retaining bolts.

Caster is adjusted by turning the front and rear adjusting bolts in the opposite direction. Camber is adjusted by turning both bolts an

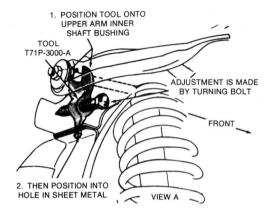

1. POSITION TOOL ONTO UPPER ARM INNER SHAFT BUSHING

TOOL T71P-3000-A

ADJUSTMENT IS MADE BY TURNING BOLT

FRONT

2. THEN POSITION INTO HOLE IN SHEET METAL

VIEW A

Front end alignment adjusting tool

equal amount in the same direction. Following the adjustments, tighten the pivot shaft retaining bolts, remove the adjusting tools, and recheck caster and camber.

Prior to adjusting toe-in, align the straight-ahead marks at the base of the steering wheel and the head of the steering column. Loosen both the clamp at the outer end of the rack bellows and the tie-rod jam nuts. Using suitable pliers (i.e. vise-grips), turn the inner tie-rod shafts to adjust toe-in. Turn the shafts an equal amount in the opposite direction, to maintain steering wheel spoke alignment. Following the adjustment, hold the inner shafts with pliers, and tighten the jam nuts.

FRONT SUSPENSION TROUBLESHOOTING

Hard Ride

1. Excessive tire pressure.
2. Shock absorbers malfunctioning.
3. Broken spring.
4. Worn suspension bushings.

Car Veers to One Side

1. Unequal tire pressures.
2. Incorrect caster, camber, or toe-in.
3. Unequal spring rates.
4. Unequal shock absorber control.
5. Incorrect steering axis inclination (bent spindle).
6. Damaged suspension components or bushings.
7. Incorrect tracking.
8. Dragging brake.
9. Grease on brake lining.

Wander

1. Incorrect or unequal tire pressures.
2. Incorrect caster or toe-in.

3. Excessively worn or damaged suspension components.

Hard or Erratic Steering

1. Insufficient tire pressure.
2. Lack of lubrication.
3. Binding or damaged steering column, steering gear, or linkage.
4. Worn or damaged suspension components.

Tires Wear in Center

1. Excessive tire pressure.

Tires Wear on Both Edges

1. Insufficient tire pressure.

Tires Wear Evenly on One Edge

1. Incorrect camber or toe-in.
2. Bent or damaged suspension components.

Tires Wear Unevenly on One Edge

1. Insufficient tire pressure.
2. Incorrect camber or toe-in.
3. Out-of-round wheel and/or tire.
4. Loose steering linkage.
5. Severe cornering.

Tires Wear Unequally

1. Unequal tire pressure.
2. Unequal tire size.
3. Incorrect toe-in or camber.
4. Loose or bent steering linkage.

Squeal on Cornering

1. Insufficient tire pressure.
2. Incorrect toe-in or camber.
3. Severe cornering.

REAR SUSPENSION

The Mustang II employs a semi-elliptic leaf spring rear suspension. The axle housing is supported by a pair of conventional, longitudinally mounted leaf springs. The housing is secured to the center of the springs by two U-bolts, retaining plates, spring pads and nuts. Each spring is suspended from the underbody side rail by a hanger at the front and a shackle at the rear. A pair of staggered mounted, telescopic shock absorbers are mounted (one in front of and one to the rear of the axle housing) between the leaf spring retaining plates and brackets welded to the crossmember.

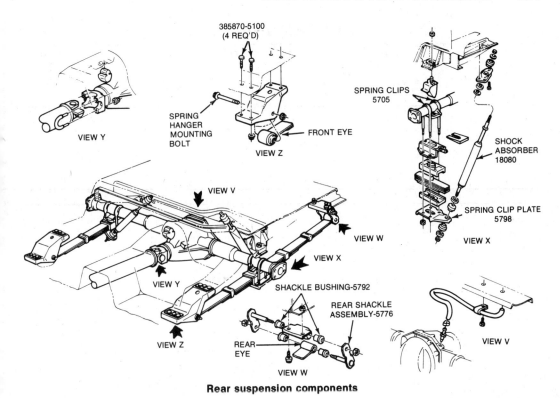

Rear suspension components

Leaf Spring

REMOVAL AND INSTALLATION

1. Raise the rear of the vehicle and position safety stands under the rear axle assembly and the underbody of the car.

2. Disconnect the bottom of the shock absorber from the spring plate.

3. Remove the spring clip plate attaching nuts and remove the spring clip plate.

4. Place a floor jack under the rear axle and raise it just enough to remove the load from the rear springs.

5. Remove the two rear shackle attaching nuts and remove the rear shackle.

6. Remove the nut and bolt which attach the front of the spring to the spring hanger and lower the spring from under the car.

NOTE: *All used attaching nuts and bolts that were removed from the vehicle must be discarded and replaced with new parts.*

7. To install, position the spring under the car and install the rear shackle.

8. Install the rear shackle attaching bolts finger-tight.

9. Position the front eye of the spring in the front hanger and install the front hanger nut, bolt, and washer. Tighten the nut and bolt finger-tight.

10. Lower the rear axle assembly until it rests on the springs.

11. Install the spring clip plate and tighten its attaching nuts.

12. Place safety stands under the rear axle assembly and remove them from beneath the body of the car.

13. Lower the car until the springs are in their approximate curb load position.

14. Tighten the rear shackle and front hanger attaching bolts and nuts.

15. Remove the safety stands and lower the car.

Rear Shock Absorber

Replace any shock absorber with a damaged or dented body, bent piston rod or fluid leakage. With the shock absorber still installed, rock the suspension up and down and make sure that when you let go, the car does not continue to rock up and down more than once. Once removed, you may check the shock absorber by extending and compressing it by hand. Depending on the factory calibrated valving of the shock, the shock should offer substantial resistance in both directions without seizing. The resistance does not have to be exactly even, but it should be

Front Wheel Alignment

| Year | Model | CAMBER | | CASTER | | Toe-in (in.) | Wheel Pivot Ratio (deg) | |
		Range (deg)	Pref Setting (deg)	Range (deg)	Pref Setting (deg)		Inner Wheel	Outer Wheel
'74	All	¼N to 1¾P	¾P	½N to 1½P	½P	0–¼	20	18.84
'75	All	⅛N to 1⅞P	⅞P	½N to 1½P	½P	0–¼	20	18.84
'76–78	All	⅛P to 1⅝P	⅞P	¼N to 1¼P	½P	0–¼	20	18.84

P Positive
N Negative

close. Also, check the shock for air pockets or areas of no resistance.

REMOVAL AND INSTALLATION

1. Disconnect the lower end of the shock absorber from the spring plate.
2. Remove the three bolts retaining the shock absorber mounting bracket at the upper end of the shock.
3. Compress and remove shock from car.
4. Transfer the mounting bracket to a new shock.
5. Position the shock absorber on the car and install the attaching parts.

STEERING

The steering gear is of the rack and pinion type. The gear input shaft is connected to the steering shaft by means of a flexible cable. A pinion gear, machined on the input shaft, engages the rack and rotation of the input shaft pinion causes the rack to move laterally.

The tie-rod is attached at each end of the rack joint. This allows the tie-rods to move with the front suspension. The gear is sealed at each end with rubber bellows. The steering gear is filled with approximately 5 oz of SAE-90 E.P. type oil at initial assembly and

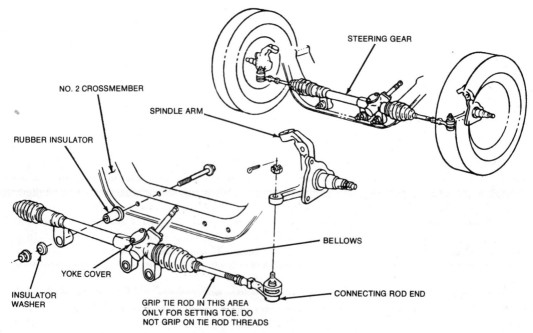

Rack and pinion manual steering linkage

checking or refilling is not required unless fluid leakage is evident or repairs become necessary.

If the steering linkage, front suspension, and steering column components are in good condition, there should be no more than ⅜ in. free-play in the steering wheel when measured at the rim of the wheel.

If a loud knock is heard when turning the steering wheel from lock-to-lock, the pinion bearing preload should be checked. A faint knock from the steering wheel when driving on very rough roads is normal and not an indication of a steering defect.

CAUTION: *When the front wheels of the vehicle are suspended completely off the ground, do not turn the wheels quickly or forcefully from lock to lock. This could cause a buildup of hydraulic pressure within the steering gear which could damage or blow out the bellows.*

Power Steering

Integral power rack and pinion steering is a hydraulic-mechanical unit, which uses an integral piston and rack design. Internal valving directs the flow of fluid from the pump and controls the pressure, as required. The unit contains a rotary hydraulic fluid control valve integrated to the input shaft of the steering gear and a boost cylinder integrated with the rack.

Steering Wheel
REMOVAL AND INSTALLATION

1. Disconnect the negative battery cable.
2. Remove the steering wheel crash pad by removing the two attaching screws from behind the steering wheel. Disconnect the horn wires from the crash pad.
3. Remove the steering wheel attaching

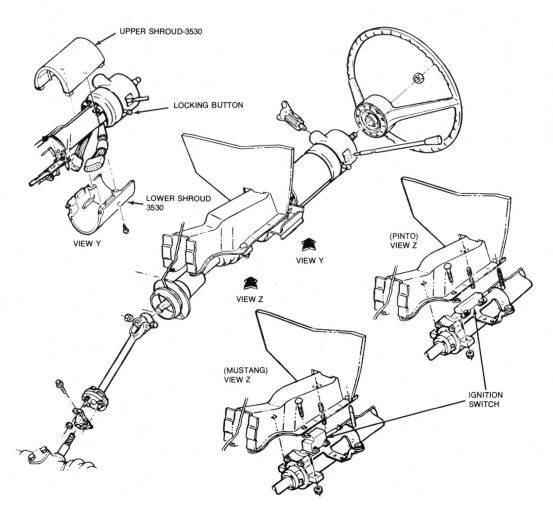

Steering column and related parts

TOOL T67L-3600-A

Steering wheel removal

nut. Make sure that the front wheels are pointing straight-ahead and that the alignment marks on the steering wheel and steering shaft are aligned.

4. Using a screw-type steering wheel puller (as shown in the illustration), remove the steering wheel.

NOTE: *The use of a knock-off type puller or striking the shaft with a heavy instrument could damage the shaft or bearings.*

5. To install, align the marks on the steering wheel and shaft. Install the wheel on the shaft.

6. Install the steering wheel attaching nut and torque it to 30–40 ft lbs.

7. Install the crash pad and connect the horn wires.

8. Connect the negative battery cable.

Turn Signal and Flasher Switch
REMOVAL AND INSTALLATION

1. Remove the steering wheel as previously outlined.

2. Remove the turn signal lever by unscrewing it from the steering column.

3. Snap off the lower steering column shroud.

4. Disconnect the steering column wiring connectors from the steering column by lifting up on the tabs and removing the connectors from the brackets.

5. Remove the three screws which attach the head of the switch to the top of the steering column.

6. Pull the switch and wire assembly up and out of the steering column. A thin wire attached to the connector will make it easy to pull it down through the column on installation.

7. On 1977–78 vehicles, remove the plastic cover sleeve from the wiring before removing the switch and wires from the top of the column. Install the plastic cover sleeve over the wiring harness in reinstallation.

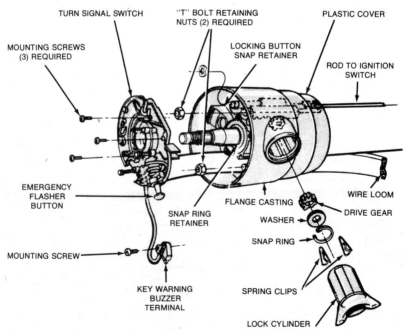

Turn signal and flasher switch removal

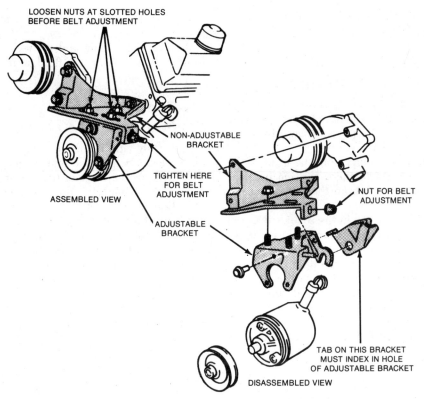

LOOSEN NUTS AT SLOTTED HOLES
BEFORE BELT ADJUSTMENT

NON-ADJUSTABLE
BRACKET

TIGHTEN HERE
FOR BELT
ADJUSTMENT

NUT FOR BELT
ADJUSTMENT

ASSEMBLED VIEW

ADJUSTABLE
BRACKET

TAB ON THIS BRACKET
MUST INDEX IN HOLE
OF ADJUSTABLE BRACKET

DISASSEMBLED VIEW

Typical power steering pump mounting—V8 unit shown

8. To install, position the switch and wires in the steering column and work the wires down the steering column.

9. Secure the wires and connectors to the base of the steering column.

10. Connect the wire connectors at the base of the column.

11. Install the switch head attaching screws. Install the shroud.

12. Install the turn signal lever.

13. Install the steering wheel.

Column-Mounted Wiper Washer Switch

REMOVAL AND INSTALLATION

Mid-1975–78

1. Using an allen wrench, remove the retaining screw and remove the turn signal arm.

2. Find the turn signal terminal connector under the dash and while inserting a screwdriver under each side successively, twist the connector to pull it apart.

3. Remove the two screws holding the lower instrument panel shield.

4. Remove the two screws and separate the two halves of the steering column cover.

5. Pull the wiring cover out from the bottom and remove it.

6. Insert a screwdriver under the wiring shield, push the tang and pry on the shield to free it.

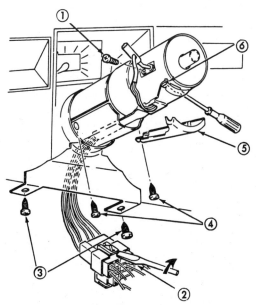

Column-mounted windshield wiper/washer switch. Circled numbers refer to steps in text.

7. Remove the arm and its wiring harness. Installation is the reverse of removal.

Power Steering Pump
REMOVAL AND INSTALLATION

1. Disconnect the fluid return hose at the reservoir, and drain the fluid from the pump.

2. Disconnect the pressure hose from the pump.

3. Remove the bolts from the front of the pump attaching it to the mounting bracket. Disconnect the belt from the pulley and remove the pump.

4. Install the pump in the reverse order of removal. Torque the attaching bolts to 30–45 ft lbs.

5. Fill the reservoir with fluid.

6. To bleed the system, turn the steering wheel from stop-to-stop several times. Do not hold the steering wheel in the far left or right position.

7. Recheck the fluid level and add fluid as necessary.

8. Start the engine and allow it to run for several minutes.

9. Stop the engine and recheck the fluid level in the reservoir; add fluid, as necessary.

Tie-Rod Ends
REMOVAL AND INSTALLATION

1. Firmly apply the parking brake and place blocks behind the rear wheels.

2. Jack up the front of the car and install jackstands beneath the frame members.

3. Remove the cotter pin and castellated nut from the tie-rod end ball joint. Pull the ball joint from the socket in the spindle arm.

4. Loosen the jam nut on the tie-rod. Unscrew the tie-rod end from the tie-rod, taking care to record the number of turns needed to remove the rod end.

5. Reverse the above procedure to install, taking care to turn the tie-rod end the correct amount of turns onto the tie-rod. This is necessary to maintain proper toe-in.

Brakes

HYDRAULIC SYSTEM

All Mustang II models utilize a dual hydraulic brake circuit in accordance with Federal safety regulations. Each circuit is independent of the other, incorporating a tandem master cylinder, a pressure differential warning valve, and, on disc brake models, a proportioning valve. One circuit services the front brakes (rear of master cylinder) and the other, the rear brakes (front of master cylinder). In case of a leak or other hydraulic failure, $1/2$ braking efficiency will be maintained. A brake system failure will decentralize the pressure differential warning valve, actuating a warning light on the dash. A proportioning valve located between the rear brake system inlet and outlet ports in the pressure differential warning valve serves to regulate the rear brake hydraulic pressure on disc brake models to prevent premature rear wheel lockup during hard braking.

In normal operation, the hydraulic system functions as follows:

When the brake pedal is depressed, the master cylinder pistons move forward, displacing the brake fluid. Due to the fact that the fluid volume is constant, the displacement results in increased hydraulic pressure. This pressure is exerted upon the wheel cylinders and/or caliper pistons, thus forcing the brake shoes or friction pads against the drums or discs.

When the brake pedal is released, hydraulic pressure drops. On drum brakes, the brake return springs, and on disc brakes, the wobbling action of the disc returns the shoes or disc pads to their retracted positions and force the displaced fluid back into the master cylinder. On disc brakes, in addition to the wobbling action of the disc, the piston seals retracting from their stretched position help return the disc pads to their released position.

Master Cylinder
REMOVAL AND INSTALLATION
Non-Power Brakes

1. Working from inside the car below the instrument panel, disconnect the master cylinder pushrod from the brake pedal assembly. The pushrod cannot be removed from the master cylinder.

2. Disconnect the stoplight switch wires at the connector. Remove the spring retainer. Slide the stoplight switch off the brake pedal pin just far enough to clear the end of the pin, then lift and remove the switch from the pin. Take care not to damage the switch during removal.

3. Loosen the master cylinder attaching

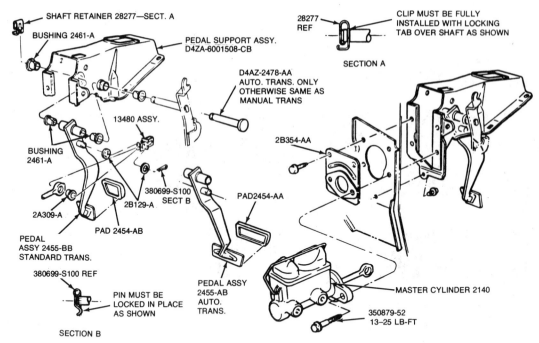

SHAFT RETAINER 28277—SECT. A

BUSHING 2461-A

PEDAL SUPPORT ASSY.
D4ZA-6001508-CB

28277
REF

CLIP MUST BE FULLY
INSTALLED WITH LOCKING
TAB OVER SHAFT AS SHOWN

SECTION A

D4AZ-2478-AA
AUTO. TRANS. ONLY
OTHERWISE SAME AS
MANUAL TRANS

13480 ASSY.

2B354-AA

BUSHING
2461-A

380699-S100
SECT B

2B129-A

PAD2454-AA

2A309-A

PAD 2454-AB

PEDAL
ASSY 2455-BB
STANDARD TRANS.

380699-S100 REF

PIN MUST BE
LOCKED IN PLACE
AS SHOWN

PEDAL ASSY
2455-AB
AUTO.
TRANS.

MASTER CYLINDER 2140

350879-52
13–25 LB-FT

SECTION B

Master cylinder and brake pedal components—non-power brakes

nuts from inside the engine compartment. Slide the master cylinder pushrod, nylon washers and bushings off the brake pedal pin.

4. Remove the brake tubes from the primary and secondary outlet ports of the master cylinder, and mark them for reassembly.

5. Remove the locknuts and lockwashers securing the master cylinder to the dash and lift the cylinder forward and upward from the car.

6. To install, position the rubber boot on the pushrod and secure the boot to the master cylinder. Carefully insert the boot through the dash panel opening and position the master cylinder and master cylinder mounting gasket (if so equipped) on the dash panel studs.

7. Install the attaching nuts and leave them loose.

8. Coat the nylon bushings with light (10W) engine oil. Install the nylon washer and bushing on the brake pedal pin.

9. Position the stoplight switch and pushrod on the brake pedal pin. Install the nylon bushing and washer and secure them in position with the spring retainer.

10. Connect the wires at the stoplight switch connector.

11. Tighten the master cylinder attaching nuts and connect the brake lines at the master cylinder.

12. Fill the master cylinder with brake fluid meeting SAE 70R3 specifications to within $1/4$ in. of the top of the dual reservoirs.

13. Bleed the master cylinder and both the primary and secondary brake hydraulic systems as outlined under "Hydraulic System Bleeding."

14. Centralize the pressure differential valve as outlined under "Differential Valve Centering."

15. Operate the brakes several times and check for leakage.

Power Brakes

1. Disconnect and plug the brake tubes from the primary and secondary outlet ports of the master cylinder.

2. Remove the two attaching nuts and slide the master cylinder forward and away from the vacuum booster assembly.

3. On all but 1978 models, prior to installation, measure the distance from the outer end of the booster pushrod to the master cylinder mounting surface. This distance should be just under 1 in., with a slight 5 lb pressure exerted against the pushrod.

4. Position the master cylinder over the booster pushrod and onto the two studs on the booster assembly. Install the attaching nuts and torque to 13–25 ft lbs.

5. Connect the brake tubes to the master cylinder.

6. Fill the master cylinder with brake fluid

meeting SAE 70R3 specifications to within
$1/4$ in. of the top of the dual reservoirs.

7. Bleed the master cylinder and the primary and secondary hydraulic systems as outlined under "Hydraulic System Bleeding."

8. Centralize the pressure differential valve as outlined under "Differential Valve Centering."

9. Operate the brakes several times and check for leakage.

MASTER CYLINDER OVERHAUL

Referring to the accompanying exploded view of the dual master cylinder components, disassemble the unit as follows: Clean the exterior of the cylinder and remove the filler cover and diaphragm. Any brake fluid remaining in the cylinder should be poured out and discarded. Remove the secondary piston stop bolt from the bottom of the cylinder and remove the bleed screw, if required. With the primary piston depressed, remove the snap-ring from its retaining groove at the rear of the cylinder bore. Withdraw the pushrod and the primary piston assembly from the bore.

NOTE: *Do not remove the screw which retains the primary return spring retainer,* *return spring, primary cup and protector on the primary piston. The assembly is adjusted at the factory and should not be disassembled.*

Remove the secondary piston assembly.

NOTE: *Do not remove the outlet tube seats, outlet check valves and outlet check valve springs from the cylinder body.*

All components should be cleaned in clean isopropyl alcohol or clean brake fluid and inspected for chipping, excessive wear and damage. Check to ensure that all recesses, openings and passageways are clear and free of foreign matter. Dirt and cleaning solvent may be removed by using compressed air. After cleaning, keep all parts on a clean surface. Inspect the cylinder bore for etching, pitting, scoring or rusting. If necessary, the cylinder bore may be honed to repair damage, but never to a diameter greater than the original diameter plus .003 in.

During the assembly operation, be sure to use all parts supplied with the master cylinder repair kit. With the exception of the master cylinder body, submerge all parts in extra heavy duty brake fluid. Carefully insert the complete secondary piston and return spring assembly into the cylinder bore and install the primary piston assembly into the bore.

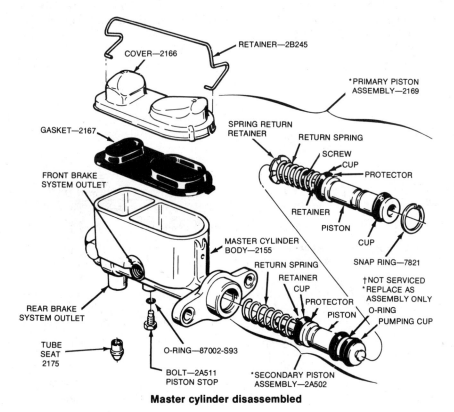

Master cylinder disassembled

With the primary piston depressed, install the snap-ring into its groove in the cylinder bore. Install the pushrod, boot and retainer (if equipped), then install the pushrod assembly into the primary piston. Be sure that the retainer is properly seated and is holding the pushrod securely. Position the inner end of the pushrod boot (if equipped) in the master cylinder body retaining groove. Install the secondary piston stop bolt and O-ring at the bottom of the master cylinder body. Install the bleed screw (if equipped) and position the gasket on the master cylinder filler cover. Be sure that the gasket is securely seated. Install the cover and secure with the retainer.

Bleeding

NOTE: *The front and rear hydraulic systems are independent. if it is known that only one system has air in it, only that system has to be bled. Always bleed the brakes in a sequence that starts with the wheel cylinder farthest from the master cylinder and ends with the wheel cylinder or caliper closest to the master cylinder.*

1. Fill the master cylinder with brake fluid.

2. Install a 3/8 in. box-end wrench to the bleeder screw on the right rear wheel.

3. Push a piece of small-diameter rubber tubing over the bleeder screw until it is flush against the wrench. Submerge the other end of the rubber tubing in a glass jar partially filled with clean brake fluid. Make sure that the rubber tube fits on the bleeder screw snugly.

4. Have a friend apply pressure to the brake pedal. Open the bleeder screw and ob-

serve the bottle of brake fluid. If bubbles appear in the glass jar, there is air in the system. When your friend has pushed the pedal to the floor, immediately close the bleeder screw before he releases the pedal.

5. Repeat this procedure until no bubbles appear in the jar. Refill the master cylinder.

6. Repeat this procedure on the left rear, right front and left front wheels, in that order. Periodically refill the master cylinder so that it does not run dry.

7. Center the pressure differential warning valve as outlined in the "Pressure Differential Warning Valve" section.

PRESSURE DIFFERENTIAL WARNING VALVE CENTERING

Since the introduction of dual master cylinders to the hydraulic brake system, a pressure differential warning signal has been added. This signal consists of a warning light on the dashboard activated by a differential pressure switch located below the master cylinder. The signal indicates a hydraulic pressure differential between the front and rear brakes of 80–150 psi, and should warn the driver that a hydraulic failure has occurred.

After repairing and bleeding any part of the hydraulic system the warning light may remain on due to the pressure differential valve remaining in the off-center position. To centralize the valve a pressure difference must be created in the opposite branch of the hydraulic system that was repaired or bled last.

NOTE: *Front wheel balancing of cars equipped with disc brakes may also cause a pressure differential in the front branch of the system.*

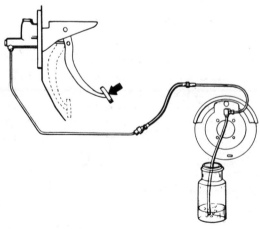

Bleeding hydraulic system

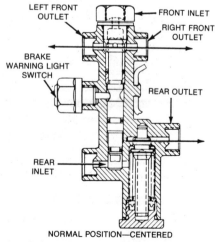

LEFT FRONT OUTLET — FRONT INLET — RIGHT FRONT OUTLET — BRAKE WARNING LIGHT SWITCH — REAR OUTLET — REAR INLET

NORMAL POSITION—CENTERED

Sectional view of pressure differential valve

To centralize the valve:

1. Turn the ignition to either the "acc" or "on" position.

2. Check the fluid level in the master cylinder reservoirs. Fill to within 1/4 in. of the top if necessary.

3. Depress the brake pedal firmly. The valve will centralize itself causing the brake warning light to go out.

4. Turn the ignition off.

5. Prior to driving the vehicle, check the operation of the brakes and obtain a firm pedal.

BRAKE SYSTEM

All Mustang II models are equipped with front disc brakes and rear drum brakes. Power assist is available on most models.

Front Disc Brakes

Instead of the traditional expanding brakes that press outward against a circular drum, disc brake systems utilize a cast iron disc with brake pads (linings or shoes). Braking effect is achieved in a manner similar to the way that you would squeeze a spinning phonograph record between your fingers. The disc (rotor) is a one-piece casting with cooling fins between the two braking surfaces. This enables air to circulate between the braking surfaces, making them less sensitive to heat buildup and more resistant to fade. Dirt and water do not affect braking action since such contaminants are thrown off by the centrifugal action of the rotor or scraped off by the pads. Also, the equal clamping action of the brake pads tends to ensure uniform, straight-line stops. All disc brakes are inherently self-adjusting.

Sliding caliper disc brakes are used at the front of all models. The name of this system is derived from the sliding action of the brake caliper on the anchor plate during braking. The plate-like brake rotor is attached to and mounted on the car by the front wheel hub. A brake caliper anchor plate, attached to the front wheel spindle, mounts over the top of, but does not touch, the rotor. The caliper is mounted in the middle of the large opening in the anchor plate. When the brake pedal is depressed, and hydraulic force is generated, the piston in the caliper forces the inboard brake pad inward and into contact with the

DUST SHIELD

ANCHOR PLATE

CALIPER ASSEMBLY

KEY RETAINER SCREW

KEY

CALIPER SUPPORT SPRING

OUTER BRAKE SHOE AND LINING ASSEMBLY

HUB AND ROTOR ASSEMBLY

Sliding caliper disc brake assembly

brake rotor. The caliper now begins to act like a C-clamp, with the inboard shoe and the piston acting as the adjustable screw. Since there is only a small amount of clearance between the brake pads and the rotor, the inboard shoe contacts the rotor almost as soon as the brake pedal is depressed. As the brake pedal is depressed farther, it increases the amount of hydraulic pressure sent to the piston in the caliper. Since the inboard shoe is already in contact with the brake rotor, it cannot be moved. As the caliper pushes on the inboard brake shoe, the increased hydraulic pressure forces the back of the caliper housing away from the back of the piston. This causes the caliper to slide inward on the anchor plate and force the outboard brake pad into contact with the rotor. Thus the name sliding caliper. This happens very quickly, so both pads contact the rotor at about the same time.

DISC BRAKE PAD REMOVAL AND INSTALLATION

1. Remove approximately $^2/_3$ of the fluid from the rear reservoir of the tandem master cylinder. Raise the vehicle, taking proper safety precautions. Install jackstands beneath the front jacking points. Block the rear wheels.

2. Remove the wheel and tire assembly.

3. Remove the key retaining screw from the caliper retaining key.

4. Slide the retaining key and support spring either inward or outward from the anchor plate. To remove the key and spring, a hammer and drift may be used, taking care not to damage the key in the process.

5. Lift the caliper assembly away from the anchor plate by pushing the caliper downward against the anchor plate and rotating the upper end upward out of the anchor plate. Be careful not to stretch or twist the flexible brake hose. Safety wire the caliper to the suspension arm.

6. Remove the inner shoe and lining assembly from the anchor plate. The inner shoe antirattle clip may become displaced at this time and should be repositioned on the anchor plate. Lightly tap on the outer shoe and lining assembly to free it from the caliper.

7. Clean the caliper, anchor plate, and disc assemblies, and inspect them for brake fluid leakage, excessive wear or signs of dam-

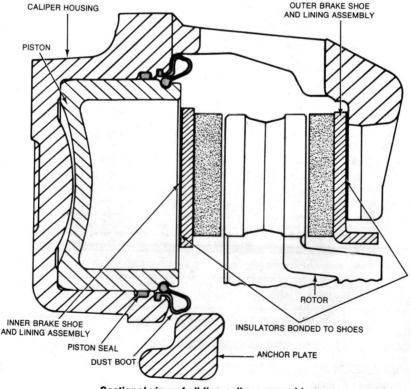

Sectional view of sliding caliper assembly

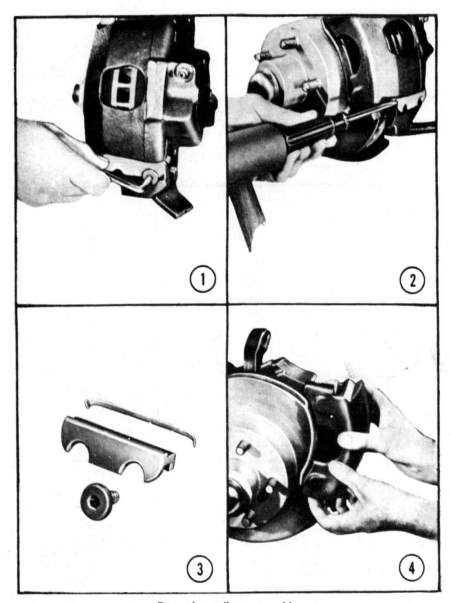

Removing caliper assembly

age. Replace the pads if either of them is worn to within $1/32$ in. of the rivet heads.

8. To install new pads, use a 4 in. C-clamp and a block of wood $1^3/4$ in. x 1 in. and approximately $3/4$ in. thick to seat the caliper hydraulic piston in its bore. This must be done in order to provide clearance for the caliper to fit over the rotor when new linings are installed.

9. At this point, the antirattle clip should be in its place on the lower inner brake shoe support of the anchor plate with the pigtail of the clip toward the inside of the anchor plate.

Position the inner brake shoe and lining assembly on the anchor plate with the pad toward the disc.

10. Install the outer brake shoe with the lower flange ends against the caliper leg abutments and the brake shoe upper flanges over the shoulders on the caliper legs. The shoe is installed correctly when its flanges fit snugly against the machined surfaces of the shoulders.

11. Remove the C-clamp used to seat the caliper piston in its bore. The piston will remain seated.

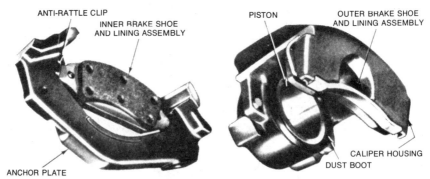

Caliper and outer shoe removed from anchor plate

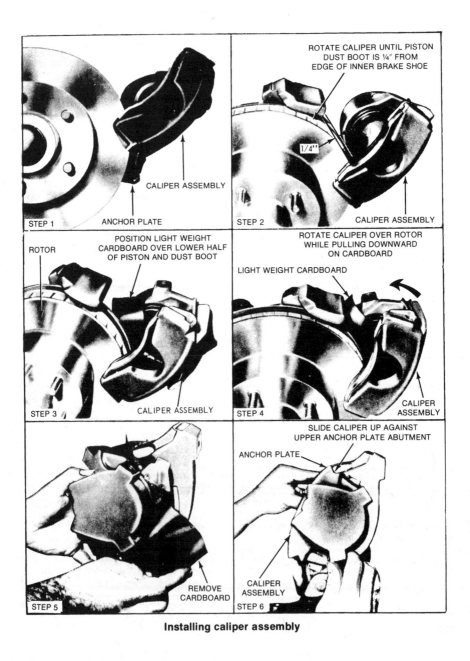

Installing caliper assembly

12. Position the caliper housing lower V-groove on the anchor plate lower abutment surface.

13. Pivot the caliper housing upward toward the disc until the outer edge of the piston dust boot is about ¹/₄ in. from the upper edge of the inboard pad.

14. In order to prevent pinching of the dust boot between the piston and the inboard pad during installation of the caliper, place a clean piece of thin cardboard between the inboard pad and the lower half of the piston dust boot.

15. Rotate the caliper housing toward the disc until a slight resistance is felt. At this point, pull the cardboard downward toward the disc centerline while rotating the caliper over the disc. Then remove the cardboard and complete the rotation of the caliper down over the disc.

16. Slide the caliper up against the upper abutment surfaces of the anchor plate and center the caliper over the lower anchor plate abutment.

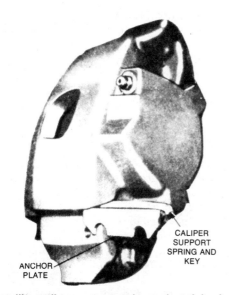

Installing caliper support spring and retaining key

17. Position the caliper support spring and key in the key slot and slide them into the opening between the lower end of the caliper and the lower anchor plate abutment until the key semicircular slot is centered over the retaining screw threaded hole in the anchor plate.

18. Install the key retaining screw and torque to 12–116 ft lbs.

19. Check the fluid level in the master cylinder and fill as necessary. Install the reser-voir cover. Depress the brake pedal several times to properly seat the caliper and pads. Check for leakage around the caliper and flexible brake hose.

20. Install the wheel and tire assembly and torque the nuts to 70–115 ft lbs. Install the wheel cover.

21. Lower the car. Make sure that you obtain a firm brake pedal and then road-test the car for proper brake operation.

DISC BRAKE CALIPER REMOVAL, OVERHAUL AND INSTALLATION

1. Raise the vehicle and place jackstands underneath the front jacking points. Block the rear wheels.

2. Remove the wheel and tire assembly.

3. Disconnect the flexible brake hose from the caliper. To disconnect the hose, loosen the tube fitting which connects the end of the hose to the brake tube at its bracket on the frame. Remove the horseshoe clip from the hose and bracket, disengage the hose, and plug the end. Then unscrew the entire hose assembly from the caliper.

4. Remove the key retaining screw from the caliper retaining key.

5. Slide the retaining key and support spring either inward or outward from the anchor plate. To remove the key and spring, a hammer and drift may be used, taking care not to damage the key in the process.

6. Lift the caliper assembly away from the anchor plate by pushing the caliper downward against the anchor plate and rotating the upper end upward out of the anchor plate.

7. Remove the piston by applying compressed air to the fluid inlet port with a rubber-tipped nozzle. Place a towel or thick cloth over the piston before applying air pressure to prevent damage to the piston. If the piston is seized in the bore and cannot be forced from the caliper, lightly tap around the outside of the caliper while applying air pressure.

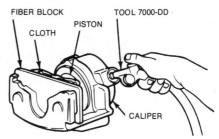

Removing piston from caliper

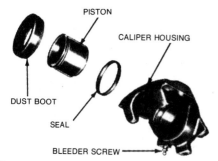

PISTON

CALIPER HOUSING

DUST BOOT

SEAL

BLEEDER SCREW

Caliper disassembled

CAUTION: *Do not attempt to catch the piston with your hand.*

8. Remove the dust boot from the caliper assembly.

9. Remove the piston seal from the cylinder and discard it.

10. Clean all metal parts with isopropyl alcohol or a suitable non-petroleum solvent and dry them with compressed air. Be sure that there is no foreign material in the bore or component parts. Inspect the piston and bore for excessive wear or damage. Replace the piston if it is pitted, scored, or if the chrome plating is wearing off.

11. Lubricate all new rubber parts in brake fluid. Install the piston seal in the cylinder groove, being careful not to twist it. Install the dust boot by setting the flange squarely in the outer groove of the bore.

12. Coat the piston with brake fluid and install it in the bore. Work the dust boot around the outside of the piston, making sure that the boot lip is seated in the piston groove.

13. Install the caliper as outlined in Steps 12–18 in the sliding caliper "Disc Pad Removal and Installation" procedure.

14. Thread the flexible brake hose and gasket onto the caliper fitting. Torque the fitting to 12–20 ft lbs. Place the upper end of the flexible brake hose in its bracket and install the horseshoe clip. Remove the plug from the brake tube and connect the tube to the hose. Torque the tube fitting nut to 10–15 ft lbs.

15. Bleed the brake system as outlined under "Hydraulic System Bleeding."

16. Check the fluid level in the master cylinder and fill as necessary. Install the reservoir cover. Depress the brake pedal several times to properly seat the caliper and shoes. Check for leakage around the caliper and the flexible brake hose.

17. Install the wheel and tire assembly

and torque the nuts to 70–115 ft lbs. Install the wheel cover.

18. Lower the car. Make sure that you obtain a firm brake pedal and then road-test the car for proper brake operation.

BRAKE DISC REMOVAL AND INSTALLATION

1. Raise the front of the vehicle and install jackstands beneath the front jacking points. Place blocks in back of the rear wheels.

2. Remove the wheel and tire assembly.

3. Remove the caliper from its mount as described under Steps 3–6 of "Disc Caliper Removal, Overhaul and Installation." Wire the caliper out of the way to the upper control arm, taking care not to twist or damage the flexible brake hose. Do not remove the anchor plate. Insert folded cardboard or wood between the brake pads to keep the piston seated.

4. Remove the grease cap from the hub. Remove the cotter pin, nut lock, and adjusting nut from the spindle.

5. Remove the outer wheel bearing and flat washer from the hub by first pulling the hub and disc assembly out far enough to loosen the bearing, then pushing it back in and removing the bearing and washer. Slide the hub and disc assembly off the spindle.

NOTE: *If a new disc is being installed, remove the protective coating with carburetor degreaser, and pack a new set of wheel bearings with wheel bearing grease. If the original disc is being installed, make sure that the grease in the hub is clean and adequate. Also make sure that the inner bearing and grease retainer are lubricated and in good condition, and that the disc braking surfaces are clean.*

6. Slide the hub and disc assembly onto the spindle. Install the outer wheel bearing and flat washer and adjusting nut on the spindle. Tighten the adjusting nut finger-tight, so that the hub and rotor may spin freely.

Inspect the disc (rotor) for scoring or corrosion. Minor scores or rust spots may be removed with a fine emery cloth. If the braking area is excessively scored or rusted, the disc must be replaced. Check the disc for warpage (run-out). Tighten the wheel bearing adjusting nut so that the end-play is taken up. Make sure that the disc can still be rotated. Then, handspin the disc and check for wobbling or an out-of-round condition. Minor run-out may be corrected by machining. Maximum allowable run-out is 0.003 in. Readjust the wheel bearing to specifications.

7. Install the caliper to its mount as described under Steps 12–18 of "Disc Brake Pad Removal and Installation."

8. Install the wheel and tire assembly.

9. Adjust the wheel bearing as outlined under "Wheel Bearing Ajustment."

10. Remove the jackstands, lower the car, and tighten the wheel lug nuts to 70–115 ft lbs.

11. Apply the brakes several times to properly position the brake pads. Roadtest the car for proper brake operation.

Front Wheel Bearings

ADJUSTMENT

The front wheels each rotate on a set of opposed, tapered roller bearings as shown in the accompanying illustration. The grease retainer at the inside of the hub prevents lubricant from leaking into the brake drum.

Adjustment of the wheel bearings is accomplished as follows: Lift the car so that the wheel and tire are clear of the ground, then remove the grease cap and remove excess grease from the end of the spindle. Remove the cotter pin and nut lock shown in the illustration. Rotate the wheel, hub and drum assembly while tightening the adjusting nut to 17–25 ft lbs in order to seat the bearings. Back off the adjusting nut one half turn, then retighten the adjusting nut to 10–15 in. lbs (*inch-pounds*). Locate the nut lock on the adjusting nut so that the castellations on the lock are lined up with the cotter pin hole in the spindle. Install a new cotter pin, bending the ends of the cotter pin around the castellated flange of the nut lock. Check the front wheel for proper rotation, then install the grease cap. If the wheel still does not rotate properly, inspect and clean or replace the wheel bearings and cups.

REMOVAL, REPACKING AND INSTALLATION

1. Raise the front of the car and support it with safety stands.

2. Remove the front wheels.

NOTE: *In order to remove the rotor, the caliper and anchor plate must be removed from the car.*

3. Loosen, but do not remove, the upper anchor plate attaching bolt with a ¾ in. socket.

4. Using a ⅝ in. socket, remove the lower anchor plate attaching bolt.

NOTE: *When the caliper is removed from the car it must be wired out of the way of the rotor. Also, the brake pads will fall out of the caliper if they are not held in place when the caliper is removed. You will have to insert a small piece of wood or a folded piece of heavy cardboard between the shoes to hold them in place. Have a piece of wire and a piece of wood handy before you start the next step.*

5. Hold the caliper in place and remove the upper anchor plate attaching bolt.

6. Slide the caliper and anchor plate assembly off the rotor, inserting the block of wood between the brake pads as they become visible above the rotor.

7. When the anchor plate is clear of the rotor, wire it out of the way.

8. Remove the dust cap from the rotor hub by either prying it off with a screwdriver or pulling it off with a pair of channel-lock pliers.

9. Remove the cotter pin and the nut lock from the spindle.

10. Loosen the bearing adjusting nut until it is at the end of the spindle.

11. Grasp the rotor with a rag and pull it outward, push it inward.

12. Remove the adjusting nut and the outer bearing.

13. Remove the rotor from the spindle.

WITH WHEEL ROTATING, TORQUE ADJUSTING NUT, TO 17–25 FT-LBS

BACK ADJUSTING NUT OFF ½ TURN

TIGHTEN ADJUSTING NUT TO 10–15 IN.-LBS.

INSTALL THE LOCK AND A NEW COTTER PIN

Front wheel bearing adjustment

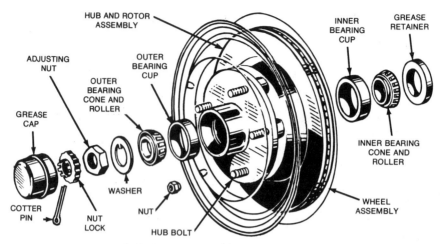

Front hub, bearing and grease retainer

Removing inner grease seal

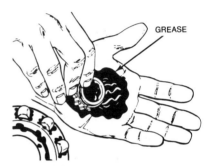

Packing wheel bearings

14. Place the rotor and tire on a clean, paper-covered surface with the wheel studs facing upward.

15. Working through the hole in the center of the wheel hub, tap the grease seal out of the rear of the hub with a screwdriver or drift.

NOTE: *Be careful not to damage the inner bearing while knocking out the grease seal.*

16. Remove the grease seal and bearing from under the rotor, and discard the grease seal.

17. Clean the inner and outer bearings and the wheel hub with suitable solvent. Remove all old grease.

18. Thoroughly dry and wipe clean all components.

19. Clean all old grease from the spindle on the car.

20. Carefully check the bearings for any sign of scoring or other damage. If the roller bearings or bearing cages are damaged, the bearing and the corresponding bearing cup in the rotor hub must be replaced. The bearing cups must be driven out of the rotor hub to be removed. The outer bearing cup is driven out of the front of the rotor from the rear and vice versa for the inner bearing cup.

21. Whether you are reinstalling the old bearings or installing new ones, the bearings must be packed with wheel bearing grease. To do this, place a glob of grease in your left palm, then, holding one of the bearings in your right hand, drag the edge of the bearing heavily through the grease. This must be done to work as much grease as possible through the roller bearings and cage. Turn the bearing and continue to pull it through the grease until the grease is packed between the bearings and the cage all the way around the circumference of the bearing. Repeat this operation until all of the bearings are packed with grease.

22. Pack the inside of the rotor hub with a moderate amount of grease, between the bearing cups. Do not overload the hub with grease.

23. Apply a small amount of grease to the spindle.

24. Place the rotor, face down, on a protected surface and install the inner bearing.

25. Coat the lip of a new grease seal with a

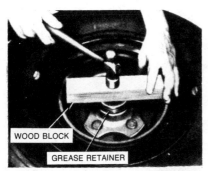

WOOD BLOCK

GREASE RETAINER

Installing inner grease seal

small amount of grease and position it on the rotor.

26. Place a block of wood on top of the grease seal and tap on the block with a hammer to install the seal. Turn the block of wood to different positions to seat it squarely in the hub.

27. Position the rotor on the spindle.

28. Install the outer bearing and washer on the spindle, inside the rotor hub.

29. Install the bearing adjusting nut and tighten it to 17–25 ft lbs while spinning the rotor. This will seat the bearing.

30. Back off the adjusting nut one half turn.

31. Tighten the adjusting nut to 10–15 in. lbs.

32. Install the nut lock on the adjusting nut so that two of the slots align with the hole in the spindle.

33. Install a new cotter pin and bend the ends back so that they will not interfere with the dust cap.

34. Install the dust cap.

35. Install the front tires if they were removed.

Drum Brakes

The drum brakes installed on the rear of all Mustang II models employ single-anchor, internal-expanding, and self-adjusting brake assemblies. The automatic adjuster continuously maintains correct operating clearance between the linings and the drums by adjusting the brake in small increments in direct proportion to lining wear. When applying the brakes while backing up, the linings tend to follow the rotating drum counterclockwise, thus forcing the upper end of the primary shoe against the anchor pin. Simultaneously, the wheel cylinder pushes the upper end of the secondary shoe and cable guide outward, away from the anchor pin.

This movement of the secondary shoe causes the cable to pull the adjusting lever upward and against the end of the tooth on the adjusting screw starwheel. As lining wear increases, the upward travel of the adjusting lever also increases. When the linings have worn sufficiently to allow the lever to move upward far enough, it passes over the end of the tooth and engages it. Upon release of the brakes, the adjusting spring pulls the adjuster lever downward, turning the starwheel and expanding the brakes.

DRUM BRAKE INSPECTION

1. Raise the front or rear of the car and support the car with safety stands. Make sure that the parking brake is not on.

2. To check the rear brakes, remove the lug nuts which attach the wheels to the axle shaft and remove the tires and wheels from the car. Using a pair of pliers, remove the tinnerman nuts from the wheel studs. Pull the brake drum off the axle shaft. If the brakes are adjusted too tightly to remove the drum, see Step 3. If you can remove the drum, see Step 4.

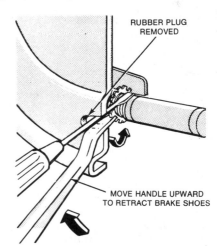

RUBBER PLUG
REMOVED

MOVE HANDLE UPWARD
TO RETRACT BRAKE SHOES

Backing off drum brake adjustment

3. If the brakes are too tight to remove the drum, get under the car (make sure that you have safety stands under the car to support it) and remove the rubber plug from the bottom of the brake backing plate. Shine a flashlight into the slot in the plate. You will see the top of the adjusting screw starwheel and the adjusting lever for the automatic brake adjusting mechanism. To back off on the adjusting screw, you must first insert a small, thin screwdriver or a piece of firm wire (coathanger wire) into the adjusting slot and push

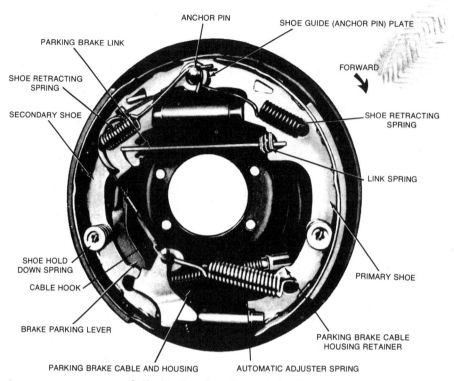

ANCHOR PIN

SHOE GUIDE (ANCHOR PIN) PLATE

PARKING BRAKE LINK

FORWARD

SHOE RETRACTING SPRING

SHOE RETRACTING SPRING

SECONDARY SHOE

LINK SPRING

SHOE HOLD DOWN SPRING

CABLE HOOK

PRIMARY SHOE

BRAKE PARKING LEVER

PARKING BRAKE CABLE HOUSING RETAINER

PARKING BRAKE CABLE AND HOUSING

AUTOMATIC ADJUSTER SPRING

Self-adjusting drum brake assembly

the adjusting lever sway from the adjusting screw. Then, insert a brake adjusting spoon into the slot and engage the top of the starwheel. Lift up on the bottom of the adjusting spoon to force the adjusting screw starwheel downward. Repeat this operation until the brake drum is free of the brake shoes and can be pulled off.

4. Clean the brake shoes and the inside of the brake drum. There must be at least $1/16$ in. of brake lining above the heads of the brake shoe attaching rivets. The lining should not be cracked or contaminated with grease or brake fluid. If there is grease or brake fluid on the lining, it must be replaced and the source of the leak must be found and corrected. Brake fluid on the lining means leaking wheel cylinders. Grease on the brake lining means a leaking axle seal. If the lining is slightly glazed but otherwise in good condition, it can be cleaned up with medium sandpaper. Lift up the bottom of the wheel cylinder boots and inspect the ends of the wheel cylinders. A small amount of fluid in the end of the cylinders should be considered normal. If fluid runs out of the cylinder when the boots are lifted, however, the wheel cylinder must be rebuilt or replaced. Examine the inside of the brake drum; it should have a smooth, dull finish. If excessive brake shoe

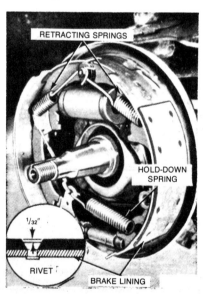

RETRACTING SPRINGS

HOLD-DOWN SPRING

$1/32''$

RIVET

BRAKE LINING

Inspecting linings for wear

wear caused grooves to wear in the drum, it must be machined or replaced. If the inside of the drum is slightly glazed, but otherwise good, it can be cleaned up with medium sandpaper.

5. If no repairs are required, install the drum and wheel. If the brake adjustment was changed to remove the drum, adjust the brakes until the drum will just fit over the

brakes. After the wheel is installed it will be necessary to complete the adjustment. See "Brake Adjustment" later in this chapter.

BRAKE DRUM REMOVAL AND INSTALLATION

Follow Steps 3 and 5 under "Drum Brake Inspection."

BRAKE SHOE REMOVAL AND INSTALLATION

NOTE: *If you are not thoroughly familiar with the procedures involved in brake replacement, only disassemble and assemble one side at a time, leaving the other wheel intact as a reference.*

1. Remove the wheel and brake drum as described above. Then, install a clamp over the ends of the wheel cylinder, as shown, to keep the wheel cylinder pistons in position.

2. Remove the shoe-to-anchor springs with the type of tool shown in the illustration. Unhook the cable eye from the anchor pin.

3. Remove the shoe guide (anchor pin) plate (see the illustration above pointing out all parts).

4. Remove the shoe hold-down springs, shoes, adjusting screw, pivot nut, socket, and automatic adjustment parts.

5. Remove the parking brake link and spring and retainer. Disconnect the parking brake cable from the parking brake lever.

6. After removing the rear brake secondary shoe, disconnect the parking brake lever at the shoe by removing the retainer clip and spring washer.

7. To install new shoes, first assemble

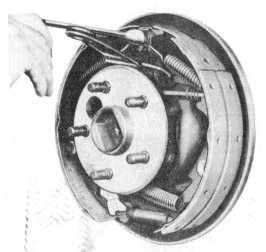

Clamping brake cylinder and removing retracting spring

the parking brake lever to the secondary shoe by putting it into position and then securing it with the spring washer and retaining clip. (A tang on the parking brake lever engages the secondary shoe.

8. Apply a light coating of high temperature grease to the points where the brake shoes ride against the backing plate in normal application and release of the shoes.

9. Then, position the shoes on the backing plate, making sure the primary shoe (which has the shorter lining) faces toward the front of the car, and the secondary shoe faces toward the rear. Secure assemblies with the hold-down springs. Then, install the parking brake link, spring, and retainer. Back off the parking brake adjustment, and then connect the parking brake cable to the parking brake lever.

10. Install the shoe guide (anchor pin) plate onto the anchor pin.

11. Position the cable eye over the anchor pin; make sure the crimped side is toward the drum.

12. Install the spring running from the primary shoe to the anchor, using a special tool designed for that purpose.

CAUTION: *Make sure the spring does not slide off the tool during this procedure, as personal injury could result.*

13. Install the cable guide onto the secondary shoe web with the flanged hole fitted into the hole in the secondary shoe web. Thread the cable around the cable guide groove. *Make sure the cable is positioned in this groove and not between the guide and the shoe web.*

14. Install both secondary shoe-to-anchor springs with a brake service tool. *Make sure that the cable eye is not cocked or binding on the anchor pin when installed, and that all parts are flat on the anchor pin.*

15. Remove the brake cylinder clamp.

16. Apply a thin, uniform coating of a lubricant specifically designed for this use to the threads and socket end of the adjusting screw. Turn the ajusting screw into the adjusting pivot nut to the limit of the threads, and then back off ½ turn. *Make sure the socket end of the adjusting screw is stamped "R" or "L" for right and left sides of the vehicle, and that the adjusting screw is on the proper side.*

17. Place the adjusting socket on the screw and install the assembly between the shoe ends with the toothed wheel of the adjusting screw nearest the secondary shoe.

TOOL 2086-L

TOOL LM-119

Disengaging return spring

18. Hook the cable hook into the hole in the adjusting lever. Make sure you are using the right lever—they, too, are stamped "R" and "L".

19. Position the hooked end of the adjuster spring fully into the large hole in the primary shoe web. Then connect the loop end of the spring to the adjuster lever hole.

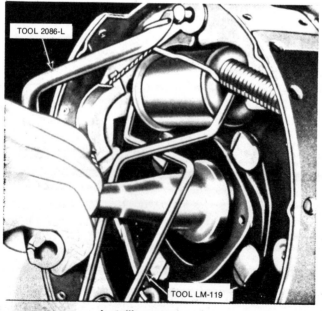

TOOL 2086-L

TOOL LM-119

Installing return spring

Finally, pull the adjuster lever, cable, and automatic adjuster spring down and to the rear to engage the pivot hook in the large hole in the secondary shoe web.

20. Check the action of the adjuster as follows:

A. Grab the cable between the cable guide and the adjuster lever and pull it toward the secondary shoe web far enough to lift the lever past a tooth on the adjusting screw wheel. The lever should snap into position behind the next tooth.

B. When the cable is released, the adjuster lever should return to its original position under the tension of the lever spring. This return action of the lever will turn the adjusting screw one tooth.

If pulling the cable does not produce this action, or if the lever action is sluggish instead of positive, check the position of the lever on the adjusting screw toothed wheel.

With the brake anchor at the top, the lever should contact the adjusting wheel $3/16$ in. (plus or minus $1/32$ in.) above the centerline of the screw. If the contact point is below this centerline, the lever will not lock on the teeth in the adjusting screw wheel, and the screw will not be turned. If the dimension is not correct, check for improperly assembled parts or worn cable end fittings, worn or stretched cables, worn cable guides, or a worn pivot hook. Reassemble or replace parts as necessary.

21. Be sure the upper ends of the brake shoes are seated against the anchor pin and that the shoes are centered on the backing plate. If they are not seated, brake off the parking brake system adjustment to obtain .005–.025 in. play after overcoming the load of the parking brake link spring.

DRUM BRAKE ADJUSTMENT

NOTE: *Drum brakes installed in the Mustang II are self-adjusting. All that is normally required to adjust the brakes is to apply them moderately hard several times while carefully backing the car in Reverse. However, if this action proves unsatisfactory, or if it proves necessary to re-adjust the brakes after replacing the linings or removing the drum, the following procedure may be used.*

1. Raise the car and support it with safety stands.

2. Remove the rubber plug from the adjusting slot on the backing plate.

3. Insert a brake adjusting spoon into the slot and engage the lowest possible tooth on the starwheel. Move the end of the brake spoon downward to move the starwheel upward and expand the adjusting screw. Repeat this operation until the brakes lock the wheel.

4. Insert a small screwdriver or piece of firm wire (coathanger wire) into the adjusting slot and push the automatic adjuster lever out and free of the starwheel on the adjusting screw.

5. Holding the adjusting lever out of the way, engage the topmost tooth possible on the starwheel with a brake adjusting spoon. Move the end of the adjusting spoon upward to move the adjusting screw starwheel downward an contact the adjusting screw. Back off the adjusting screw starwheel until the wheel spins freely with a minimum of drag. Keep track of the number of turns the starwheel is backed off.

6. Repeat this operation for the other side. When backing off the brakes on the other side, the adjusting lever must be backed off the same number of turns to prevent side-to-side brake pull.

7. Repeat this operation on the other set of brakes.

8. When all brakes are adjusted, make several stops, while backing the car, to equalize all of the wheels.

9. Road-test the car.

REAR WHEEL CYLINDER REMOVAL AND INSTALLATION

1. Remove the brake shoes.

2. Loosen the brake line at the rear of the cylinder. Do not pull the line away from the cylinder as it may bend or crack.

3. Remove the bolts and lockwashers attaching the wheel cylinder to the backing plate and remove the cylinder.

4. Poition a new or overhauled wheel cylinder on the backing plate and install the cylinder attaching bolts and lockwashers.

5. Attach the brake line to the cylinder. Carefully thread the connection to the cylinder.

6. Install the brake shoes.

REAR WHEEL CYLINDER OVERHAUL

Since the travel of the pistons in the wheel cylinder changes when new brake shoes are installed, it is possible for previously good wheel cylinders to start leaking after new brakes are installed. Therefore, to save yourself the expense of having to replace new

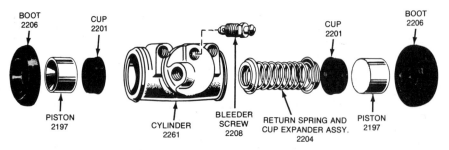

BOOT 2206   CUP 2201   CUP 2201   BOOT 2206

PISTON 2197   CYLINDER 2261   BLEEDER SCREW 2208   RETURN SPRING AND CUP EXPANDER ASSY. 2204   PISTON 2197

Rear wheel cylinder disassembled

brakes which become saturated with brake fluid and the aggravation of having to take everything apart again, it is strongly recommended that wheel cylinders be rebuilt every time new brake shoes are installed. This is especially true on high-mileage cars.

1. Remove the brakes.

2. Place a bucket or old newspapers under the brake backing plate to catch the brake fluid which will run out of the wheel cylinder.

3. Remove the boots from the ends of the wheel cylinders.

4. Push one piston toward the center of the cylinder to force the opposite piston and cup out the other end of the cylinder. Reach in the open end of the cylinder and push the spring, cup, and piston out of the cylinder.

5. Remove the bleeder screw from the rear of the cylinder, on the back of the backing plate.

6. Inspect the inside of the wheel cylinder. It is is scored in any way, the cylinder must be honed with a wheel cylinder hone or fine emery paper, and finished with crocus cloth if emergy paper is used. If the inside of the cylinder is excessively worn, the cylinder will have to be replaced, as only 0.003 in. of material can be removed from the cylinder walls. When honing or cleaning the wheel cylinders, keep a small amount of brake fluid in the cylinder to serve as a lubricant.

7. Clean any foreign matter from the pistons. The sides of the pistons must be smooth for the wheel cylinders to operate properly.

8. Clean the cylinder bore with alcohol and a lint-free rag. Pull the rag through the bore several times to remove all foreign matter and dry the cylinder.

9. Install the bleeder screw and the return spring in the cylinder.

10. Coat new cylinder cups with new brake fluid and install them in the cylinder. Make sure that they are square in the bore or they will leak.

11. Install the pistons in the cylinder after coating them with new brake fluid.

12. Coat the insides of the boots with new brake fluid and install them on the cylinder. Install the brakes.

PARKING BRAKE

CABLE ADJUSTMENT

1. Release the parking brake. Make sure that it is fully released. Place blocks in front of the front wheels.

2. Place the transmission in Neutral. Place a jack under the rear axle and raise the wheels just off the ground. If the supension is off-loaded, the cables may stretch, giving a faulty adjustment.

3. Pry up the rear of the parking brake handle boot cover between the front seats to expose the equalizer rod and adjusting nut. Loosen the locknut, then tighten the adjusting nut against the cable equalizer rod sufficiently to cause brake drag when the rear wheel is spun by hand. Next, loosen the adjusting nut until the rear wheels spin freely again. Then, tighten the locknut to 7–10 ft lbs. Snap the boot cover down.

4. Lower the car and check the adjustment. The parking brake should hold the car on a steep grade when pulled up to the third or fourth notch.

NOTE: *If the parking brake cannot be satisfactorily adjusted, the cable may be stretched and in need of replacement, the rear brakes may need adjustment, or the rear linings may be in need of replacement.*

CABLE REPLACEMENT

1. Completely release the parking brake. Loosen the adjusting nut. Loosen the lug nuts a few turns.

2. Raise the car and install jackstands beneath the reinforced box member areas.

3. Disconnect the cable from the equalizer.

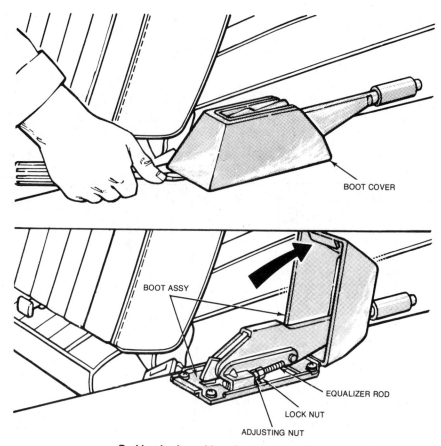

Parking brake cable adjustment location

4. Compress the retainer prongs and pull the cable back through the cable brackets sufficiently to release the cable.

5. Remove the clip attaching the cable to the bracket bolt.

6. Remove the rear wheel and tire assemblies. Remove the rear brake drums.

7. Remove the self-adjuster springs and the cable retainers from the backing plates.

8. Disconnect the cable ends from the parking brake levers on the secondary brake shoes.

9. Compress the cable retainer prongs

Brake Specifications

All measurements given are (in.) unless noted

Year	Model	Lug Nut Torque (ft/lb)	Master Cylinder Bore	Brake Disc		Brake Drum			Minimum Lining Thickness	
				Minimum Thickness	Maximum Run-Out	Diameter	Max Machine O/S	Max Wear Limit	Front	Rear
1974–78	All	70–115	.938	.810	.003	9.0	9.060	—	—	$\frac{1}{32}$ ①

① Above rivet heads

NOTE: *Minimum lining thickness is as recommended by the manufacturer. Because of variations in state inspection regulations, the minimum allowable thickness may be different than recommended by the manufacturer.*

PARKING BRAKE ADJUSTMENT PROCEDURE

ADJUST THE TENSION NUT "A" TO DEVELOP 60-85 LB FORCE 1.5 IN. BACK FROM THE FORWARD EDGE OF THE HANDLE—WITH THE HANDLE 40° UP FROM ITS RELEASED POSITION (8TH NOTCH).

THIS ADJUSTMENT MUST BE PERFORMED WITH THE VEHICLE WEIGHT ON THE AXLE AND NOT ON AN EXTERNAL BODY CARRIER.

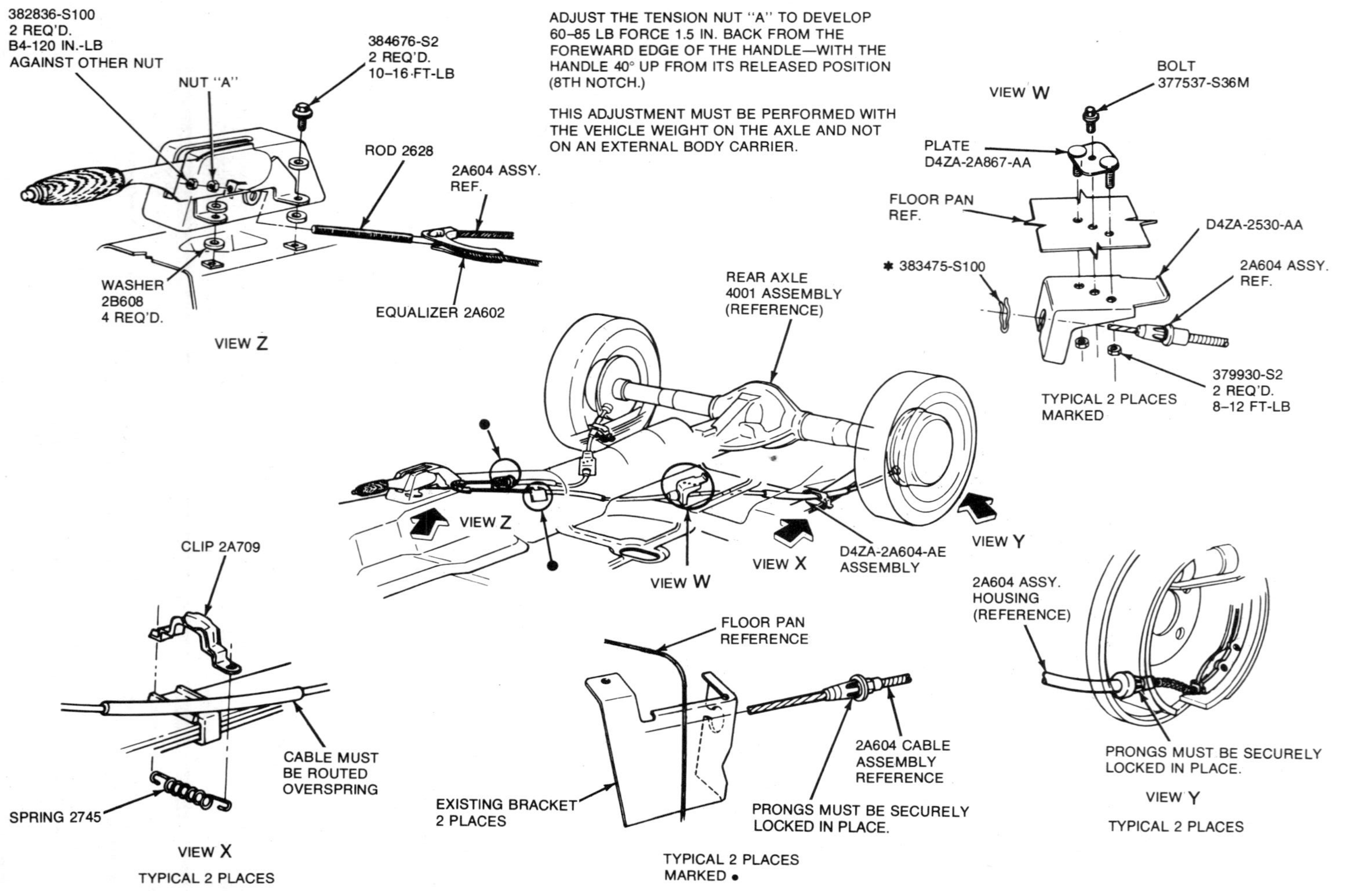

BOLT
377537-S36M

VIEW W

PLATE
D4ZA-2A867-AA

FLOOR PAN
REF.

* 383475-S100

D4ZA-2530-AA

2A604 ASSY.
REF.

379930-S2
2 REQ'D.
8-12 FT-LB

TYPICAL 2 PLACES
MARKED ●

PRONGS MUST BE SECURELY
LOCKED IN PLACE.

VIEW Y
TYPICAL 2 PLACES

VIEW Y

2A604 ASSY.
HOUSING
(REFERENCE)

D4ZA-2A604-AE
ASSEMBLY

VIEW X

REAR AXLE
4001 ASSEMBLY
(REFERENCE)

VIEW W

2A604 CABLE
ASSEMBLY
REFERENCE

FLOOR PAN
REFERENCE

PRONGS MUST BE SECURELY
LOCKED IN PLACE.

TYPICAL 2 PLACES
MARKED ●

EXISTING BRACKET
2 PLACES

Parking brake cable routing

382836-S100
2 REQ'D.
84-120 IN.-LB
AGAINST OTHER NUT

NUT "A"

384676-S2
2 REQ'D.
10-16 FT-LB

ROD 2628

2A604 ASSY.
REF.

EQUALIZER 2A602

VIEW Z

WASHER
2B608
4 REQ'D.

VIEW Z

CLIP 2A709

CABLE MUST
BE ROUTED
OVERSPRING

VIEW X
TYPICAL 2 PLACES

SPRING 2745

* COLOR RED FOR IDENTIFICATION

and pull the cable ends from the backing plates.

10. Remove the cable(s) from the vehicle.

11. To install, insert the cable ends through the backing plates and pull them into the rear brake assemblies so that the retainer prongs are securely seated in the backing plate holes.

12. Connect the cable end to the parking brake levers on the secondary brake shoes.

13. Install the cable retainers and the self-adjuster springs on the rear brake assemblies.

14. Position the cable in the retainers on the rear suspension and install the retainer spring.

15. Position the cable in the bolt-on brackets and insert the retaining clips.

16. Position the cable in the retainer brackets and pull forward until the retainer prongs are securely seated in the bracket holes.

17. Connect the cable at the equalizer.

18. Install the brake drums and wheel and tire assemblies. Remove the jackstands and lower the car.

19. Adjust the parking brake as outlined under cable adjustment.

Body

You can repair most minor auto body damage yourself. Minor damage usually falls into one of several categories: (1) small scratches and dings in the paint that can be repaired without the use of body filler, (2) deep scratches and dents that require body filler, but do not require pulling, or hammering metal back into shape and (3) rust-out repairs. The repair sequences illustrated in this chapter are typical of these types of repairs. If you want to get involved in more complicated repairs including pulling or hammering sheet metal back into shape, you will probably need more detailed instructions. Chilton's *Minor Auto Body Repair, 2nd Edition* is a comprehensive guide to repairing auto body damage yourself.

TOOLS AND SUPPLIES

The list of tools and equipment you may need to fix minor body damage ranges from very basic hand tools to a wide assortment of specialized body tools. Most minor scratches, dings and rust holes can be fixed using an electric drill, wire wheel or grinder attachment, half-round plastic file, sanding block, various grades of sandpaper (#36, which is coarse through #600, which is fine) in both wet and dry types, auto body plastic,

primer, touch-up paint, spreaders, newspaper and masking tape.

Most manufacturers of auto body repair products began supplying materials to professionals. Their knowledge of the best, most-used products has been translated into body repair kits for the do-it-yourselfer. Kits are available from a number of manufacturers and contain the necessary materials in the required amounts for the repair identified on the package.

Kits are available for a wide variety of uses, including:

- Rusted out metal
- All purpose kit for dents and holes
- Dents and deep scratches
- Fiberglass repair kit
- Epoxy kit for restyling.

Kits offer the advantage of buying what you need for the job. There is little waste and little chance of materials going bad from not being used. The same manufacturers also merchandise all of the individual products used—spreaders, dent pullers, fiberglass cloth, polyester resin, cream hardener, body filler, body files, sandpaper, sanding discs and holders, primer, spray paint, etc.

CAUTION: *Most of the products you will be using contain harmful chemicals, so be extremely careful. Always read the complete label before opening the containers. When* *you put them away for future use, be sure they are out of children's reach!*

Most auto body repair kits contain all the materials you need to do the job right in the kit. So, if you have a small rust spot or dent you want to fix, check the contents of the kit before you run out and buy any additional tools.

ALIGNING BODY PANELS

Doors

There are several methods of adjusting doors. Your vehicle will probably use one of those illustrated.

Whenever a door is removed and is to be reinstalled, you should matchmark the position of the hinges on the door pillars. The holes of the hinges and/or the hinge attaching points are usually oversize to permit alignment of doors. The striker plate is also moveable, through oversize holes, permitting up-and-down, in-and-out and fore-and-aft movement. Fore-and-aft movement is made by adding or subtracting shims from behind the striker and pillar post. The striker should be adjusted so that the door closes fully and remains closed, yet enters the lock freely.

DOOR HINGES

Don't try to cover up poor door adjustment with a striker plate adjustment. The gap on each side of the door should be equal and uniform and there should be no metal-to-metal contact as the door is opened or closed.

1. Determine which hinge bolts must be loosened to move the door in the desired direction.

2. Loosen the hinge bolt(s) just enough to allow the door to be moved with a padded pry bar.

3. Move the door a small amount and check the fit, after tightening the bolts. Be sure that there is no bind or interference with adjacent panels.

4. Repeat this until the door is properly positioned, and tighten all the bolts securely.

Hood, Trunk or Tailgate

As with doors, the outline of hinges should be scribed before removal. The hood and trunk can be aligned by loosening the hinge bolts in their slotted mounting holes and moving the hood or trunk lid as necessary.

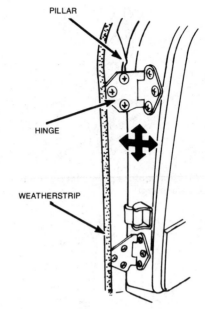

Door hinge adjustment

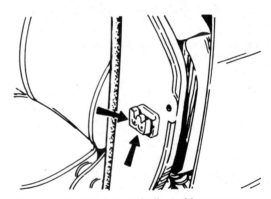

Move the door striker as indicated by arrows

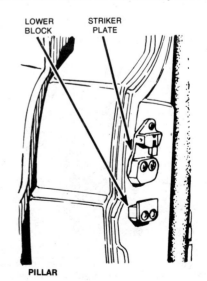

Striker plate and lower block

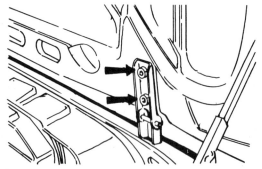

Loosen the hinge boots to permit fore-and-aft and horizontal adjustment

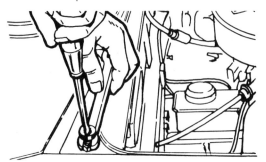

The hood is adjusted vertically by stop-screws at the front and/or rear

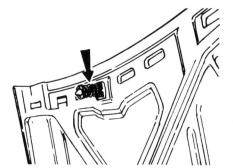

The hood pin can be adjusted for proper lock engagement

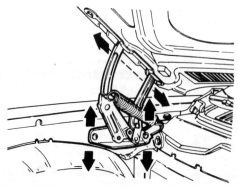

The height of the hood at the rear is adjusted by loosening the bolts that attach the hinge to the body and moving the hood up or down

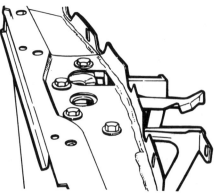

The base of the hood lock can also be repositioned slightly to give more positive lock engagement

The hood and trunk have adjustable catch locations to regulate lock engagement. Bumpers at the front and/or rear of the hood provide a vertical adjustment and the hood lockpin can be adjusted for proper engagement.

The tailgate on the station wagon can be adjusted by loosening the hinge bolts in their slotted mounting holes and moving the tailgate on its hinges. The latchplate and latch striker at the bottom of the tailgate opening can be adjusted to stop rattle. An adjustable bumper is located on each side.

RUST, UNDERCOATING, AND RUSTPROOFING

Rust

Rust is an electrochemical process. It works on ferrous metals (iron and steel) from the inside out due to exposure of unprotected surfaces to air and moisture. The possibility of rust exists practically nationwide—anywhere humidity, industrial pollution or chemical salts are present, rust can form. In coastal areas, the problem is high humidity and salt air; in snowy areas, the problem is chemical salt (de-icer) used to keep the roads clear, and in industrial areas, sulphur dioxide is present in the air from industrial pollution and is changed to sulphuric acid when it rains. The rusting process is accelerated by high temperatures, especially in snowy areas, when vehicles are driven over slushy roads and then left overnight in a heated garage.

Automotive styling also can be a contributor to rust formation. Spot welding of panels creates small pockets that trap moisture and form an environment for rust formation. Fortunately, auto manufacturers have been working hard to increase the corrosion protection of their products. Galvanized sheet metal enjoys much wider use, along with the increased use of plastic and various rust retardant coatings. Manufacturers are also designing out areas in the body where rust-forming moisture can collect.

To prevent rust, you must stop it before it gets started. On new vehicles, there are two ways to accomplish this.

First, the car or truck should be treated with a commercial rustproofing compound. There are many different brands of franchised rustproofers, but most processes involve spraying a waxy "self-healing" compound under the chassis, inside rocker panels, inside doors and fender liners and similar places where rust is likely to form. Prices for a quality rustproofing job range from $100–$250, depending on the area, the brand name and the size of the vehicle.

Ideally, the vehicle should be rustproofed as soon as possible following the purchase. The surfaces of the car or truck have begun to oxidize and deteriorate during shipping. In addition, the car may have sat on a dealer's lot or on a lot at the factory, and once the rust has progressed past the stage of light, powdery surface oxidation rustproofing is not likely to be worthwhile. Professional rustproofers feel that once rust has formed, rustproofing will simply seal in moisture already present. Most franchised rustproofing operations offer a 3–5 year warranty against rust-through, but will not support that warranty if the rustproofing is not applied within three months of the date of manufacture.

Undercoating should not be mistaken for rustproofing. Undercoating is a black, tar-like substance that is applied to the underside of a vehicle. Its basic function is to deaden noises that are transmitted from under the car. It simply cannot get into the crevices and seams where moisture tends to collect. In fact, it may clog up drainage holes and ventilation passages. Some undercoatings also tend to crack or peel with age and only create more moisture and corrosion attracting pockets.

The second thing you should do immediately after purchasing the car is apply a paint sealant. A sealant is a petroleum based product marketed under a wide variety of brand names. It has the same protective properties as a good wax, but bonds to the paint with a chemically inert layer that seals it from the air. If air can't get at the surface, oxidation cannot start.

The paint sealant kit consists of a base coat and a conditioning coat that should be applied every 6–8 months, depending on the manufacturer. The base coat must be applied before waxing, or the wax must first be removed.

Third, keep a garden hose handy for your car in winter. Use it a few times on nice days during the winter for underneath areas, and it will pay big dividends when spring arrives. Spraying under the fenders and other areas which even car washes don't reach will help remove road salt, dirt and other build-ups which help breed rust. Adjust the nozzle to a high-force spray. An old brush will help break up residue, permitting it to be washed away more easily.

It's a somewhat messy job, but worth it in the long run because rust often starts in those hidden areas.

At the same time, wash grime off the door sills and, more importantly, the under portions of the doors, plus the tailgate if you have a station wagon or truck. Applying a coat of wax to those areas at least once before and once during winter will help fend off rust.

When applying the wax to the under parts of the doors, you will note small drain holes. These holes often are plugged with undercoating or dirt. Make sure they are cleaned out to prevent water build-up inside the doors. A small punch or penknife will do the job.

Water from the high-pressure sprays in car washes sometimes can get into the housings for parking and taillights, so take a close look. If they contain water merely loosen the retaining screws and the water should run out.

Repairing Scratches and Small Dents

Step 1. This dent (arrow) is typical of a deep scratch or minor dent. If deep enough, the dent or scratch can be pulled out or hammered out from behind. In this case no straightening is necessary

Step 2. Using an 80-grit grinding disc on an electric drill grind the paint from the surrounding area down to bare metal. This will provide a rough surface for the body filler to grab

Step 3. The area should look like this when you're finished grinding

Step 4. Mix the body filler and cream hardener according to the directions

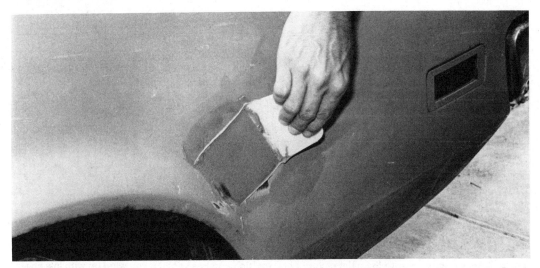

Step 5. Spread the body filler evenly over the entire area. Be sure to cover the area completely

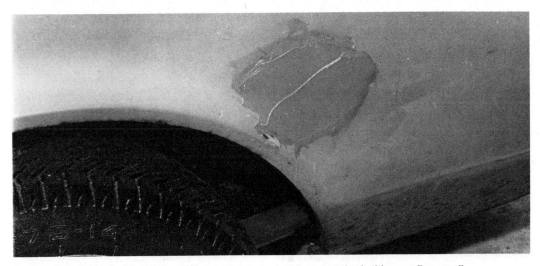

Step 6. Let the body filler dry until the surface can just be scratched with your fingernail

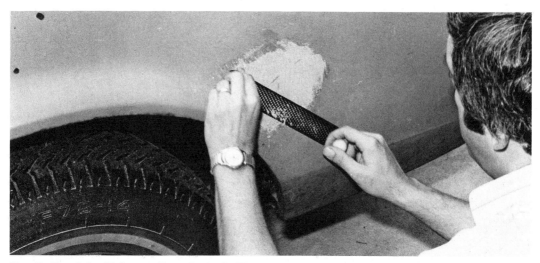

Step 7. Knock the high spots from the body filler with a body file

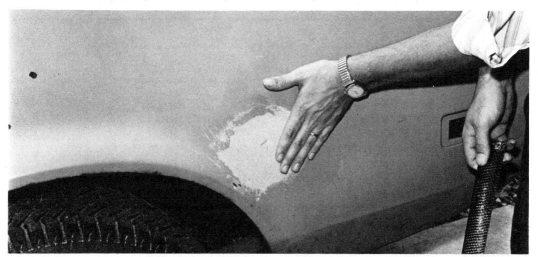

Step 8. Check frequently with the palm of your hand for high and low spots. If you wind up with low spots, you may have to apply another layer of filler

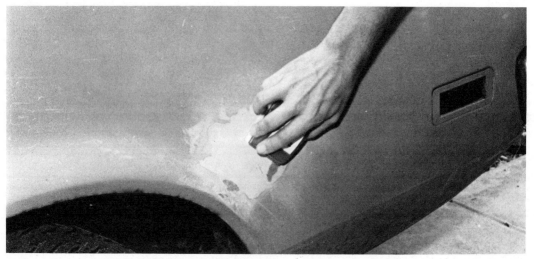

Step 9. Block sand the entire area with 320 grit paper

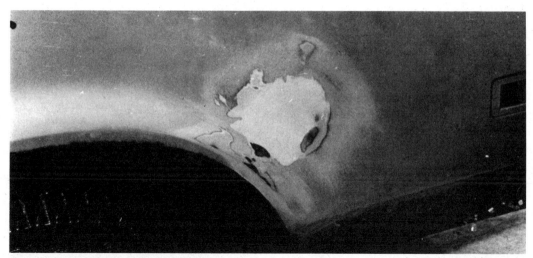

Step 10. When you're finished, the repair should look like this. Note the sand marks extending 2—3 inches out from the repaired area

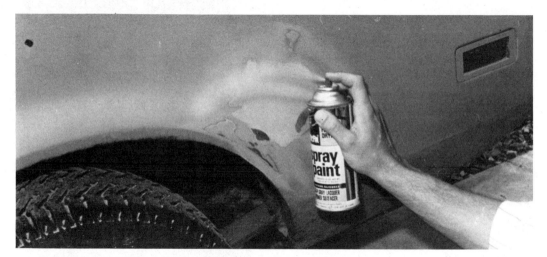

Step 11. Prime the entire area with automotive primer

Step 12. The finished repair ready for the final paint coat. Note that the primer has covered the sanding marks (see Step 10). A repair of this size should be able to be spotpainted with good results

REPAIRING RUST HOLES

One thing you have to remember about rust: even if you grind away all the rusted metal in a panel, and repair the area with any of the kits available, *eventually* the rust will return. There are two reasons for this. One, rust is a chemical reaction that causes pressure under the repair from the inside out. That's how the blisters form. Two, the back side of the panel (and the repair) is wide open to moisture, and unpainted body filler acts like a sponge. That's why the best solution to rust problems is to remove the rusted panel and install a new one or have the rusted area cut out and a new piece of sheet metal welded in its place. The trouble with welding is the expense; sometimes it will cost more than the car or truck is worth.

One of the better solutions to do-it-yourself rust repair is the process using a fiberglass cloth repair kit (shown here). This will give a strong repair that resists cracking and moisture and is relatively easy to use. It can be used on large or small holes and also can be applied over contoured surfaces.

Step 1. Rust areas such as this are common and are easily fixed

Step 2. Grind away all traces of rust with a 24-grit grinding disc. Be sure to grind back 3—4 inches from the edge of the hole down to bare metal and be sure all traces of rust are removed

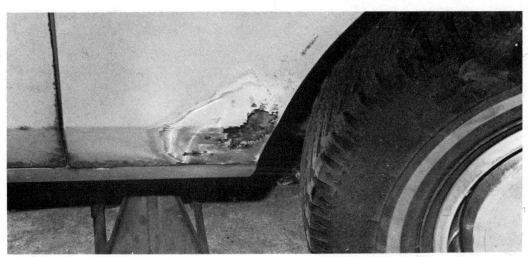

Step 3. Be sure all rust is removed from the edges of the metal. The edges must be ground back to un-rusted metal

Step 4. If you are going to use release film, cut a piece about 2″ larger than the area you have sanded. Place the film over the repair and mark the sanded area on the film. Avoid any unnecessary wrinkling of the film

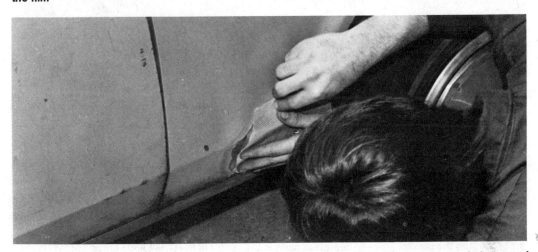

Step 5. Cut 2 pieces of fiberglass matte. One piece should be about 1″ smaller than the sanded area and the second piece should be 1″ smaller than the first. Use sharp scissors to avoid loose ends

Step 6. Check the dimensions of the release film and cloth by holding them up to the repair area

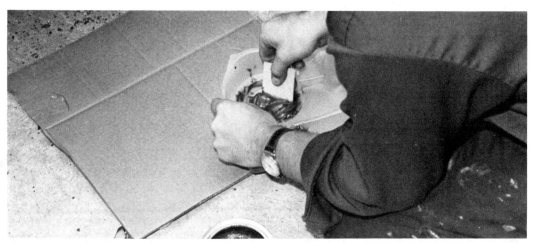

Step 7. Mix enough repair jelly and cream hardener in the mixing tray to saturate the fiberglass material or fill the repair area. Follow the directions on the container

Step 8. Lay the release sheet on a flat surface and spread an even layer of filler, large enough to cover the repair. Lay the smaller piece of fiberglass cloth in the center of the sheet and spread another layer of repair jelly over the fiberglass cloth. Repeat the operation for the larger piece of cloth. If the fiberglass cloth is not used, spread the repair jelly on the release film, concentrated in the middle of the repair

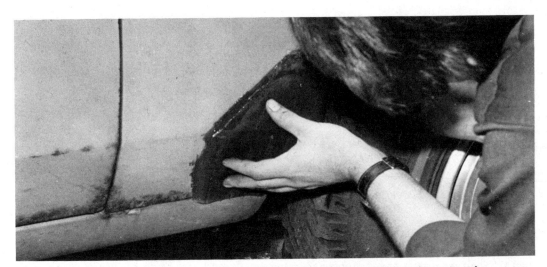

Step 9. Place the repair material over the repair area, with the release film facing outward

Step 10. Use a spreader and work from the center outward to smooth the material, following the body contours. Be sure to remove all air bubbles

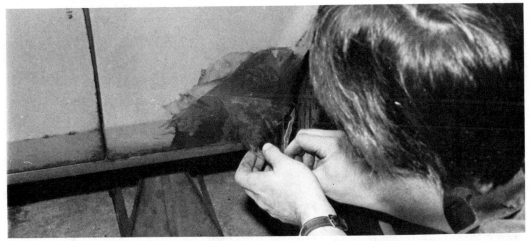

Step 11. Wait until the repair has dried tack-free and peel off the release sheet. The ideal working temperature is 65—90° F. Cooler or warmer temperatures or high humidity may require additional curing time

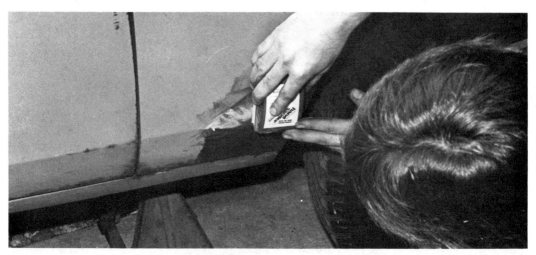

Step 12. Sand and feather-edge the entire area. The initial sanding can be done with a sanding disc on an electric drill if care is used. Finish the sanding with a block sander

Step 13. When the area is sanded smooth, mix some topcoat and hardener and apply it directly with a spreader. This will give a smooth finish and prevent the glass matte from showing through the paint

Step 14. Block sand the topcoat with finishing sandpaper

Step 15. To finish this repair, grind out the surface rust along the top edge of the rocker panel

Step 16. Mix some more repair jelly and cream hardener and apply it directly over the surface

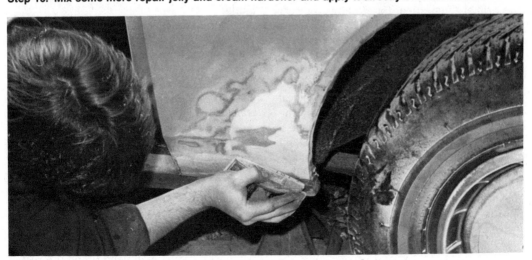

Step 17. When it dries tack-free, block sand the surface smooth

Step 18. If necessary, mask off adjacent panels and spray the entire repair with primer. You are now ready for a color coat

AUTO BODY CARE

There are hundreds—maybe thousands—of products on the market, all designed to protect or aid your car's finish in some manner. There are as many different products as there are ways to use them, but they all have one thing in common—the surface must be clean.

Washing

The primary ingredient for washing your car is water, preferably "soft" water. In many areas of the country, the local water supply is "hard" containing many minerals. The little rings or film that is left on your car's surface after it has dried is the result of "hard" water.

Since you usually can't change the local water supply, the next best thing is to dry the surface before it has a chance to dry itself.

Into the water you usually add soap. Don't use detergents or common, coarse soaps. Your car's paint never truly dries out, but is always evaporating residual oils into the air. Harsh detergents will remove these oils, causing the paint to dry faster than normal. Instead use warm water and a non-detergent soap made especially for waxed surfaces or a liquid soap made for waxed surfaces or a liquid soap made for washing dishes by hand.

Other products that can be used on painted surfaces include baking soda or plain soda water for stubborn dirt.

Wash the car completely, starting at the top, and rinse it completely clean. Abrasive grit should be loaded off under water pressure; scrubbing grit off will scratch the finish. The best washing tool is a sponge, cleaning mitt or soft towel. Whichever you choose, replace it often as each tends to absorb grease and dirt.

Other ways to get a better wash include:

• Don't wash your car in the sun or when the finish is hot.

• Use water pressure to remove caked-on dirt.

• Remove tree-sap and bird effluence immediately. Such substances will eat through wax, polish and paint.

One of the best implements to dry your car is a turkish towel or an old, soft bath towel. Anything with a deep nap will hold any dirt in suspension and not grind it into the paint.

Harder cloths will only grind the grit into the paint making more scratches. Always start drying at the top, followed by the hood and trunk and sides. You'll find there's always more dirt near the rocker panels and wheelwells which will wind up on the rest of the car if you dry these areas first.

Cleaners, Waxes and Polishes

Before going any farther you should know the function of various products.

Cleaners—remove the top layer of dead pigment or paint.

Rubbing or polishing compounds—used to remove stubborn dirt, get rid of minor scratches, smooth away imperfections and partially restore badly weathered paint.

Polishes—contain no abrasives or waxes; they shine the paint by adding oils to the paint.

Waxes—are a protective coating for the polish.

CLEANERS AND COMPOUNDS

Before you apply any wax, you'll have to remove oxidation, road film and other types of pollutants that washing alone will not remove.

The paint on your car never dries completely. There are always residual oils evaporating from the paint into the air. When enough oils are present in the paint, it has a healthy shine (gloss). When too many oils evaporate the paint takes on a whitish cast known as oxidation. The idea of polishing and waxing is to keep enough oil present in the painted surface to prevent oxidation; but when it occurs, the only recourse is to remove the top layer of "dead" paint, exposing the healthy paint underneath.

Products to remove oxidation and road film are sold under a variety of generic names—polishes, cleaner, rubbing compound, cleaner/polish, polish/cleaner, self-polishing wax, pre-wax cleaner, finish restorer and many more. Regardless of name there are two types of cleaners—abrasive cleaners (sometimes called polishing or rubbing compounds) that remove oxidation by grinding away the top layer of "dead" paint, or chemical cleaners that dissolve the "dead" pigment, allowing it to be wiped away.

Abrasive cleaners, by their nature, leave thousands of minute scratches in the finish, which must be polished out later. These should only be used in extreme cases, but are usually the only thing to use on badly oxidized paint finishes. Chemical cleaners are much milder but are not strong enough for severe cases of oxidation or weathered paint.

The most popular cleaners are liquid or paste abrasive polishing and rubbing compounds. Polishing compounds have a finer abrasive grit for medium duty work. Rubbing compounds are a coarser abrasive and for heavy duty work. Unless you are familiar with how to use compounds, be very careful. Excessive rubbing with any type of compound or cleaner can grind right through the paint to primer or bare metal. Follow the directions on the container—depending on type, the cleaner may or may not be OK for your paint. For example, some cleaners are not formulated for acrylic lacquer finishes.

When a small area needs compounding or heavy polishing, it's best to do the job by hand. Some people prefer a powered buffer for large areas. Avoid cutting through the paint along styling edges on the body. Small, hand operations where the compound is applied and rubbed using cloth folded into a thick ball allow you to work in straight lines along such edges.

To avoid cutting through on the edges when using a power buffer, try masking tape. Just cover the edge with tape while using power. Then finish the job by hand with the tape removed. Even then work carefully. The paint tends to be a lot thinner along the sharp ridges stamped into the panels.

Whether compounding by machine or by hand, only work on a small area and apply the compound sparingly. If the materials are spread too thin, or allowed to sit too long, they dry out. Once dry they lose the ability to deliver a smooth, clean finish. Also, dried out polish tends to cause the buffer to stick in one spot. This in turn can burn or cut through the finish.

WAXES AND POLISHES

Your car's finish can be protected in a number of ways. A cleaner/wax or polish/cleaner followed by wax or variations of each all provide good results. The two-step approach (polish followed by wax) is probably slightly better but consumes more time and effort. Properly fed with oils, your paint should never need cleaning, but despite the best polishing job, it won't last unless it's protected with wax. Without wax, polish must be renewed at least once a month to prevent oxidation. Years ago (some still swear by it today), the best wax was made from the Brazilian palm, the Carnuba, favored for its vegetable base and high melting point. However, modern synthetic waxes are harder, which means they protect against moisture better, and chemically inert silicone is used for a long lasting protection. The only problem with silicone wax is that it penetrates all layers of paint. To repaint or touch up a panel or car protected by silicone wax, you have to completely strip the finish to avoid "fish-eyes."

Under normal conditions, silicone waxes will last 4–6 months, but you have to be careful of wax build-up from too much waxing. Too thick a coat of wax is just as bad as no wax at all; it stops the paint from breathing.

Combination cleaners/waxes have become popular lately because they remove the old layer of wax plus light oxidation, while putting on a fresh coat of wax at the same time. Some cleaners/waxes contain abrasive cleaners which require caution, although many cleaner/waxes use a chemical cleaner.

Applying Wax or Polish

You may view polishing and waxing your car as a pleasant way to spend an afternoon, or as a boring chore, but it has to be done to keep the paint on your car. Caring for the paint doesn't require special tools, but you should follow a few rules.

1. Use a good quality wax.
2. Before applying any wax or polish, be sure the surface is completely clean. Just because the car looks clean, doesn't mean it's ready for polish or wax.
3. If the finish on your car is weathered, dull, or oxidized, it will probably have to be compounded to remove the old or oxidized paint. If the paint is simply dulled from lack of care, one of the non-abrasive cleaners known as polishing compounds will do the trick. If the paint is severely scratched or really dull, you'll probably have to use a rubbing compound to prepare the finish for waxing. If you're not sure which one to use, use the polishing compound, since you can easily ruin the finish by using too strong a compound.
4. Don't apply wax, polish or compound in direct sunlight, even if the directions on the can say you can. Most waxes will not cure properly in bright sunlight and you'll probably end up with a blotchy looking finish.
5. Don't rub the wax off too soon. The result will be a wet, dull looking finish. Let the wax dry thoroughly before buffing it off.
6. A constant debate among car enthusiasts is how wax should be applied. Some maintain pastes or liquids should be applied in a circular motion, but body shop experts have long thought that this approach results in barely detectable circular abrasions, especially on cars that are waxed frequently. They

advise rubbing in straight lines, especially if any kind of cleaner is involved.

7. If an applicator is not supplied with the wax, use a piece of soft cheesecloth or very soft lint-free material. The same applies to buffing the surface.

SPECIAL SURFACES

One-step combination cleaner and wax formulas shouldn't be used on many of the special surfaces which abound on cars. The one-step materials contain abrasives to achieve a clean surface under the wax top coat. The abrasives are so mild that you could clean a car every week for a couple of years without fear of rubbing through the paint. But this same level of abrasiveness might, through repeated use, damage decals used for special trim effects. This includes wide stripes, wood-grain trim and other appliques.

Painted plastics must be cleaned with care. If a cleaner is too aggressive it will cut through the paint and expose the primer. If bright trim such as polished aluminum or chrome is painted, cleaning must be performed with even greater care. If rubbing compound is being used, it will cut faster than polish.

Abrasive cleaners will dull an acrylic finish. The best way to clean these newer finishes is with a non-abrasive liquid polish. Only dirt and oxidation, not paint, will be removed.

Taking a few minutes to read the instructions on the can of polish or wax will help prevent making serious mistakes. Not all preparations will work on all surfaces. And some are intended for power application while others will only work when applied by hand.

Don't get the idea that just pouring on some polish and then hitting it with a buffer will suffice. Power equipment speeds the operation. But it also adds a measure of risk. It's very easy to damage the finish if you use the wrong methods or materials.

Caring for Chrome

Read the label on the container. Many products are formulated specifically for chrome, but others contain abrasives that will scratch the chrome finish. If it isn't recommended for chrome, don't use it.

Never use steel wool or kitchen soap pads to clean chrome. Be careful not to get chrome cleaner on paint or interior vinyl surfaces. If you do, get it off immediately.

Troubleshooting

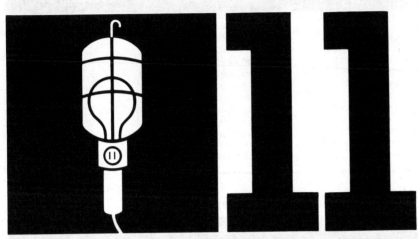

11

This section is designed to aid in the quick, accurate diagnosis of automotive problems. While automotive repairs can be made by many people, accurate troubleshooting is a rare skill for the amateur and professional alike.

In its simplest state, troubleshooting is an exercise in logic. It is essential to realize that an automobile is really composed of a series of systems. Some of these systems are interrelated; others are not. Automobiles operate within a framework of logical rules and physical laws, and the key to troubleshooting is a good understanding of all the automotive systems.

This section breaks the car or truck down into its component systems, allowing the problem to be isolated. The charts and diagnostic road maps list the most common problems and the most probable causes of trouble. Obviously it would be impossible to list every possible problem that could happen along with every possible cause, but it will locate MOST problems and eliminate a lot of unnecessary guesswork. The systematic format will locate problems within a given system, but, because many automotive systems are interrelated, the solution to your particular problem may be found in a number of systems on the car or truck.

USING THE TROUBLESHOOTING CHARTS

This book contains all of the specific information that the average do-it-yourself mechanic needs to repair and maintain his or her car or truck. The troubleshooting charts are designed to be used in conjunction with the specific procedures and information in the text. For instance, troubleshooting a point-type ignition system is fairly standard for all models, but you may be directed to the text to find procedures for troubleshooting an individual type of electronic ignition. You will also have to refer to the specification charts throughout the book for specifications applicable to your car or truck.

TOOLS AND EQUIPMENT

The tools illustrated in Chapter 1 (plus two more diagnostic pieces) will be adequate to troubleshoot most problems. The two other tools needed are a voltmeter and an ohmmeter. These can be purchased separately or in combination, known as a VOM meter.

In the event that other tools are required, they will be noted in the procedures.

Troubleshooting Engine Problems

See Chapters 2, 3, 4 for more information and service procedures.

Index to Systems

System	To Test	Group
Battery	Engine need not be running	1
Starting system	Engine need not be running	2
Primary electrical system	Engine need not be running	3
Secondary electrical system	Engine need not be running	4
Fuel system	Engine need not be running	5
Engine compression	Engine need not be running	6
Engine vacuum	Engine must be running	7
Secondary electrical system	Engine must be running	8
Valve train	Engine must be running	9
Exhaust system	Engine must be running	10
Cooling system	Engine must be running	11
Engine lubrication	Engine must be running	12

Index to Problems

Problem: Symptom	Begin at Specific Diagnosis, Number ____
Engine Won't Start:	
Starter doesn't turn	1.1, 2.1
Starter turns, engine doesn't	2.1
Starter turns engine very slowly	1.1, 2.4
Starter turns engine normally	3.1, 4.1
Starter turns engine very quickly	6.1
Engine fires intermittently	4.1
Engine fires consistently	5.1, 6.1
Engine Runs Poorly:	
Hard starting	3.1, 4.1, 5.1, 8.1
Rough idle	4.1, 5.1, 8.1
Stalling	3.1, 4.1, 5.1, 8.1
Engine dies at high speeds	4.1, 5.1
Hesitation (on acceleration from standing stop)	5.1, 8.1
Poor pickup	4.1, 5.1, 8.1
Lack of power	3.1, 4.1, 5.1, 8.1
Backfire through the carburetor	4.1, 8.1, 9.1
Backfire through the exhaust	4.1, 8.1, 9.1
Blue exhaust gases	6.1, 7.1
Black exhaust gases	5.1
Running on (after the ignition is shut off)	3.1, 8.1
Susceptible to moisture	4.1
Engine misfires under load	4.1, 7.1, 8.4, 9.1
Engine misfires at speed	4.1, 8.4
Engine misfires at idle	3.1, 4.1, 5.1, 7.1, 8.4

Sample Section

Test and Procedure	Results and Indications	Proceed to
4.1—Check for spark: Hold each spark plug wire approximately ¼" from ground with gloves or a heavy, dry rag. Crank the engine and observe the spark.	If no spark is evident:	4.2
	If spark is good in some cases:	4.3
	If spark is good in all cases:	4.6

Specific Diagnosis

This section is arranged so that following each test, instructions are given to proceed to another, until a problem is diagnosed.

Section 1—Battery

Test and Procedure	Results and Indications	Proceed to
1.1—Inspect the battery visually for case condition (corrosion, cracks) and water level.	If case is cracked, replace battery:	**1.4**
	If the case is intact, remove corrosion with a solution of baking soda and water (**CAUTION**: *do not get the solution into the battery*), and fill with water:	**1.2**

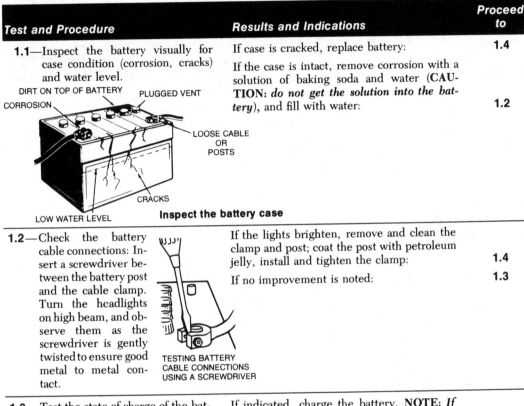

DIRT ON TOP OF BATTERY
PLUGGED VENT
CORROSION
LOOSE CABLE OR POSTS
CRACKS
LOW WATER LEVEL

Inspect the battery case

Test and Procedure	Results and Indications	Proceed to
1.2—Check the battery cable connections: Insert a screwdriver between the battery post and the cable clamp. Turn the headlights on high beam, and observe them as the screwdriver is gently twisted to ensure good metal to metal contact.	If the lights brighten, remove and clean the clamp and post; coat the post with petroleum jelly, install and tighten the clamp:	**1.4**
	If no improvement is noted:	**1.3**

TESTING BATTERY CABLE CONNECTIONS USING A SCREWDRIVER

Test and Procedure	Results and Indications	Proceed to
1.3—Test the state of charge of the battery using an individual cell tester or hydrometer.	If indicated, charge the battery. **NOTE:** *If no obvious reason exists for the low state of charge (i.e., battery age, prolonged storage), proceed to:*	**1.4**

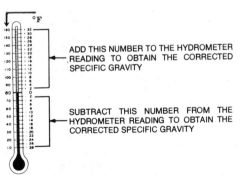

°F

ADD THIS NUMBER TO THE HYDROMETER READING TO OBTAIN THE CORRECTED SPECIFIC GRAVITY

SUBTRACT THIS NUMBER FROM THE HYDROMETER READING TO OBTAIN THE CORRECTED SPECIFIC GRAVITY

Specific Gravity (@ 80° F.)

Minimum	Battery Charge
1.260	100% Charged
1.230	75% Charged
1.200	50% Charged
1.170	25% Charged
1.140	Very Little Power Left
1.110	Completely Discharged

The effects of temperature on battery specific gravity (left) and amount of battery charge in relation to specific gravity (right)

Test and Procedure	Results and Indications	Proceed to
1.4—Visually inspect battery cables for cracking, bad connection to ground, or bad connection to starter.	If necessary, tighten connections or replace the cables:	**2.1**

Section 2—Starting System
See Chapter 3 for service procedures

Test and Procedure	Results and Indications	Proceed to

Note: Tests in Group 2 are performed with coil high tension lead disconnected to prevent accidental starting.

2.1—Test the starter motor and solenoid: Connect a jumper from the battery post of the solenoid (or relay) to the starter post of the solenoid (or relay).	If starter turns the engine normally:	**2.2**
	If the starter buzzes, or turns the engine very slowly:	**2.4**
	If no response, replace the solenoid (or relay).	**3.1**
	If the starter turns, but the engine doesn't, ensure that the flywheel ring gear is intact. If the gear is undamaged, replace the starter drive.	**3.1**
2.2—Determine whether ignition override switches are functioning properly (clutch start switch, neutral safety switch), by connecting a jumper across the switch(es), and turning the ignition switch to "start".	If starter operates, adjust or replace switch:	**3.1**
	If the starter doesn't operate:	**2.3**
2.3—Check the ignition switch "start" position: Connect a 12V test lamp or voltmeter between the starter post of the solenoid (or relay) and ground. Turn the ignition switch to the "start" position, and jiggle the key.	If the lamp doesn't light or the meter needle doesn't move when the switch is turned, check the ignition switch for loose connections, cracked insulation, or broken wires. Repair or replace as necessary:	**3.1**
	If the lamp flickers or needle moves when the key is jiggled, replace the ignition switch.	**3.3**

Checking the ignition switch "start" position

STARTER RELAY (IF EQUIPPED)

2.4—Remove and bench test the starter, according to specifications in the engine electrical section.	If the starter does not meet specifications, repair or replace as needed:	**3.1**
	If the starter is operating properly:	**2.5**
2.5—Determine whether the engine can turn freely: Remove the spark plugs, and check for water in the cylinders. Check for water on the dipstick, or oil in the radiator. Attempt to turn the engine using an 18″ flex drive and socket on the crankshaft pulley nut or bolt.	If the engine will turn freely only with the spark plugs out, and hydrostatic lock (water in the cylinders) is ruled out, check valve timing:	**9.2**
	If engine will not turn freely, and it is known that the clutch and transmission are free, the engine must be disassembled for further evaluation:	**Chapter 3**

Section 3—Primary Electrical System

Test and Procedure	Results and Indications	Proceed to
3.1—Check the ignition switch "on" position: Connect a jumper wire between the distributor side of the coil and ground, and a 12V test lamp between the switch side of the coil and ground. Remove the high tension lead from the coil. Turn the ignition switch on and jiggle the key.	If the lamp lights:	**3.2**
	If the lamp flickers when the key is jiggled, replace the ignition switch:	**3.3**
	If the lamp doesn't light, check for loose or open connections. If none are found, remove the ignition switch and check for continuity. If the switch is faulty, replace it:	**3.3**

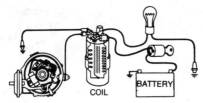

Checking the ignition switch "on" position

3.2—Check the ballast resistor or resistance wire for an open circuit, using an ohmmeter. See Chapter 3 for specific tests.	Replace the resistor or resistance wire if the resistance is zero. **NOTE:** *Some ignition systems have no ballast resistor.*	**3.3**

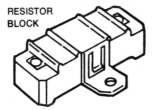

RESISTOR BLOCK

CALIBRATED RESISTANCE LEAD

Two types of resistors

3.3—On point-type ignition systems, visually inspect the breaker points for burning, pitting or excessive wear. Gray coloring of the point contact surfaces is normal. Rotate the crankshaft until the contact heel rests on a high point of the distributor cam and adjust the point gap to specifications. On electronic ignition models, remove the distributor cap and visually inspect the armature. Ensure that the armature pin is in place, and that the armature is on tight and rotates when the engine is cranked. Make sure there are no cracks, chips or rounded edges on the armature.	If the breaker points are intact, clean the contact surfaces with fine emery cloth, and adjust the point gap to specifications. If the points are worn, replace them. On electronic systems, replace any parts which appear defective. If condition persists:	**3.4**

Test and Procedure	Results and Indications	Proceed to
3.4—On point-type ignition systems, connect a dwell-meter between the distributor primary lead and ground. Crank the engine and observe the point dwell angle. On electronic ignition systems, conduct a stator (magnetic pickup assembly) test. See Chapter 3.	On point-type systems, adjust the dwell angle if necessary. **NOTE:** *Increasing the point gap decreases the dwell angle and vice-versa.*	**3.6**
	If the dwell meter shows little or no reading;	**3.5**
	On electronic ignition systems, if the stator is bad, replace the stator. If the stator is good, proceed to the other tests in Chapter 3.	

Dwell is a function of point gap

3.5—On the point-type ignition systems, check the condenser for short: connect an ohmeter across the condenser body and the pigtail lead.	If any reading other than infinite is noted, replace the condenser	**3.6**

Checking the condenser for short

3.6—Test the coil primary resistance: On point-type ignition systems, connect an ohmmeter across the coil primary terminals, and read the resistance on the low scale. Note whether an external ballast resistor or resistance wire is used. On electronic ignition systems, test the coil primary resistance as in Chapter 3.	Point-type ignition coils utilizing ballast resistors or resistance wires should have approximately 1.0 ohms resistance. Coils with internal resistors should have approximately 4.0 ohms resistance. If values far from the above are noted, replace the coil.	**4.1**

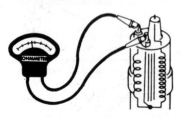

Check the coil primary resistance

Section 4—Secondary Electrical System
See Chapters 2–3 for service procedures

Test and Procedure	Results and Indications	Proceed to
4.1—Check for spark: Hold each spark plug wire approximately ¼″ from ground with gloves or a heavy, dry rag. Crank the engine, and observe the spark.	If no spark is evident:	**4.2**
	If spark is good in some cylinders:	**4.3**
	If spark is good in all cylinders:	**4.6**

Check for spark at the plugs

4.2—Check for spark at the coil high tension lead: Remove the coil high tension lead from the distributor and position it approximately ¼″ from ground. Crank the engine and observe spark. **CAUTION: This test should not be performed on engines equipped with electronic ignition.**	If the spark is good and consistent:	**4.3**
	If the spark is good but intermittent, test the primary electrical system starting at 3.3:	**3.3**
	If the spark is weak or non-existent, replace the coil high tension lead, clean and tighten all connections and retest. If no improvement is noted:	**4.4**
4.3—Visually inspect the distributor cap and rotor for burned or corroded contacts, cracks, carbon tracks, or moisture. Also check the fit of the rotor on the distributor shaft (where applicable).	If moisture is present, dry thoroughly, and retest per 4.1:	**4.1**
	If burned or excessively corroded contacts, cracks, or carbon tracks are noted, replace the defective part(s) and retest per 4.1:	**4.1**
	If the rotor and cap appear intact, or are only slightly corroded, clean the contacts thoroughly (including the cap towers and spark plug wire ends) and retest per 4.1:	
	If the spark is good in all cases:	**4.6**
	If the spark is poor in all cases:	**4.5**

Inspect the distributor cap and rotor

Test and Procedure	Results and Indications	Proceed to
4.4—Check the coil secondary resistance: On point-type systems connect an ohmmeter across the distributor side of the coil and the coil tower. Read the resistance on the high scale of the ohmmeter. On electronic ignition systems, see Chapter 3 for specific tests.	The resistance of a satisfactory coil should be between 4,000 and 10,000 ohms. If resistance is considerably higher (i.e., 40,000 ohms) replace the coil and retest per 4.1. **NOTE:** *This does not apply to high performance coils.*	

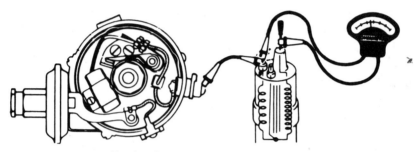

Testing the coil secondary resistance

4.5—Visually inspect the spark plug wires for cracking or brittleness. Ensure that no two wires are positioned so as to cause induction firing (adjacent and parallel). Remove each wire, one by one, and check resistance with an ohmmeter.	Replace any cracked or brittle wires. If any of the wires are defective, replace the entire set. Replace any wires with excessive resistance (over $8000\,\Omega$ per foot for suppression wire), and separate any wires that might cause induction firing.	**4.6**

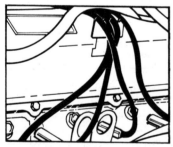

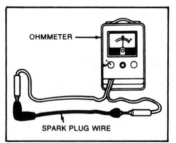

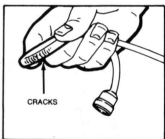

Misfiring can be the result of spark plug leads to adjacent, consecutively firing cylinders running parallel and too close together

On point-type ignition systems, check the spark plug wires as shown. On electronic ignitions, do not remove the wire from the distributor cap terminal; instead, test through the cap

Spark plug wires can be checked visually by bending them in a loop over your finger. This will reveal any cracks, burned or broken insulation. Any wire with cracked insulation should be replaced

4.6—Remove the spark plugs, noting the cylinders from which they were removed, and evaluate according to the color photos in the middle of this book.	See following.	**See following.**

Test and Procedure	Results and Indications	Proceed to
4.7—Examine the location of all the plugs.	The following diagrams illustrate some of the conditions that the location of plugs will reveal.	4.8

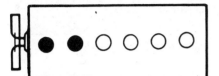

Two adjacent plugs are fouled in a 6-cylinder engine, 4-cylinder engine or either bank of a V-8. This is probably due to a blown head gasket between the two cylinders

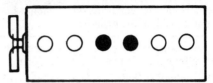

The two center plugs in a 6-cylinder engine are fouled. Raw fuel may be "boiled" out of the carburetor into the intake manifold after the engine is shut-off. Stop-start driving can also foul the center plugs, due to overly rich mixture. Proper float level, a new float needle and seat or use of an insulating spacer may help this problem

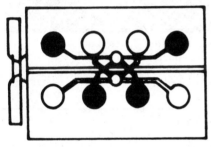

An unbalanced carburetor is indicated. Following the fuel flow on this particular design shows that the cylinders fed by the right-hand barrel are fouled from overly rich mixture, while the cylinders fed by the left-hand barrel are normal

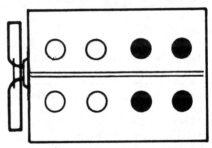

If the four rear plugs are overheated, a cooling system problem is suggested. A thorough cleaning of the cooling system may restore coolant circulation and cure the problem

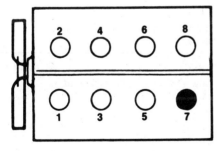

Finding one plug overheated may indicate an intake manifold leak near the affected cylinder. If the overheated plug is the second of two adjacent, consecutively firing plugs, it could be the result of ignition cross-firing. Separating the leads to these two plugs will eliminate cross-fire

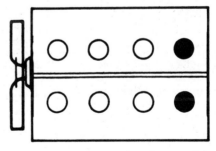

Occasionally, the two rear plugs in large, lightly used V-8's will become oil fouled. High oil consumption and smoky exhaust may also be noticed. It is probably due to plugged oil drain holes in the rear of the cylinder head, causing oil to be sucked in around the valve stems. This usually occurs in the rear cylinders first, because the engine slants that way

Test and Procedure	Results and Indications	Proceed to
4.8—Determine the static ignition timing. Using the crankshaft pulley timing marks as a guide, locate top dead center on the compression stroke of the number one cylinder.	The rotor should be pointing toward the No. 1 tower in the distributor cap, and, on electronic ignitions, the armature spoke for that cylinder should be lined up with the stator.	**4.8**
4.9—Check coil polarity: Connect a voltmeter negative lead to the coil high tension lead, and the positive lead to ground (**NOTE:** *Reverse the hook-up for positive ground systems*). Crank the engine momentarily. **Checking coil polarity**	If the voltmeter reads up-scale, the polarity is correct: If the voltmeter reads down-scale, reverse the coil polarity (switch the primary leads):	**5.1** **5.1**

Section 5—Fuel System
See Chapter 4 for service procedures

Test and Procedure	Results and Indications	Proceed to
5.1—Determine that the air filter is functioning efficiently: Hold paper elements up to a strong light, and attempt to see light through the filter.	Clean permanent air filters in solvent (or manufacturer's recommendation), and allow to dry. Replace paper elements through which light cannot be seen:	**5.2**
5.2—Determine whether a flooding condition exists: Flooding is identified by a strong gasoline odor, and excessive gasoline present in the throttle bore(s) of the carburetor. **If the engine floods repeatedly, check the choke butterfly flap**	If flooding is not evident: If flooding is evident, permit the gasoline to dry for a few moments and restart. If flooding doesn't recur: If flooding is persistent:	**5.3** **5.7** **5.5**
5.3—Check that fuel is reaching the carburetor: Detach the fuel line at the carburetor inlet. Hold the end of the line in a cup (not styrofoam), and crank the engine. 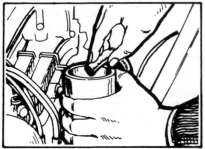 **Check the fuel pump by disconnecting the output line (fuel pump-to-carburetor) at the carburetor and operating the starter briefly**	If fuel flows smoothly: If fuel doesn't flow (**NOTE:** *Make sure that there is fuel in the tank*), or flows erratically:	**5.7** **5.4**

Test and Procedure	Results and Indications	Proceed to
5.4—Test the fuel pump: Disconnect all fuel lines from the fuel pump. Hold a finger over the input fitting, crank the engine (with electric pump, turn the ignition or pump on); and feel for suction.	If suction is evident, blow out the fuel line to the tank with low pressure compressed air until bubbling is heard from the fuel filler neck. Also blow out the carburetor fuel line (both ends disconnected):	**5.7**
	If no suction is evident, replace or repair the fuel pump: **NOTE:** *Repeated oil fouling of the spark plugs, or a no-start condition, could be the result of a ruptured vacuum booster pump diaphragm, through which oil or gasoline is being drawn into the intake manifold (where applicable).*	**5.7**
5.5—Occasionally, small specks of dirt will clog the small jets and orifices in the carburetor. With the engine cold, hold a flat piece of wood or similar material over the carburetor, where possible, and crank the engine.	If the engine starts, but runs roughly the engine is probably not run enough. If the engine won't start:	**5.9**
5.6—Check the needle and seat: Tap the carburetor in the area of the needle and seat.	If flooding stops, a gasoline additive (e.g., Gumout) will often cure the problem:	**5.7**
	If flooding continues, check the fuel pump for excessive pressure at the carburetor (according to specifications). If the pressure is normal, the needle and seat must be removed and checked, and/or the float level adjusted:	**5.7**
5.7—Test the accelerator pump by looking into the throttle bores while operating the throttle.	If the accelerator pump appears to be operating normally:	**5.8**
	If the accelerator pump is not operating, the pump must be reconditioned. Where possible, service the pump with the carburetor(s) installed on the engine. If necessary, remove the carburetor. Prior to removal:	**5.8**

Check for gas at the carburetor by looking down the carburetor throat while someone moves the accelerator

Test and Procedure	Results and Indications	Proceed to
5.8—Determine whether the carburetor main fuel system is functioning: Spray a commercial starting fluid into the carburetor while attempting to start the engine.	If the engine starts, runs for a few seconds, and dies:	**5.9**
	If the engine doesn't start:	**6.1**

Test and Procedure	Results and Indications	Proceed to
5.9—Uncommon fuel system malfunctions: See below:	If the problem is solved: If the problem remains, remove and recondition the carburetor.	**6.1**

Condition	Indication	Test	Prevailing Weather Conditions	Remedy
Vapor lock	Engine will not restart shortly after running.	Cool the components of the fuel system until the engine starts. Vapor lock can be cured faster by draping a wet cloth over a mechanical fuel pump.	Hot to very hot	Ensure that the exhaust manifold heat control valve is operating. Check with the vehicle manufacturer for the recommended solution to vapor lock on the model in question.
Carburetor icing	Engine will not idle, stalls at low speeds.	Visually inspect the throttle plate area of the throttle bores for frost.	High humidity, 32–40° F.	Ensure that the exhaust manifold heat control valve is operating, and that the intake manifold heat riser is not blocked.
Water in the fuel	Engine sputters and stalls; may not start.	Pump a small amount of fuel into a glass jar. Allow to stand, and inspect for droplets or a layer of water.	High humidity, extreme temperature changes.	For droplets, use one or two cans of commercial gas line anti-freeze. For a layer of water, the tank must be drained, and the fuel lines blown out with compressed air.

Section 6—Engine Compression
See Chapter 3 for service procedures

6.1—Test engine compression: Remove all spark plugs. Block the throttle wide open. Insert a compression gauge into a spark plug port, crank the engine to obtain the maximum reading, and record.	If compression is within limits on all cylinders:	**7.1**
	If gauge reading is extremely low on all cylinders:	**6.2**
	If gauge reading is low on one or two cylinders: (If gauge readings are identical and low on two or more adjacent cylinders, the head gasket must be replaced.)	**6.2**

Checking compression

6.2—Test engine compression (wet): Squirt approximately 30 cc. of engine oil into each cylinder, and retest per 6.1.	If the readings improve, worn or cracked rings or broken pistons are indicated:	**See Chapter 3**
	If the readings do not improve, burned or excessively carboned valves or a jumped timing chain are indicated: NOTE: *A jumped timing chain is often indicated by difficult cranking.*	**7.1**

Section 7—Engine Vacuum
See Chapter 3 for service procedures

Test and Procedure	Results and Indications	Proceed to
7.1—Attach a vacuum gauge to the intake manifold beyond the throttle plate. Start the engine, and observe the action of the needle over the range of engine speeds.	See below.	**See below**

INDICATION: normal engine in good condition

Proceed to: 8.1

Normal engine
Gauge reading: steady, from 17–22 in./Hg.

INDICATION: sticking valves or ignition miss

Proceed to: 9.1, 8.3

Sticking valves
Gauge reading: intermittent fluctuation at idle

INDICATION: late ignition or valve timing, low compression, stuck throttle valve, leaking carburetor or manifold gasket

Proceed to: 6.1

Incorrect valve timing
Gauge reading: low (10–15 in./Hg) but steady

INDICATION: improper carburetor adjustment or minor intake leak.

Proceed to: 7.2

Carburetor requires adjustment
Gauge reading: drifting needle

INDICATION: ignition miss, blown cylinder head gasket, leaking valve or weak valve spring

Proceed to: 8.3, 6.1

Blown head gasket
Gauge reading: needle fluctuates as engine speed increases

INDICATION: burnt valve or faulty valve clearance. Needle will fall when defective valve operates

Proceed to: 9.1

Burnt or leaking valves
Gauge reading: steady needle, but drops regularly

INDICATION: choked muffler, excessive back pressure in system

Proceed to: 10.1

Clogged exhaust system
Gauge reading: gradual drop in reading at idle

INDICATION: worn valve guides

Proceed to: 9.1

Worn valve guides
Gauge reading: needle vibrates excessively at idle, but steadies as engine speed increases

White pointer = steady gauge hand   Black pointer = fluctuating gauge hand

Test and Procedure	Results and Indications	Proceed to
7.2—Attach a vacuum gauge per 7.1, and test for an intake manifold leak. Squirt a small amount of oil around the intake manifold gaskets, carburetor gaskets, plugs and fittings. Observe the action of the vacuum gauge.	If the reading improves, replace the indicated gasket, or seal the indicated fitting or plug: If the reading remains low:	**8.1** **7.3**
7.3—Test all vacuum hoses and accessories for leaks as described in 7.2. Also check the carburetor body (dashpots, automatic choke mechanism, throttle shafts) for leaks in the same manner.	If the reading improves, service or replace the offending part(s): If the reading remains low:	**8.1** **6.1**

Section 8—Secondary Electrical System
See Chapter 2 for service procedures

Test and Procedure	Results and Indications	Proceed to
8.1—Remove the distributor cap and check to make sure that the rotor turns when the engine is cranked. Visually inspect the distributor components.	Clean, tighten or replace any components which appear defective.	**8.2**
8.2—Connect a timing light (per manufacturer's recommendation) and check the dynamic ignition timing. Disconnect and plug the vacuum hose(s) to the distributor if specified, start the engine, and observe the timing marks at the specified engine speed.	If the timing is not correct, adjust to specifications by rotating the distributor in the engine: (Advance timing by rotating distributor opposite normal direction of rotor rotation, retard timing by rotating distributor in same direction as rotor rotation.)	**8.3**
8.3—Check the operation of the distributor advance mechanism(s): To test the mechanical advance, disconnect the vacuum lines from the distributor advance unit and observe the timing marks with a timing light as the engine speed is increased from idle. If the mark moves smoothly, without hesitation, it may be assumed that the mechanical advance is functioning properly. To test vacuum advance and/or retard systems, alternately crimp and release the vacuum line, and observe the timing mark for movement. If movement is noted, the system is operating.	If the systems are functioning: If the systems are not functioning, remove the distributor, and test on a distributor tester:	**8.4** **8.4**
8.4—Locate an ignition miss: With the engine running, remove each spark plug wire, one at a time, until one is found that doesn't cause the engine to roughen and slow down.	When the missing cylinder is identified:	**4.1**

Section 9—Valve Train
See Chapter 3 for service procedures

Test and Procedure	Results and Indications	Proceed to
9.1—Evaluate the valve train: Remove the valve cover, and ensure that the valves are adjusted to specifications. A mechanic's stethoscope may be used to aid in the diagnosis of the valve train. By pushing the probe on or near push rods or rockers, valve noise often can be isolated. A timing light also may be used to diagnose valve problems. Connect the light according to manufacturer's recommendations, and start the engine. Vary the firing moment of the light by increasing the engine speed (and therefore the ignition advance), and moving the trigger from cylinder to cylinder. Observe the movement of each valve.	Sticking valves or erratic valve train motion can be observed with the timing light. The cylinder head must be disassembled for repairs.	**See Chapter 3**
9.2—Check the valve timing: Locate top dead center of the No. 1 piston, and install a degree wheel or tape on the crankshaft pulley or damper with zero corresponding to an index mark on the engine. Rotate the crankshaft in its direction of rotation, and observe the opening of the No. 1 cylinder intake valve. The opening should correspond with the correct mark on the degree wheel according to specifications.	If the timing is not correct, the timing cover must be removed for further investigation.	**See Chapter 3**

Section 10—Exhaust System

Test and Procedure	Results and Indications	Proceed to
10.1—Determine whether the exhaust manifold heat control valve is operating: Operate the valve by hand to determine whether it is free to move. If the valve is free, run the engine to operating temperature and observe the action of the valve, to ensure that it is opening.	If the valve sticks, spray it with a suitable solvent, open and close the valve to free it, and retest. If the valve functions properly: If the valve does not free, or does not operate, replace the valve:	 **10.2** **10.2**
10.2—Ensure that there are no exhaust restrictions: Visually inspect the exhaust system for kinks, dents, or crushing. Also note that gases are flowing freely from the tailpipe at all engine speeds, indicating no restriction in the muffler or resonator.	Replace any damaged portion of the system:	**11.1**

Section 11—Cooling System
See Chapter 3 for service procedures

Test and Procedure	Results and Indications	Proceed to
11.1—Visually inspect the fan belt for glazing, cracks, and fraying, and replace if necessary. Tighten the belt so that the longest span has approximately ½″ play at its midpoint under thumb pressure (see Chapter 1).	Replace or tighten the fan belt as necessary: **Checking belt tension**	**11.2**
11.2—Check the fluid level of the cooling system.	If full or slightly low, fill as necessary: If extremely low:	**11.5** **11.3**
11.3—Visually inspect the external portions of the cooling system (radiator, radiator hoses, thermostat elbow, water pump seals, heater hoses, etc.) for leaks. If none are found, pressurize the cooling system to 14–15 psi.	If cooling system holds the pressure: If cooling system loses pressure rapidly, reinspect external parts of the system for leaks under pressure. If none are found, check dipstick for coolant in crankcase. If no coolant is present, but pressure loss continues: If coolant is evident in crankcase, remove cylinder head(s), and check gasket(s). If gaskets are intact, block and cylinder head(s) should be checked for cracks or holes. If the gasket(s) is blown, replace, and purge the crankcase of coolant: NOTE: *Occasionally, due to atmospheric and driving conditions, condensation of water can occur in the crankcase. This causes the oil to appear milky white. To remedy, run the engine until hot, and change the oil and oil filter.*	**11.5** **11.4** **12.6**
11.4—Check for combustion leaks into the cooling system: Pressurize the cooling system as above. Start the engine, and observe the pressure gauge. If the needle fluctuates, remove each spark plug wire, one at a time, noting which cylinder(s) reduce or eliminate the fluctuation.	Cylinders which reduce or eliminate the fluctuation, when the spark plug wire is removed, are leaking into the cooling system. Replace the head gasket on the affected cylinder bank(s). 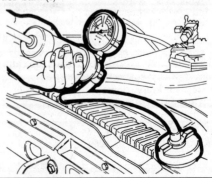 **Pressurizing the cooling system**	

Test and Procedure	Results and Indications	Proceed to
11.5—Check the radiator pressure cap: Attach a radiator pressure tester to the radiator cap (wet the seal prior to installation). Quickly pump up the pressure, noting the point at which the cap releases.	If the cap releases within ± 1 psi of the specified rating, it is operating properly:	**11.6**
	If the cap releases at more than ± 1 psi of the specified rating, it should be replaced:	**11.6**

Checking radiator pressure cap

Test and Procedure	Results and Indications	Proceed to
11.6—Test the thermostat: Start the engine cold, remove the radiator cap, and insert a thermometer into the radiator. Allow the engine to idle. After a short while, there will be a sudden, rapid increase in coolant temperature. The temperature at which this sharp rise stops is the thermostat opening temperature.	If the thermostat opens at or about the specified temperature:	**11.7**
	If the temperature doesn't increase: (If the temperature increases slowly and gradually, replace the thermostat.)	**11.7**
11.7—Check the water pump: Remove the thermostat elbow and the thermostat, disconnect the coil high tension lead (to prevent starting), and crank the engine momentarily.	If coolant flows, replace the thermostat and retest per 11.6:	**11.6**
	If coolant doesn't flow, reverse flush the cooling system to alleviate any blockage that might exist. If system is not blocked, and coolant will not flow, replace the water pump.	

Section 12—Lubrication
See Chapter 3 for service procedures

Test and Procedure	Results and Indications	Proceed to
12.1—Check the oil pressure gauge or warning light: If the gauge shows low pressure, or the light is on for no obvious reason, remove the oil pressure sender. Install an accurate oil pressure gauge and run the engine momentarily.	If oil pressure builds normally, run engine for a few moments to determine that it is functioning normally, and replace the sender.	—
	If the pressure remains low:	**12.2**
	If the pressure surges:	**12.3**
	If the oil pressure is zero:	**12.3**
12.2—Visually inspect the oil: If the oil is watery or very thin, milky, or foamy, replace the oil and oil filter.	If the oil is normal:	**12.3**
	If after replacing oil the pressure remains low:	**12.3**
	If after replacing oil the pressure becomes normal:	—

Test and Procedure	Results and Indications	Proceed to
12.3—Inspect the oil pressure relief valve and spring, to ensure that it is not sticking or stuck. Remove and thoroughly clean the valve, spring, and the valve body.	If the oil pressure improves: If no improvement is noted:	— **12.4**
12.4—Check to ensure that the oil pump is not cavitating (sucking air instead of oil): See that the crankcase is neither over nor underfull, and that the pickup in the sump is in the proper position and free from sludge.	Fill or drain the crankcase to the proper capacity, and clean the pickup screen in solvent if necessary. If no improvement is noted:	**12.5**
12.5—Inspect the oil pump drive and the oil pump:	If the pump drive or the oil pump appear to be defective, service as necessary and retest per 12.1: If the pump drive and pump appear to be operating normally, the engine should be disassembled to determine where blockage exists:	**12.1** **See Chapter 3**
12.6—Purge the engine of ethylene glycol coolant: Completely drain the crankcase and the oil filter. Obtain a commercial butyl cellosolve base solvent, designated for this purpose, and follow the instructions precisely. Following this, install a new oil filter and refill the crankcase with the proper weight oil. The next oil and filter change should follow shortly thereafter (1000 miles).		

TROUBLESHOOTING EMISSION CONTROL SYSTEMS

See Chapter 4 for procedures applicable to individual emission control systems used on specific combinations of engine/transmission/model.

TROUBLESHOOTING THE CARBURETOR
See Chapter 4 for service procedures

Carburetor problems cannot be effectively isolated unless all other engine systems (particularly ignition and emission) are functioning properly and the engine is properly tuned.

Condition	Possible Cause
Engine cranks, but does not start	1. Improper starting procedure 2. No fuel in tank 3. Clogged fuel line or filter 4. Defective fuel pump 5. Choke valve not closing properly 6. Engine flooded 7. Choke valve not unloading 8. Throttle linkage not making full travel 9. Stuck needle or float 10. Leaking float needle or seat 11. Improper float adjustment
Engine stalls	1. Improperly adjusted idle speed or mixture **Engine hot** 2. Improperly adjusted dashpot 3. Defective or improperly adjusted solenoid 4. Incorrect fuel level in fuel bowl 5. Fuel pump pressure too high 6. Leaking float needle seat 7. Secondary throttle valve stuck open 8. Air or fuel leaks 9. Idle air bleeds plugged or missing 10. Idle passages plugged **Engine Cold** 11. Incorrectly adjusted choke 12. Improperly adjusted fast idle speed 13. Air leaks 14. Plugged idle or idle air passages 15. Stuck choke valve or binding linkage 16. Stuck secondary throttle valves 17. Engine flooding—high fuel level 18. Leaking or misaligned float
Engine hesitates on acceleration	1. Clogged fuel filter 2. Leaking fuel pump diaphragm 3. Low fuel pump pressure 4. Secondary throttle valves stuck, bent or misadjusted 5. Sticking or binding air valve 6. Defective accelerator pump 7. Vacuum leaks 8. Clogged air filter 9. Incorrect choke adjustment (engine cold)
Engine feels sluggish or flat on acceleration	1. Improperly adjusted idle speed or mixture 2. Clogged fuel filter 3. Defective accelerator pump 4. Dirty, plugged or incorrect main metering jets 5. Bent or sticking main metering rods 6. Sticking throttle valves 7. Stuck heat riser 8. Binding or stuck air valve 9. Dirty, plugged or incorrect secondary jets 10. Bent or sticking secondary metering rods. 11. Throttle body or manifold heat passages plugged 12. Improperly adjusted choke or choke vacuum break.
Carburetor floods	1. Defective fuel pump. Pressure too high. 2. Stuck choke valve 3. Dirty, worn or damaged float or needle valve/seat 4. Incorrect float/fuel level 5. Leaking float bowl

Condition	Possible Cause
Engine idles roughly and stalls	1. Incorrect idle speed 2. Clogged fuel filter 3. Dirt in fuel system or carburetor 4. Loose carburetor screws or attaching bolts 5. Broken carburetor gaskets 6. Air leaks 7. Dirty carburetor 8. Worn idle mixture needles 9. Throttle valves stuck open 10. Incorrectly adjusted float or fuel level 11. Clogged air filter
Engine runs unevenly or surges	1. Defective fuel pump 2. Dirty or clogged fuel filter 3. Plugged, loose or incorrect main metering jets or rods 4. Air leaks 5. Bent or sticking main metering rods 6. Stuck power piston 7. Incorrect float adjustment 8. Incorrect idle speed or mixture 9. Dirty or plugged idle system passages 10. Hard, brittle or broken gaskets 11. Loose attaching or mounting screws 12. Stuck or misaligned secondary throttle valves
Poor fuel economy	1. Poor driving habits 2. Stuck choke valve 3. Binding choke linkage 4. Stuck heat riser 5. Incorrect idle mixture 6. Defective accelerator pump 7. Air leaks 8. Plugged, loose or incorrect main metering jets 9. Improperly adjusted float or fuel level 10. Bent, misaligned or fuel-clogged float 11. Leaking float needle seat 12. Fuel leak 13. Accelerator pump discharge ball not seating properly 14. Incorrect main jets
Engine lacks high speed performance or power	1. Incorrect throttle linkage adjustment 2. Stuck or binding power piston 3. Defective accelerator pump 4. Air leaks 5. Incorrect float setting or fuel level 6. Dirty, plugged, worn or incorrect main metering jets or rods 7. Binding or sticking air valve 8. Brittle or cracked gaskets 9. Bent, incorrect or improperly adjusted secondary metering rods 10. Clogged fuel filter 11. Clogged air filter 12. Defective fuel pump

TROUBLESHOOTING FUEL INJECTION PROBLEMS

Each fuel injection system has its own unique components and test procedures, for which it is impossible to generalize. Refer to Chapter 4 of this Repair & Tune-Up Guide for specific test and repair procedures, if the vehicle is equipped with fuel injection.

TROUBLESHOOTING ELECTRICAL PROBLEMS

See Chapter 5 for service procedures

For any electrical system to operate, it must make a complete circuit. This simply means that the power flow from the battery must make a complete circle. When an electrical component is operating, power flows from the battery to the component, passes through the component causing it to perform its function (lighting a light bulb), and then returns to the battery through the ground of the circuit. This ground is usually (but not always) the metal part of the car or truck on which the electrical component is mounted.

Perhaps the easiest way to visualize this is to think of connecting a light bulb with two wires attached to it to the battery. If one of the two wires attached to the light bulb were attached to the negative post of the battery and the other were attached to the positive post of the battery, you would have a complete circuit. Current from the battery would flow to the light bulb, causing it to light, and return to the negative post of the battery.

The normal automotive circuit differs from this simple example in two ways. First, instead of having a return wire from the bulb to the battery, the light bulb returns the current to the battery through the chassis of the vehicle. Since the negative battery cable is attached to the chassis and the chassis is made of electrically conductive metal, the chassis of the vehicle can serve as a ground wire to complete the circuit. Secondly, most automotive circuits contain switches to turn components on and off as required.

Every complete circuit from a power source must include a component which is using the power from the power source. If you were to disconnect the light bulb from the wires and touch the two wires together (don't do this) the power supply wire to the component would be grounded before the normal ground connection for the circuit.

Because grounding a wire from a power source makes a complete circuit—less the required component to use the power—this phenomenon is called a short circuit. Common causes are: broken insulation (exposing the metal wire to a metal part of the car or truck), or a shorted switch.

Some electrical components which require a large amount of current to operate also have a relay in their circuit. Since these circuits carry a large amount of current, the thickness of the wire in the circuit (gauge size) is also greater. If this large wire were connected from the component to the control switch on the instrument panel, and then back to the component, a voltage drop would occur in the circuit. To prevent this potential drop in voltage, an electromagnetic switch (relay) is used. The large wires in the circuit are connected from the battery to one side of the relay, and from the opposite side of the relay to the component. The relay is normally open, preventing current from passing through the circuit. An additional, smaller, wire is connected from the relay to the control switch for the circuit. When the control switch is turned on, it grounds the smaller wire from the relay and completes the circuit. This closes the relay and allows current to flow from the battery to the component. The horn, headlight, and starter circuits are three which use relays.

It is possible for larger surges of current to pass through the electrical system of your car or truck. If this surge of current were to reach an electrical component, it could burn it out. To prevent this, fuses, circuit breakers or fusible links are connected into the current supply wires of most of the major electrical systems. When an electrical current of excessive power passes through the component's fuse, the fuse blows out and breaks the circuit, saving the component from destruction.

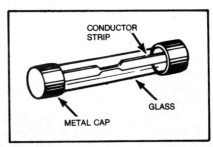

Typical automotive fuse

A circuit breaker is basically a self-repairing fuse. The circuit breaker opens the circuit the same way a fuse does. However, when either the short is removed from the circuit or the surge subsides, the circuit breaker resets itself and does not have to be replaced as a fuse does.

A fuse link is a wire that acts as a fuse. It is normally connected between the starter relay and the main wiring harness. This connection is usually under the hood. The fuse link (if installed) protects all the

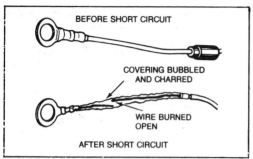

Most fusible links show a charred, melted insulation when they burn out

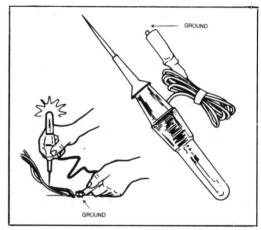

The test light will show the presence of current when touched to a hot wire and grounded at the other end

chassis electrical components, and is the probable cause of trouble when none of the electrical components function, unless the battery is disconnected or dead.

Electrical problems generally fall into one of three areas:

1. The component that is not functioning is not receiving current.

2. The component itself is not functioning.

3. The component is not properly grounded.

The electrical system can be checked with a test light and a jumper wire. A test light is a device that looks like a pointed screwdriver with a wire attached to it and has a light bulb in its handle. A jumper wire is a piece of insulated wire with an alligator clip attached to each end.

If a component is not working, you must follow a systematic plan to determine which of the three causes is the villain.

1. Turn on the switch that controls the inoperable component.

2. Disconnect the power supply wire from the component.

3. Attach the ground wire on the test light to a good metal ground.

4. Touch the probe end of the test light to the end of the power supply wire that was disconnected from the component. If the component is receiving current, the test light will go on.

NOTE: *Some components work only when the ignition switch is turned on.*

If the test light does not go on, then the problem is in the circuit between the battery and the component. This includes all the switches, fuses, and relays in the system. Follow the wire that runs back to the battery. The problem is an open circuit between the

battery and the component. If the fuse is blown and, when replaced, immediately blows again, there is a short circuit in the system which must be located and repaired. If there is a switch in the system, bypass it with a jumper wire. This is done by connecting one end of the jumper wire to the power supply wire into the switch and the other end of the jumper wire to the wire coming out of the switch. If the test light lights with the jumper wire installed, the switch or whatever was bypassed is defective.

NOTE: *Never substitute the jumper wire for the component, since it is required to use the power from the power source.*

5. If the bulb in the test light goes on, then the current is getting to the component that is not working. This eliminates the first of the three possible causes. Connect the power supply wire and connect a jumper wire from the component to a good metal ground. Do this with the switch which controls the component turned on, and also the ignition switch turned on if it is required for the component to work. If the component works with the jumper wire installed, then it has a bad ground. This is usually caused by the metal area on which the component mounts to the chassis being coated with some type of foreign matter.

6. If neither test located the source of the trouble, then the component itself is defective. Remember that for any electrical system to work, all connections must be clean and tight.

Troubleshooting Basic Turn Signal and Flasher Problems
See Chapter 5 for service procedures

Most problems in the turn signals or flasher system can be reduced to defective flashers or bulbs, which are easily replaced. Occasionally, the turn signal switch will prove defective.

F = Front   R = Rear   ● = Lights off   ○ = Lights on

Condition		Possible Cause
Turn signals light, but do not flash	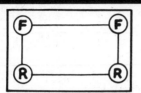	Defective flasher
No turn signals light on either side	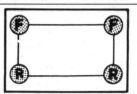	Blown fuse. Replace if defective. Defective flasher. Check by substitution. Open circuit, short circuit or poor ground.
Both turn signals on one side don't work	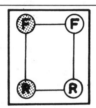	Bad bulbs. Bad ground in both (or either) housings.
One turn signal light on one side doesn't work	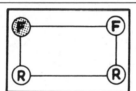	Defective bulb. Corrosion in socket. Clean contacts. Poor ground at socket.
Turn signal flashes too fast or too slowly	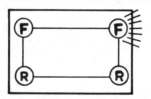	Check any bulb on the side flashing too fast. A heavy-duty bulb is probably installed in place of a regular bulb. Check the bulb flashing too slowly. A standard bulb was probably installed in place of a heavy-duty bulb. Loose connections or corrosion at the bulb socket.
Indicator lights don't work in either direction		Check if the turn signals are working. Check the dash indicator lights. Check the flasher by substitution.
One indicator light doesn't light		On systems with one dash indicator: See if the lights work on the same side. Often the filaments have been reversed in systems combining stoplights with taillights and turn signals. Check the flasher by substitution. On systems with two indicators: Check the bulbs on the same side. Check the indicator light bulb. Check the flasher by substitution.

Troubleshooting Lighting Problems
See Chapter 5 for service procedures

Condition	Possible Cause
One or more lights don't work, but others do	1. Defective bulb(s) 2. Blown fuse(s) 3. Dirty fuse clips or light sockets 4. Poor ground circuit
Lights burn out quickly	1. Incorrect voltage regulator setting or defective regulator 2. Poor battery/alternator connections
Lights go dim	1. Low/discharged battery 2. Alternator not charging 3. Corroded sockets or connections 4. Low voltage output
Lights flicker	1. Loose connection 2. Poor ground. (Run ground wire from light housing to frame) 3. Circuit breaker operating (short circuit)
Lights "flare"—Some flare is normal on acceleration—If excessive, see "Lights Burn Out Quickly"	High voltage setting
Lights glare—approaching drivers are blinded	1. Lights adjusted too high 2. Rear springs or shocks sagging 3. Rear tires soft

Troubleshooting Dash Gauge Problems
Most problems can be traced to a defective sending unit or faulty wiring. Occasionally, the gauge itself is at fault. See Chapter 5 for service procedures.

Condition	Possible Cause

COOLANT TEMPERATURE GAUGE

Gauge reads erratically or not at all	1. Loose or dirty connections 2. Defective sending unit. 3. Defective gauge. To test a bi-metal gauge, remove the wire from the sending unit. Ground the wire for an instant. If the gauge registers, replace the sending unit. To test a magnetic gauge, disconnect the wire at the sending unit. With ignition ON gauge should register COLD. Ground the wire; gauge should register HOT.

AMMETER GAUGE—TURN HEADLIGHTS ON (DO NOT START ENGINE). NOTE REACTION

Ammeter shows charge Ammeter shows discharge Ammeter does not move	1. Connections reversed on gauge 2. Ammeter is OK 3. Loose connections or faulty wiring 4. Defective gauge

Condition	Possible Cause

OIL PRESSURE GAUGE

Condition	Possible Cause
Gauge does not register or is inaccurate	1. On mechanical gauge, Bourdon tube may be bent or kinked. 2. Low oil pressure. Remove sending unit. Idle the engine briefly. If no oil flows from sending unit hole, problem is in engine. 3. Defective gauge. Remove the wire from the sending unit and ground it for an instant with the ignition ON. A good gauge will go to the top of the scale. 4. Defective wiring. Check the wiring to the gauge. If it's OK and the gauge doesn't register when grounded, replace the gauge. 5. Defective sending unit.

ALL GAUGES

Condition	Possible Cause
All gauges do not operate All gauges read low or erratically All gauges pegged	1. Blown fuse 2. Defective instrument regulator 3. Defective or dirty instrument voltage regulator 4. Loss of ground between instrument voltage regulator and frame 5. Defective instrument regulator

WARNING LIGHTS

Condition	Possible Cause
Light(s) do not come on when ignition is ON, but engine is not started Light comes on with engine running	1. Defective bulb 2. Defective wire 3. Defective sending unit. Disconnect the wire from the sending unit and ground it. Replace the sending unit if the light comes on with the ignition ON. 4. Problem in individual system 5. Defective sending unit

Troubleshooting Clutch Problems

It is false economy to replace individual clutch components. The pressure plate, clutch plate and throwout bearing should be replaced as a set, and the flywheel face inspected, whenever the clutch is overhauled. See Chapter 6 for service procedures.

Condition	Possible Cause
Clutch chatter	1. Grease on driven plate (disc) facing 2. Binding clutch linkage or cable 3. Loose, damaged facings on driven plate (disc) 4. Engine mounts loose 5. Incorrect height adjustment of pressure plate release levers 6. Clutch housing or housing to transmission adapter misalignment 7. Loose driven plate hub
Clutch grabbing	1. Oil, grease on driven plate (disc) facing 2. Broken pressure plate 3. Warped or binding driven plate. Driven plate binding on clutch shaft
Clutch slips	1. Lack of lubrication in clutch linkage or cable (linkage or cable binds, causes incomplete engagement) 2. Incorrect pedal, or linkage adjustment 3. Broken pressure plate springs 4. Weak pressure plate springs 5. Grease on driven plate facings (disc)

Troubleshooting Clutch Problems (cont.)

Condition	Possible Cause
Incomplete clutch release	1. Incorrect pedal or linkage adjustment or linkage or cable binding 2. Incorrect height adjustment on pressure plate release levers 3. Loose, broken facings on driven plate (disc) 4. Bent, dished, warped driven plate caused by overheating
Grinding, whirring grating noise when pedal is depressed	1. Worn or defective throwout bearing 2. Starter drive teeth contacting flywheel ring gear teeth. Look for milled or polished teeth on ring gear.
Squeal, howl, trumpeting noise when pedal is being released (occurs during first inch to inch and one-half of pedal travel)	Pilot bushing worn or lack of lubricant. If bushing appears OK, polish bushing with emery cloth, soak lube wick in oil, lube bushing with oil, apply film of chassis grease to clutch shaft pilot hub, reassemble. NOTE: Bushing wear may be due to misalignment of clutch housing or housing to transmission adapter
Vibration or clutch pedal pulsation with clutch disengaged (pedal fully depressed)	1. Worn or defective engine transmission mounts 2. Flywheel run out. (Flywheel run out at face not to exceed 0.005") 3. Damaged or defective clutch components

Troubleshooting Manual Transmission Problems
See Chapter 6 for service procedures

Condition	Possible Cause
Transmission jumps out of gear	1. Misalignment of transmission case or clutch housing. 2. Worn pilot bearing in crankshaft. 3. Bent transmission shaft. 4. Worn high speed sliding gear. 5. Worn teeth or end-play in clutch shaft. 6. Insufficient spring tension on shifter rail plunger. 7. Bent or loose shifter fork. 8. Gears not engaging completely. 9. Loose or worn bearings on clutch shaft or mainshaft. 10. Worn gear teeth. 11. Worn or damaged detent balls.
Transmission sticks in gear	1. Clutch not releasing fully. 2. Burred or battered teeth on clutch shaft, or sliding sleeve. 3. Burred or battered transmission mainshaft. 4. Frozen synchronizing clutch. 5. Stuck shifter rail plunger. 6. Gearshift lever twisting and binding shifter rail. 7. Battered teeth on high speed sliding gear or on sleeve. 8. Improper lubrication, or lack of lubrication. 9. Corroded transmission parts. 10. Defective mainshaft pilot bearing. 11. Locked gear bearings will give same effect as stuck in gear.
Transmission gears will not synchronize	1. Binding pilot bearing on mainshaft, will synchronize in high gear only. 2. Clutch not releasing fully. 3. Detent spring weak or broken. 4. Weak or broken springs under balls in sliding gear sleeve. 5. Binding bearing on clutch shaft, or binding countershaft. 6. Binding pilot bearing in crankshaft. 7. Badly worn gear teeth. 8. Improper lubrication. 9. Constant mesh gear not turning freely on transmission mainshaft. Will synchronize in that gear only.

Condition	Possible Cause
Gears spinning when shifting into gear from neutral	1. Clutch not releasing fully. 2. In some cases an extremely light lubricant in transmission will cause gears to continue to spin for a short time after clutch is released. 3. Binding pilot bearing in crankshaft.
Transmission noisy in all gears	1. Insufficient lubricant, or improper lubricant. 2. Worn countergear bearings. 3. Worn or damaged main drive gear or countergear. 4. Damaged main drive gear or mainshaft bearings. 5. Worn or damaged countergear anti-lash plate.
Transmission noisy in neutral only	1. Damaged main drive gear bearing. 2. Damaged or loose mainshaft pilot bearing. 3. Worn or damaged countergear anti-lash plate. 4. Worn countergear bearings.
Transmission noisy in one gear only	1. Damaged or worn constant mesh gears. 2. Worn or damaged countergear bearings. 3. Damaged or worn synchronizer.
Transmission noisy in reverse only	1. Worn or damaged reverse idler gear or idler bushing. 2. Worn or damaged mainshaft reverse gear. 3. Worn or damaged reverse countergear. 4. Damaged shift mechanism.

TROUBLESHOOTING AUTOMATIC TRANSMISSION PROBLEMS

Keeping alert to changes in the operating characteristics of the transmission (changing shift points, noises, etc.) can prevent small problems from becoming large ones. If the problem cannot be traced to loose bolts, fluid level, misadjusted linkage, clogged filters or similar problems, you should probably seek professional service.

Transmission Fluid Indications

The appearance and odor of the transmission fluid can give valuable clues to the overall condition of the transmission. Always note the appearance of the fluid when you check the fluid level or change the fluid. Rub a small amount of fluid between your fingers to feel for grit and smell the fluid on the dipstick.

If the fluid appears:	It indicates:
Clear and red colored	Normal operation
Discolored (extremely dark red or brownish) or smells burned	Band or clutch pack failure, usually caused by an overheated transmission. Hauling very heavy loads with insufficient power or failure to change the fluid often result in overheating. Do not confuse this appearance with newer fluids that have a darker red color and a strong odor (though not a burned odor).
Foamy or aerated (light in color and full of bubbles)	1. The level is too high (gear train is churning oil) 2. An internal air leak (air is mixing with the fluid). Have the transmission checked professionally.
Solid residue in the fluid	Defective bands, clutch pack or bearings. Bits of band material or metal abrasives are clinging to the dipstick. Have the transmission checked professionally.
Varnish coating on the dipstick	The transmission fluid is overheating

TROUBLESHOOTING DRIVE AXLE PROBLEMS

First, determine when the noise is most noticeable.

Drive Noise: Produced under vehicle acceleration.

Coast Noise: Produced while coasting with a closed throttle.

Float Noise: Occurs while maintaining constant speed (just enough to keep speed constant) on a level road.

External Noise Elimination

It is advisable to make a thorough road test to determine whether the noise originates in the rear axle or whether it originates from the tires, engine, transmission, wheel bearings or road surface. Noise originating from other places cannot be corrected by servicing the rear axle.

ROAD NOISE

Brick or rough surfaced concrete roads produce noises that seem to come from the rear axle. Road noise is usually identical in Drive or Coast and driving on a different type of road will tell whether the road is the problem.

TIRE NOISE

Tire noise can be mistaken as rear axle noise, even though the tires on the front are at fault. Snow tread and mud tread tires or tires worn unevenly will frequently cause vibrations which seem to originate elsewhere; *temporarily, and for test purposes only,* inflate the tires to 40–50 lbs. This will significantly alter the noise produced by the tires, but will not alter noise from the rear axle. Noises from the rear axle will normally cease at speeds below 30 mph on coast, while tire noise will continue at lower tone as speed is decreased. The rear axle noise will usually change from drive conditions to coast conditions, while tire noise will not. Do not forget to lower the tire pressure to normal after the test is complete.

ENGINE/TRANSMISSION NOISE

Determine at what speed the noise is most pronounced, then stop in a quiet place. With the transmission in Neutral, run the engine through speeds corresponding to road speeds where the noise was noticed. Noises produced with the vehicle standing still are coming from the engine or transmission.

FRONT WHEEL BEARINGS

Front wheel bearing noises, sometimes confused with rear axle noises, will not change when comparing drive and coast conditions. While holding the speed steady, lightly apply the footbrake. This will often cause wheel bearing noise to lessen, as some of the weight is taken off the bearing. Front wheel bearings are easily checked by jacking up the wheels and spinning the wheels. Shaking the wheels will also determine if the wheel bearings are excessively loose.

REAR AXLE NOISES

Eliminating other possible sources can narrow the cause to the rear axle, which normally produces noise from worn gears or bearings. Gear noises tend to peak in a narrow speed range, while bearing noises will usually vary in pitch with engine speeds.

Noise Diagnosis

The Noise Is:	Most Probably Produced By:
1. Identical under Drive or Coast	Road surface, tires or front wheel bearings
2. Different depending on road surface	Road surface or tires
3. Lower as speed is lowered	Tires
4. Similar when standing or moving	Engine or transmission
5. A vibration	Unbalanced tires, rear wheel bearing, unbalanced driveshaft or worn U-joint
6. A knock or click about every two tire revolutions	Rear wheel bearing
7. Most pronounced on turns	Damaged differential gears
8. A steady low-pitched whirring or scraping, starting at low speeds	Damaged or worn pinion bearing
9. A chattering vibration on turns	Wrong differential lubricant or worn clutch plates (limited slip rear axle)
10. Noticed only in Drive, Coast or Float conditions	Worn ring gear and/or pinion gear

Troubleshooting Steering & Suspension Problems

Condition	Possible Cause
Hard steering (wheel is hard to turn)	1. Improper tire pressure 2. Loose or glazed pump drive belt 3. Low or incorrect fluid 4. Loose, bent or poorly lubricated front end parts 5. Improper front end alignment (excessive caster) 6. Bind in steering column or linkage 7. Kinked hydraulic hose 8. Air in hydraulic system 9. Low pump output or leaks in system 10. Obstruction in lines 11. Pump valves sticking or out of adjustment 12. Incorrect wheel alignment
Loose steering (too much play in steering wheel)	1. Loose wheel bearings 2. Faulty shocks 3. Worn linkage or suspension components 4. Loose steering gear mounting or linkage points 5. Steering mechanism worn or improperly adjusted 6. Valve spool improperly adjusted 7. Worn ball joints, tie-rod ends, etc.
Veers or wanders (pulls to one side with hands off steering wheel)	1. Improper tire pressure 2. Improper front end alignment 3. Dragging or improperly adjusted brakes 4. Bent frame 5. Improper rear end alignment 6. Faulty shocks or springs 7. Loose or bent front end components 8. Play in Pitman arm 9. Steering gear mountings loose 10. Loose wheel bearings 11. Binding Pitman arm 12. Spool valve sticking or improperly adjusted 13. Worn ball joints
Wheel oscillation or vibration transmitted through steering wheel	1. Low or uneven tire pressure 2. Loose wheel bearings 3. Improper front end alignment 4. Bent spindle 5. Worn, bent or broken front end components 6. Tires out of round or out of balance 7. Excessive lateral runout in disc brake rotor 8. Loose or bent shock absorber or strut
Noises (see also "Troubleshooting Drive Axle Problems")	1. Loose belts 2. Low fluid, air in system 3. Foreign matter in system 4. Improper lubrication 5. Interference or chafing in linkage 6. Steering gear mountings loose 7. Incorrect adjustment or wear in gear box 8. Faulty valves or wear in pump 9. Kinked hydraulic lines 10. Worn wheel bearings
Poor return of steering	1. Over-inflated tires 2. Improperly aligned front end (excessive caster) 3. Binding in steering column 4. No lubrication in front end 5. Steering gear adjusted too tight
Uneven tire wear (see "How To Read Tire Wear")	1. Incorrect tire pressure 2. Improperly aligned front end 3. Tires out-of-balance 4. Bent or worn suspension parts

HOW TO READ TIRE WEAR

The way your tires wear is a good indicator of other parts of the suspension. Abnormal wear patterns are often caused by the need for simple tire maintenance, or for front end alignment.

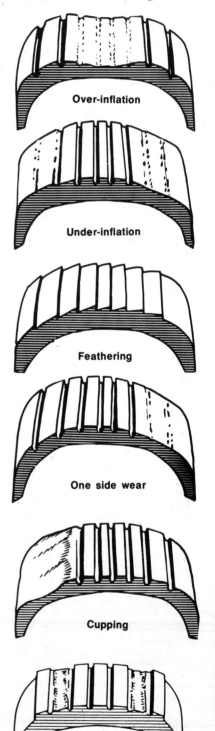

Excessive wear at the center of the tread indicates that the air pressure in the tire is consistently too high. The tire is riding on the center of the tread and wearing it prematurely. Occasionally, this wear pattern can result from outrageously wide tires on narrow rims. The cure for this is to replace either the tires or the wheels.

Over-inflation

This type of wear usually results from consistent under-inflation. When a tire is under-inflated, there is too much contact with the road by the outer treads, which wear prematurely. When this type of wear occurs, and the tire pressure is known to be consistently correct, a bent or worn steering component or the need for wheel alignment could be indicated.

Under-inflation

Feathering is a condition when the edge of each tread rib develops a slightly rounded edge on one side and a sharp edge on the other. By running your hand over the tire, you can usually feel the sharper edges before you'll be able to see them. The most common causes of feathering are incorrect toe-in setting or deteriorated bushings in the front suspension.

Feathering

When an inner or outer rib wears faster than the rest of the tire, the need for wheel alignment is indicated. There is excessive camber in the front suspension, causing the wheel to lean too much putting excessive load on one side of the tire. Misalignment could also be due to sagging springs, worn ball joints, or worn control arm bushings. Be sure the vehicle is loaded the way it's normally driven when you have the wheels aligned.

One side wear

Cups or scalloped dips appearing around the edge of the tread almost always indicate worn (sometimes bent) suspension parts. Adjustment of wheel alignment alone will seldom cure the problem. Any worn component that connects the wheel to the suspension can cause this type of wear. Occasionally, wheels that are out of balance will wear like this, but wheel imbalance usually shows up as bald spots between the outside edges and center of the tread.

Cupping

Second-rib wear is usually found only in radial tires, and appears where the steel belts end in relation to the tread. It can be kept to a minimum by paying careful attention to tire pressure and frequently rotating the tires. This is often considered normal wear but excessive amounts indicate that the tires are too wide for the wheels.

Second-rib wear

Troubleshooting Disc Brake Problems

Condition	Possible Cause
Noise—groan—brake noise emanating when slowly releasing brakes (creep-groan)	Not detrimental to function of disc brakes—no corrective action required. (This noise may be eliminated by slightly increasing or decreasing brake pedal efforts.)
Rattle—brake noise or rattle emanating at low speeds on rough roads, (front wheels only).	1. Shoe anti-rattle spring missing or not properly positioned. 2. Excessive clearance between shoe and caliper. 3. Soft or broken caliper seals. 4. Deformed or misaligned disc. 5. Loose caliper.
Scraping	1. Mounting bolts too long. 2. Loose wheel bearings. 3. Bent, loose, or misaligned splash shield.
Front brakes heat up during driving and fail to release	1. Operator riding brake pedal. 2. Stop light switch improperly adjusted. 3. Sticking pedal linkage. 4. Frozen or seized piston. 5. Residual pressure valve in master cylinder. 6. Power brake malfunction. 7. Proportioning valve malfunction.
Leaky brake caliper	1. Damaged or worn caliper piston seal. 2. Scores or corrosion on surface of cylinder bore.
Grabbing or uneven brake action—Brakes pull to one side	1. Causes listed under "Brakes Pull". 2. Power brake malfunction. 3. Low fluid level in master cylinder. 4. Air in hydraulic system. 5. Brake fluid, oil or grease on linings. 6. Unmatched linings. 7. Distorted brake pads. 8. Frozen or seized pistons. 9. Incorrect tire pressure. 10. Front end out of alignment. 11. Broken rear spring. 12. Brake caliper pistons sticking. 13. Restricted hose or line. 14. Caliper not in proper alignment to braking disc. 15. Stuck or malfunctioning metering valve. 16. Soft or broken caliper seals. 17. Loose caliper.
Brake pedal can be depressed without braking effect	1. Air in hydraulic system or improper bleeding procedure. 2. Leak past primary cup in master cylinder. 3. Leak in system. 4. Rear brakes out of adjustment. 5. Bleeder screw open.
Excessive pedal travel	1. Air, leak, or insufficient fluid in system or caliper. 2. Warped or excessively tapered shoe and lining assembly. 3. Excessive disc runout. 4. Rear brake adjustment required. 5. Loose wheel bearing adjustment. 6. Damaged caliper piston seal. 7. Improper brake fluid (boil). 8. Power brake malfunction. 9. Weak or soft hoses.

Troubleshooting Disc Brake Problems (cont.)

Condition	Possible Cause
Brake roughness or chatter (pedal pumping)	1. Excessive thickness variation of braking disc. 2. Excessive lateral runout of braking disc. 3. Rear brake drums out-of-round. 4. Excessive front bearing clearance.
Excessive pedal effort	1. Brake fluid, oil or grease on linings. 2. Incorrect lining. 3. Frozen or seized pistons. 4. Power brake malfunction. 5. Kinked or collapsed hose or line. 6. Stuck metering valve. 7. Scored caliper or master cylinder bore. 8. Seized caliper pistons.
Brake pedal fades (pedal travel increases with foot on brake)	1. Rough master cylinder or caliper bore. 2. Loose or broken hydraulic lines/connections. 3. Air in hydraulic system. 4. Fluid level low. 5. Weak or soft hoses. 6. Inferior quality brake shoes or fluid. 7. Worn master cylinder piston cups or seals.

Troubleshooting Drum Brakes

Condition	Possible Cause
Pedal goes to floor	1. Fluid low in reservoir. 2. Air in hydraulic system. 3. Improperly adjusted brake. 4. Leaking wheel cylinders. 5. Loose or broken brake lines. 6. Leaking or worn master cylinder. 7. Excessively worn brake lining.
Spongy brake pedal	1. Air in hydraulic system. 2. Improper brake fluid (low boiling point). 3. Excessively worn or cracked brake drums. 4. Broken pedal pivot bushing.
Brakes pulling	1. Contaminated lining. 2. Front end out of alignment. 3. Incorrect brake adjustment. 4. Unmatched brake lining. 5. Brake drums out of round. 6. Brake shoes distorted. 7. Restricted brake hose or line. 8. Broken rear spring. 9. Worn brake linings. 10. Uneven lining wear. 11. Glazed brake lining. 12. Excessive brake lining dust. 13. Heat spotted brake drums. 14. Weak brake return springs. 15. Faulty automatic adjusters. 16. Low or incorrect tire pressure.

Condition	Possible Cause
Squealing brakes	1. Glazed brake lining. 2. Saturated brake lining. 3. Weak or broken brake shoe retaining spring. 4. Broken or weak brake shoe return spring. 5. Incorrect brake lining. 6. Distorted brake shoes. 7. Bent support plate. 8. Dust in brakes or scored brake drums. 9. Linings worn below limit. 10. Uneven brake lining wear. 11. Heat spotted brake drums.
Chirping brakes	1. Out of round drum or eccentric axle flange pilot.
Dragging brakes	1. Incorrect wheel or parking brake adjustment. 2. Parking brakes engaged or improperly adjusted. 3. Weak or broken brake shoe return spring. 4. Brake pedal binding. 5. Master cylinder cup sticking. 6. Obstructed master cylinder relief port. 7. Saturated brake lining. 8. Bent or out of round brake drum. 9. Contaminated or improper brake fluid. 10. Sticking wheel cylinder pistons. 11. Driver riding brake pedal. 12. Defective proportioning valve. 13. Insufficient brake shoe lubricant.
Hard pedal	1. Brake booster inoperative. 2. Incorrect brake lining. 3. Restricted brake line or hose. 4. Frozen brake pedal linkage. 5. Stuck wheel cylinder. 6. Binding pedal linkage. 7. Faulty proportioning valve.
Wheel locks	1. Contaminated brake lining. 2. Loose or torn brake lining. 3. Wheel cylinder cups sticking. 4. Incorrect wheel bearing adjustment. 5. Faulty proportioning valve.
Brakes fade (high speed)	1. Incorrect lining. 2. Overheated brake drums. 3. Incorrect brake fluid (low boiling temperature). 4. Saturated brake lining. 5. Leak in hydraulic system. 6. Faulty automatic adjusters.
Pedal pulsates	1. Bent or out of round brake drum.
Brake chatter and shoe knock	1. Out of round brake drum. 2. Loose support plate. 3. Bent support plate. 4. Distorted brake shoes. 5. Machine grooves in contact face of brake drum (Shoe Knock). 6. Contaminated brake lining. 7. Missing or loose components. 8. Incorrect lining material. 9. Out-of-round brake drums. 10. Heat spotted or scored brake drums. 11. Out-of-balance wheels.

Troubleshooting Drum Brakes (cont.)

Condition	Possible Cause
Brakes do not self adjust	1. Adjuster screw frozen in thread. 2. Adjuster screw corroded at thrust washer. 3. Adjuster lever does not engage star wheel. 4. Adjuster installed on wrong wheel.
Brake light glows	1. Leak in the hydraulic system. 2. Air in the system. 3. Improperly adjusted master cylinder pushrod. 4. Uneven lining wear. 5. Failure to center combination valve or proportioning valve.

Appendix

General Conversion Table

Multiply by	To convert	To	
2.54	Inches	Centimeters	.3937
30.48	Feet	Centimeters	.0328
.914	Yards	Meters	1.094
1.609	Miles	Kilometers	.621
6.45	Square inches	Square cm.	.155
.836	Square yards	Square meters	1.196
16.39	Cubic inches	Cubic cm.	.061
28.3	Cubic feet	Liters	.0353
.4536	Pounds	Kilograms	2.2045
3.785	Gallons	Liters	.264
.068	Lbs./sq. in. (psi)	Atmospheres	14.7
.138	Foot pounds	Kg. m.	7.23
1.014	H.P. (DIN)	H.P. (SAE)	.9861
—	To obtain	From	Multiply by

Note: 1 cm. equals 10 mm.; 1 mm. equals .0394″.

Conversion—Common Fractions to Decimals and Millimeters

Common Fractions	Decimal Fractions	Millimeters (approx.)	Common Fractions	Decimal Fractions	Millimeters (approx.)	Common Fractions	Decimal Fractions	Millimeters (approx.)
1/128	.008	0.20	11/32	.344	8.73	43/64	.672	17.07
1/64	.016	0.40	23/64	.359	9.13	11/16	.688	17.46
1/32	.031	0.79	3/8	.375	9.53	45/64	.703	17.86
3/64	.047	1.19	25/64	.391	9.92	23/32	.719	18.26
1/16	.063	1.59	13/32	.406	10.32	47/64	.734	18.65
5/64	.078	1.98	27/64	.422	10.72	3/4	.750	19.05
3/32	.094	2.38	7/16	.438	11.11	49/64	.766	19.45
7/64	.109	2.78	29/64	.453	11.51	25/32	.781	19.84
1/8	.125	3.18	15/32	.469	11.91	51/64	.797	20.24
9/64	.141	3.57	31/64	.484	12.30	13/16	.813	20.64
5/32	.156	3.97	1/2	.500	12.70	53/64	.828	21.03
11/64	.172	4.37	33/64	.516	13.10	27/32	.844	21.43
3/16	.188	4.76	17/32	.531	13.49	55/64	.859	21.83
13/64	.203	5.16	35/64	.547	13.89	7/8	.875	22.23
7/32	.219	5.56	9/16	.563	14.29	57/64	.891	22.62
15/64	.234	5.95	37/64	.578	14.68	29/32	.906	23.02
1/4	.250	6.35	19/32	.594	15.08	59/64	.922	23.42
17/64	.266	6.75	39/64	.609	15.48	15/16	.938	23.81
9/32	.281	7.14	5/8	.625	15.88	61/64	.953	24.21
19/64	.297	7.54	41/64	.641	16.27	31/32	.969	24.61
5/16	.313	7.94	21/32	.656	16.67	63/64	.984	25.00
21/64	.328	8.33						

Conversion—Millimeters to Decimal Inches

mm	inches	mm	inches	mm	inches	mm	inches	mm	inches
1	.039 370	31	1.220 470	61	2.401 570	91	3.582 670	210	8.267 700
2	.078 740	32	1.259 840	62	2.440 940	92	3.622 040	220	8.661 400
3	.118 110	33	1.299 210	63	2.480 310	93	3.661 410	230	9.055 100
4	.157 480	34	1.338 580	64	2.519 680	94	3.700 780	240	9.448 800
5	.196 850	35	1.377 949	65	2.559 050	95	3.740 150	250	9.842 500
6	.236 220	36	1.417 319	66	2.598 420	96	3.779 520	260	10.236 200
7	.275 590	37	1.456 689	67	2.637 790	97	3.818 890	270	10.629 900
8	.314 960	38	1.496 050	68	2.677 160	98	3.858 260	280	11.032 600
9	.354 330	39	1.535 430	69	2.716 530	99	3.897 630	290	11.417 300
10	.393 700	40	1.574 800	70	2.755 900	100	3.937 000	300	11.811 000
11	.433 070	41	1.614 170	71	2.795 270	105	4.133 848	310	12.204 700
12	.472 440	42	1.653 540	72	2.834 640	110	4.330 700	320	12.598 400
13	.511 810	43	1.692 910	73	2.874 010	115	4.527 550	330	12.992 100
14	.551 180	44	1.732 280	74	2.913 380	120	4.724 400	340	13.385 800
15	.590 550	45	1.771 650	75	2.952 750	125	4.921 250	350	13.779 500
16	.629 920	46	1.811 020	76	2.992 120	130	5.118 100	360	14.173 200
17	.669 290	47	1.850 390	77	3.031 490	135	5.314 950	370	14.566 900
18	.708 660	48	1.889 760	78	3.070 860	140	5.511 800	380	14.960 600
19	.748 030	49	1.929 130	79	3.110 230	145	5.708 650	390	15.354 300
20	.787 400	50	1.968 500	80	3.149 600	150	5.905 500	400	15.748 000
21	.826 770	51	2.007 870	81	3.188 970	155	6.102 350	500	19.685 000
22	.866 140	52	2.047 240	82	3.228 340	160	6.299 200	600	23.622 000
23	.905 510	53	2.086 610	83	3.267 710	165	6.496 050	700	27.559 000
24	.944 880	54	2.125 980	84	3.307 080	170	6.692 900	800	31.496 000
25	.984 250	55	2.165 350	85	3.346 450	175	6.889 750	900	35.433 000
26	1.023 620	56	2.204 720	86	3.385 820	180	7.086 600	1000	39.370 000
27	1.062 990	57	2.244 090	87	3.425 190	185	7.283 450	2000	78.740 000
28	1.102 360	58	2.283 460	88	3.464 560	190	7.480 300	3000	118.110 000
29	1.141 730	59	2.322 830	89	3.503 903	195	7.677 150	4000	157.480 000
30	1.181 100	60	2.362 200	90	3.543 300	200	7.874 000	5000	196.850 000

To change decimal millimeters to decimal inches, position the decimal point where desired on either side of the millimeter measurement shown and reset the inches decimal by the same number of digits in the same direction. For example, to convert 0.001 mm to decimal inches, reset the decimal behind the 1 mm (shown on the chart) to 0.001; change the decimal inch equivalent (0.039″ shown) to 0.000039″.

Tap Drill Sizes

National Fine or S.A.E.

Screw & Tap Size	Threads Per Inch	Use Drill Number
No. 5	44	37
No. 6	40	33
No. 8	36	29
No. 10	32	21
No. 12	28	15
¼	28	3
5/16	24	1
3/8	24	Q
7/16	20	W
½	20	29/64
9/16	18	33/64
5/8	18	37/64
¾	16	11/16
7/8	14	13/16
1⅛	12	1 3/64
1¼	12	1 11/64
1½	12	1 27/64

Tap Drill Sizes

National Coarse or U.S.S.

Screw & Tap Size	Threads Per Inch	Use Drill Number
No. 5	40	39
No. 6	32	36
No. 8	32	29
No. 10	24	25
No. 12	24	17
¼	20	8
5/16	18	F
3/8	16	5/16
7/16	14	U
½	13	27/64
9/16	12	31/64
5/8	11	17/32
¾	10	21/32
7/8	9	49/64
1	8	7/8
1⅛	7	63/64
1¼	7	1 7/64
1½	6	1 11/32

Decimal Equivalent Size of the Number Drills

Drill No.	Decimal Equivalent	Drill No.	Decimal Equivalent	Drill No.	Decimal Equivalent
80	.0135	53	.0595	26	.1470
79	.0145	52	.0635	25	.1495
78	.0160	51	.0670	24	.1520
77	.0180	50	.0700	23	.1540
76	.0200	49	.0730	22	.1570
75	.0210	48	.0760	21	.1590
74	.0225	47	.0785	20	.1610
73	.0240	46	.0810	19	.1660
72	.0250	45	.0820	18	.1695
71	.0260	44	.0860	17	.1730
70	.0280	43	.0890	16	.1770
69	.0292	42	.0935	15	.1800
68	.0310	41	.0960	14	.1820
67	.0320	40	.0980	13	.1850
66	.0330	39	.0995	12	.1890
65	.0350	38	.1015	11	.1910
64	.0360	37	.1040	10	.1935
63	.0370	36	.1065	9	.1960
62	.0380	35	.1100	8	.1990
61	.0390	34	.1110	7	.2010
60	.0400	33	.1130	6	.2040
59	.0410	32	.1160	5	.2055
58	.0420	31	.1200	4	.2090
57	.0430	30	.1285	3	.2130
56	.0465	29	.1360	2	.2210
55	.0520	28	.1405	1	.2280
54	.0550	27	.1440		

Decimal Equivalent Size of the Letter Drills

Letter Drill	Decimal Equivalent	Letter Drill	Decimal Equivalent	Letter Drill	Decimal Equivalent
A	.234	J	.277	S	.348
B	.238	K	.281	T	.358
C	.242	L	.290	U	.368
D	.246	M	.295	V	.377
E	.250	N	.302	W	.386
F	.257	O	.316	X	.397
G	.261	P	.323	Y	.404
H	.266	Q	.332	Z	.413
I	.272	R	.339		

Anti-Freeze Chart

Temperatures Shown in Degrees Fahrenheit +32 is Freezing

Cooling System Capacity Quarts	Quarts of ETHYLENE GLYCOL Needed for Protection to Temperatures Shown Below													
	1	2	3	4	5	6	7	8	9	10	11	12	13	14
10	+24°	+16°	+ 4°	−12°	−34°	−62°								
11	+25	+18	+ 8	− 6	−23	−47		For capacities over 30 quarts divide true capacity by 3. Find quarts Anti-Freeze for the ⅓ and multiply by 3 for quarts to add.						
12	+26	+19	+10	0	−15	−34	−57°							
13	+27	+21	+13	+ 3	− 9	−25	−45							
14			+15	+ 6	− 5	−18	−34							
15			+16	+ 8	0	−12	−26							
16			+17	+10	+ 2	− 8	−19	−34	−52°					
17			+18	+12	+ 5	− 4	−14	−27	−42					
18			+19	+14	+ 7	0	−10	−21	−34	−50°				
19			+20	+15	+ 9	+ 2	− 7	−16	−28	−42				
20				+16	+10	+ 4	− 3	−12	−22	−34	−48°			
21				+17	+12	+ 6	0	− 9	−17	−28	−41			
22				+18	+13	+ 8	+ 2	− 6	−14	−23	−34	−47°		
23				+19	+14	+ 9	+ 4	− 3	−10	−19	−29	−40		
24				+19	+15	+10	+ 5	0	− 8	−15	−23	−34	−46°	
25				+20	+16	+12	+ 7	+ 1	− 5	−12	−20	−29	−40	−50°
26					+17	+13	+ 8	+ 3	− 3	− 9	−16	−25	−34	−44
27					+18	+14	+ 9	+ 5	− 1	− 7	−13	−21	−29	−39
28					+18	+15	+10	+ 6	+ 1	− 5	−11	−18	−25	−34
29					+19	+16	+12	+ 7	+ 2	− 3	− 8	−15	−22	−29
30					+20	+17	+13	+ 8	+ 4	− 1	− 6	−12	−18	−25

For capacities under 10 quarts multiply true capacity by 3. Find quarts Anti-Freeze for the tripled volume and divide by 3 for quarts to add.

To Increase the Freezing Protection of Anti-Freeze Solutions Already Installed

Cooling System Capacity Quarts	Number of Quarts of ETHYLENE GLYCOL Anti-Freeze Required to Increase Protection													
	From +20° F. to					From +10° F. to					From 0° F. to			
	0°	−10°	−20°	−30°	−40°	0°	−10°	−20°	−30°	−40°	−10°	−20°	−30°	−40°
10	1¾	2¼	3	3½	3¾	¾	1½	2¼	2¾	3¼	¾	1½	2	2½
12	2	2¾	3½	4	4½	1	1¾	2½	3¼	3¾	1	1¾	2½	3¼
14	2¼	3¼	4	4¾	5½	1¼	2	3	3¾	4½	1	2	3	3½
16	2½	3½	4½	5¼	6	1¼	2½	3½	4¼	5¼	1¼	2¼	3¼	4
18	3	4	5	6	7	1½	2¾	4	5	5¾	1½	2½	3¾	4¾
20	3¼	4½	5¾	6¾	7½	1¾	3	4¼	5½	6½	1½	2¾	4¼	5¼
22	3½	5	6¼	7¼	8¼	1¾	3¼	4¾	6	7¼	1¾	3¼	4½	5½
24	4	5½	7	8	9	2	3½	5	6½	7½	1¾	3½	5	6
26	4¼	6	7½	8¾	10	2	4	5½	7	8¼	2	3¾	5½	6¾
28	4½	6¼	8	9½	10½	2¼	4¼	6	7½	9	2	4	5¾	7¼
30	5	6¾	8½	10	11½	2½	4½	6½	8	9½	2¼	4¼	6¼	7¾

Test radiator solution with proper hydrometer. Determine from the table the number of quarts of solution to be drawn off from a full cooling system and replace with undiluted anti-freeze, to give the desired increased protection. For example, to increase protection of a 22-quart cooling system containing Ethylene Glycol (permanent type) anti-freeze, from +20° F. to −20° F. will require the replacement of 6¼ quarts of solution with undiluted anti-freeze.

Index

Chilton's Repair & Tune-Up Guides

The Complete line covers domestic cars, imports, trucks, vans, RV's and 4-wheel drive vehicles.

────────────────── IMPORTANT ──────────────────

- **All vehicles are listed alphabetically by individual model names rather than by manufacturer.**
- **Numerical model names follow the alphabetical model name listing.**

Model Name	RTUG Title	Part No.
Accord	Honda 1973–84	6980
Alliance	Renault 1975–85	7165
AMX	AMC 1975–82	7199
Aries 1981–82	Chrysler K-Car 1981–82	7163
Arrow	Champ/Arrow/Sapporo 1978–83	7041
Arrow Pick-Ups	D-50/Arrow Pick-Up 1979–82	7032
Aspen 1976–80	Aspen/Volare 1976–80	6637
Astre 1975–77	GM Subcompact 1971–80	6935
Barracuda 1965–72	Barracuda/Challenger 1965–72	5807
Bavaria	BMW 1970–82	6844
Bel Air 1968–75	Chevrolet 1968–83	7135
Belvedere 1968–70	Roadrunner/Satellite/Belvedere/GTX 1968–73	5821
Biscayne 1968–71	Chevrolet 1968–83	7135
Blazer 1969–82	Blazer/Jimmy 1969–82	6931
Bobcat 1975–80	Pinto/Bobcat 1971–80	7027
Bonneville 1975–83	Buick/Olds/Pontiac 1975–83	7308
BRAT	Subaru 1970–84	6982
Bronco 1966–83	Ford Bronco 1966–83	7140
Bronco II 1984	Ford Bronco II 1984	7408
Brookwood 1968–72	Chevrolet 1968–83	7135
Brougham 1974–75	Valiant/Duster 1968–76	6326
B-210 1974–78	Datsun 1200, etc. 1973–84	7197
Caballero 1964–82	Chevrolet Mid-Size 1964–84	6840
Camaro 1967–81	Camaro 1967–81	6735
Camaro 1982–83	Camaro 1982–83	7317
Camry 1983–84	Toyota Corona, etc. 1970–84	7004
Capri 1970–77	Capri 1970–77	6695
Capri 1979–83	Mustang/Capri 1979–83	6963
Caprice 1975–83	Chevrolet 1968–83	7135
Caravan 1984–85	Caravan/Voyager 1984–85	7482
Carina 1972–73	Toyota Corolla, etc. 1970–83	7036
Catalina 1975–83	Buick/Olds/Pontiac 1975–83	7308
Cavalier 1982	GM J-Car 1982	7059
Celebrity 1982–83	GM A-Body 1982–83	7309
Celica 1971–83	Toyota Celica/Supra 1971–83	7043
Century, front wheel drive 1982–83	GM A-Body 1982–83	7309
Century, rear wheel drive 1975–83	Century/Regal 1975–83	7307
Challenger 1965–72	Barracuda/Challenger 1965–72	5807
Challenger 1977–83	Colt/Challenger/Vista 1971–83	7037
Champ	Champ/Arrow/Sapporo 1978–83	7041
Charger 2.2 1982–84	Omni/Horizon 1978–84	6845
Cherokee 1974–84	Jeep Wagoneer, etc. 1962–84	6739
Chevelle 1964–77	Chevrolet Mid-Size 1964–84	6840
Chevette 1976–84	Chevette/T-1000 1976–84	6836
Chevy Pick-Ups 1970–84	Chevrolet/GMC Pick-Ups/Suburban 1970–84	6936
Chevy Vans 1967–84	Chevy/GMC Vans 1967–84	6930
Chevy II 1962–68	Chevy II/Nova 1962–79	6841
Cimarron 1982	GM J-Car 1982	7059
Citation 1980–83	GM X-Body 1980–83	7049
Civic	Honda 1973–84	6980
Colt	Colt/Challenger/Vista 1971–83	7037
Comet 1971–77	Maverick/Comet 1971–77	6634
Commando 1971–73	Jeep Wagoneer, Commando, Cherokee, Truck 1962–84	6739
Concord	AMC 1975–82	7199
Continental 1982–85	Ford/Mercury Mid-Size 1971–85	6696
Corolla 1968–70	Toyota 1966–70	5795
Corolla 1970–84	Toyota Corolla, etc. 1970–84	7036
Corona 1966–70	Toyota 1966–70	5795
Corona 1970–81	Toyota Corona, etc. 1970–84	7004
Corsa	Corvair 1960–69	6691
Corvair 1960–69	Corvair 1960–69	6691
Corvette 1953–62	Corvette 1953–62	6576
Corvette 1963–84	Corvette 1963–84	6843
Cosmo	Mazda 1971–84	6981
Cougar 1967–71	Mustang/Cougar 1965–73	6542
Cougar 1972–85	Ford/Mercury Mid-Size 1971–85	6696
Country Sedan 1968–81	Ford/Mercury/Lincoln 1968–85	6842
Country Squire 1968–83	Ford/Mercury/Lincoln 1968–85	6842
Courier 1972–82	Ford Courier 1972–82	6983
Cressida 1978–84	Toyota Corona, etc. 1970–84	7004
Crown 1966–70	Toyota 1966–70	5795
Crown 1970–72	Toyota Corona, etc. 1970–84	7004
Crown Victoria 1981–85	Ford/Mercury/Lincoln 1968–85	6842
Cutlass 1970–82	Cutlass 1970–82	6933
Cutlass Ciera 1982–83	GM A-Body 1982–83	7309
Dart 1968–76	Dart/Demon 1968–76	6324
Dasher	VW Front Wheel Drive 1974–83	6962
Datsun Pick-Ups 1961–72	Datsun 1961–72	5790
Datsun Pick-Ups 1970–83	Datsun Pick-Ups 1970–83	6816
Demon 1971–76	Dart/Demon 1968–76	6324
deVille 1967–84	Cadillac 1967–84	7462
Dodge Pick-Ups 1967–84	Dodge/Plymouth Trucks 1967–84	7459
Dodge Vans	Dodge/Plymouth Vans 1967–84	6934
Duster 1970–76	Valiant/Duster 1968–76	6326
D-50 Pick-Up 1979–81	D-50/Arrow Pick-Ups 1979–81	7032
Eagle	AMC 1975–82	7199
El Camino 1964–82	Chevrolet Mid-Size 1964–82	6840
Eldorado 1967–84	Cadillac 1967–84	7462
Electra 1975–84	Buick/Olds/Pontiac 1975–85	7308
Elite 1974–76	Ford/Mercury Mid-Size 1971–85	6696
Encore	Renault 1975–85	7165
Escort, EXP 1981–85	Ford/Mercury Front Wheel Drive 1981–85	7055
Fairlane 1962–70	Fairlane/Torino 1962–75	6320
Fairmont 1978–83	Fairmont/Zephyr 1978–83	6965
FF-1	Subaru 1970–84	6982
Fiat, all models	Fiat 1969–81	7042
Fiesta	Fiesta 1978–80	6846
Firebird 1967–81	Firebird 1967–81	5996
Firebird 1982–83	Firebird 1982–83	7345
Firenza 1982	GM J-Car 1982	7059
Fleetwood 1967–84	Cadillac 1967–84	7462
Ford Pick-Ups 1965–84	Ford Pick-ups 1965–84	6913
Ford Vans	Ford Vans 1961–84	6849
Fuego	Renault 1975–85	7165
Fury 1968–76	Plymouth 1968–76	6552
F-10 1977–78	Datsun F-10, etc. 1977–82	7196
F-85 1970–72	Cutlass 1970–82	6933
Galaxie 1968–81	Ford/Mercury/Lincoln 1968–85	6842
GLC	Mazda 1971–84	6981
GMC Pick-Ups 1970–84	Chevrolet/GMC Pick-Ups/Suburban 1970–84	6936
GMC Vans	Chevrolet/GMC Vans 1967–84	6930
Gordini	Renault 1975–85	7165
Granada 1975–82	Granada/Monarch 1975–82	6937
Grand Coupe, Gran Fury, Gran Sedan	Plymouth 1968–76	6552
Grand Am 1974–80	Pontiac Mid-Size 1974–83	7346
Grand Prix 1974–83	Pontiac Mid-Size 1974–83	7346
Grand Safari 1975–85	Buick/Olds/Pontiac 1975–85	7308
Grand Ville 1975–83	Buick/Olds/Pontiac 1975–83	7308
Greenbriar	Corvair 1960–69	6691
Gremlin	AMC 1975–82	7199
GTO 1968–73	Tempest/GTO/LeMans 1968–73	5905
GTO 1974	Pontiac Mid-Size 1974–83	7346
GTX 1968–71	Roadrunner/Satellite/Belvedere/GTX 1968–73	5821
GT6	Triumph 1969–73	5910
G.T.350, G.T.500	Mustang/Cougar 1965–73	6542
Horizon 1978–84	Omni/Horizon 1978–84	6845
Hornet	AMC 1975–82	7199
Impala 1968–78	Chevrolet 1968–83	7135
Jeep CJ	Jeep CJ 1945–84	6817
Jeep Pick-Ups	Jeep Wagoneer, Commando, Cherokee, Truck 1962–84	6739
Jeepster 1966–70	Jeep Wagoneer, Commando, Cherokee, Truck 1962–84	6739
Jetta	VW Front Wheel Drive 1974–83	6962
Jimmy	Blazer/Jimmy 1969–82	6931
Kingswood 1968–81	Chevrolet 1968–83	7135
Lakewood	Corvair 1960–69	6691
Lancer	Champ/Arrow/Sapporo 1977–83	7041
Land Cruiser 1966–70	Toyota 1966–70	5795
Land Cruiser 1970–83	Toyota Trucks 1970–83	7035
LeBaron 1982	Chrysler K-Car 1981–82	7163
LeCar	Renault 1975–85	7165
LeMans 1968–73	Tempest/GTO/LeMans 1968–73	5905
LeMans, Grand LeMans 1974–83	Pontiac Mid-Size 1974–83	7346
LeSabre 1975–85	Buick/Olds/Pontiac 1975–85	7308
Lincoln 1968–85	Ford/Mercury/Lincoln 1968–85	6842
LTD 1968–81	Ford/Mercury/Lincoln 1968–85	6842
LTD II 1977–79	Ford/Mercury Mid-Size 1971–85	6696
LUV 1972–81	Chevrolet LUV 1972–81	6815
Lynx, LN-7 1981–85	Ford/Mercury Front Wheel Drive 1981–85	7055
Mach I 1968–73	Mustang/Cougar 1965–73	6542
Malibu	Chevrolet Mid-Size 1964–84	6840
Matador	AMC 1975–82	7199
Maverick 1970–77	Maverick/Comet 1970–77	6634
Maxima 1980–84	Datsun 200SX, etc. 1973–84	7170
Mercury (Full-Size) 1968–85	Ford/Mercury/Lincoln 1968–85	6842
MG	MG 1961–81	6780
Mk.II 1969–70	Toyota 1966–70	5795
Mk.II 1970–76	Toyota Corona, etc. 1970–84	7004
Monaco 1968–77	Dodge 1968–77	6554
Monarch 1975–80	Granada/Monarch 1975–82	6937
Monte Carlo 1970–84	Chevrolet Mid-Size 1964–84	6840
Montego 1971–78	Ford/Mercury Mid-Size 1971–85	6696
Monza 1968–69	Corvair 1960–69	6691
Monza 1975–80	GM Subcompact 1971–80	6935
Mustang 1965–73	Mustang/Cougar 1965–73	6542
Mustang 1979–83	Mustang/Capri 1979–83	6963
Mustang II 1974–78	Mustang II 1974–78	6812
Nova	Chevy II/Nova 1962–79	6841
Omega 1980–81	GM X-Body 1980–83	7049
Omni 1978–84	Omni/Horizon 1978–84	6845
Opel	Opel 1964–70	5792
Opel 1971–75	Opel 1971–75	6575
Pacer	AMC 1975–82	7199
Patrol 1961–69	Datsun 1961–72	5790
Peugeot	Peugeot 1970–74	5982
Phoenix 1980–83	GM X-Body 1980–83	7049
Pinto 1971–80	Pinto/Bobcat 1971–80	7027

continued on next page

Model Name	RTUG Title	Part No.	Model Name	RTUG Title	Part No.
Plymouth Vans 1974–84	Dodge/Plymouth Vans 1967–84	6934	Z-28 1982–83	Camaro 1982–83	7317
Polara 1968–77	Dodge 1968–77	6554	4-4-2 1970–80	Cutlass 1970–82	6933
Prelude	Honda 1973–84	6980	024 1978–84	Omni/Horizon 1978–84	6845
PV-444, 544	Volvo 1956–69	6529	3.0S, 3.0Si, 3.0CS	BMW 1970–82	6844
P-1800	Volvo 1956–69	6529	6.9 1978–79	Mercedes-Benz 1974–84	6809
Quantum 1974–84	VW Front Wheel Drive 1974–84	6962	88, 98	Buick/Olds/Pontiac 1975–83	7308
Rabbit	VW Front Wheel Drive 1974–84	6962	99 1969–75	SAAB 99 1969–75	5988
Ramcharger	Dodge/Plymouth Trucks 1967–84	7459	100 LS, 100GL	Audi 1970–73	5902
Ranchero 1967–70	Fairlane/Torino 1962–70	6320	122, 122S	Volvo 1956–69	6529
Ranchero 1971–78	Ford/Mercury Mid-Size 1971–85	6696	142, 144, 145, 164	Volvo 1956–69	6529
Ranch Wagon	Ford/Mercury/Lincoln 1968–85	6842		Volvo 1970–84	7040
Ranger Pick-Up 1983–84	Ford Ranger 1983–84	7338	190E, 190D 1984	Mercedes-Benz 1974–84	6809
Regal 1975–85	Century/Regal 1975–85	7307	190C, 190DC 1961–66	Mercedes-Benz 1959–70	6065
Reliant 1981–85	Chrysler K-Car 1981–85	7163	200, 200D	Mercedes-Benz 1959–70	6065
Roadrunner 1968–73	Roadrunner/Satellite/Belvedere/GTX 1968–73	5821	200SX 1977–84	Datsun 200SX, etc. 1973–84	7170
RX-2, RX-3, RX-4	Mazda 1971–84	6981	210 1979–81	Datsun 1200, etc. 1971–84	7197
RX-7	RX-7 1979–81	7031	220D, 220B, 220Sb, 220SEb	Mercedes-Benz 1959–70	6065
R-12, 15, 17, 18, 18i	Renault 1975–85	7165	220/8 1968–73	Mercedes-Benz 1968–73	5907
Sapporo 1977–83	Champ/Arrow/Saporro 1978–83	7041	230 1974–78	Mercedes-Benz 1974–84	6809
Satellite 1968–73	Roadrunner/Satellite/Belvedere/GTX 1968–73	5821	230S, 230SL	Mercedes-Benz 1959–70	6065
Scamp 1971–76	Valiant/Duster 1968–76	6326	230/8 1968–69	Mercedes-Benz 1968–73	5907
Scamp 1982	Omni/Horizon 1978–84	6845	240D 1974–79	Mercedes-Benz 1974–84	6809
Scirocco	VW Front Wheel Drive 1974–83	6962	240Z, 260Z, 280Z, 280ZX, 300ZX	Datsun Z & ZX 1970–84	6932
Scout 1967–73	International Scout 1967–73	5912	242, 244, 245, 262, 264, 265	Volvo 1970–84	7040
Scrambler 1981–84	Jeep CJ 1981–84	6817	250C, 250/8	Mercedes-Benz 1968–73	5907
Sentra 1982–84	Datsun 1200, etc. 1973–84	7197	250S, 250SE, 250SL	Mercedes-Benz 1959–70	6065
Seville 1967–84	Cadillac 1967–84	7462	280, 280C, 280S/8, 280SE, 280SE/8, 280SEL, 280SEL/8 280SL	Mercedes-Benz 1968–73	5907
Skyhawk 1975–80	GM Subcompact 1971–80	6935	280, 280C, 280CE, 280E, 280S, 280SE, 300CD, 300D, 300SD	Mercedes-Benz 1974–84	6809
Skyhawk 1982	GM J-Car 1982	7059	300SE, 1961–63	Mercedes-Benz 1959–70	6065
Skylark 1980–83	GM X-Body 1980–83	7049	300SEL, 3.5, 4.5, 6.3, 300SEL/8	Mercedes-Benz 1968–73	5907
Spirit	AMC 1975–82	7199	300TD 1979	Mercedes-Benz 1974–84	6809
Sport Wagon	Renault 1975–85	7165	304	Peugeot 1970–74	5982
Stanza	Datsun F-10, etc. 1977–82	7196	310, 311 1962–69	Datsun 1961–72	5790
Starfire 1975–80	GM Subcompact 1971–80	6935	310 1979–82	Datsun F-10, etc. 1977–82	7196
Starlet 1981–84	Toyota Corolla, etc. 1970–84	7036	320i	BMW 1970–82	6844
Suburban 1968–76	Plymouth 1968–76	6552	350SL 1972	Mercedes-Benz 1968–73	5907
Suburban 1970–84	Chevy/GMC Pick-Ups/Suburban 1970–84	6936	380SEC, 380SL, 380SLC, 380SEL	Mercedes-Benz 1974–84	6809
Sunbird 1975–80	GM Subcompact 1971–80	6935	400 1982	Chrysler K-Car 1981–82	7163
Super 90	Audi 1970–73	5902	410, 411, 1963–68	Datsun 1961–72	5790
Supra 1979–84	Toyota Celica/Supra 1971–84	7043	411, 412	VW 1970–81	7081
SX-4	AMC 1975–82	7199	450SLC 1973	Mercedes-Benz 1968–73	5907
S-10 Blazer, S-15 Jimmy 1982–85	Chevy S-10 Blazer/GMC S-15 Jimmy 1982–85	7383	450SE, 450SEL, 450SEL 6.9, 450SL, 450SLC	Mercedes-Benz 1974–84	6809
S-10, S-15 Pick-Ups 1982–85	Chevy S-10/GMC S-15 Pick-Ups 1982–85	7310	500SEC, 500SEL	Mercedes-Benz 1974–84	6809
TC-3 1978–82	Omni/Horizon/Rampage 1978–84	6845	504	Peugeot 1970–74	5982
Tempest 1968–73	Tempest/GTO/LeMans 1968–73	5905	510 1968–71	Datsun 1961–72	5790
Tempo 1984–85	Ford/Mercury Front Wheel Drive 1981–85	7055	510 1973, 1978–80	Datsun 200SX, etc. 1973–84	7170
Tercel 1980–84	Toyota Corolla, etc. 1970–84	7036	528i, 530i	BMW 1970–82	6844
Thunderbird 1977–83	Ford/Mercury Mid-Size 1971–83	6696	600	Honda 1973–84	6980
Topaz 1983–85	Ford/Mercury Front Wheel Drive 1981–85	7055	610 1973–76	Datsun 200SX, etc. 1973–84	7170
Torino 1968–71	Fairlane/Torino 1962–75	6320	626	Mazda 1971–84	6981
Torino, Gran Torino 1971–76	Ford/Mercury Mid-Size 1971–83	6696	630 CSi, 633 CSi	BMW 1970–82	6844
Townsman 1968–72	Chevrolet 1968–83	7135	710 1974–77	Datsun 200SX, etc. 1973–84	7170
Toyota Pick-Ups 1966–70	Toyota 1966–70	5795	733i	BMW 1970–82	6844
Toyota Pick-Ups 1970–83	Toyota Trucks 1970–83	7035	760, 760GLE	Volvo 1970–84	7040
Toyota Van 1984	Toyota Corona, etc. 1970–84	7004	808 (1300, 1600)	Mazda 1971–84	6981
Trail Duster 1974–84	Dodge/Plymouth Trucks 1967–84	7459	810 1977–80	Datsun 200SX, etc. 1973–84	7170
Triumph, all models	Triumph 1969–73	5910	900, 900 Turbo 1976–85	SAAB 900 1976–85	7572
Turismo 1982–84	Omni/Horizon 1978–84	6845	911, 914	Porsche 1969–73	5822
T-37 1971	Tempest/GTO/LeMans 1968–73	5905	924, 928	Porsche 924/928 1976–81	7048
Vega 1971–77	GM Subcompact 1971–80	6935	1000 1981–84	Chevette/1000 1976–84	6836
Ventura 1974–79	Pontiac Mid-Size 1974–84	7346	1200 1500, 1600, 2000	Datsun 1961–72	5790
Versailles 1978–80	Ford/Mercury Mid-Size 1971–83	6696	1200 1973	Datsun 1200, etc. 1973–84	7197
VIP 1969–74	Plymouth 1968–76	6552	1400, 1600, 1800 GL/DL/GF	Subaru 1970–84	6982
Vista Cruiser 1970–72	Cutlass 1970–82	6933	1500, 1600, 1600–2, 1800	BMW 1970–82	6844
Volare 1976–80	Aspen/Volare 1976–80	6637	1800, 1800S	Volvo 1956–69	6529
Voyager 1984	Caravan/Voyager 1984	7482	2000, 2002, 2002Ti, 2002Tii, 2500, 2800	BMW 1970–82	6844
VW All models 1949–71	VW 1949–71	5796	2000 1982	GM J-Car 1982	7059
VW Types 1, 2, 3	VW 1970–81	6837	4000, 5000	Audi 4000/5000 1978–81	7028
Wagoneer 1962–84	Jeep Wagoneer, Commando, Cherokee, Truck 1962–84	6739	6000 1982–83	GM A-Body 1982–83	7309
XL 1968–75	Ford/Mercury/Lincoln 1968–85	6842			
XR-7 1977–83	Ford/Mercury Mid-Size 1971–83	6696			
Zephyr 1978–80	Fairmont/Zephyr 1978–83	6965			
Z-28 1967–81	Camaro 1967–81	6735			

Spanish Language Repair & Tune-Up Guides

Chevrolet/GMC Pick-ups 1970–82	Part No. 7468
Ford Pick-ups 1965–82	Part No. 7469
Toyota 1970–79	Part No. 7467
Chevrolet 1968–79	Part No. 7082
Datsun 1973–80	Part No. 7083
Ford 1968–79	Part No. 7084
Rabbit/Scirocco 1975–78	Part No. 7089
Volkswagen 1970–79	Part No. 7081

Chilton's Repair & Tune-Up Guides are available at your local retailer or by mailing a check or money order for **$11.95** plus **$1.75** to cover postage and handling to:

Chilton Book Company
Dept. DM
Radnor, PA 19089

NOTE: When ordering be sure to include your name & address, book part No. & title.